From Shaman to Psychotherapist

A History of the Treatment of Mental Illness

Walter Bromberg, M.D.

Henry Regnery Company • Chicago

Library of Congress Cataloging in Publication Data

Bromberg, Walter, 1900-
   From shaman to psychotherapist.

   First and 3d ed. published in 1937 and 1954 respec-
tively under title: The mind of man; 2d ed. published
in 1954 under title: Man above humanity.
   Includes bibliographical references and index.
   1. Psychotherapy—History.   I. Title.
[DNLM: 1. Psychotherapy—History.   WM11.1 B868f]
RC480.B7   1975   616.8'914'09   75-13216
ISBN 0-8092-8349-2
ISBN 0-8092-8147-3 pbk.

Published by Henry Regnery Company
180 North Michigan Avenue, Chicago, Illinois 60601
Manufactured in the United States of America
Library of Congress Card Number: 75-13216
International Standard Book Number: 0-8092-8349-2 (cloth)
                                    0-8092-8147-3 (paper)

Published simultaneously in Canada by
Fitzhenry & Whiteside Limited
150 Lesmill Road
Don Mills, Ontario M3B 2T5
Canada

Contents

Preface

This volume relates the story of healing by mental means; its origins, evolution, and possible fate.

Measured in terms of man's 7,000-year-old attempt to cure his bodily and mental ills through magic, art, and science, psychotherapy is our most recent endeavor. Scarcely two hundred years old, organized psychiatry and clinical psychology have treated and tried to understand the most elusive of emotional disturbances, the most complex of mental operations. These human problems always tormented man but they were dealt with under names other than psychotherapy. As the scientific elaboration of this field grew, fascination with this chess game of the whys of human behavior took precedence in psychiatry and psychology. Psychotherapy tagged along as the art of helping the sufferer and his society.

Psychotherapy antedates psychiatry; the history of psychotherapy is the story of *doing* as opposed to *thinking* about doing. It developed around personal and social needs to do something for the distraught, the obsessed, the deluded, the frenzied. In answering urgent cries for help by the anxiety-laden, mental healing and psychotherapy became involved with strange bedfellows—religion, faith healing, folk medicine, occultism, self-help, the euphoria of personality enlargement.

Here were healing methods that paid little attention to logical form or scientific proof; their business was to relieve, not to offer complicated theories. In time, however, empirical methods that worked successfully began to be scrutinized for their theoretical backgrounds. Explanations were sought in terms of hypotheses, comparisons were made to secure scientific validation, logic was employed to find reasons for success. In short, a "science" of mental healing developed. Since psychotherapy included obscure, anachronistic methods and a melange of religiophilosophic ideas, mental scientists strove to nail down "facts," discard irrelevancies, test theories. They tried to isolate what was magic and what were predictable psychological forces.

So a division slowly developed; those who wore the mantle of Psychotherapy were physicians and psychologists; the others were Mental Healers. But whether science or art, that bundle of astute, informed, intuitive or bungling practices aimed and still aims to alter ideas, behavior, and emotion in patients.

Still, even the trained therapist works in a contradictory world of theories and practices. Dr. Roy Grinker, one of the deans of American psychiatry, recently admonished the profession for "galloping off in all directions at once." Grinker's point is well taken, but the outlook is for continuation of this discord. Was mental healing as a human endeavor ever stabilized? Will it ever be stabilized?

The history to be detailed may eventually lead to one school or theory, or it may not. In any event, the record, if it does not foretell the future, will surely illuminate the past.

This volume is a fourth edition of *The Mind of Man*, originally published by Harper & Bros. in 1937, of the second edition titled *Man Above Humanity*, J. B. Lippincott, 1954, and of the third edition, *The Mind of Man*, Harper Bros. Torchbook Series, 1958. All acknowledgements in earlier editions continue in force. In the present work, it is a pleasure to acknowledge the assistance of Malcolm MacFail in research on some philosophical implications and on recent Esalen developments. Michael Bennett, librarian of the Sacramento Medical Society, was very helpful in providing historical material otherwise inaccessible and the librarians of the California State Library are also to be thanked for their assistance. For the tedious and exacting task of typing this manuscript, I am indebted to Lucy Calvetti, R.N., my secretary.

Finally, to patients over the years, on whom I have tried some of the therapeutic techniques discussed, and to colleagues and teachers with whom I have worked, I express my appreciation and gratitude.

The opinions of the author and the selection of material cited, however, are his own responsibility.

Walter Bromberg, M.D., L.F., A.P.A.
Sacramento, California
November 1974

1

Beginnings

How can the sprawling, chaotic, yet vigorous and human story of mental healing be told in logical sequence and chronologic order? Although we speak of psychotherapy as an identifiable group of activities clustering around knowledge of man's psychic apparatus, it had no clearcut beginning as such. For one thing, psychotherapy and mental healing were influenced indirectly, and sometimes directly, by political philosophies, religions and neo-religions, mythologies and folklore, science and theories of ego function, as well as economic and cultural realignments. At one extremity the techniques employed touched on magic, mysticism, religious submission to a Divine Will and idealism, while on the other, methods relied on biochemistry, neurology, psychology, psychoanalysis, and existentialism. The figures through whom mental healing evolved ran the gamut of monks and medicine men, kings and quacks, prophets and gurus, physicians and psychologists, including men of every degree of genius and mediocrity. Their actions were inspired by human nobility, scientific curiosity, workaday patience. The amount of energy expended is incalculable. This vibrant "living" quality of psychotherapy makes the writing of a sequential history of this subject difficult. But there was some kind of a beginning.

But even establishing a beginning meets with difficulties. The deeper we search, the less clear the trail becomes; the more we probe, the more speculation and interpretation replace exact information. Any analysis of what happened in the past should heed the historian's warning:

> Only a part of what was observed in the past was remembered by those who observed it; only a part of what was remembered was recorded; only a part of what was recorded has survived; only a part of what has survived has come to the historian's attention; only a part of what has come to their attention is credible; and only a part of what is credible has been grasped.... History as told...is only the historian's expressed part of the understood part of the credible part of the discovered part of history-as-recorded.[1]

No one can say when the attention of prehistoric man was consciously deflected from physical suffering to psychological pain—when he looked beyond the ache of a torn muscle to the existence of mental torment. Primitive man was threatened by injury and destruction on all sides; pain had to be accepted as a prerequisite of life. In a blind hit-or-miss fashion, the caveman found gums that soothed his bleeding flesh and infusions of berries or leaves that eased his pain. As Victor Robinson has reconstructed it:

> Early man moistened his bruises with saliva, he extracted the thorns which lodged in his flesh, he used a pointed stick to dig sand fleas from his skin, he put leaves or mud or clay on his wounds, he tasted herbs and some he spat out and some he swallowed, he was rubbed or stroked when in pain, his broken bones were splinted with branches.[2]

How and when the transition from treating bodily ills to ministering to mental anguish occurred, no one knows. How did early man of the Pleistocene Age a million years ago, give or take a thousand, view displeasure and mental pain? Paleontologists, working with remnants of the Stone Age and later, hypothecate that bits of bone, teeth of animals, vertebrae of snakes found in amulet bags contained some magic force, some magic law, that contributed mental ease to their possessors.[3] That some type of practitioner, the shaman of the Bronze Age, used this magical aid through "dreams, controlled breathing, repetition," as well as amulets which embodied this force, seems reasonable.[4] Did early man borrow from his universe the concept of an external, all-powerful force, which could be harnessed to help his fellow man in pain and sorrow? The answer seems to lie in the concept of *mana*, a force that lay beyond the observable world, and which grew crops, avenged enemies, and healed the ill. This power, which we call supernatural, and the techniques to invoke it, which we call magical, probably represents the earliest form of psychotherapy.

The concept of *mana*, introduced by Codrington in his studies of Melanesians,[5] has been generally accepted as the raw material out of which primitive religions evolved. *Mana* represents a supernatural impersonal power, also present in today's so-called primitive religions; the *manitou* of the Algonquins, *wakonda* of the Sioux, *orenda* of the Iroquois —which could be appealed to for good or ill.[6]

The shaman or medicine man, by virtue of his special gifts and acquaintance with the supernatural world, was able to harness this force to heal the sick, divine the weather, and undo mischief. The shaman combined early religious concepts with a shrewd knowledge of his fellow man to become, in Coon's words, "an all-purpose expert in human relations." Armed with the power of the *taboo* and his skill in invoking the Great Spirit or *mana*, it is assumed that the early medicine man served as physical and mental healer. "The shaman's profession," writes Coon, "not prostitution, is the oldest." From this matrix arose, presumably, the close relation between magic and religion,[7] for "magical law" was as real to early man as is biophysical science to us. The evolution of medicine man to priest, of the invocation of *mana* to prayer and ritual to gods or God, condenses the whole story of the growth of faith healing.

The ordinary man ceded his interest in healing and in cosmic problems to the priests and the magicians, who by tradition and through knowledge were in close contact with divinity. Through a gradual extension of this role, humanity's suffering was broadly accepted by the priest-physician as his proper responsibility. Mental healing and the religious spirit were inextricably mixed in their psychological origins.

Magic conveyed by amulets, charms, words, and ritual was the chief vehicle for healing in the ancient world. The priest-caste of Mesopotamia and Egypt, in using them, could be called the first psychotherapists. Fragmentary medical writings about Imhotep the Egyptian physician (3000 B.C., the Ebers papyrus) and the Babylonian Code of Hammurabi (about 2000 B.C.) contained a mixture of sober advice and magic, detailed measures for driving out demons, and prescriptions for the use of opium and olive oil.

Castiglioni, the medical historian, concluded that the medicine of Mesopotamia, "which is perhaps the most ancient of which we have clear knowledge...was dominated by magical concepts and priestly practice."[8] Similarly, according to Japanese tradition,[9] the gods who created the islands of Japan gave birth to Amaterasu, Goddess of Light, ancestor of all the rulers of Japan, who in turn gave birth to a physician, Suku-na-biko, the giver of charms against evil spirits.

Magic, then, was the first therapeutic principle, an irreducible element in mental healing. It is an attitude within the recipient who hopes for results, no matter how improbable. It will be found to have been an essential aspect of healing in antiquity, among nonliterate and sophisticated groups even today. Reliance on magical thinking is still abundantly present in those deeper layers of our minds subject to fantasy and out of control of the reasonable ego. In the healing arts the influence of magical thinking colors the effect of medicines, injections, and the like, as every physician and every pharmacist is aware from daily experience.

Magic is the infantile wish of the human race for accomplishment of the impossible; its universal presence depends less on proof of previous successes than on an ineradicable human wish.

Beyond the magic wish, another ingredient, faith, was needed. Faith can be thought of as an extension of magical wishing, with the important difference that in human experience its premises cannot be considered as illusory. Although it appears to rest on the same emotionally toned wish for bounty, faith, unlike magic, feeds upon belief and, one may say, upon proof. Faith requires mental work in the "faithful" for its consummation, whereas magic confers on the recipient the results of activity, having its origin beyond the ken of man. Faith is critical to some degree, since it is related to a body of impressive occurrences, world-accepted legends, or historical precedents. Its possibilities of success increase with successes following acts of faith. Ducasse summarizes his analysis of religious faith:

> "Faith" then apparently means not only (a) very firm belief, either supported or insufficiently supported by evidence; but in addition either (b) that the content of the belief tends to be made true by the very act of believing it firmly; or (c) that the content of the belief is of such a nature that firm belief of it tends to have certain valuable results.

Yet, the medicine man's effectiveness depended on other factors than his own skill; it depended on the accepted beliefs of his culture. As Caudill points out, reasoning from anthropologic studies of American Indian religious healers, the strength of the medicine man comes,

> not only from the interpersonal ties between doctor and patient but also from the re-inforcing effect of... participation of the entire community in his treatment.[10]

Notes to Chapter 1

1. Louis Gottschalk, *Understanding History: A Primer of Historical Method*, New York, Knopf, 1950, p. 46.

2. Victor Robinson, *The Story of Medicine*, New York, Boni, 1931, p. 1.
3. R. R. Schmidt, *The Dawn of the Human Mind*, translated by R.A.S. Macalister, London, Sidgwick & Jackson, 1936, p. 210.
4. Carleton Coon, *The Story of Man*, 2nd. ed., New York, A. A. Knopf, 1962, p. 105.
5. R. H. Codrington, *The Melanesians*, Oxford, Clarendon Press, 1891, p. 119.
6. R. R. Marett, *The Threshold of Religion*, 2nd ed., New York, Macmillan, 1914, p. 97.
7. C. J. Ducasse, *A Philosophical Scrutiny of Religion*, New York, Ronald, 1952, p. 63.
8. Arturo Castiglioni, *A History of Medicine*, translated from the Italian and edited by E. B. Krumbhaar, 2nd ed., New York, Knopf, 1947.
9. Ilza Veith, "Ancient Japanese Medicine," *Ciba Symposium*, Summit, N. J., 2:1191, February-March, 1950.
10. William Caudill, "Applied Anthropology in Medicine," in *Anthropology To-Day*, Chicago, University of Chicago Press, 1953, p. 773.

2

The Roots of Mental Healing

THROUGHOUT history, every therapist, whether medicine man, priest, or physician, had his "public," whose world view coincided with his own. If it was accepted that one or several spirits and gods ruled the universe, the individual who tapped that source of good and evil was accepted as close to divinity. If divine, he could cure diseases. In Assyrian-Babylonian times (two or three millennia before the Christian era), Ea, god of the deep, Anu, god of heaven, and Bel, god of the earth, controlled man's destiny; they sent Marduk, son of Ea, with a healing message for the insane. Clay tablets, translated by archeologists, read,

> Take a bucket, fill it with water from the mouth of the river, impart to this the exalted magic power, sprinkle the man with it.... May insanity be dispelled. May Ea's word drive it out. [1]

The magic of words, a potent weapon against evil spirits, has lasted for thousands of years; even today the Rx at the head of every medical prescription derives from the figure ♃ , a symbol of prayer to Jupiter.

The mysterious power of the "word" was represented in ancient cabalistic philosophy, which hoped to find the key to the universe, the secret beyond the secrets of revelation.[2] The kabbalah (cabala), a sect of mystical Jews, and the Christian Gnostics both furthered an alphabetical and numerical mysticism in which the mysterious power of the twenty-two letters of the Hebrew alphabet would furnish the key to eternal transcendence. The "Heavenly Alphabet" was an implement of divine powers in "which every wall is removed from the spiritual eye."[3] This was the meaning that Cornelius Agrippa (1486?-1535), an otherwise enlightened medieval scholar, attributed to knowing the true pronunciation of the name "Jehovah." Such a person "had the world in his mouth."[4] From antiquity through the Middle Ages, the magic of words was passed on as a potent therapeutic weapon. The Venerable Bede, Anglo-Saxon theologian (circa 700 A.D.), recommended the following for gout:

> I pronounce the great name in which are consolidated things as Eaz, Azuf, Threux, Bain, Choog, Go go, now, now, quick, quick....

From cabalistic words to amulets, charms, and talismans, the vehicle of magic spread to numbers. To witness a passage in one of the *Anglo-Saxon Leechdoms*, "There are three days in the year which we call *Aegyptiaci*, that is, in our tongue, dangerous days; in which by no means, for no occasion, neither man's nor beasts' blood must be diminished."[5] The Venerable Bede, in his *Medesyns Approbate for Mortal Sekeness*, counseled, "[Whoever] of mankynde letteth hyme blode upon any of these iii dayes he shall be dede withynne five days nexte that followyn. These be iii forbode dayes." Indeed, the psychological undercurrent in medical practice to comparatively modern times was intimately related to the Pythagorean philosophy of numbers.

There were four varieties of bodily humors (blood, phlegm, yellow bile, black bile); four natural elements (fire, air, earth, and water); there were critical days in a disease and three forbidden days. Concoctions were given three times, prayers said over the patient seven times on seven days, ad infinitum.

Magical properties passed to precious stones. The

adamant (diamonds) drove off nocturnal specters, routed black venom, mended quarrels, and cured the insane. Agates worn as amulets were notoriously hostile to demons and magical illusions (hallucinations). The psychological substratum beneath jewels, charms, and amulets was the displacement of an idea to the object. The charm was anthrompomorphized, or rather spiritized as an active force against evil spirits. In time, evil forces causing specific diseases could be routed by invoking the proper charm. The doctrine of "signatures," reappearing in the medieval medicine of Paracelsus, was a further development wherein each disease carried a "signature," cured by use of the proper fetish.

Sources of information about treatment of mental disease in the ancient world—the tablets of Babylonia, the papyrus scrolls of Egypt, the Zendavesta of Persia—reveal a combination of religious, hygienic, and rational (naturalistic) attitudes. This is reflected in Greek writings as well as those of the ancient Hebrews. Pre-Hippocratic medicine began, in Brock's words, "on the periphery rather than the center of the Greek world"[6] and Sigerist, the eminent historian of medicine, points out that "religious medicine is timeless...Greece was no exception."[7]

Throughout the ancient world, "psychotherapy" as it is known today was imbedded in religious ritual and mysticism. Although Greek physicians brought a scientific spirit into treatment by mental means, even their thinking was based on Mesopotamian, Egyptian, Indian, and Minoan practices.[8] As early as 1140 B.C. the Chinese maintained institutions for the insane and Hindu physicians treated some forms of madness with "kindness and consideration" (1400 B.C.). It is probable that if more records of early civilizations in Asia Minor were available, as is the case in the voluminous Talmudic and Biblical writings, much would be known of the practice of "psychiatry" in ancient days. For example, the Talmud cites an incantation:

> He who enters a town and is afraid of the Evil Eye, let him take his right thumb in his left hand, his left thumb in his

right hand and say the following: "I, son of B, come from the seed of Joseph against whom the Evil Eye has no power."[9]

But practical health measures were part of Talmudic therapy also, to witness:

> Thirteen things are said concerning bread eaten in the morning; it protects from heat, cold, injurious spirits and demons; it makes the simple wise and helps him win a lawsuit....[10]

Still, magic was inveighed against by the Rabbis; "the charmer who charms snakes...the consulter with familiar spirits" was guilty of infraction of the Laws of the Torah; divination and magic were, though prevalent, a "heathen practice." Dr. Cohen, translator of the Talmud, remarks,

> The Talmud reveals very clearly a conflict between the pure, rational doctrines of the Bible and the debased beliefs and superstitions which pervaded the world in which the Jews live.[11]

The ultimate healing power came from God, ministered through His priests and Rabbis. For proof, Talmudists pointed to Chronicles II in the Old Testament, where the fate of Asa, King of Israel, is recorded:

He died in the "one and fortieth year of his reign" because he "sought not to the Lord but to physicians."[12] It is stated in Deuteronomy that "the Lord will smite thee with madness...the Lord will take away all sickness."[13]

It was in the golden age of Hellenic culture that the conglomerate mixture of ritual and rationalism was brought to fruition under the Aesculapian physicians. Historians believe the Aesculapians represented but one school of priest-physicians, where observation of disease and prayer for the removal of symptoms developed side by side.[14] Other cults, such as the Dioscure, who prayed to Castor and Pollux, used psychological methods, including dream interpretation and incubation, but the cult of Asclepius dominated the scene.[15] The Edelsteins, who translated from the original Greek, described the process of "incubation": The patient, having entered the temple or the halls especially built for incubation, lay down on the floor on a pallet. In these impressive surroundings, the god Asclepius revealed himself directly to everyone who needed his help. The god was seen by the incubant in a dream, whereupon the patient entered into personal contact with him, and he proceeded to heal the disease brought to his attention or advised a treatment to be followed. Sometimes ventriloquism on the part of the priest-attendants aided the patient's spirit to converse with his Aesculapian god. Another description, contributed by Sigerist, states: "The gods healed by appearing to the patient, fondling him, giving verbal orders, or had him touched by a dog, snake, or caused the patient to dream; when he awoke, he was cured."[16]

Diagnosis through interpretation of dreams apparently has a long history in antiquity, as does "temple sleep." In general, dreams were relied on to divine the nature of an illness and to foretell the future. Freud, who twenty centuries later penetratingly turned his attention to the psychological meaning of dreams, points out that interpretation of dreams through associations was freely utilized by Artemidoros of Daldianus, but that the interpretation was through the associations of the *interpreter*, not the patient.[17] An inscription on stone tablets discovered at Epidaurus relates a case history of an incubation treatment:

> Agestratos suffered from insomnia on account of headaches. As soon as he came to the *abaton* he fell asleep and had a dream. He thought that the god cured him of his headache and, making him stand up, taught him wrestling. When day came he departed cured, and after a short time he competed at the Nemean games and was victor in wrestling.[18]

Similar techniques were employed at the site of oracles. Kouretas, a professor at the University of Athens, translated a description of the practice at the Oracle of Trophonius, where the therapy was conducted in a cave whose atmosphere was so fearsome that patients were "obliged to remain silent on the subject all their lives on pain of death (and) not to divulge their treatment at the hands of the holy diviners."[19] The record states: "One Timorchus, while in the cave . . . at the same time he heard a crash and was struck on the head, and the sutures parted and released his soul."

Of the physicians, the most famous was Hippocrates, who, at Cos, practiced a "rational supernaturalism."[20] Although there is a question as to whether the physicians of Hippocrates' time followed the priestly operations of the Aesclepiadiae, Hippocrates, the Father of Medicine, is believed to have worked at one of these temples of health, the temple at Cos. The most celebrated physician of the ancient world, Hippocrates inveighed against "charms, amulets and other such vulgarity." His collected works, *Corpus Hippocraticum* (considered by some the work of several men), contain the foundation stones of modern medicine and the earliest unmodified statement of naturalism in medicine: "It is nature itself that finds the way; though untaught and uninstructed, it does what is proper" *(Epidemics VI, 5)*. Discontented with the supernaturalism that passed for medical theory in his time, the Father of Medicine insisted that disease should be looked upon as arising from bodily (natural) sources. With regard to the disease "called Sacred" (epilepsy), Hippocrates wrote:

> It appears to me to be nowise more divine nor more sacred than other disease, but has a natural cause from which it originates like other affections. Men regard its nature and cause as divine from ignorance and wonder, because it is not at all like to other diseases.[21]

The writings of Hippocrates exerted a lasting influence on medicine for a millennium or more. He contributed a high moral tone to the therapeutic aspect of medicine. Though his clinical observations were more medical than psychiatric, his influence proved to be significant in the evolution of psychiatric thinking. In effect, Hippocrates laid the ground for its readmission within the purview of clinical medicine. For example, hysteria was shrewdly considered by him to be due to the movement of the womb (*hysteron*) throughout the body. He antedated by two thousand years the modern findings of the place of sexuality in the neurosis. Although Hippocrates prescribed the traditional tight bandage around the abdomen for hysterical paroxysms, with fumigation by warm vapors conveyed through a funnel into the vagina, he astutely advised as a more practical remedy for hysteria "to indulge the intentions of nature and to light the torch of Hymen."

The amazing persistence of healing ideas common to the ancient world may be judged by an experience of this writer in the 1930s in New York. A young Sephardic Jewess appeared at the clinic of the Beth Israel Hospital complaining of a group of symptoms diagnosed as hysterical. They had been treated unsuccessfully by medication and modern "psychotherapy." Her parents, after a further trial, in their anxiety wrote to the Chief Rabbi in Salonika, Greece, from whose Jewish population of centuries standing the parents had emigrated. The Rabbi responded, sending her some herbs with instructions to have the young virgin straddle over a pan of steaming water in which the herbs had been steeped.

Later centuries, rich in Greek intellectualism, exerted only a minor influence on mental healing. Aristotle's (384-322 B.C.) analysis of psychological functions, which held for centuries as the foundation of academic psychology, had little to do with practical healing methods. Socrates' appeal to reason, Plato's idealism, the genius of Greek philosophers, apparently touched only the educated, elite Greek citizen. However, mental disease as a natural problem did not escape the attention of the Greek psychologist-philosophers. Plato suggested that mental disorder was partly somatic, partly moral, and partly divine in origin, "caused by 1, the result of love, 2, the result of great trouble, 3, from the Muses," and offered an essentially sensible therapy. The curative effect of words, of "beautiful logic," was advised by Plato in the case of one Charmides, who

had lately complained of a heaviness in his head...

Charmides asking me whether I knew of a remedy? I replied, it is a certain leaf, and a certain incantation in addition to medicine.... The soul is cured by certain incantations, and these incantations are beautiful reasons.[22]

As the glory of classic Greece declined, other areas developed medical centers. Alexandrian physicians made great strides in anatomy, pathology, and physiology. Brock states that the "greatest advance...between the time of Hippocrates and Galen, (500 to 600 years) was probably made by Alexandrian physicians."[23] The flow of classic culture from Greece to Rome brought Hippocratic medicine in its train. Here, for a century or two, it met opposition from Roman patricians, for the practice of medicine was regarded as a profession worthy only of slaves and foreigners. New healing methods and concepts brought to Rome by Greek physicians were feared: Garrison quotes Pliny the Elder's complaining at the invasion of "Greeklings" (physicians) that Romans with their household gods for every disease had "got on for 600 years without doctors." If one abandoned domestic simples, herbals, and religious observances, Pliny observed, the Greeks "would murder us by means of their Physicke."[24] Such an exclusive and isolationist point of view allowed little room in ancient Rome for the development of a psychotherapeutic attitude.

In the first century B.C., a physician named Asclepiades succeeded in impressing Romans of the virtue of Greek medicine to the point where he is said to have had Mark Antony and Cicero as patients. His political tact apparently dispelled the contempt noble Romans felt for the itinerant Greek physician who was despised for "accepting compensation for his services."[25] Asclepiades engaged in a controversy with the Hippocratic theory of humors by proposing a therapeutic scheme opposed to the healing power of nature that ultimately led to the Methodist school. For the next century or two, various schools of medicine, the Empiricists, Dogmatists, Methodists or Pneumatists, and Eclectics opposed each other in theory. The issue was whether Humoralism (hot, cold, dry, moist body fluids), Solidism (solid particles in the body), or Pneumatism (vital air circulating through the body) could explain health and disease: the Eclectics (as they do in today's psychotherapy), appropriated the best of all theories. In all this "welter of theorizing," as Garrison puts it, the names of Soranus, Celsus, and Galen stand out as epitomizing medicine of that age. [26]

Of the authors whose works have been translated, the contribution of Aulus Cornelius Celsus (25 B.C.–50 A.D.), touched most closely on treatment of mental illnesses. Celsus, whom Garrison calls a "private *litterateur*," not a physician, wrote in Latin. His *De Medicina* prescribed the management of mental cases with refreshing clarity.

> Those...violent, it is expedient to fetter. Ancients held them in darkness [which] quiets the spirit but there is no difference, dark or light. [After a day] the head is shaved, fomented with verbena; pour rose oil over the head and in nostrils...or rose rue pounded in vinegar...hold to the nose. [27]

On the other hand, Celsus prescribed black hellebore for depression, and "if hilarious, white hellebore." But for delusional patients:

> If however, it is the mind that deceives the madman, he is best treated by certain tortures. When he says or does anything wrong, he is to be coerced by starvation, fetters and flogging. He is to be forced both to fix his attention and to learn something and to memorize it; for thus...little by little he will be forced by fear to consider what he is doing.... To be thoroughly frightened is beneficial in this illness and so, in general, is anything which thoroughly agitates the spirit.

Notes to Chapter 2

1. Benjamin L. Gordon, *Medicine Throughout Antiquity,* Philadelphia, F. A. Davis, 1949, p. 163.
2. Josef Kastein, *History and Destiny of the Jews,* trans. by Huntley Paterson, New York, Viking, 1933.

3. Louis Ginzburg, "Cabala," in *The Jewish Encyclopedia*, New York, Funk, 1907, Vol. 3, p. 456.
4. Lynn Thorndike, *The Place of Magic in the Intellectual History of Europe*, New York, Columbia, 1925, p. 21.
5. J. F. Payne, *English Medicine in Anglo-Saxon Times*, Oxford, Clarendon Press, 1904.
6. Arthur J. Brock, *Greek Medicine*, trans. by A. J. Brock, London, J. M. Dent & Sons, 1929, p. 4.
7. Henry E. Sigerist, *A History of Medicine*, Volume II, New York, Oxford Univ. Press, p. 44.
8. C.N.B. Camac, *Imhotep to Harvey: Backgrounds to Medical History*. New York, Hoeber, 1931.
9. Rev. Dr. A. Cohen, *Everyman's Talmud*, New York, E. P. Dutton & Co., 1949, p. 274.
10. *Ibid.* p. 246.
11. *Ibid.*, p. 274.
12. II Chronicles, 16:12–13.
13. Deuteronomy, 7:15.
14. Sigerist, p. 67.
15. E. J. Edelstein and Ludwig Edelstein, *Asclepius*, Baltimore, Johns Hopkins Press, Vol. 2, 1945.
16. Sigerist, p. 67.
17. Sigmund Freud, *The Interpretation of Dreams*, trans. A. A. Brill, New York, Macmillan, 1933, p. 107.
18. Douglas Guthrie, *A History of Medicine*, Philadelphia, Lippincott, 1946, p. 44.
19. D. Kouretas, "The Oracle of Trophonius," *Brit. J. Psych.* 113, 1967, p. 144.
20. Ludwig Edelstein, "Greek Medicine in Its Relation to Religion and Magic," *Bull. Hist. of Med.* 5:201, 1937.
21. Francis Adams, *The Genuine Works of Hippocrates*, Vols. 1 and 2, New York, Wood, 1886.
22. La Rue Van Hook, *Greek Life and Thought*, New York, Columbia University Press, 1923, p. 252.
23. Brock; p. 13.
24. Fielding H. Garrison, *An Introduction to the History of Medicine*, 3rd. ed., Phila., Saunders, 1921, p. 96.
25. Brock, p. 13.
26. Garrison, p. 20.
27. Garrison, p. 96.

3

Rationalism and Religion

The enlightened treatment of mental cases, outlined with meticulous care by Celsus, and within a century by Galen, did not reach the lower classes of Roman society. The records indicate little recognition of the difference between somatic and psychological troubles or their treatment. The Roman gentleman of means had small interest in the sufferings of the masses and less in their life and comfort. Cicero (circa 100 B.C.) wrote:

> All gains made by hired labourers are dishonorable and base, for what we buy of them is their labour, not their artistic skill... the very gain itself does but increase the slavishness of the work.... [1]

Militarily and politically the Romans were supreme, their feats of engineering outstanding, their orators and writers vitalizing. Latin authors dealt with many aspects of medicolegal problems, with epidemiology, sanitation, nutrition, hygiene; philosophers wrote on morals, the ethics of man, and his political institutions. But psychotherapy as a predominant medical interest was nonexistent. It was not until pride in Roman efficiency softened and the Roman Empire began to crumble and paganism gave way to Christianity (A.D. 392) that traces of a humane spirit toward the mentally distraught appeared. The zeal of the early Christians, spreading doctrines of poverty, obedience, and charity, paved the way for acceptance of the monastic tradition of humility and humaneness.

As noted, the literate of Rome held the lowly born citizen in contempt. Tacitus dryly describes a therapeutic scene:

> ...a second petitioner, who suffered a withered hand pleaded his case too.... Would Caesar tread upon him with the royal foot?... With a smiling expression, and surrounded by an expectant crowd of bystanders, he did what was asked. Instantly, the cripple recovered the use of his hand.[2]

Similarly, Lucian, writing of the traveling quack:

> You are similar to the fake physicians who buy themselves silver cupping-glasses, lancets with gold handles...but they do not know how to use the tools....[3]

If slaves and common citizens were treated at all, it was by the salves and philtres of "wise women," by army surgeons, professional poisoners, and drug peddlers.

As Christianity gathered adherents in Europe, attitudes changed toward the mentally ill. If the early years of the first millennium can be characterized, even in the light of its diversity, Meecham's comments would be apt:

> That age was one of extraordinary religious quest. National and ancestral faith had failed. The mind of the West hungered for a new knowledge.[4]

Still the influence of old pagan cults did not disappear; they were woven into Christian doctrine, surfacing in a new form of magic—demonology. For the first few centuries of the Christian era, magic "was identified with demons."[5]

During the first millennium, the doctrines of the Early Church, which taught that the aim of life hinged on a mystical and eventual reunion with God, exerted another effect on the development of mental healing. By accenting forbearance toward pain and the mutability of earthly pursuits, the Church retarded the progress of medical investigation throughout the Dark Ages and later. Though this is true, it is also true that the responsibilities and the dangers confronting man as he contemplated his soul—his relation to God, his guilt, his needs for renunciation and efforts at salvation—did bring into focus those psychological deflections akin to disturbances now recognized as nervous afflictions.

In spite of the pseudo-physicians who thronged toward Rome, the inheritors of Greek medicine continued their interminable argument. To judge from their writings, the Dogmatists, the Methodists, and the Empiricists supported their own schools and reviled the others. The most influential of them all was Galen, who flourished in Rome during the latter part of the 2nd century A.D. He extended the ideas of Hippocrates (humoral theory) with those of the "pneumatists" into a body of writing that lasted for seventeen centuries. Garrison states that the authority of Galen, to whose works all debates were referred during the Dark and Middle Ages, "prevented the advancement of medical science" until the Renaissance.[6]

Sigerist, in his introduction to the translated works of Galen, characterizes Galen's writing as "verbose, turgid and quibbling" in contrast to Hippocrates' "clarity and simplicity."[7] Nevertheless, Galen was an anatomist, physiologist, neurologist, and above all, an authority on everything medical. In spite of his dogmatism, he understood the psychology of his patients and his recommendations for treatment appealed to the upper-class Romans.

Galen, whom another translator calls the "great synthetiser"[8] was born in Pergamum, Greece, where he absorbed the ancient cultures and developed an enthusiasm for Hippocrates. By the time he transferred his activities to Rome, whatever his theoretical writings proclaimed, his therapy was naturalistic. In his discussion of depression and anxiety, he counseled:

> Apotherapeutic exercise, the result of well-completed exercise, is suitable in grief and in wakefulness... such conditions are relieved by gentle massage with plenty of oil, by temperate baths, by slow exercise without violent tension with numerous rest periods interposed....
>
> The oil—a relaxing oil as Sabine (Italy) and fir seed, fully ripe at the time Arcturus rises (September) in Rome or Mysteria in Athens.[9]

The "Rational" system of medicine, extended to mental diseases, appears in other writings of the time. Aretaeus, a Greek of the second century A.D., advised consideration of the peculiarities of the patient:

> It is better to agree with some than to oppose them; those who will not eat are to be placed among those who eat; the educated should be forced to read and repeat what they learned.[10]

Caelius Aurelianus, a Roman who translated the work of Soranus of Ephesus in the fifth century A.D., reflects the rational system of treatment, while he quibbles with his predecessors.

> Asclepiades in Book I of his *Acute Diseases* says that phrenitis is a stoppage... in the membranes of the brain frequently without any feeling of pain and accompanied by loss of reason....
>
> It would be better therefore for Asclepiades to describe the disease in clear and suitable language and not with reference to an obscure and confusing "stoppage." In fact this stoppage may not even exist, as we shall show in a treatise we are planning to write against the sects.[11]

Thanks to the translation of Drabkin, a definitive picture of treatment for mania in the early Dark Ages can be obtained through Aurelianus. In great detail the latter indicates the need for a

> light and warm room... the bed firmly fastened down... rubbing the patient's limbs gently... instruct the

servants to give the patient a sympathetic hearing... if he is excited, bind him. First cover his limbs with wool and then fasten with a bandage... do not give food until the end of the first three-day period... perform a venesection at the end of the three-day period... when the highest stage of the attack is reached, cut the patient's hair and apply cupping....

and so on until the "disease declines."[12]

The rules for after-treatment were equally detailed, rational, and curiously modern:

when the mental aberration is reduced, give him a bath of olive oil with the addition of a decoction of marshmallow... prescribe walking and vocal exercise... let him see a stage performance... give him problems appropriate to his particular craft... give him questions on commonplace matters or let him play checkers....

The forces at work in the early Christian era conditioned the type of therapy used. While the Italian schools of medicine at Salerno (9th to 12th century A.D.) after the decline of Rome depended on Hippocrates' and Galen's writings, faith cures were also popular. Castiglioni points out that while lay physicians, schooled in Greek medicine in Salerno and elsewhere in Italy, worked their rational methods on patients, nearby Monte Cassino's priests employed religious faith.[13] The chain of faith healing, from primitive *mana* to the amulets of polytheistic religions to the faith in God of Judeo-Christian theology, came into full force late in the Dark Ages. This healing force, discovered and organized and exploited by the Church of Rome, was the most significant contribution to mental healing in the Western world until the rise of psychological science in the eighteenth century.

Under the leadership of the Church, faith became a ubiquitous force. The Church's position as molder of social consciousness in the medieval period is well summarized by Worcester and McComb:

Religion, knowledge, science, art, philosophy, and even

the chief pleasures of life, were in her keeping. When people went to the theatre, it was to witness the mysteries of the Christian religion. When they traveled, it was to go on a pilgrimage to Christ's tomb. From the cradle to the grave, on week-days and Sundays, the Church surrounded human life.[14]

For this leadership the Church exacted the price of implicit obedience. In healing, as well as in other aspects of contemporary activity, faith in the Church played a dominant role.

With the fall of the Roman Empire, leadership in medical matters passed to Constantinople. Here, Greek medicine was kept alive, and the flourishing Arabians made progress in surgery, pharmacy, and the companion sciences astronomy, mathematics, and botany. The effect of Mohammedan, Persian, and Jewish influences on medicine in the so-called "Arabic" period was noteworthy. The Arabic period was distinguished by much writing, its main influence deriving from Greek medicine. Two names out of many characterized the extended period; Avicenna in Baghdad (980–1036 A.D.) and Maimonides in Cordova, Spain (1135–1204 A.D.). Although Avicenna wrote a "gigantic tome" covering all of medical practice, few of his works involved mental healing. Historians characterize his books as a "miracle of syllogism" that "appealed to the medieval mind."[15]

Maimonides, on the other hand, stressed physical and mental hygiene. A Jew who wrote in Arabic, Maimonides brought his knowledge of Greek medicine into combination with his Talmudic learning. "Emotional experiences caused marked changes in the body," he wrote; "the thought brings worry to the spirit over what is going to come or happen in the future."[16] Yet, his prescription to "help digestion, strengthen heart and brain...delay aging...liquify white fluid...remove tension...help sex life...and expand the soul," implied the same shotgun quality of Galenic and Grecian medication:

Rx:
1 Myrobalan from Kabul,
Belilegium—one ounce each,
Myrobalanus embliu, two ounces,
Citron,
Ox Tongue,
Lavender Flower,
Bitter costus root and Aconite,
Red rose flowers,
Asparagus,
Pistachio seed....[17]

The centuries covered by this panoramic historical sketch are difficult to compress. Garrison makes the point that while Western Europe was still trifling with charms, amulets, and relics in their faith healing, "many of the Jewish and Mohammedan physicians were beginning to look upon these things with a certain secret contempt."[18] Hospitals in Cairo developed into specialized centers; the Arabians were much ahead of their contemporaries in Western Europe in their treatment of the insane. The religious fervor of Saint Augustine, the ethical pronouncements of Rabbi Maimonides, the increasing accent on introspection in the examination of the inner life of man had an indirect influence on mental healing. Moreover, hospitals developing in such disparate areas as Lyon and Paris, France; Salerno, Italy; Baghdad; Cairo; and Valencia, Spain, during the period from the fifth to twelfth century indicates the benevolent interest of physicians, priests, and philosophers in the mentally ill.[19] Indeed, from our vantage point, the more that comes to light, the less dark appear the "Dark Ages."

The tangled strands of psychotherapy during this vast period can be separated into two main streams—rational therapy with an accent on bodily hygiene, and mystical faith healing under the canopy of the Christian, Moslem, and Jewish faiths. The main vehicle, stimulated by the spread of Christianity in the Western world, was the refinement and specificity of belief. Jesus taught that faith alone was enough; "Thy faith hath made thee whole."[20] Although Jesus also healed with the Word—"He cast out the spirits with his Word"[21]—healing by direct faith was an even further simplification of psychotherapy beyond the various symbolic vehicles of healing. Revealed religion purified healing through faith by indicating that the "light of faith is a gift supernaturally bestowed upon the understanding" of man, a "gratuitous" gift waiting only upon acceptance of God.[22] For when Jesus healed he was using the faith of those who came to him:

> They brought unto him all sick people . . . with divers diseases and torments, and those which were possessed with devils, and those which were lunatick, and those that had the palsy; and he healed them.[23]

Centuries later this faith was recognized by scholastics as "an act of the intellect assenting to a Divine truth owing to the movement of the will, which is itself moved by the Grace of God" (St. Thomas). Healing through faith was concretized over many centuries of Western life. Theology and a radical change in attitude toward mental life were responsible elements: in Mumford's words, "an assertion of the primacy of the person, and a shift from outer circumstances to inner values.[24]

Throughout this psychological transformation, the continuity of underlying magical influence active in faith healing can be seen in the accessory techniques used by early Christian healers. The laying on of hands, for example, was a healing tradition of great antiquity (Ebers papyrus), evolving apparently from the Oriental custom of treatment by massage with oil, water, or saliva. This custom may have arisen from the use by Egyptians of aromatic oils for purposes of sensual stimulation.[25] In the Book of Mark there is a description of the use of oil as a healing agent.[26] The intermediary substance, oil or saliva, used by the ancient healer cemented the therapeutic bond between patient and priest-physician, since saliva (spittle) was an effective agent for breaking a charm or warding off evil. The significance of the magical cleansing element in lustrum (spittle), acknowledged in antiquity, is seen in the Greek tragedy when King Oedipus proclaims the curse, "From fellowship of prayer or sacrifice or lustral rite is excommunicated."[27] Purification by water, oil, or spittle (the lustral rite) is an expiatory act containing within it a healing connotation.

In the early days of Western Europe, healing through spiritual abstractions was mixed with pagan wizardry. The medical therapy of early Britain is illustrated in the poem "Lorica" (A.D. 830), studied by Singer, to be used against "demons, all poisons, envy...and sudden death."[28] It names each anatomic part, asking divine blessing and protection for each. To Singer it represented "classical science in the last stage of degeneration."

Medical folklore, always popular, was rampant in Europe during the early Christian Era. The Church, set against this kind of therapy, insisted upon substituting exorcism for the magical formulas and herb concoctions of the leeches. Before the Norman invasion of England in A.D. 1066, leechdom was synonymous with medicine in Britain. The *Leech Book of Blad*, one of the collections of folk medicine still extant, describes medical prescriptions for mental cases, for a "fiend, sick man or demoniac" that are in form a medley of herbal tradition, magic, and faith:

> When a devil possessed the man or controls him from within with disease: a spew drink or emetic, lupin, bishop-wort, henbane, corpleek: pound these together, add ale for a liquid, let it stand for a night, add fifty bibcorns of cathartic grains and holy water—to be drunk out of a church bell.[29]

Those espousing healing by faith alone had to battle the forces of native medical "science." Anglo-Saxon physicians, known as "leeches," developed an enormous list of medicaments, derived in large part from the "wise women" who occupied a role similar to that of the medicine man in earlier civilizations, but without his priestly attributes. The "wise women" had neither learning nor written precepts. They kept their pedestrian art alive from generation to generation through word of mouth. Gradually their herb recipes became interlarded with magic, bits of astrology, prayer, and superstitious doggerel. Reviled by the learned of her generation, it was the "wise woman," nevertheless, to whom sufferers went when the advice and the physic of the physician-leech were of no avail. Today, among some persons, a deep respect for the magic of grandmother's household remedies survives the barrage of scientific rationale in our generation.

Leechdom was finally subordinated when the higher clergy proclaimed that only the Church could work miraculous cures through the exorcising of devils from sufferers. But the appeal of the leech and his magic was strong, as was the combined appeal of religious ritual, magic, and the royal healing touch. A medical treatise of the fourteenth century advises the making of a "cramp-ring" for the falling sickness (epilepsy) in imitation of the cramp-rings made of gold and silver given by King Edward the Confessor and his successors. The ring, when formed of coins, was "hallowed" by the Plantagenet and the Tudor kings on Good Friday and given to supplicants for their curative value. The medical prescription, modernized somewhat, advises for the "Crampe":

> Take...on Gude Friday, at five parish churches, five of the first penyes that is offered at the crosse, of each church the first penye: then take them all and go before the crosse and say V. pater nosters in the worschip of fife wondes (of the crucified Jesus) and bear them on V days and say each day in the same wise...and then go make a ryng there without alloy of other metal, and write within Jasper, Batasar, Altrapa and write without, c. nazarenus (Christ of Nazareth); and sithen take it fra the goldsmyth upon a Fridai, and say V. pater nosters as thu did before and use it alway afterward.[30]

As late as 1518, the College of Physicians in London agreed that rings consecrated by the King were charms against "Spasms"; amulets, against "slander and calumny."

The problem of control over the depredations of Satan was settled, to the Church's satisfaction at least, at the Council of Toledo in the fifth century.[31] The Church Fathers followed St. Augustine in his discussion of "miraculous healing":

> demonic seizures can be cured only by miracles, whereas diseases... can also be overcome by human medical effort.[32]

So, for many of Satan's hordes, nervous disorders such as hysteria ceased "to be a disease—it became a visible token of bewitchment and thus fell within the domain of the Church."[33] Slowly during the centuries, evil, through the influence of the Devil, became equated with madness. Subtly, black magic, demon possession, and witchcraft invaded Europe. There was no cure but exorcism. In a sense, the struggle between the magic of the common people —leechdom—and that of the Devil—witchcraft—was joined. The Church took full responsibility for the necessary downfall of Satan and in so doing became the unwitting psychotherapists of the medieval period.

But the theology of the Patristic followers of St. Augustine was not unmixed with the ethic of kindliness and mercy. For the medieval hospital movement epitomized a tradition of humane treatment of patients, in particular mental patients. Monastic medicine, encouraged by Pope Innocent III in 1198, flourished in such hospitals as that established by the Knights of St. John on the Island of Rhodes (1311) in the days of the Crusades. Nursing groups were established in hospitals along the route to the Holy Land through France, Switzerland, Italy, in the eleventh, the twelfth, and the thirteenth centuries. Within their walls, religious orders brought tranquility and humaneness, piety and tenderness, to their charges. Because madmen and simples, uncared for by an organized group, roamed the highways, the butt of derision or neglect, the monasteries manned by religious orders assumed the burden of the maniacal or the feebleminded patient. One of the first hospitals devoted to mental patients exclusively was the colony established in Gheel, Belgium, in the thirteenth century. The colony plan was a step forward in the treatment of mental patients, since it stressed other than purely custodial features.

The colony at Gheel centered in a shrine to St. Dymphna.[34] According to the legend, Dymphna was the daughter of a pagan Irish king about the year A.D. 600. Influenced by her mother, a devout Catholic, Dymphna had decided to consecrate her life to God. Upon the death of her mother, the King proposed incestuous marriage to his daughter. She fled to the Continent, and when she refused to yield, he slew her in insane rage. Because she had triumphed over the incestuous desires of a father made mad by demons, she became the saint of those with mental maladies. On the spot where Dymphna fell, an infirmary and a church were erected. Patients were brought there to receive benefits from the relics of St. Dymphna contained in the hospital. Some patients remained at the shrine, being boarded out to peasants in the neighborhood. Retarded children, left for a longer while, were given work in the fields and the households under the benevolent guidance of the country folk and the healing influence of the spirit of St. Dymphna. In this way the "colony" plan or "boarding-out system" for treating defectives evolved and is in active existence today.

The monastic tradition of treatment through loving care and gentleness was particularly applicable to mental cases. The early hospitals conducted by The Sisters of the Society of Hospitalers did not attempt any physical treatment, principally because of injunctions by the Holy See against monks engaging in healing by worldly means. These "sick houses" provided good food, rest, and spiritual calm for their patients in an atmosphere of humility and service. But there is other evidence to show that the management of mental cases rested on a spirit of humanitarianism. The connotation of "barbarousness" commonly associated with the Dark Ages is not entirely merited, at least in the management of mental cases. Evidence from the early French romances reflects the tradition of humaneness and a realistic conception of mental disease. Study of this literature, Wright comments,[35] reveals the notion of curability of insanity through physical and mental means with little mention of demonology. In England, one of the Arthurian legends that details the story of Sir Launcelot's madness reflects the practical handling of madmen in the Dark Ages.

The story relates that hard upon a precipitating emotional shock, Sir Launcelot became mad and exiled himself from his customary haunts. While wandering in a forest, he was found by Sir Blaunt and his aide, a dwarf, who conveyed him to the castle:

> And so they took...Sir Launcelot...to the castle; and then they bound his hands and his feet, and gave him good meals and good drink, and brought him back again to his strength and his fairness; but in his wits they could not bring him again, nor to know himself. Thus Sir Launcelot was there more than a year and a half.[36]

Subsequently, Launcelot wandered off, returning to the forest and by "adventure came into the city of Corbin, where Dame Elaine was that had borne Galahad, Sir Launcelot's son." As was the custom, the wandering madman was reviled by the youths of the town:

> And so when he was entered into the town, he ran through the town into the castle, and then all the young men of the city ran after Sir Launcelot, and there they threw turfs at him, and gave him many said strokes; and, as Sir Launcelot might reach any of them, he threw them, so that they would never more come into his hands; for of some he break their legs, and some their arms, and so fled into the castle. And then came out knights and squires for to rescue Sir Launcelot, and when they beheld him, and looked upon his person, they thought they saw never so goodly a man; and when they saw so many wounds upon him, they all

deemed that he had been a man of worship. And they then ordained clothes unto his body, and straw underneath him, and a little house, and then every day they would throw him meat, and set him drink; but there were few or none that would bring meat to his hands.

The kindness of Launcelot's rescuers required a complement of magic and faith for his eventual recovery. The resolution of the case occurred, so the story relates, when Dame Brisen applied an enchantment:

> "Sir," said Dame Brisen, "we must be wise and ware how we deal with him for this knight is out of mind; and if that we awake him rudely, what he will do we all know not, but ye shall abide, and I shall throw such an enchantment on him, that he shall now awake within the space of an hour."

and a priest wrought a miracle through faith:

> ...and so they bear him into a tower, and so into the chamber, where as was the holy vessel of Sancgreal; and, by force Sir Launcelot was laid by that holy vessel. And then there came a holy man and uncovered the vessel; and so, by miracle, and by virtue of that holy vessel, Sir Launcelot was healed and recovered.

The naturalistic treatment attitudes toward the insane reflected in these Arthurian legends are mirrored in the historic work of a Franciscan monk, Bartholomeus Anglicus. Bartholomew, professor of theology at Magdeburg and later serving in England, was the author of a nineteen-volume encyclopedia called *De Proprietatibus Rerum* (Of the Nature of Things). Written on parchment in 1275, it had the distinction of being printed by Caxton; later it was translated into many languages and became one of the first books to be widely published after the invention of printing. It had a tremendous vogue, especially among the clergy, being used as a household manual by those who were called upon to give counsel in medical as well as in spiritual affairs.

The seventh book of Bartholomew's *De Proprietatibus*, which dealt with mental illnesses, was most probably based on current knowledge and practice.[37] One is struck by the reasonableness of the viewpoint expressed and the restrained treatment prescribed, considering the therapy accorded "frenzied" patients several centuries later by medical men. Treatment recommended by Bartholomew noted that

> the diet shall be full scarce as crumbs of bread oft washed in vinegar and that he be well controlled or be bound in a dark place. He [the madman] should not see many people nor should he be shown pictures for they will probably make his state worse. All those about him should be required to be still and silent and they must not answer his nice [foolish] words.... The most important thing is to secure sleep for him and for this ointment and balming [use of balsams] applied to the head may be effective.[38]

For the melancholics he counseled:

> The medicine [treatment] of them is that they be bound that they hurt not themselves and other men and such patients must be refreshed and comforted and withdrawn from cause of any matter of busy thoughts and they must be gladded with instruments of music and some deal be occupied.

There was little of magic and no hint of demonology in the writings of Bartholomew on mental illnesses. With the hysteria of witchcraft seething around him, and ecclesiastic authorities and lawmakers putting demented, deluded witches to the rack, Bartholomew and his fellow monks and nuns plodded on, nursing, observing, helping patients by methods singularly like those used in modern hospitals.

The crosscurrents, then as now, flowed from different premises, bringing antipodal attitudes into view. One of these arose from the mountebanks who plied their trade in most of Europe.

The absence of controlled medical practice in medieval days left the field of healing open to all those who could obtain the public ear. Moreover, there was no unity of medical opinion or practice; Arabian medicine did not grow, and Galenic physicians refused to budge from the tests of Galen, the "True Physition." In this confusion, the art of healing was the open prey of "itinerant toothdrawers and prittle-prattling barbers." The medical act of 1511 in England promulgated by Henry VIII, was aimed against a

> grete multitude of ignorant persons . . . common artificers, smyths, wevers and women [who] boldly take upon them grete curis [cures] . . . in which they partely use socery [sorcery] and witchcrafte

and partly medicine of a noisome type. The barbarities of therapy among "tinkers, tooth-drawers, horse gelders and horse leechers" need not be detailed. A supply of leech-doms and a taste for showmanship sufficed to embark one on a healer's career. The public was warned to be wary of the following self-appointed physicians:

> Runagate Jews, the cut-throats and robbers of Christians, slowbellied monks, who have made escape from their cloisters, simoniacal and perjured shavelings, busy Sir John Lack-Latins, thrasonical and unlettered chemists, shifting and outcast pettifoggers, lightheaded and trivial druggers and apothecaries, sun-shunning mechanics, stage players, jugglers, peddlers, prittle-prattling barbers, filthy graziers, curious bath-keepers, common shifters and cogging cavaliers, bragging soldiers, lazy clowns, one-eyed or lamed fencers, toothless and tattling old wives. . . . [39]

Against this band of "dolts, idiots and buzzards," men like Burton mourned, "All the world knows that there is no virtue in charms, &c, but a strong conceit and opinion alone . . . which takes away the cause of the malady from the parts affected."[40]

One of the sources from which these "haters of all good learning" drew their *materia medica* was alchemy, the chemical science of the Middle Ages. Alchemists, intrigued by the search for the elixir that would confer everlasting life, and for the secret formula that would transmute lead into gold, drifted off into mysticism. In their dimly lit laboratories they detached themselves from any practical quest and delved into secrets that lay just beyond the veil. They came to be regarded as magicians whose murky solutions contained the answer to life's riddles. Magic and divination crept into the practice of alchemy. The secrets of the "wise women" were mixed with those of alchemy and necromancy to form black magic, which was the life stuff of the charlatan's practices.

Through the itinerant physician Paracelsus,[41] alchemy was brought into medieval healing. Theophrastus Bombastus von Hohenheim, called Paracelsus (1443–1541), was a vivid figure of his time, "half-genius and half rogue." Alone, he all but transformed the complexion of medical treatment in medieval times and after. He dared to lecture in the vernacular German, taking the results of his thought and experiments directly to the people. Paracelsus insisted that only minerals such as sulfur, lead, mercury, iron, and other chemical compounds of proved activity were to be used in medical treatment, in place of the innocuous roots, herbs, extracts, and tinctures of the traditional school of Galen. Bombastic in speech and positive to the point of vituperation, Paracelsus demolished the authoritarianism of medieval physicians:

> By what right, I ask, can that sausage stuffer [the Galenic physician] and the sordid concocter of the pharmacopeia give himself out as a dispenser.... If you would put aside these your incapacities and would examine...how the stars rule diseases and health, then...you would learn that your whole foundation amounted to nothing but fantasy and private opinion.

He insisted that iron received its magnetic power from the heavenly bodies and that the

> Arcanum of the heavens ruled human destinies as it ruled health...Luna leads the brain. What relates to the spleen flows thither by means of Saturn.... So, too, kidneys are governed by Venus, the liver by Jupiter, the bile by Mars.

The truculent Paracelsus approached the treatment of the mentally unbalanced with the same vigor he used to attack his compatriots. To "remove mania in a miraculous way," he prescribed a half drachm of "one ounce olei comphore, 1 drachm olei musci," to be drunk by the patient in small doses or denuding the skin with

2½ ounces of aqua forte,
½   ounce of a solution of salis communalis,
3   drachms of mercuri sublimati;
Mix and dissolve with heat. Place on the skin [of scalp or fingers] until it peels off the skin. . . . [41]

A peripatetic physician, Paracelsus wandered everywhere, treating everyone while he buffeted his contemporaries with his diatribes against Galenic medicine. Actually, however, his approach to mental troubles was more realistic than his rantings indicate.[42] But more than that, Paracelsus' introduction of minerals in his treatment—mercury, iron, lead, sulphur, arsenic, copper—led to a widespread use of chemicals in the service of medicine. His significance for the history of psychotherapy lies, oddly enough, in his dalliance with astrology and magnetism. The use of the magnet for bodily ailments led to mesmerism and beyond. Paracelsus caught a glimpse of the importance of imagination within the patient, in Galdston's words, thus starting a "series of stages in the progressive development . . . of modern psychotherapy via magnetism, mesmerism, hypnotism, suggestion, psycho-catharsis and psychoanalysis."[43]

Undoubtedly Paracelsus has been unappreciated in the history of psychotherapy, for as a "man of the people and of the earth,"[44] he broke into the circle of priestly, even royal, faith healers. For generations the healing touch was regarded as the property of kings. English kings since Edward the Confessor, as well as European monarchs, Clovis the Frank in the fifth century and Henry IV and Louis IX in later years, enjoyed "the king's touch." The English kings chiefly exercised their power on scrofula (the king's evil), but some extended their activity to all types of illnesses and all manner of patients. In the *Parliamentary Journal* for July 2, 1660, there is an entry:

His sacred majesty, on Monday last, touched 250, in the banqueting house; among whom, when his majesty was delivering the gold, one shuffled himself in, out of an hope of profit, which had not been stroked.

The practice of the king's touch faded with the removal of the Stuart line from the British throne, but a worthy successor arose in the figure of the commoner, Valentine Greatrakes. Greatrakes, a veteran of Cromwell's army in retirement in the country, was seized one day with an inspiration to heal. The "stroaker" explained how he became aware of

an impulse, or a strange persuasion in my own mind (of which I am not able to give any rational account to another) which...suggested to me that there was bestowed on me a gift of curing king's evil.[45]

Greatrakes was astounded no less than his patients at his success. Stimulated, he continued treating "the Ague...and...the Falling sickness," delighted to see the "pains slip and fly from place to place until they did run out." The procedure consisted of stroking the skin gently or vigorously while saying, "God Almighty heal and strengthen you for Jesus' sake." Greatrakes claimed that under energetic massage even the most malignant evil spirit would vanish and the devil would go "like a well bred dog." Greatrakes, the "Irish stroaker," became a national figure.

His book reported cures through testimonials of scientists of the day. Robert Boyle, a Fellow of the Royal Society, wrote of Greatrakes' curing "a man who could not move his hand, it being to his thinking dead." Others recounted cures of

twenty several persons in Fits of the Falling-sickness, or Convulsions, or Hysterical passion (for I am not wise enough to distinguish them).

Greatrakes had his detractors, who demanded investigations of his cures, but he came through unscathed because of the "gift of God" and his princely bearing. Other commoners who aspired to the divine touch were not so revered. Some years before the "Irish stroaker," James Leverett claimed he could heal "all manner of diseases... by stroaking or touching with his hands" by virtue of his being "the 7th son of a 7th son."[46] Denounced as an "Impostour and cousener of the King's people," Leverett was brought before the Star Chamber in 1637, yet his "manual exercise" helped many. Without the divine aura that surrounded Greatrakes, Leverett did not attain the popularity of the former. Still, the healing touch, until then invested in royal and priestly hands, passed to a long line of digital healers through the efforts of Leverett, Greatrakes, and others. The transposition of faith from sovereign to subject seems to have been a nodal point in the evolution of faith healing, little noticed at the time, but of great importance in retrospect.

The displacement of faith healing from kings to laymen proceeded irregularly for several centuries, sometimes covertly, sometimes openly in a flood of spiritual enthusiasm. It achieved its full flowering during the Renaissance, a vigorous growth during the middle 1800s, and a continued bloom into the eternal present.

Notes to Chapter 3

1. Harry Elmer Barnes, *The History of Western Civilization*, Vol. 1, New York, Harcourt, Brace & Co., p. 309.
2. Scarborough, *Roman Medicine*, Trans. by K. Wellesley, Ithaca, Cornell Univ. Press, 1969, p. 208.
3. Scarborough, p. 99.
4. Henry G. Meecham, *Light from Ancient Letters*, London, Geo. Allen & Unwin, 1923, p. 150.
5. Arturo Castiglioni, *Adventures of the Mind*. Trans. V. Gianturio, New York, A. A. Knopf, 1946, p. 215.
6. Garrison, p. 106.
7. *Galen's Hygiene, De Sanitate Tuenda*, trans. Robt. M. Green, M.D. Intro. by Henry Sigerist. Springfield, Ill., Chas. C. Thomas, 1951.
8. Brock, p. 18.
9. *Galen's Hygiene* (trans. R. M. Green).
10. Whitwell, p. 160.

11. Gaelius Aurelianus. *On Acute and On Chronic Diseases*, edited and trans. by I. E. Drabkin, Chicago, Univ. of Chi. Press, 1950, p. 7.
12. Aurelianus, p. 543 et seq.
13. Arturo Castiglioni. *Clio Medica* VI, *Italian Medicine*, ed. E. B. Krumbhaar, New York, Hoeber, 1932, p. 12.
14. Elwood Worcester, Samuel McComb, and I. H. Coriat. *Religion and Medicine, the Moral Control of Nervous Disorders*, New York, Moffat, 1908.
15. Garrison, p. 120.
16. Moses Ben Maimon (Maimonides), *The Preservation of Youth*, trans. from the Arabic by Hirsch L. Gordon, Philosophical Library.
17. Moses Ben Maimon, p. 56.
18. F. H. Garrison: p. 128.
19. Alexander and Selesnick, p. 64 et seq.
20. Matt. 9:22.
21. Matt. 8:16.
22. "Faith," in *Catholic Encyclopedia*, Vol. 5, p. 756, New York, Appleton, 1909.
23. Matt. 4:24.
24. Lewis Mumford, *The Condition of Man*, New York, Harcourt, 1944.
25. Edward L. Margetts: *Personal Communication*.
26. Mark 6:13.
27. Sophocles, *The Theban Plays*, trans. E. F. Watling, Harmondsworth, Middlesex, England, Penguin, 1947, p. 32.
28. C. J. Singer: *From Magic to Science: Essays on the Scientific Twilight*, New York, Liveright, 1928.
29. Rev. Oswald Cockayne, *Leechdoms, Wortcunning and Starcraft of Early England, being a collection of documents for the most part never before printed, illustrating the history of science in this country before the Norman Conquest*, London, Longmans, 1864.
30. Raymond Crawfurd, "The Blessing of Cramp-Rings; a Chapter in the History of the Treatment of Epilepsy" in *Studies in the History and Method of Science*, edited by C. J. Singer, Vol. 1, Oxford, Clarendon Press, 1917.
31. Louis Coulange, *The Life of the Devil*, trans. by S. H. Guest, New York, A. A. Knopf, 1930.
32. Ilza Veith, *Hysteria, the History of a Disease*. Chicago, Univ. of Chicago Press, 1965, p. 46.
33. Veith, p. 56.
34. A. J. Kilgour, "Colony Gheel," *Am. J. Psychiat.* 92: 959, 1936.
35. E. A. Wright, "Medieval attitudes towards mental illness," *Bull. Hist. Med.* 7: 352, 1939.
36. Sir Thomas Malory, *The Arthurian Tales*, from the text edition of 1634, R. B. Anderson, Editor-in-Chief, London, Norroena Society, 1906.
37. Lynn Thorndike, *A History of Magic and Experimental Science*, p. 406.
38. Bartholomeus Anglicus, *De Proprietatibus Rerum*, Book 7, *On Medicine*, translated and annotated with an Introductory Essay by J. J. Walsh, Vol. 40, Froben Press, October to December, 1933. (A

parchment manuscript is in the library of the Academy of Medicine, New York, dated 1360, entitled: "De Proprietatibus Rerum," Libri XVIII, Opus Theologicum et Philosophicum, by Bartholomei Anglici, Ordanis Frere Minorum.)

39. The Anatomyes of the True Physition and Counterfeit Montebanks, London, 1602.
40. Robert Burton, *The Anatomy of Melancholy,* London, Bell, 1906.
41. Paracelsus, *Four Treatises of Theophrastus von Hohenheim Called Paracelsus* (The Diseases that Deprive Man of His Reason, Such as St. Vitus' Dance, Falling Sickness, Melancholy and Insanity and their Correct Treatment), trans. by Gregory Zilboorg from the original German. Also Temkin, Rosen, and Sigerist. Baltimore, Johns Hopkins Press, 1941.
42. George Mora, *Paracelsus: On the Occasion of the 400th. Anniversary of his Book, "Diseases that Deprive Man of His Reason (1567)." American J. Psych.* 124:803, Dec. 1967.
43. Iago Galdston, "The Psychiatry of Paracelsus," *Bull. Hist. Med.* Vol. 24, May-June, 1950, pp. 205, 213.
44. Zilboorg, *Paracelsus,* p. 130.
45. Richard Hunter and Ida Macalpine, *Three Hundreds Years of Psychiatry,* London, Oxford Press, 1963, p. 178.
46. Hunter and Macalpine, p. 151.

4

The Devil's Dominion

THE advent of witchcraft in Western Europe as a religious, legal, and psychopathological phenomenon during the early years of the second millennium had a direct impact on psychotherapy. Witchcraft itself is as old as man; its roots, according to Murray,[1] are in the folk religion of prehistoric Europe. But its eruption into a "cause" during the medieval years and later turned the Church's zeal into a witch hunt with its grisly train of torture and death.

Early churchmen fought the malevolent demons for more than fourteen centuries. In A.D. 563, the Council of Braga decreed that anyone who believed in the virtue of the devil to create thunder and lightning, tempests and droughts, was "anathema," or if anyone believed in the influence of the stars on the body and the soul of man, "let him be anathema also." St. Augustine, in the fifth century, wrote: "All diseases of Christians are to be ascribed to these demons. Chiefly do they torment fresh-baptized Christians, yea, even the guiltless newborn infants."

The reformer, Martin Luther, declared that the devil "stirs up arguments and quarrels, arms the murderer against his brother, urges rebellion, foments war, brings to birth storms, hale and diseases."

There were strong emotional reasons for the widespread belief in the malevolence of Satan's hordes. Life for the peasant masses was circumscribed. Their physical existence belonged to the feudal master, their spiritual being was entrusted to the Church. But their fantasy life was uncontrolled, and folklore, fairy tales, and witches' stories became outlets for the peasant's fantasy. The gigantic fallacy of the Covenant of Satan, the flying cult of Diana, and the thousand oddities of witchcraft had the stamp of reality.

Not only the ignorant, suggestible element in medieval society believed in witchcraft; it was common among men of learning and intelligence. Kings, priests, lawyers, judges, noblemen, scholars, artists—all believed firmly in this gigantic delusion: among them stood Lord Bacon, Sir Walter Raleigh, Sir Thomas Browne, Mathew Hale, and so on.[2]

The Devil satisfied a deep need in mankind. On him was heaped all the "badness in this world." Theologians taught that Lucifer and his fallen angels, driven from Heaven, were dedicated to evil from the start. Moreover, the Devil could work magic and change his form in the twinkling of an eye, invade people, turn into an animal, carry his evildoing into every cranny of God's world. This magic aspect of the Devil made him a formidable foe. The works of the exorcising churchmen appeared all the more miraculous in this light. The arch enemy of the race was, and is, tireless in his efforts to undo good, as Lewis so charmingly described recently.[3] The early Christian fathers saw their duty clearly. Humanity had to be preserved from these "thousand demons to the right and ten thousand to the left." A malevolent angel, Tertullian insisted, was in constant attendance upon every person, and only the most energetic Christian action could combat its evil influence.[4]

It was vital then for the Church to stamp out these heretics and destroyers of society. The inquisitors were originally drawn from the Franciscan and the Dominican Orders and sent to aid the local courts in adjudicating cases, for example, of "Sorcery, Satanism and apostasy," for which crimes the secular court usually decreed death. Inquisitorial interest was predominately in heretics and the political implications of Satanism, which Summers in 1928 declared to be identical with the "absolutism of any revolutionary of today... [of] Lenin, Trotsky, Zinoviev and their fellows."[5] Later, the Church, through its inquisitorial representatives, increased its activity beyond that of apostates, hoping to quell the plan of witches and their black leader to destroy the true Church and set the standard of Satan on high.

The Church fathers felt the need of an authoritative work that would set down rules and regulations for the discovery, the apprehension, and the conviction of witches and sorcerers throughout the Christian world. This need was met by the work known as the *Malleus Maleficarum*, or *The Witches' Hammer*, by Fr. Henry Kramer and Fr. James Sprenger, of the Order of Preachers, which appeared in Latin in 1484, accompanied by a laudatory papal bull of Pope Innocent VIII. For two centuries this book was the bible of the inquisitors.[6]

The papal bull authorizing the work of the inquisitors Kramer and Sprenger tells in measured phrases the need for their work:

THE BULL OF INNOCENT VIII

Innocent, Bishop, Servant of the servants
of God, for an eternal remembrance.

Desiring with the most heartfelt anxiety, even as Our Apostleship requires that the Catholic Faith should especially in this Our day increase and flourish everywhere, and that all heretical depravity should be driven far from the frontiers and bournes of the Faithful....

It had indeed lately come to Our ears, not without inflicting Us with bitter sorrow, that in some parts of Northern Germany as well as in the provinces, townships, territories, and dioceses of Mainz, Cologne, Treves, Salzburg and Bremen, many persons of both sexes, unmindful of their own salvation and straying from the Catholic Faith, have abandoned themselves to evil, Incubi, Succubi, and their incantations, spells, conjurations and other accursed charms and crafts, enormities and horrid offenses, has slain infants yet in the mother's womb as also the offspring of cattle, have blasted produce of the earth...afflict and torment men and women...hinder men from performing the sexual act and women from conceiving.

Our dear sons, Henry Kramer and James Sprenger, Professors of Theology, of the Orders of Friars Preachers, have been by Letters Apostolic delegated as Inquisitors of these heretical pravities....

Wherefore, We, as is Our duty, being wholly desirous of removing all hindrances and obstacles by which the good work of the Inquisitors may be let and tarded...[that the Inquisitors may not be] molested or hindered by any authority whatsoever....

(Given at Rome, at S. Peter's, on the 9 December of the Year of the Incarnation of R. Lord, 1,484....)

To the inquisitors, witchcraft was the creed of all who fought against established order, who undermined religious institutions and, as Summers says, "set on high the red standard of revolution." The Church had to fight not only defections in its ranks and ward off the attacks of those sincere few who were branded agnostics, but also those who nurtured subversive ideas against the state. Philosophers of the day who spoke for the abolition of private properties and the overthrow of monarchies, or who dreamt of the destruction of the feudal system, were fair game for the inquisitors. They, like the religious heretics, belonged to the hosts of the devil, their souls given over to the powers of darkness and obstructionism. It is against these that Summers speaks when he says:

In fact, heresy was one huge revolutionary body exploiting its forces through a hundred different channels and having as its object chaos and destruction...the teachings of the Waldenses and the Albigenses, the Henricians, The Poor Men of Lyons...were in reality the same dark fraternity just as The Third Internationals, The Anarchists, The

Nihilists, and the Bolsheviks are in every sense, save the mere label, entirely identical.[7]

This attitude toward political thought extended naturally toward other abnormal aspects of human behavior, including mental illnesses. The *Malleus Maleficarum* gave the approbation of authority to the idea that demon-possession was the cause of mental as well as all other types of human disturbances.

The *Malleus Maleficarum* is divided into three parts. The first part answers the question of the existence of witches through devious argumentation, chiefly on the Scriptures, the Canons, and the works of the scholastics, St. Thomas, St. Augustine, and numerous medieval theologians. The authors disposed of the obvious objection that witchcraft and magic are self-delusions or products of the imagination. Only God can change man and since the Almighty with His permission allows devils to exist, therefore devils actually change, inhabit, and possess man. The tome goes on carefully to define the acts to be considered those of witchcraft, telling how to handle witnesses, how to controvert the arguments of laymen, how to obtain confessions or, failing that, force an acceptance through torture.

Throughout the whole volume, and indeed the whole of medieval demonology, runs the idea that women are closely allied to sin, the Devil, and witchcraft. The Church argued from the doctrine of primal sin that it was to the devil's advantage to encourage carnal pleasures. The female sex was a natural ally to concupiscence. The authors of the *Malleus Maleficarum* affirm:

> All witchcraft comes from carnal lust, which is in woman insatiable. (See Proverbs XXX: There are three things that are never satisfied, yea, a fourth thing which says not, It is enough; that is the mouth of womb.) Wherefore, for the sake of fulfilling their lusts they consort even with devils.

In the section entitled "Remedies, Prescribed for Those Who Are Bewitched by the Limitation of the Generative Power," is found:

Although far more women are witches than men, as shown in the first part of the work, yet men are more often bewitched than women and the reason for this resides in the fact that God allows the devil more power over the venereal act through which the original sin is handed down in other human actions.

The misogynic tone of demonology rested on a characteristic medieval attitude toward women, which Havelock Ellis points out was expressed in the aphorism, "woman is a temple built over a sewer." It is small wonder that half-crazed witches, buoyed by an intense masochism and incontinence with the prevailing value judgment toward women, freely related their phantasmagoria. Consider the case of

a young girl witch who had been converted, whose aunt also had been burned in the diocese of Strasburg. And she added that she had become a witch by the method in which her aunt had first tried to seduce her.

For one day her aunt ordered her to go upstairs with her, and at her command to go into a room where she found fifteen young men clothed in green garments after the manner of German Knights. And her aunt said to her: "Choose whom you wish from these young men, and I will give him to you, and he will take you for his wife" ... and when she said she did not wish for any of them, she was sorely beaten and at last consented, and was initiated according to the aforesaid ceremony. She said also that she was often transported by night with her aunt over vast distances, even from Strasburg to Cologne.[8]

There is also the following case report:

Another, named Walpurgis was notorious for her power of preserving silence and used to teach other women how to achieve a like quality of silence by cooking their first-born sons in an oven. Many such examples are to our hand.[9]

The medical use of witchcraft developed into an art and science. Clinical cases[10] were reported extensively describing the interrogation of the devil and techniques of exorcism. Signs of possession were detailed for the benefit of medical men and jurists.[11] Exorcists apparently were not above using a little trickery in their deliverance of witches. Ventriloquism was an important aid to the monks in making vivid their conversations with demons.

The treatment of choice was exorcism, but first the pathology of Satan's works had to be mastered. The important discovery was made that the devil had a regular technique for enamoring and seducing his followers. The pact of Satan and the coven were in time uncovered. The Convention (small coven) of the Sabbat, the midnight meetings of witches with their master, was believed in implicitly by many. Each witch who testified confirmed the details. The activities of the coven and the pact constituted irrefutable legal proof of witchcraft to the satisfaction of the most meticulous.

The Witches' Sabbat or Coven was a ceremony in which Satan at intervals renewed his compact with the witches, binding them to eternal evil. The witches, walking or flying through the air, were met in a group by the devil on some lonely moor, where they indicated their allegiance to him by stories of their wickedness, depravity, and psychosexual perversion. The coven was sealed by the "reverential kiss, *osculum infame* ... on the Devil's fundament."[12] The details, described in medieval writings, were of a frenzy of bestiality, whipped up and given direction by the devil, who, besieged by palpitating, quivering witches, seized them to satisfy his carnal lust.[13] Accounts relate that the witches stood "waving their bellies" in a most sensuous dance, writhing in sexual torment and delight, while the fever grew to intense proportions and the wind of terror "froze their naked bodies."

Orgies of perversion and unspeakable cruelty, frenzies of undisguised sadomasochism, were imputed by common consent to the Prince of Evil. Magistrates and theologians were moved by the evidence, zealous to show the witch as she really was:

> an evil liver; a social pest and parasite, the devotee of a
> loathly and obscene creed; an adept at poisoning, blackmail,

and other creeping crimes; a member of a powerful secret organization inimical to Church and State; a blasphemer in word and deed; swaying the villagers by terror and superstition; a charlatan and a quack sometimes; a bawd; an abortionist; the dark counsellor of lewd court ladies and adulterous gallants; a minister to vice and inconceivable corruption; battening upon the filth and foulest passions of the age.[14]

As records of cases of witchcraft accumulated, learned doctors hastened to publish their experiences, hoping to assist others in the diagnosing of the possessed. Sammarinus, in his treatise on exorcism, states that the symptoms that, for a theologian, denote a demoniac are:

1. If he feigns to be mad, and the strength and size of his body continually grow and augment.

2. If he speaks in a language, be it Greek, Latin or any other, which he has never learnt.

3. If he becomes dumb, deaf, insane, blind, which are the signs contained in Holy Scripture.

The signs for physicians indicating possession were no less numerous or less precise. Here are those enumerated by Baptiste Codronchus:

1. If the disease is such that the doctors cannot discover or diagnose it.

2. If he loses his appetite, and vomits whatever meat he has taken; if his stomach is as if narrowed and drawn in, and if there seems to him to be some mysterious heavy thing inside himself.

3. If he becomes impotent in the arts of Venus.

4. If he feels a great lack of strength throughout his whole body, with extreme languor. If he feels stupid in his mind, and takes pleasure in uttering stupidities and idiocies, as do melancholics.[15]

A final diagnostic sign was the Devil's Mark or Witch's Mark, otherwise known as the *Stigmata Diaboli*. These were blemishes on the skin indicating points of contact with Satan. A medical authority of the 1700s describes the mark as

> sometimes like a blew spot, or a little tate, or reid spots, like flea biting; sometimes also the flesh is sunk in, and hollow, and this is put in secret places, and among the hair of the head, or eye-brows, within the lips, under the arm-pits, and in the most secret parts of the body.[16]

Under the impetus of *The Witches' Hammer,* witch finding in the sixteenth and the seventeenth centuries passed from an art to a medicolegal science. Early editions of the *Malleus Maleficarum* were printed in miniature form so that "inquisitors might carry it in their pockets and read it under the table."[17] The inquisitorial boards were composed of clergymen, judges, professors—men of standing learned in the science of witchcraft. Their opinions were authoritative and final; their techniques of witch hunting and torture were the approved legal procedure of the day. Sir Thomas Browne, author of the famous *Religio Medici* (1643), when questioned by the judge, laid down the proposal as an accepted scientific fact "that the Devil in such cases did work upon the Bodies of Men and Women, upon a Natural Foundation to stir up, and excite such humours superabounding in their Bodies to a great excess."[18]

The foot-crushing by the Spanish boot, the torture on the rack, the immersion in cold water were not aimed at the witch but at the evil spirit imprisoned within the subject's body. The purpose of torture was to drive the demon out of the subject's body until he came forth admitting defeat. Medical records of the medieval period explain how baffling illnesses were cleared up in the most unexpected manner by the willingness of a devil to admit he was plaguing the body of the patient. A case attributed to the great surgeon, Ambrose Paré, one of the most rational physicians of medieval times, illustrates the literalness with which the devil was regarded as the cause of mental and physical disease. The doctor had been called to attend a young nobleman who had convulsions which involved different parts of his body such as the left arm, or the right, or on occasion only a single finger, one loin or both, or his spine, and then his whole body would become so suddenly convulsed and disturbed that four servants would have difficulty in keeping him in bed. His brain, however, was in no way agitated or tormented, his speech was free, his mind was not confused, and his sensations, particularly in the regions of the convulsions, remained intact. . . .

At the end of the third month it was discovered that it was the devil who was the cause of the malady. This was learned from a statement made by the devil himself, speaking through the lips of the patient in profuse Greek and Latin. . . .

This devil, forced to talk frankly by means of religious services and exorcisms, stated that he was a spirit. . . . He was then interrogated as to what kind of spirit he was, and by what means and by what means and by virtue of what authority he tormented the young nobleman. . . .

[He] stated that he was relegated to the body of our patient by someone whose name he did not want to give, that he entered it through the patient's feet and went up to the level of the brain, and that he would leave the patient also through the latter's feet but not until the day set by previous agreement. . . . [19]

Communications with possessing demons sometimes were reported as long colloquies between demon and exorcist, and sometimes as peremptory commands, accompanied by prayer, "Depart, O Satan, from him," during the exorcism, or "Accursed Devil, hear thy doom . . . depart with thy works from this servant" of the Lord.[20] The abundant demonologic art of the medieval period often pictures devils departing from the mouth and other parts of the body. In view of the devil's declamation in the above-quoted case by Paré, that he would leave through the patient's feet, it is interesting to read the description of exorcism by a Fiji Islander, as reported by a missionary, Rev. L. Fison (circa 1870):

He passed his hands over the patient's body till he detected the spirit by a peculiar fluttering sensation in his finger ends. He then endeavored to bring it down to one of the extremities, a foot or hand. Much patience and care were required, because the spirits are very cunning.[21]

The medicine man continued:

When you have got the demon into a leg or an arm you can grasp with your fingers, you must take care or he will escape you.... But when you have drawn him down to a finger or a toe, you must pull him out with a sudden jerk, and throw him away, and blow after him lest he should return.

So alarming was the spread of Satan's influence that King James I, while in Scotland, interested himself in several cases. One was that of Geillis Duncane, a maid who was observed to leave her house nightly to perform miracles. Her master, suspecting that she was involved with the devil, examined and tormented her by "binding and wrinching her head with a corde," without result as far as confession was concerned. She was then brought before proper authorities and examined in the presence of the king. After a diligent search the examiners found the mark of the devil in her "fore crag or foreparte of her throate." At this Geillis confessed, accusing Agnes Sampson and others of teaching her to have traffic with the devil. The king's counselors examined Agnes Sampson for marks on her body indicating contact with the devil. After careful search the devil's mark was found on her external genitals. This was irrefutable evidence, since it was established that the devil, when he makes a pact with his subjects, binds it by licking them with his "tung" in some "privy" part.[22]

It is not surprising that the clergy exerted a direct influence on mental disorders through witchcraft, since physical ailments were relegated to physicians, whereas those of the "soule" (mind) remained in the hands of divines. Hunter and Macalpine, in their invaluable compilation of medieval and Renaissance writers on madness,[23] point out that sources of the history of psychiatry go beyond the work of physicians, to the clergy, philosophers, philanthropists, men of letters, to be found in parliamentary acts and reports, unpublished manuscripts and so on. Perusal of their material shows that while many clerics wrote of

> *Demoniacus* ... he or they the which be mad and possessed of the devyll or devyls and theyre propertie to hurt and kyll them selfe, or ... any other thynge.... [24]

others, such as John Downame (1609), "puritan divine of London," called for "silence ... whereas ... crosse speeches and perverse replies, make the chollericke man proceed from anger to rage ... to fury and madness...."[25] "Spiritual Physicke," or psychotherapy, in spite of the pandemic of exorcism, was never entirely absent among the "ministers to a mind diseased."

While the devil held dominion over the insane, influences were stirring that were eventually to dissolve the mass delusion of witchcraft. The liberal atmosphere of the Renaissance, the stimulus to individual thought and experiment during the sixteenth and seventeenth centuries, provided the background for dissolution of the grand illusion. Increased activities in mathematical and astronomical sciences, in literature, architecture, philosophy, exploration and colonization, all indicated the new spirit which had one reflection in a reorientation of implicit medieval reliance on supernaturalism.

A significant factor was the spread of printing and its reflection on the reading public. Scholars estimate that during the 1550s forty percent of the masses were literate, "for laborers a fraction of 1%, ... the merchant class ... read English and [had] some training in Latin."[26] Books were being bought; new ideas were promulgated; a sixteenth-century encyclopedia, Sebastian Munster's *Cosmography,* which appeared in 1544, ran through thirty-five editions until 1628, and was translated into German, Latin, Italian, and Czech.[27]

Enlightenment was forthcoming. Francis Bacon (1561–1626) was already writing in 1605: "We come ... now to that knowledge ... which is the knowledge of ourselves; which deserveth the more accurate handling...."[28] And: "Medicine is a Science, which hath beene more professed, than labored, and yet more labored, than advanced; the labor having been in my judgment, rather in circle, than in progression."

Undoubtedly the invention of the printing press stimulated experimentation and discussion, and a half century after the first books were written, articles and tomes came from the presses in increasing numbers. Heinrich Laehr computes that from 1459 to 1800 fifteen thousand authors wrote articles on philosophy, medicine, psychology, forensic medicine, psychiatry, and neurology.[29] By analyzing the enormous compilation by Laehr, one may see the increasing interest in neuropsychiatric subjects. This bibliography, of course, does not include the thousands of tracts, pamphlets, and letters that were written on all aspects of magic, faith healing, demonology, etc. Thus, in the fifteenth century, about six items on neuropsychiatric treatment appeared; in the sixteenth century, this number had increased to 250 items; in the seventeenth century, 1,800 items appeared; and in the eighteenth century, the number had increased to 3,000 items. The range of interest in psychiatric symptomatology is matched only by the complexity of treatments offered. All the prescriptions of the ancients with their commentaries (added over fifteen hundred years) were copied and recopied in the medical works of European writers of the sixteenth and seventeenth centuries. To these were added the findings of demonologists, interspersed with old wives' tales, philosophic theories and herb lore in one conglomerate therapeutic mixture. For example, in Ronsseus' *Miscellanea* s. epist. med (1618), the subheadings were:

> Of Mania; Therapy of Mania; A Fall Heals Mania; Daemonomania; Practices do not Rectify so-Called Second

Nature (Habits); Fornication brings about a Disease Manifested in Deadly Convulsions in Several Districts of Luneburg; Hydrophobia; Hydrocephalus; Tabes Dorsalis....

The Renaissance opened horizons in medicine and psychiatry. Although the countryside had its quota of "deceiving sorcerers" who preyed on the peasants with nostrums and salves and leftover astrological charms, the universities were bringing science into contact with medicine. A work by Thomas Willis, professor at Oxford (1660), whose name lives in neurology as the discoverer of the Circle of Willis, contained the following table of contents:

Of the Convulsive Diseases; Pathological Affect of Hysteria; Of the Mind of Brutes; Manifestations of the Physiological and Pathological Aspects as Melancholia, Mania, and Stupidities and Imbecility; Anatomy of the Brain; Chemical Theories; Recommendation of Diversion in Melancholia; Occupational Therapy including Mathematics and Chemistry; Change of Location; Farming; Ought not to be Left to Themselves; Beatings and Chains for Maniacs only in Institutions; Imbecility Depends Mostly on Changes in the Brain.... [30]

Psychotherapy was still, during the Renaissance, in a muddled state, divided between philosophers, clergymen, and enlightened physicians and "roving phisicians." In the middle of the seventeenth century, John Halle, a surgeon of Maidstone, England, wrote "An Historicall Expostulation: Against the beastle Abusers (of Surgery and Physic) in our time..." in which he gravely set down an accusation against

...one Robert Haris, professynge and pretendyng an highe knowledge in physike; under cloke wherof he deceaved mervaylouslie with vyle sorcerie...[and] one Thomas Lufkyn...[who] by roving abroad, became a phisician, a chirugien, a sothsayer, an astronomier, a phisiognomier, a palmister, a sothsayer, a fortune devyner and I can not tell what. This beastliest beguiler by his sorcery...this divell incarnate.... [31]

Or let us glance at the more garish work of Karl F. Paullini, called *Flagellum Salutis* (1698), whose table of contents reads as follows:

> Strange tales how by beatings all kinds of incurable cases have been easily and quickly cured; In the new editions has been added miraculous cures by music (F. E. Neidter); Life has been prolonged up to 115 years by the breath of young girls (F. H. Cohauser, Stuttgart); Deals with the usefulness of voluntary beatings in many diseases of the head; Beatings in melancholia; in frenzy; in paralysis; in epilepsy; in facial expression of feebleminded; in hardness of hearing; in toothache; in dumbness; hysterical crying; in nymphomania; sleepwalking....

A century later, George Baglivi, a prominent Italian physician, expressed in his widely read *Practice of Physic* a humanism and enlightenment that presaged modern psychotherapy

> I can scarce express what influence the physician's words have upon the patient's life, and how much they sway the fancy; for a physician that has his tongue well hung, and is master of the art of perswading, fastens... such a vertue upon his remedies and raises the faith and hopes of the patient... that sometimes he masters difficult diseases with the silliest remedies.[32]

There is no straight line of progress in psychotherapy and there was none during the seventeenth century. The eddies of sorcery and those of rational science swirled in the same stream. While Baglivi in Italy and Robert Burton (author of *The Anatomy of Melancholy*) preached gentleness and moderation in the management of mental patients, King Charles II on his deathbed (1685) was bled, a hot iron "applied to his head, a loathsome volatile salt, extracted from human skulls, forced into his mouth."[33] Against this medical medievalism, clergymen were gradually coming to consider mental illness as due to the "Soules Conflict."[34] So Richard Sibbs, Preacher at Grey's Inn, Cambridge, wrote:

If there were no enemie in the world, nor Devill in hell, we carry within us, that if it be let loose will trouble us more than all the world besides....

But first, supernaturalism in the form of witchcraft had to be scotched. The empirical, experimental, reality-testing attitude that the science of Copernicus, Kepler, and Newton was advancing in physics and astronomy, had not yet touched the infant art of psychiatry and psychotherapy.

As skepticism became more prevalent, learned men ventured to discuss witchcraft with some freedom. Education was preparing men to scrutinize old shibboleths. "The old fabric of ecclesiastical education housed a new lay clientele... [they studied] not to become priests... but more effective laymen."[35] To speak against the Church required intellectual courage; Reginald Scot, Squire from Kent, one such man, earned the wrath of King James I. Prefacing the latter's famous *Daemonologie*, the King, who caught the import of Scot's dissent, wrote:

> The fearful aboundinge at this time in this countrie of these detestable slaves of the Devill, the Witches or enchanters, hath moved me... to dispatch in post, this following treatise... against the damnable opinions of two principally in our age... the one called SCOT, an Englishman, is not ashamed in publike print to deny, that ther can be such a thing as Witchcraft.... The other called Vviervs [Wierus], a German Phisition sets out a publick apologie for all these craftesfolkes.[36]

Scot, who published his *Discoverie of Witchcraft*[37] seven years earlier (1584), had openly stated:

> The common people have become so assotted and bewitched, with whatsoever poets have feigned of witchcraft, either in earnest, in jest, or else in derision; and with whatsoever lowd liers and couseners [swindlers]... that they thinke it heresie to doubt in anie part of the matter; speciallie bicause they find this word witchcraft expressed in the scriptures.

The significance of Scot's book for psychiatry resides in his insistence upon natural explanations for the weird self-confessed experiences of witches. He collected examples of mysteries attributed to witches, and showed by logic and by scientific, philosophic, and even theologic argument that they could all be explained on naturalistic grounds. In place of the torture chamber, what these bedeviled, starved, ignorant suspects needed was "physick, food and necessaries." Scot's views were attacked on all sides. Even Montague Summers, the twentieth-century witch finder, expresses his belated contempt of Scot's work by saying, "[He] covers his atheism with the thinnest of ear and in fact wholly and essentially denies the supernatural."

Sexual activities loomed large in the Devil's domain: it was here that Reginald Scot was most effective. The theory of Incubi and Succubi is integral to understanding Satan's sexual powers.

Incubus was the name given to the male demon who visited women at night, forcing them into sexual congress against their will, while *succubus* was a female spirit who visited men for a similar purpose. Incubi and succubi were accounted to be the cause of night terrors, violent dreams, and nightmares. The incubus caused a sensation of weight on the chest, difficulty in breathing, terror, and a feeling of strangulation in sleeping persons, especially women, presumably because of the weight of the devil on the body of the sleeper. The incubus was regarded as a demon with a material body. It was believed, for reasons not difficult to understand, that the incubi particularly chose virgins and virtuous women to molest but did not cavil at the goodwife. The authors of *Malleus Maleficarum,* discussing a case of "Phantom pregnancy," blame incubi for the nocturnal activities that produced such diseases:

> At times also women think they have been made pregnant by an Incubus, and their bellies grow to an enormous size; but when the time of parturition comes, their swelling

is relieved by no more than the explosion of a great quantity of wind.... And it is very easy for the devil to cause these and even greater disorders in the stomach.

But to Scot these explanations were cloaks for lechery, a deception fed to an ignorant and trusting populace to gloss over the amours of young (and older) adventurers. Thus Scot in exposing

Bishop Sylvanus, his lecherie opened and covered againe, how maides having yellow haire are most combred with Incubus, how married men are bewitched to use other men's wives, and to refuse their own

relates the case of an incubus that came to a lady's bedside and made "hot loove unto hir." The lady, being offended, cried out loudly, and the company came and found the incubus under her bed in the likeness of Bishop Sylvanus. The defamation of Sylvanus continued until one day this infamy was purged by a devil who made a confession at the tomb of St. Jerome. Scot's caustic comment on this tale is, "Oh excellent peace of witchcraft or cousening wrought by Sylvanus!"

Troublesome incubi, although occasionally discovered to be youths bent on erotic adventures, were more often recognized as demons lying with married women even while their husbands were abed with them. Chaucer seems to have caught the humor of the situation when he writes in *The Wife of Bath's Tale:*

Women may go saufly up and doun,
In every bush, or under every tree;
There is noon other incubus but hee,
And he ne wol doon hem but dishonour.[38]

Incubi and Succubi were but one aspect of sexual deviltry. Impotence, for example, was also due to the malefactions of the Evil One. The *Malleus Maleficarum* dealt with it in detail, advancing the ingenious theory of "glamor" to account for this distressing disability. A *glamor* was a devil in the form of a man but so transformed as to be without his sexual organs. In this state of deprivation the glamor would replace the intended victim without the latter's knowledge. The victim, turned into a sexless being, needed only to find someone who would exorcise the demon to regain his virility. Parenthetically, it is interesting to note how the original castrative meaning of "glamor" has been displaced through the intermediate meaning of "deceptive allure" to the present connotation of "exciting, stimulating, or colorful." A case of glamor is reported by Kramer and Sprenger:

> A certain young man had an intrigue with a girl. Wishing to leave her, he lost his member; that is to say, some glamor was cast over it so that he could see or touch nothing but his smooth body. In his worry over this he went to a tavern to drink wine: and...got into conversation with another woman who was there, and told her the cause of his sadness, explaining everything and demonstrating in his body that it was so. The woman was astute, and asked whether he suspected anyone; and when he named such a one,...she said: "If persuasion is not enough, you must use some violence, to induce her to restore to you your health." So in the evening the young man watched the way...the witch was in the habit of going, and, finding her, prayed her to restore him the health of his body. And when she maintained that she was innocent and knew nothing about it, he fell upon her, and winding a towel tightly around her neck, choked her, saying: "Unless you give me back my health, you shall die at my hands." Then she, being unable to cry out, and with her face already swelling and growing black, said: "Let me go, and I will heal you." The young man then relaxed the pressure of the towel, and the witch touched him with her hand between the thighs, saying: "Now, you have what you desire." And the young man, as he afterwards said, plainly felt, before he had verified it by looking or touching, that his member had been restored to him by the mere touch of the witch.[39]

The authors warn, however, that the male organ was taken away "not indeed by actually despoiling the human body of it, but by concealing it with some glamor."

Reginald Scot was not a physician, and he was more

concerned with the injustices done to suspected witches during the trials in inquisitorial courts than in understanding the psychological basis of witchcraft. For the law, far more than medicine, held the fate of demonologic psychopathology in its iron control. Besides Scot, there were other disbelievers in the universe of demons. Paracelsus had supplied an ingenious explanation to the incubus legend:

> Incubi are male, succubae female creatures. They are the outgrowths of an intense and lewd imagination of men and women, formed of the semen of those who commit the unnatural sin of Onan.... This semen, born from imagination, may be taken away by spirits that wander about by night, and that may carry it to a place where they may hatch it out.[40]

Another iconoclast, Cornelius Agrippa von Nettesheim (1486–1535), had earlier been a strong advocate of magic. Later, he attacked the disease of demonology. Hated and persecuted by his colleagues for his attack on the delusion of witchcraft, Agrippa, in his mature years, wrote a volume, *On the Uncertainty and Vanity of All Sciences (i.e., Occultism and Magic)*, decrying witchcraft and magic, and declaring that their advocacy would benefit neither science, the Church, nor the state. While advocate of the city of Metz, Agrippa was able to put some of his convictions into practice. At one time he vanquished a particularly cruel judge, the Inquisitor Savini, and Agrippa's pupils hailed his triumph with delight. One Brennon wrote him: "All the poor women who were in prison are free and those who fled [the city] have returned. Savini sits in his monastery cell biting his nails and does not care to go out."[41] Eventually the monks of Metz accused him of belonging to the devil and of inviting the Master of Hell into his rooms. He was arrested twice and finally forced to flee to Grenoble.

The second of the two whose "damnable" opinions caused King James I so much vexation was Johann Wierus (Wier, Weyer) (1515–1576), born in Germany, a student of medicine under the preceptorship of Cornelius Agrippa.

Although widely interested in philosophy and the classics, Weyer devoted himself to the practice of medicine throughout his life. His great work, *De Praestigiis Daemonum* (1563),[42] is a volume in which he lays open with prophetic psychiatric insight the fallacies of demonology. He was both attacked by the Church and acclaimed by his followers for two centuries after the publication of his work. Bodin, a scholar of proportions, particularly castigated Weyer as one who "armed himself against God" and was skeptical at the evidence of "the most notorious of existing facts."[43] Montague Summers retained the vigor of his attack on disbelievers when he dubbed Weyer's work that of a "natural skeptic, a man without imagination, an ineffective little soul, a myopic squireen."

Weyer, a gentle physician and a loyal churchman, could and did lash out at the corrupt and slothful practice he witnessed about him.[44] His zeal, unlike Scot's, which was that of the reformer, arose from seasoned clinical observation and the desire to find the "shining truth" in an age of darkness. From experience he wrote that priests and monks

> are, in the main, ignorant and bold. (The good and pious ones which I hold in high esteem, I except.) They claim to understand the healing art and they lie to those who seek help that their sicknesses are derived from witchery... and the ignorant and clumsy physicians blame all sicknesses which they are unable to cure or which they have treated wrongly, on witchery.

Johann Weyer's method of study was that of clinical science. His practice was to search out cases of demonic possession and investigate, taking notes on every aspect of the phenomenon. He did not speculate, he studied patients. Hence his views have a freshness and a freedom from emotional bias rare in Weyer's day. Weyer insisted on *individualization* of cases. People should not be "molded in accordance with one definite model, as is the custom of many inept people, liars, imposters and various other grand masters of superstition and impiety."[45] Weyer's plea that the patient be regarded as an individual heralded a medical psychology that three centuries later regarded patients as individuals with an emotional life and a set of reactions specific unto themselves. Weyer introduced a practical, clinical attitude, presaging the perception of individual differences and individual emotional needs.

Weyer's system of treatment for the possessed is summarized in his works. He cautioned the physician who believed the patient to be possessed to examine him carefully in body and spirit. If the body were at first freed from demons, then more attention could be given to the physical aspect of healing. Weyer counseled (at this point he apologized for going counter to the Church) that the possessed first be taught about the deceptions of the demons. Official prayers are to be said for them. Fasting is effective because "if you are full of food and lazy, the demon has a special likeness for you." Alms should be given according to the patient's means. Every person was to be treated individually. In cases of impotence he advised the patient first to consult a doctor "to see if there is any other natural reason." If the cause is deeper, he should wait for three years until he considered it a reason for divorce. During this time he should give alms eagerly, should pray and make contrition, but should not fast.

Notions of demonology did not obscure Weyer's understanding of his cases. For example, when he dealt with the incubus question, he explained it as a nightmare due to the combined effects of indigestion and imagination:

> What is called Incubus is nothing than the condition which you call in this country "mare" and in England nightmare.... Why should not melancholic women, when they are lying on their backs asleep, once in a while imagine and assert that they were raped by an evil spirit?[46]

Yet Weyer was hooted down except by a few. For, as Binz says, "Weyer was talking like a rational human being to the inmates of a gigantic insane asylum, and undoubtedly with the same success."

Persistent, gentle, clearheaded, Weyer paved the way for a clinical psychiatry. Zilboorg, who recently "discovered" Weyer's importance in the history of psychiatry, with justice calls him the "first psychiatrist."[47] Only patient investigation and unbiased judgment could have allowed him to solve, according to psychiatric principles, cases that the medieval world accepted as due to demons.

Others followed Weyer, the German "Phisition," as the tide of rationality flowed on. One Father Spee, a German monk, published a volume in 1623 in which he denounced the prejudice-ridden magistrates of Germany and France. Starting in the traditional manner with the affirmation of belief in witches, Spee, his profession of faith made, was able then to demonstrate the absurdities of the doctrine of demonology. With admirable candor he said, "We who have to do with such people in prisons and have examined them often and carefully (not to say curiously), have sometimes found our minds perplexed." In an anonymous entry in a volume, *Cautio Criminalis* (1631), the monk was less circumspect. Here he pleaded:

> Why do you search so diligently for sorcerers? I will show you at once where they are. Take the Capuchins, the Jesuits, all the religious orders, and torture them—they will confess. If some deny, repeat it a few times—they will confess. Should a few still be obstinate, exorcise them, shave them, only keep on torturing—they will give in. If you want more, take the Canons, the Doctors, the Bishops of the Church— they will confess.... If you want still more, I will torture you and then you me. I will confess the crimes you will have confessed and so we shall all be sorcerers together.[48]

Father Spee's interest was chiefly in the legalities centering in the reality of confessions by witches. What he did, in effect, was to point out to the inquisitors that a wizard or a witch under trial must necessarily be suggestible. And therein he hit upon a vital point in the psychology of witch-making. A wizard on trial, besieged by questions, hammered at, grilled for hours, taken to the rack, grilled again and then taken back to the torture chamber, all the while being adjured to tell the truth, prayed at, shouted at, derided, mocked, was not a fit subject to give correct testimony.

Reginald Scot, Father Spee, and Adam Tanner in turn pointed out the absurdity of rules of evidence used against witches. Father Spee was joined by other members of the German church in urging that doctors and theologians should be consulted before the judiciary took steps in prosecuting cases of witchcraft. In the late 1600s, Robert Burton, divine turned psychiatrist, satirized the "cunning men and witches" who claimed a "St. Catherine's Wheel printed in the roof of the mouth" as proof of their satanic association.[49] The St. Catherine's wheel, an instrument of torture, characterized by spikes projecting from a wheel's circumference, was so named in memory of the Saint's martyrdom. The "cunning men" and witches, appropriating the place of wise women in providing therapy through enchantment, were castigated by Burton: "Tis a common practice of some men to go first to a witch, and then to a physician; if one cannot, the other shall; if they cannot bend Heaven, they will try Hell." Doubt was arising on all sides as to the validity of self-confession among witches and the ubiquity of witches and the devil's ability to cause disease by possession.

Early in the eighteenth century, liberalists of France entered upon a campaign of mockery of witchcraft. They thrust the rapiers of their wit at it, puncturing the bombastic conceit of the clergy and subduing the glee of the witch-pursuing mob. The Encyclopedists and other French writers such as Voltaire and Rousseau insisted again and again that belief in witchcraft was a "species of madness." The subtle influence of the Age of Reason was extending itself.

Not everyone gave up demonic possession as a "revealed" cause of man's troubles. Although medical men dismissed demonology as cause of disease, John Wesley mourned the passing of witchcraft:

It is true that the English have given up all... witches. I

am sorry for it.... Giving up witchcraft is in effect giving up the Bible.[49]

By the middle of the eighteenth century, medical attitudes were fixed in relation to mental illnesses caused by demons. Professor William Cullen, a leader in medical education in Great Britain, wrote in his *First Lines of Physick* (1769) that "we do not allow that there is any true demonomania.... In my opinion the species [of demonomania]...are melancholy or mania, feigned diseases or diseases falsely lived by spectators."[50]

A note reminiscent of the "glamors" of the *Malleus Maleficarum* creeps into his discussion of nervous ailments when Cullen writes, "Anaphrodisia magica is a fictitious species." Still, Robert Whytt, a contemporary of Cullen's, adopts a less reverential tone in discussing "the incubus or nightmare": "I shall just remark that a plethora, as well as other causes may so affect the nerves of the stomach as to give rise to the incubus."[51]

The demise of Satan and his nefarious works was enacted into law in England in 1736. In the reign of George II, an Act of Parliament repealed

> ...the statute made in the First Year of the Reign of King James the First intituled An Act against Conjuration, Witchcraft and dealing with evil and wicked Spirits...shall ...from the Twenty Fourth Day of June next, be repealed and utterly void and of non-effect...[52]

In the exploration of currents of mental healing, the digression into witchcraft was forced by an odd psychological turn of events. Until the seventeenth century, demonology was the psychological modality within which certain mental aberrations were perceived. Even if the examination and the disposition of witches were universally aimed at the salvation of society from evil, and in no way consciously turned toward the problem of treating individual mental patients, it still occupies a significant place in the history of mental healing.

In retrospect it seems clear that the emotional energies bent on detecting and punishing witches were similar to those energies that during the late Reformation period spurred humanitarian enterprises. Such ambivalent tendencies can be observed in society's handling of other large sociopsychological problems. The reaction of humanitarianism in public dealing with criminals and the insane during the eighteenth century was the other side of the coin. Sympathy replaced hate toward malefactors of a century or two earlier. Demonology was a way station in society's adaptation to its psychological problems. The cosmology of Satanism contained a satisfactory explanation for the manifestations of evil and "sin" in man: a screen on which to visualize cause and effect in human behavior. But when interest in man's soul passed from ecclesiastical to secular hands, science entertained other explanations.

Notes to Chapter 4

1. M. A. Murray, *The Witch-cult in Western Europe: A Study in Anthropology.* Oxford, Clarendon Press, 1921, p. 10.
2. M. A. Murray, p. 10.
3. C. S. Lewis, *The Screwtape Letters,* New York, Macmillan, 1943.
4. Quintus Tertullianus, *Apologetic and Practical Treatises,* edited by Rev. C. Dodgson, Oxford, Library of Fathers, 1854.
5. Montague Summers, Introduction to *Malleus Maleficarum,* London, John Rodker, 1928, p. xvii.
6. Henry Kramer and James Sprenger, *Malleus Maleficarum,* translated by the Rev. Montague Summers from the edition of 1489, "The Hammer of Witches which destroyeth Witches and their heresy as with a two-edged sword by Fr. Henry Kramer and Fr. James Sprenger, of the Order of Preachers, Inquisitors," with introduction and notes, London, Rodker, 1928.
7. Montague Summers, *The History of Witchcraft and Demonology,* London, Kegan Paul, Trench, Trubner & Co. Ltd., 1926, p. 45.
8. Kramer and Sprenger, p. 100.
9. Kramer and Sprenger, p. 102.
10. J. W. Wickwar, *Witchcraft and the Black Art, A Book Dealing with the Psychology and Folklore of the Witches,* New York, McBride, 1926.
11. Maurice Garcon and Jean Vinchon, *The Devil, An Historical, Critical and Medical Study,* translated by S. H. Guest, New York, Dutton, 1930.
12. Montague Summers, p. 137.

13. Ian Ferguson, *The Philosophy of Witchcraft*, New York, Appleton, 1925; C. W. Oliver, *An Analysis of Magic and Witchcraft*, London, Rider, 1928.
14. Montague Summers, p. xiv.
15. Maurice Garcon and Jean Vinchon, p. 82.
16. Montague Summers, p. 70.
17. E. T. Withington, "Dr. John Weyer and the Witch Mania," in *Studies in the History and Method of Science*, edited by C. J. Singer, Oxford, Clarendon Press, 1917, p. 201.
18. G. L. Kittredge, *Witchcraft in Old and New England*, Cambridge, Mass., Harvard, 1928, p. 334.
19. G. Zilboorg, *The Medical Man and the Witch during the Renaissance*, Vol. 2 of *Publications of the Institute of the History of Medicine*, Baltimore, Johns Hopkins Press, 1935, pp. 84-87. (Zilboorg has found this same case quoted by other medievalists.)
20. Kramer and Sprenger, p. 183.
21. R. H. Codrington, *The Melanesians*, Oxford, Clarendon Press, 1891, p. 198.
22. King James I, *Daemonologie* (1597). Contains also "Newes from Scotland declaring the Damnable Life and Death of Doctor Fian, a notable Sorcerer who was burned at Edenbrough in January last (1591)," London, John Lane, and New York, Dutton, 1924.
23. Richard Hunter and Ida Macalpine. *Three Hundred Years of Psychiatry* (1535–1860), London, Oxford Univ. Press, 1963, p. viii.
24. Andrew Boorde (Bishop of Chichester (1490–1549), quoted in Hunter and Macalpine, p. 13.
25. John Downame, *Spiritual physicke to cure diseases of the soule arising from superflutie of choller, prescribed out of God's word* (1600), quoted in Hunter and Macalpine, p. 55.
26. Dennis Hay, "The Early Renaissance in England," in *From the Renaissance to the Counter Reformation*, ed. with intro. by Chas. H. Carter, New York, Random House, 1965, p. 99.
27. Gerald Strauss, "A Sixteenth-Century Encyclopedia," in *The Early Renaissance in England*, p. 145.
28. Francis Bacon. *The Two Books... Of the proficience and advancement of learning, divine and human*, 1605, quoted in Hunter and Macalpine, p. 78.
29. Heinrich Laehr, *Die Literatur der Psychiatrie, Neurologie und Psychologie von 1459–1799*, Akademie der Wissenschaften zu Berlin, Berlin, Reimber, 1900.
30. *Ibid.*
31. John Halle, *An Historicall Expostulation: Against beastle abusers, bothe of Chyrurgerie, and Physyke, in oure tyme: with a boodlye Doctrine and Instruction, necessarye to be marked and followed*...Thomas Marsh, London, 1565, pp. 6, 8.
32. George Baglivi, *The Practice of Physick Reduced to the Ancient Way of Observations*, in Latin, Rome, 1696. Printed in London, 1704, p. 189.
33. Thomas Babington Macaulay, *The History of England*, Vol. 1, Phila., J. B. Lippincott & Co., 1880, p. 340.

34. Richard Sibbs, *The soules conflict with it selfe... A Treatise of the inward disquietments of distressed spirits...*, London, Dawlman, 1635, in Hunter and Macalpine, p. 110.
35. Dennis Hay, p. 99.
36. King James I, *Op. cit.*
37. Reginald Scot, *The Discoverie of Witchcraft,* with an introduction by the Rev. Montague Summers, reprinted by John Rodker, Suffolk, 1930.
38. Geoffrey Chaucer, "The Tale of the Wyf of Bathe," in *The Works of Geoffrey Chaucer,* edited by W. W. Skeat, ed. 2, Oxford Univ. Press, 1900, Vol. 4, p. 345.
39. Kramer and Sprenger, p. 119.
40. Paracelsus, *De Morbis Invisibilus,* quoted by H. M. Pachter, *Magic into Science, The Story of Paracelsus,* New York, Schuman, 1951, p. 74.
41. Reginald Scot, *Op. cit.*
42. Johann Wierus, *De Praestigiis Daemonum et Incantationibus, ac Veneficiis,* Libri V, 1563 (translations by Zilboorg and Binz).
43. W. E. H. Lecky, *History of the Rise and Influence of the Spirit of Rationalism in Europe,* Vol. I, New York, Appleton, 1866, p. 109.
44. Carl Binz, *Doktor Johann Weyer, ein rheinischer Arzt der erste Bekampfer des Hexenwahns,* ed. 2, Berlin, Hirschwald, 1896.
45. *Ibid.*
46. Modified after G. Zilboorg, *Op. cit.*
47. G. Zilboorg, p. 205.
48. E. T. Withington, p. 204.
49. E. T. Withington, p. 223.
50. William Cullen, *First Lines of the Practice of Psychic,* Edinburgh, Creech, 1779–1784.
51. Robert Whytt, *Observations on the Nature, Causes and Cure of those Disorders Commonly called Nervous, Hypochondriac or Hysteric,* ed. 3, Edinburgh, Balfour, 1767.
52. Hunter and Macalpine, p. 357.

5

Science Enters Mental Healing

THE transition from supernaturalism to rationalism in searching for the causes of mental and physical aberrations was slower in clerical than in medical hands. In the 1690s Cotton Mather viewed with alarm the invasion of New England by the Invisible World: "Another Wo that may be Look'd for is, the Devil being let Loose in preternatural Operations...perhaps in Possessions and Obsessions,"[1] whereas Robert Burton, seventy years earlier, had stated that only to the "prepared bosom" of the physician-friend could the melancholic patient profitably confide his troubles.[2]

The intellectualism and humanitarianism of the eighteenth century provided a background for the evolution of psychotherapy. "The old theological measure of probability disappeared," summarized Lecky, "replaced by a shrewd secular common sense."[3] The token spirit of the Age of Reason, with its skepticism toward revealed religion, combined with the rise of a clinical sense among medical men to constitute the chief factors for the entrance of medicine into mental healing.

Among literate persons and in Western Europe, ideas attained a new validity and mobility. In Europe, Adam Smith the economist, Goethe the universal genius, Pestalozzi the pioneer in modern education, Beccaria the penal reformer, Rousseau, Montesquieu—all wrote, conversed, argued, and pleaded for the right of man to improve his lot by the application of civilization's accumulated knowledge. The intellectual ferment of the century was most apparent among the aristocracy, in whose salons philosophers (this term included scientists and social reformers) expounded their views and disseminated knowledge, receiving adulation in return. But preoccupation with issues of the day, with the validity of revelation, of miracles, of tolerance for deistic ideas or even atheism, of skepticism toward ten centuries of dogma, did not remain the exclusive property of one class or one nation. English Deism and rationalism were hailed in France, Voltaire's skepticism was admired in England, Holland's tolerance of religious differences was adumbrated in the American colonies. While Voltaire cried, "Your study is Man, that labyrinth you explore," the Quakers in England astonished "all Christendom by behaving like Christians."[4]

In France, the "Salonnieres," a "vital part of the nation's intellectual life,"[5] not only touched on every aspect of the current knowledge of arts and sciences, but embarked on discussions of the new psychology. Condillac's formulation that sensation passed through the sense organs to result in higher mental forms attracted much attention. A salon chronicler[6] described how Mme. Necker, mother of Baroness de Staël, vivaciously discussed recent theories of sensation with M. Diderot, the French encyclopedist:

> "M. Diderot," Madam Necker said, "Did you not tell me that it was possible to explain thought by the succession of sensations?" ... Answered M. Diderot, "All nature is nothing but a series of progressive sensations; the stone feels, but very feebly; the plant feels more than the stone, the oyster feels more than the plant, and so on till I reach man. Weak sensations leave no trace of themselves behind. The light impress of my finger on a hard body could not be preserved, but stronger sensations do actually produce a remem-

brance—remembrance which is nothing other than thought."

Psychology, which was to have an indirect but potent influence on psychotherapy in the nineteenth and twentieth centuries, was being forged out of the philosophic theories relating to the "mind." Descartes (1596–1650), for example, assumed that nerve tubes that conducted "animal spirits" were responsible for mental functions. (The nerves extending to the brain were thought of as "tubes" that transmitted mechanical motion, i.e., impulses.) Others, such as Spinoza (1632–1677), regarded mind and matter as one substance (monism). English philosophers thought of the mind in terms of sensation—experience and reflection thereon (Locke, 1632–1704), while Hume (1711–1776) argued that associations determined thinking, an idea extended by Hartley (1705–1757) to include a physiological notion, that connections in the brain between "centers for ideas" was the basis for thinking.

While philosophers were evolving a *reasoned* structure for mental life, a physiology of the brain and nervous system was developing to account for the transmission of nerve impulses in health and disease. By the late eighteenth century, William Cullen, an influential figure at the University of Edinburgh, wrote of "motions in the animal economy,"[7] by which he meant "nerve motions" or impulses. This became known as the "neurosis" theory of disease: accurately stated, Cullen's notion was that diseases that did not depend on physical conditions—infections, tumors, and the like—were caused by "neuroses":

> ...those affections on sense or motion...which do not depend upon topical affection of organs but upon general affection of the nervous system.

As a clinician, Cullen was concerned with understanding the bewildering array of mental and physical ailments with their overlapping symptoms. Attempting to bring order into medical diagnosis, he divided all diseases into four classes: *Pyrexiae* (febrile diseases), *Neuroses* (nervous conditions), *Cachexiae* (wasting diseases), and *Locales* (local diseases). This overview of clinical states he combined with the then new notion of the "Nervous Power... a subtile very moveable fluid..." which operated in "a manner we do not clearly understand...."[8] How "Nervous Power" worked depended on experimental studies under way during the eighteenth century.

The basic function of muscle irritability investigated by von Haller, the regeneration of nerve tracts (Spallanzani), Volta's use of electricity in inducing muscular contractions, the analysis of types of skulls (Blumenbach) were fundamental findings that bore directly on the infant fields of Neurology and Psychiatry. The nature of nerve impulse, the difference between sensory and motor impulses and the relation of the mind to all of this led to much speculation.

Significant for the field of psychotherapy was thinking centering on the "motions... in the animal economy," which we may identify as nerve impulses. Moreover, much information on the brain, especially following head injuries, had been accumulated by surgeons. They knew of skull (*contra coup*) fracture, of its effect on the crossed tracts in the brain, of the co-ordination function of the cerebellum, of the conduction of sensory impulses in the nerves, of paralysis following cerebral hemorrhage, and so on. Indeed, experimentalists on the brain and spinal nerves in monkeys, some 1500 years before Cullen, had come to grips with the problem of anatomy of the brain, the significance of the ventricles, the pineal body, cervical nerves, even localization of sensation and movement in the cortex (Galen). The Renaissance witnessed dissections of the brain with an elucidation of anatomical details by such men as Sylvius, Leonardo da Vinci, Malphigi, and a host of others.[9]

Although many were well informed in anatomy and physiology of the nervous system, the nature of the nerve impulse eluded them; it was conceived as the movement of "vital spirits" (Stahl), "a certain power" (Whytt), "Vital Sympathy" (Cudsworth), "specific energy of the nerves"

(Muller—1826). Their quest led through Gall and his Phrenology, over a century to the modern view of the nerve impulse as a minute electrical charge accompanied by intricate chemical changes along the nerves. This development led, during the eighteenth and nineteenth centuries, to a "neurology" that was still distant from mental healing. For clinical medicine, unevenly developed, had not yet united with treatment of the insane.

It was inevitable that interest should pass from religious criticism to philosophy and later to psychology and neurology. Emanuel Swedenborg, the Swedish scientist-mystic who "resolved, cost what it may, to trace out the nature of the human soul,"[10] delved into the anatomy of the cortical substance. The search for the soul led him to the modern concept that "brain activity is combined activity of individual (cortical) cells. The cerebral cortex is the seat of soul."[11] Search for the place of abode of the "soul" with its neurologic connotations was still distant from everyday medical interest. We shall see later how a rudimentary neurology struggled with these questions as the school of "neuropathology" developed in the latter part of the eighteenth century. But clinical medicine was too unevenly developed in the eighteenth century to nurture a union between humanitarianism and medical science in regard to mental disease. Lack of conformity in the theory of medical treatment, antagonisms growing out of ignorance, were characteristic. Weikard, a German, wrote in his autobiography of the state of medicine in mid-century:

> What confusion when we regard the therapy of different nations! The French bleed, use enemas, astringents, purges, water, always want to dilute. The English give salts and herbs, minerals.... The Viennese praise their new remedies, the good effects of which the other sons of Aesculpaius never can confirm. The other Germans mill about, try first this and that, and in therapy do as they do in other things, imitate and admire the foreigner.... Almost every province, every university has its own routine. Where shall an impartial physician seek his information?[12]

Meanwhile, the scientific spirit activated physicians such as Linnaeus (1707–1778), the Swedish physician and botanist who revolutionized biologic science by suggesting a classification of animals and plants based on similarities of structure or function. In the same period, Cuvier, the father of paleontology, brought order into the science of comparative zoology. De Sauvages (1706–1767), a prominent clinician, classified diseases, following Linnaeus, into 10 classes, 295 genera, and 24,000 species. [13] The encyclopedic fervor exemplified by the French Encyclopedists was both a product and an indicator of intellectual activity of the eighteenth century. Leaders in medicine were immersed in classifying the body of medical knowledge that had been accumulating. The urge for cataloguing the bewildering array of human illnesses developed as a reaction to the spotty medical knowledge of earlier centuries and fitted the psychological trend of the time—to recount and capitalize the gains "made by civilization prior to the Industrial Age." [14] Cullen for all his classification attempts, was unable to correlate his "neurosis" theory of disease with a therapy to match. He accepted the Hippocratic theory that hysteria was due to a displacement of the ovary. "In what manner," Cullen wrote, "the uterus and in particular the ovaria...rise upwards to the brain so as to cause convulsions...I cannot explain." Their obeisance made to the Father of Medicine, physicians of Cullen's time preferred to treat hysteria with evil-tasting medicine and indulgent benevolence rather than to probe into the emotional or the sexual life of the patient. The renowned Sydenham prescribed for hysteria: "Let eight ounces of Blood be taken away. Apply Plaister of Galbanum to the Navel. Next A.M. Two drams cochia the greater, cafloreum powder 2 grains, Balsam of Peru, 3 drops, etc." [15]

The struggle to account for inexplicable nervous symptoms continued for decades. Cullen, of whom Pinel wrote, "One English nosologist, Cullen, made sound remarks on the specific character of the delirious mania...but...(also) futile explanations and gratuitous theories," [16] nevertheless was not entirely unaware of the need for a psychology in psychiatry.[17] "I must take notice," Cullen remarks, in the Introduction to his text,

> that to many of you I may appear to deal in Metaphysics;...in so far as some analysis of the faculties of the human mind, some account of its general operations is to be so called. I employ Metaphysics because every physiologist has employed them; they have been employed to corrupt and destroy Physiology to a great degree.

Psychology (metaphysics) beckoned students of neurosis in their clinical studies. Consider the suggestion of a French physician who, in studying the confusing symptoms of nymphomania, pointed out that "one of the principal points to which a physician ought to attach himself is the study of the effects of the imagination"[18] in obscure illnesses of women. For imagination was "the mother of the greater part of the passions and of their excesses" that eventuated in the disease nymphomania. This condition, incidentally, was in actuality a broad category; as reconstructed from de Bienville's description, it was a combination of puberty longings, adult libidinal sensations, masturbation, leukorrhea, endocervicitis, vulvovaginitis, depression, schizophrenia, and psychopathic behavior patterns.

The atmosphere of the times, particularly in France, England, and to a degree in Germany, lent itself to a loosening hold of theology on psychology and science.

There is general agreement that scientific discoveries of the seventeenth century, in combination with a "free play of mind" (Shaftesbury) in matters of religion, formed an antisupernatural climate of opinion. The *Honnête Homme*, the man of clear perceptions and unfettered thinking, became the "man of parts and sense . . . the moral norm of the age." Sainte-Beuve, a friend of Mme. de Staël, caught the sprightly tone of a society that had provided the intellectual's haven, as he tells in his memoirs of a salon conversation, " . . . these two holding the magic racquets of the discussion, and sending back to each other, for hours at a time, without ever missing, the ball of a thousand related thoughts."[19]

The English Deists, who conceived of God as a benevolent being, as opposed to the orthodox picture of a severe, condemning judge, were much admired in France; their ideas were eagerly and secretly discussed in the Parisian salons.[20] The Earl of Shaftesbury, in defining an urbane and a tolerant Deity, "matched," comments Barnes, "that of a typical English gentleman of the eighteenth century."[21] Deism or "natural religion" formed the philosophic background for the French and the American revolutions, since a benevolent God was primarily concerned with men's happiness in the "now." The doctrine that "all men were created equal" and entitled to "liberty and equality" followed from the deistic position. Humanitarianism encompassed the wish to improve social relations, and hence conferred sanction on emotional and social problems as worthy of attention.

The "free play of mind" spread from earnest philosophers to the populace. A contemporary observer wrote: "...the philosophies were read...[and] many teachers were infected with unbelief."[22] A "philosophy of amoralism" was abroad. More than that, social deterioration lived alongside intellectual brilliance. "If you have a spark of genius," wrote Rousseau, "go and spend a year in Paris. Soon you will be all that you can ever be or else...nothing at all." Yet Paris in the 1780s was also a maelstrom of "juvenile delinquency, petty thieves, professional criminals, prostitutes, male and female...."[23]

Out of this ferment arose Philippe Pinel, liberator of the insane at Bicêtre. In the city of 100,000, Bicêtre in the 1780s was the catch basin for the city's insane, prostitutes, aged derelicts, and criminals. For the "dispossessed, demoralized, degraded and bitter-spirited people" of Paris, Bicêtre was a living grave.[24]

The situation was no better in England, where in public hospitals, patients were placed "two in one bed...patients were seldom washed, for washing was considered 'weakening.' "[25] In London, as in Paris, "the streets belonged to the poor" while aristocrats enjoyed a "brilliant period in the fine arts."

The flow of events during the eighteenth and nineteenth centuries resulted in a vast change in the concept of mental disease and its treatment. Clinical medicine and pathology finally became involved in the mystery of brain and spinal cord function and neurology was aborning. But what was the effect of psychology, or more accurately, medical psychology, on the treatment of that "Class and Set of Distempers...these nervous Disorders?"[26] A generalized answer can be given in the words of psychologist T. V. Moore, writing in 1944: "American psychiatry has definitely turned its back on psychology and gone to neurology for information about the mind of man."[27] Certainly in the late 1700s psychology and neurology were far apart, each concerned with its own problems. But Moore's answer needs some modification, for psychological principles were beginning to appear in clinical psychotherapy. With the twentieth century, however, medical psychology exerted a tremendous impact on psychotherapy and mental health activities. The results of this impact will be presented in a later chapter.

Not unmindful of the experiments, medical observations and introspection of dozens of physicians and philosophers, it can be said that a mystic, Emanuel Swedenborg, brought the "mind" and brain together in a meaningful synthesis in the 1740s. A member of the Royal Swedish Academy of Medicine, a Deist[28] on the order of Voltaire, Swedenborg conceived of the gray matter in the cortex to be the seat of consciousness, perception, sensation, and thought, while the gray matter in the medulla oblongata and spinal cord regulated automatic and habitual movement.[29] A layman, well read in the physiology of his time, Swedenborg isolated the mind from the soul. Mind operated in the "organic, cortical substance" of the brain, while the Soul was a "faculty distinct from the intellectual mind." Essentially a religionist, his plea for Deism—"the one God...who gave man reason for a reason"—was matched by his psychology: "Soul, mind and body...were all part of nature and obeyed natural laws."[30]

Men had always wondered how the mind functioned: the eighteenth century saw many attempts to unite a philosophy of mind with the physiology of the brain, which formed the basis for the field of psychology. When Doctor David Hartley, a British physician (1705–1757) speculated that "vibrations" coursed along the nerves as the "immediate Instrument of Sensation and Motion" and that these sensations "presented Ideas to the Mind," he laid a persuasive background for a physiological psychology.[31] The notion of a soul was dispensed with in the ensuing half century as the association-of-ideas theory gained adherents as well as dissidents. Among the latter, the Scottish philosophers, such as Reid (1785), denied that mental life consisted of a passive field of associations but extolled human reason as a primary innate gift,[32] an *apriori* function (Kant). And the Mills, James and his son John Stuart, doubting the presence of a soul as a mental phenomenon, still argued for an "active, synthetic" principle in the mind in addition to associations.[33]

But none of this thinking, or even the subsequent experimentation of transmission of nerve impulses, played a direct role in psychotherapy at the turn of the nineteenth century. Oddly, the crude relationship between feelings, ideas, emotions, and brain structure—a "faculty psychology"—that impinged on mental healing did develop out of the discredited *craniology* of Franz Gall.

A graduate of the University of Vienna, Doctor Gall had been obsessed with a chance observation that fellow students whose eyes were prominent proved to have the best memories. From this observation, he reasoned that the frontal lobes of the brain were related to prominent eyes: he determined to study the brain itself. At the time (1796) the structure of the brain was unknown: it was considered to be a formless, pulpy mass. The nerve fibers were known to originate in the walls of the ventricles, united in some way by the spinal fluid. Soemmering, a German authority, and his contemporaries felt that the quantity of spinal fluid secreted was directly related to the degree of intelligence.[34] But Gall, tracing the spinal fiber bundles into the brain by the method of unfolding the layers of gray matter and separating the bundles of white matter, demonstrated the nervous system to have a design and, presumably, a meaning.

He studied the differences in convolutions between the brains of animals and of human beings, and postulated differences in mental capacity in direct proportion to the quantity of convolutional (gray) matter. Gall was one of the first to demonstrate the paucity of cortex in the idiots, accounting for their mental weakness. His contemporary, Christian Reil, is quoted as saying that Gall demonstrated in his dissections of the nervous system "more than I conceived a man could discover in the course of a long life."

From his conviction that higher mental functions were connected with convolutions of the cerebrum, Gall postulated that certain areas in the frontal lobes served specific functions, as arithmetic, music, language, etc. By comparing the internal concavities of the skull corresponding to the convexities of the brain substance, and noting the relative size of various areas or "organs" of the cortex, Gall pointed to organs of *courage, memory, observation, liberality, copulative urge,* and so on.[35] Classifying hundreds of skulls in relation to the history of temperament (behavior), character (personality function), and powers (intelligence) of their possessors, Gall felt that he had validated his findings. He used a series of unit functions in various degrees of dominance or deficiency to account for the infinite gradations of human behavior and disposition. These units were described as "PROPENSITIES, (Amativeness, Philo-progenitiveness, Concentrativeness, etc.), SENTIMENTS, Lower (Self-Esteem) and Superior (Benevolent, Veneration...) FACULTIES, Perception (Form, Size, Weight...Language...), Reflective (Comparison, Causality...)."

Forbidden by the emperor to continue his "blasphemous researches" on the brain in Vienna, Gall traveled to Germany and then to France, where, in 1808, he prepared an anatomic work for the Institute of France.[36] Neurologists were much impressed; Flourens, an experimentalist of cerebral physiology, stated, on viewing Gall's dissections, "it seemed to me that I had never seen that organ [the brain]."

The scientific community welcomed Gall's researches on the brain. A Dr. Loder wrote:

> I am ashamed and angry with myself for having like the rest, of having sliced hundreds of brains as we cut a cheese and for having missed seeing the forest for the trees....[37]

Not only physicians but the literati took to the new *science* of craniology. Gall, now with a Boswell in his train, was invited to lecture everywhere. "I experienced the most flattering reception," he wrote. "Sovereigns, ministers, philosophers, legislators, artists, seconded my design." His Boswell was Johann Christoph Spurzheim, a candidate for the clergy, who became fascinated with Gall's work. Traveling with Gall, Spurzheim, a pompous man with a facile tongue, publicized craniology—soon to be called phrenology—to the point where it soared off into charlatanism, but not before Gall was welcomed into France in 1807 by Cuvier, Flourens, and Saint Hilaire of the Institute of France. In Paris, Gall's success was great but an English physician (Barclay) grumbled, "Imagine saying that a lot of gray material (convolutions)...contains...separate organs of the mind."[38]

Actually, Gall's researches represented a type of constitutional psychiatry. As Spurzheim, his associate, put it, "Configuration and organic constitution proclaim innate disposition and capacities of action."[39] When to the early constitutional psychiatry was added a "phrenological mode of considering cerebral organization," Gall felt he had enriched medicine by indicating how dominance or inferiority of the various mental faculties and sentiments could be accurately gauged, how "determinate characters" could be outlined and powers of the brain projected to the outside world for all to see and comprehend.

As Gall's social successes mounted, his scientific standing became murky. While Parisians took Gall and his "organic" descriptions to their hearts, Pinel became engaged in an academic quarrel with Gall concerning the seat of insanity. A contemporary journalist wrote, "Great indeed was the ardor excited among Parisians by the presence of the men, who... could tell their fortunes by their heads," but Pinel insisted on hearing from Gall how exaggeration of the various faculties of the brain could cause insanity when, for example, the hypochondriac's disorder was in the nerves of his stomach.

Phrenology, as it was evolving from craniology, maintained a reputable medical position for a time. Dr. Elliotson lectured before the Phrenological Society (1823) on a celebrated murderer, a "poor wretch... [whose] bumps of amativeness, destructiveness, acquisitiveness" were overdeveloped. The *Lancet* in 1824 noted that Dr. Willis was preparing to give a series of lectures on phrenology, which the editors hoped "would include the dissection of the brain according to Gall's system."[40]

A committee of five was appointed to examine Gall's anatomical studies. The committee was favorably impressed but Napoleon was not: "Away with this pettifogging German with his skull bumps and passions and sentiments!" When the Emperor Napoleon showed his displeasure, scientists fell in line; from 1810 onwards, medical men in France lost interest in Gall's conclusions that mental faculties lay under the skull bumps. A few acknowledged his anatomical discoveries but it was Spurzheim who developed the "faculty" aspect of craniology; it was Spurzheim also who popularized the term "phrenology." The parting of the ways occurred in 1813 when Spurzheim moved to England and to international acclaim, while Gall remained in Paris to finish his six volumes on the *Anatomy and Physiology of the Nervous System*.[41] He died in 1828. Phrenology met a varying fate. The *Edinburgh Review* set down the phrenology doctrine as a "piece of thorough quackery," while a journalist for the *Birmingham Journal* wrote: "This man is the greatest moral philosopher that Europe has produced."[42]

Spurzheim's zeal carried him and phrenology into popular areas, a journey that will be pursued later in this book. Aside from Gall's anatomical dissections and findings, *craniology* with its extension *phrenology* marked a nodal point in the history of psychotherapy. It did not enter into mental healing directly but Gall's uniting sentiments and propensities (amativeness, combativeness, secretiveness, and the like) with the skull, turned attention to the *use* one made of his inborn cranial heritage. More than that, Gall made craniology a subject for popular discussion. George Eliot, for example, became an ardent phrenologist, feeling her creative skill grow under the influence of phrenology. Parisian wits like Charles Villers lampooned Gall: "... everybody in Vienna was trembling for its head and fearing to put it in Dr. Gall's cabinet." M. Denis, the Emperor's librarian, willed his cranium "for M. Gall's scalpel."

Another discipline that purported to be scientific and fanned out into a fad was called *physiognomy* by its inventor Johann Casper Lavater, a Swiss theologian.[43] His theory, which came to him as an intuitive flash, stated that "all passive and active movements... all traits whereby suffering or acting [of] man can be perceived..." are reflected in the face, hence the name, *physiognomy*, he gave his science. Lavater's four-volume *Fragments on Physiognomy* (1775) detailed instruments for measuring the brow, techniques for obtaining outlines of the head and face, which he brought into relation with phrenology. Lavater's "science" fell into disrepute but not before it intrigued the public; fashionable gentlemen in Paris engraved their physiognomies on their snuffboxes.

Popular interest in phrenology remained high for decades after neurologists withdrew from it. Dr. Durbin, President of Dickinson College in Pennsylvania, commented on visiting Dr. Gall's craniology collection in Paris (1844): "The head of Bacon is majestic, the head of Voltaire full in the region of the ears—what we would look for in the prince of persifleurs." And an American psychiatrist in 1849 upheld phrenology as a "true science" in its relation to significant cerebral lobes:

> ...Bare mention of the fundamental principles of the science...[a] mind composed of a plurality of faculties, dependent upon the brain...is sufficient to solve the whole mystery attached to "moral insanity."[44]

The advent of craniology had been preceded by considerable experimentation during the eighteenth and early nineteenth centuries on the brain and nervous system. Some outstanding accomplishments were Rolando's autopsies of the brain (1809); Galvani's demonstration of the response to the electrical current of a severed frog's leg (1780); the discovery of the sensory and motor functions of nerve trunks by Bell (1807) and Magendie (1822) and Flourens' experiments on birds analyzing cerebellar functions (1822).[45] This and other work constituted the rudiments of the science of neurology.

For physicians, however, the jungle of confusing symptoms presented by patients—headache, muscle spasms, tics, paralyses, neuralgias, muscular atrophies, syncope, wasted limbs, rheumatic conditions—strained their diagnostic resources. Details of physiologic-psychologic study, as the specific function of sensory nerves and their relay paths to the brain (Müller, 1835); the influence of sympathetic nerves on blood vessels (Bernard, 1851); analysis of mental processes rather than "faculties" (Herbart, 1816), were yet to be joined with clinical neurological observations. Darwinian ideas reflected in psychological writings (Spencer, 1855) wherein nervous and mental processes were considered *adaptive* in nature through evolution,[46] even Bain's conceptualization of a "Psychology" of normal experience (1855), found no place in clinical psychiatry, no less in mental therapy at the time.

But the field of neurology, which blossomed from 1850 to the end of the century, did contribute to psychotherapy in two ways: Directly through hypnosis via Charcot and his contemporaries, and indirectly through the establishment of neurasthenia as a clinical entity. The neurologic heritage enriched mental healing, striving to understand mysterious yet persistent symptoms for which no medical basis could be found. The progress of neurology, however, was persistent. Strokes were recognized as differing from *tabes dorsalis* (Steinthal, 1844); *paralysis agitans* from hysterical tremors (Parkinson, 1817); spinal muscular atrophy from neuritis (Duchenne, 1847); multiple sclerosis from Parkinson's disease (Charcot, 1870).[47] Nevertheless, a large group of symptoms remained unclassified. Neuralgias, morbid fears, sexual impotence and a host of other ill-defined complaints for which no medical basis could be found, plagued patient and doctor alike. These cases came to be known as due to "nervous prostration, spinal irritation or cerebral neurosis" and were gladly handed over to neurologists by practitioners. "Nervous exhaustion" cases so perplexed practicing physicians, and hysterics so unnerved them, that Weir Mitchell remarked on "the disgust with which the general practitioner encounters this malady [hysteria]."[48]

The advent of a specialty called neurology had the effect of focusing on these states of "nervous debility." Social attitudes and mores had already prepared the ground for a closer look at hysteria. The "genteel tradition" imposed upon women a set of values that found expression equally in the "charming invalid" of the Victorian period and the bizarre "hysterics" described by French neurologists. The moral education of women commenced with the doctrine, divinely sanctioned, that a boundary existed between "these two great divisions of mankind," male and female, and extended to the virtues of humility, patience, and "loving deference" to their spouses. The emotions of women during the Victorian age were arranged and ordered for them, and they were advised to accept these restrictions gracefully. Under such social limitations it is not strange that the sexual and aggressive drives of women required the circuitous route of hysteria for expression. An emancipated woman, writing in 1865, complained of the universal poor health of women: "In my immense circle of friends all over the union, I can't recall more than 10 married ladies born in this country who are sound, healthy and vigorous."[49] Beyond the dangers of the nuptial chamber, the rise of education among women brought its penalties. "I see breakdowns among women of 16 to 19 in female colleges, when the nervous system is so sensitive," wrote Weir Mitchell in a slender volume, *Wear and Tear*,[50] which was to serve as a warning of the neurologic cost of "restless" living. And, in agreement on the other side of the ocean, an eminent French physician said, "If your daughter reads novels at fifteen she will have hysteria at twenty."

The secrets of "female weaknesses" remained suppressed by the dominant medical mood. Professor Meigs of Philadelphia, for example, denounced Oliver Wendell Holmes' insistence that obstetricians carried germs from the autopsy room to their patients as "jejune and fizenless dreamings of sophomore writers."[51] Well might Lydia Pinkham, whose "Greatest Medical Discovery Since the Dawn of History" brought relief to thousands of women suffering in silence, become the repository of clinical details of the causes of nervous debility. Jean Burton, Pinkham's biographer, comments that the "Pinkham files were the nearest thing to a Kinsey Survey the era produced."[52] But the ubiquitous hysterical illnesses were not confined solely to women. Charcot early pointed to hysterical symptoms among men, a view which was treated with ridicule when Freud, upon his return from Paris, remarked on this finding at the Vienna Medical Society.

Hints of the vulnerability of men to hysteria were crystallizing in the minds of American neurologists also. Civil War experiences of numerous psychiatric casualties observed by Surgeon General William Hammond, of the Union Army, and his confrères, Weir Mitchell and W. W.

Keen, were both impressive and puzzling, particularly states of exhaustion in soldiers on the battlefield. These experiences returned to Mitchell's mind when later, in civilian practice, he encountered cases of "brain-tire" and neurasthenia occurring under stress of business competition, "Railway Traveling," and a speeded-up social life.[53]

In the same year, 1869, that Beard's article on neurasthenia[54] appeared, lifting nervous exhaustion to the level of a treatable condition, Van Deusen wrote an article[55] linking "nervous prostration [neurasthenia] to insanity . . . "

Although it was acknowledged that the disease was a "product of our progress and refinement," Beard had described a complex bundle of symptoms that passed beyond hysteria to sexual and emotional spheres. Thus neurasthenics suffered from:

> tenderness of scalp; dilated pupils; sick headache; pressure pain in head; irritable eye (asthenopis); noises in ears; atonic voices; concentration inability: irritability; hopelessness; morbid fear (anthro-phobo-claustro-phobias, etc.); blushing, insomnia; tenderness of teeth; dyspepsia; sweating and dryness of skin; spinal hyperesthesia; palpitations; spasms; dysphagia; exhaustion; neuralgias; sexual disabilities; yawning; impotence, etc.[56]

Beard's treatment for this newly uncovered group of patients was generally medical in nature, a continuation of the so-called "supporting treatment"[57] for the insane, itself a reaction to the early venesection and depletion procedures. Arsenic, caffeine, ergot for "congestion of the brain and cord," blisters, phosphates, chloral, belladonna, calomel, baths, were freely administered. In addition to this regimen, honored by neurologists for eighty years, Beard added a serious consideration and an intensification of electrotherapy, already sporadically used since the eighteenth century. From the days of Benjamin Franklin, electricity had been recommended for stimulation of the nerves and improvement of blood circulation. Much experimentation with electrical conductors, storers of static current (Leyden jar), faradic and galvanic current stimulated the introduction of electricity for hysterics and melancholics. John Wesley, in speaking of Lovett's electric-spark treatment, avowed that "more nervous disorders would be cured by this single remedy...than the whole Materia Medica."[58] As early as 1767, electricity was employed in English hospitals (Middlesex Hospital), and the following year Garrison notes that an electric bath was advocated in another English hospital. Elaborate apparatuses for delivery of electric current to the head, for migraine, deafness, and other nerve diseases, are described in the literature of Mesmer's time.

When Beard espoused medical electricity for neurasthenics, enthusiasm for this treatment in neurologic disorders was high. His monograph on the subject, which covered 65 pages in the first edition, grew to a tome of 799 pages in the eighth edition.[59] In Europe, in this period, Wilhelm Erb, a leading German neurologist, developed electrotherapy to the point at which it became the mainstay of treatment for neurotics. It was of the highly regarded electrotherapy that Freud, years later, remarked that he found himself helpless with neurotic patients in the face of disappointments following its use. Variations appeared in the form of electrical vibrators (Granville's Percuteur)[60] and others, each with its proponents, intent on stimulating the "torpid centers." Treatment by electricity vied with hydrotherapy for neurasthenics. A German authority, more confident in baths than in electrical current for the treatment of hysterics, recommended that "the calm waters of the Baltic are preferable for delicate, nervous constitutions, and the North Sea, with its stronger billows, may be recommended in torpid constitutions."[61] In general, stimulating therapy, hydrotherapy, electricity, and the inevitable "tonic" were the mainstays of neurologic psychotherapy.

One significant advance encompassed in the neurasthenic concept was Beard's tolerance towards patients with sexual symptoms. He brought sexual disturbances into relation with functional nervous diseases at a time when impotence and spermatorrhea were relegated to the genitourinary surgeon or treated with dark moralism and subsequent neglect. The day had not passed when Philippe Ricord, the great Parisian venereologist, set the forlorn tone physicians employed toward men with venereal diseases: "We know when gonorrhea begins, but only God knows when it ends."[62] Ricord, whom Holmes called the "Voltaire of pelvic literature, a skeptic as to the morality of the race,"[63] expressed the prevalent difficulty of treating gonorrhea and syphilis medically as well as the gingerly disdain with which sexual inadequacies in patients were met. Extension of the neurasthenic concept to sexual neurasthenia dispelled some of this gloom and offered an attitude of assurance and naturalness in sexual matters. Beard urged that seminal emissions and masturbation were not, as was commonly thought, diseases among unmarried men but evidences of exhaustion of one of the three great reflex irritation centers—brain, stomach, and genital system. The cure was to "strengthen the constitution, advise them to live generously, work hard, keep brain and muscle active" and avoid excesses.

Beard's "total attack" in the management of neurasthenia was based on the then current theory of nervous exhaustion: The nuclei of nerve cells shrank after exhaustion (or electrical excitation) and regained their normal appearance and function after rest. Thus nutrition of the nervous system and removal of the toxins of fatigue were the main therapeutic aims. But there was more—the mind of the patient—to be cared for: "Mental treatment without medication, was as ineffective as medication without a mental method." In a meeting of the American Neurological Association in 1877, Beard related two cases of organic disease of the spine who showed relief while "sitting under blue glass."[64] He added: "Physicians of great scientific attainment...may fail when an ignorant and obscure charlatan succeeds because...wonder and awe are excited...." The discussion following his presentation was heated. Dr. Sequin arose to support his psychologic approach: "I deny, with Dr. Beard, that there is any trickery in the use of emotions to the end of curing disease." Beard was not disheartened; his book with A. D. Rockwell on sexual neurasthenia had already reached a sixth edition in 1905.[65]

While Krafft-Ebing was working on his *Psychopathia Sexualis* (1886) and Havelock Ellis (1880s) produced his studies on the *Psychology of Sex*, clinicians like Erb in Germany and Beard stressed the functional nature of sexual symptoms. Beard recognized that dismissal of sexual problems as due to "indigestion, oxaluria, imagination" were mis-diagnoses. For his freedom in bringing nervous problems to medical and public view, Beard was branded as indulging in "self-praise...not the least deference to recognized authorities...[with a] style mainly directed to the lay reader."[66]

The startling novelty of physicians carrying the secrets of sexual and nerve pathology to the public aroused opposition among conservative physicians. So eminent a man as S. Weir Mitchell of Civil War fame—author, novelist, Philadelphia aristocrat—was subject to criticism through such damning comments as "charlatan" with oblique references to "nerves coming into vogue" when his book *Wear and Tear*[67] appeared. All he tried to do was remind his countrymen in down-to-earth language that brain fatigue and nervous exhaustion were preventable diseases, susceptible to a hygienic regimen that eliminated, among other evils, "the frying pan...which reigns supreme west of the Alleghenies." In spite of being called a "popular" author[68] —a dreadful word for a doctor at that time—Mitchell moved on, detailing his recommended regimen in another popular book called *Fat and Blood*,[69] which answered all therapeutic problems of hysteria and neurasthenia through his celebrated Rest Cure. The patient, said Mitchell, must be rebuilt and retrained. She must have rest, good food and, above all, isolation. There must be no contact with relatives. She must be removed from the morbid surroundings in which her illness had developed or flourished. Instead of being waited upon hand and foot by loved ones, pampered and catered to by nurses and attendants, the patient should have only one nurse, preferably one emotionally indifferent to the family. Mitchell understood very clearly how emotional contacts could retard the progress of a case, how the hysteric feeds upon the attention and adulation she gets from those about her. Where shades had been drawn and silence preserved, the doctor increased the light day by day, as well as reading or other tasks.

The Rest Cure attained a rapid popularity throughout the medical world. From the 1880s to the period of suggestive therapeutics and the psychoanalytic infiltration into neuropsychiatric thinking, textbooks in the United States,[70] Great Britain,[71] Germany,[72] France, and elsewhere advocated the Rest Cure. Many were impressed with the adjunctive methods, massage and the painstaking management of the patient.

Notes to Chapter 5

1. Cotton Mather, *On Witchcraft, Being the Wonders of the Invisible World. . . . First published in Boston in Octo. 1692 and Now Reprinted with Additional Matter and Old Wood-Cuts for the Library of the Fantastic and Curious,* Mt. Vernon, New York, Peter Pauper Press, 1951.
2. Bergen Evans and G. Mohn, *The Psychiatry of Robert Burton,* New York, Columbia, 1944, p. 89.
3. W. E. H. Lecky, *History of the Rise and Influence of the Spirit of Rationalism in Europe,* Vol. 1, New York, Appleton, 1866, p. 111.
4. Will Durant, *The Story of Philosophy,* New York, Simon and Schuster, 1926, p. 226.
5. Will and Ariel Durant, *The Story of Civilization, Part X, Rousseau & Revolution,* New York, Simon & Schuster, 1967, p. 906.
6. R. B. Mowat, *The Age of Reason,* Boston, Houghton, 1934, p. 222.
7. William Cullen, *First lines of the Practice of Physic,* Edinburgh, Creech, 1785.
8. William Cullen, *Nosology, or a Systematic Arrangement of Diseases by Classes, Orders, Genera and Species with the Distinguishing Characteristics of Each and Outlines of the System of Sauvages, Linnaeus, Vogel, Sagar and Macbride,* translated from the original Latin, 1769, London, Bell, Bradfut & Murray, 1810.
9. Israel S. Wechsler, *A Textbook of Clinical Neurology,* with an Introduction to the History of Neurology., 7th ed., Phila., W. B. Saunders, 1952.

10. Emmanuel Swedenborg, *The Soul, or, Rational Psychology,* translated by F. Sewall, ed. 3, New York, New Church Board, 1887.
11. *Encyclopaedia Britannica,* ed. 13, 1945, Vol. 21, p. 653.
12. M. A. Weikard, *Autobiography,* 1784. Quoted in Victor Robinson, *The Story of Medicine,* New York, Boni, 1931, p. 335.
13. Garrison, *An Introduction to the History of Medicine,* ed. 3, Philadelphia, Saunders, 1921, p. 318.
14. Mowat, p. 18.
15. *Dr. Sydenham's Compleat Method of Curing Almost All Diseases,* abridged and translated from the Latin, ed. 5, London, Horne & Parker, 1713, p. 6.
16. Raymond de Saussure, "The Psychiatry of Pinel," *Ciba Symposia,* Vol. II, No. 5, Summer, 1950, p. 1233.
17. John Thompson, *An Account of the Life, Lectures, and Writings of William Cullen, M. D.,* Edinburgh, Blackwood, and London, Cadell Strand, 1832, Vol. I, p. 260.
18. J. D. T. de Bienville, *Nymphomania, or A Dissertation Concerning the Furor Uterinus,* translated from the French by E. S. Wilmot, London, J. Bew, 1775.
19. Basil Willey, *The Eighteenth Century Background,* New York, Columbia, 1941, p. 75; Sainte-Beuve, "Portraits de femmes (1845)," in Mowat, p. 224.
20. Charles Seignobos, *The Rise of European Civilization,* translated by C. A. Phillips, New York, Knopf, 1938, p. 304.
21. H. E. Barnes, *The History of Western Civilization,* New York, Harcourt, 1935, Vol. 2, p. 178.
22. W. & A. Durant, p. 901.
23. W. & A. Durant, p. 903.
24. L. S. Mercier, *The Waiting City, Paris (1782–1788),* translated by Helen Simpson, London, Harrap, 1933.
25. Louis Kronenberger, *Kings and Desperate Men: Life in 18th Century England,* New York, A. A. Knopf, 1942, p. 270.
26. George Cheyne, *The English Malady or a Treatise of Nervous Diseases of all Kinds, As Spleen, Vapours, Lowness of Spirits, Hypochondrical, and Hysterical Distempers,* London, G. Strahan, 1734.
27. T. V. Moore, "A Century of Psychology in Relationship to American Psychiatry," in *One Hundred Years of American Psychiatry,* New York, Columbia, 1944, p. 447.
28. Personal communication from Leslie Marshall, The Swedenborg Foundation, New York, 1950.
29. Brett, *History of Psychology,* ed. R. S. Peters, London, Geo. Allen & Unwin, New York, Macmillan, 1953, p. 590.
30. Emmanuel Swedenborg, *The Economy of the Animal Kingdom,* II, 1940, p. 304; Signe Toksvig, *Emmanuel Swedenborg, Scientist and Mystic,* New Haven, Yale Univ. Press, 1948.
31. David Hartley, *Observations on Man, His Frame, His Duty and his Expectations,* 4th ed., London, Johnson, 1801, Chap. I.
32. Thomas Reid, *Essay on the Intellectual Powers of Man,* Edinburgh, 1785.

33. James Mill, *Analysis of the Phenomena of the Human Mind*, London, 1829.
34. Bernard Hollander, *In Commemoration of Francis J. Gall*, Ethnological Soc., London, Medical Press, July, 1928.
35. *Exposition de la doctrine physionomique due Docteur Gall*, Paris, Heinrichs, 1804.
36. F. J. Gall and J. C. Spurzheim, *Recherches sur le système nerveux en général et sur celui du cerveau en particulier...*, Paris, Schoell, 1809.
37. John K. Winkler and Walter Bromberg, *Mind Explorers*, p. 16.
38. Winkler and Bromberg, p. 18.
39. J. C. Spurzheim, *Phrenology in Connection with the Study of Physiognomy*, London, Treuttel, Wortz & Richter, 1826.
40. *Lancet Notes:* Phrenology II: 182, February 8, 1824.
41. F. Gall, *Anatomie et physiologie du système nerveux en général et du cerveau en particulier*, Paris, 1810–1819.
42. Winkler and Bromberg, p. 21.
43. Quoted in R. D. Loewenberg, "The Significance of the Obvious, an 18th Century Controversy on Psychosomatic Principles," *Bull. Hist. Med.*, Vol. 10, 1941.
44. H. A. Buttolph, "The Relation Between Phrenology and Insanity," *Amer. Jour. Insanity*, Vol. VI, October, 1849.
45. Edwin G. Boring, *A History of Experimental Psychology*, 2nd ed., New York, Appleton-Century-Crofts, 1950, p. 27.
46. Gardner Murphy, *Historical Introduction to Modern Psychology*, New York, Harcourt, Brace, 1953.
47. F. H. Garrison, p. 692 *et seq.*
48. S. Weir Mitchell, *Wear and Tear, or, Hints for the Overworked*, Philadelphia, Lippincott, 1871.
49. Catherine Beecher, *Letters to the People on Health and Happiness*, quoted in R. T. Edes, *New England Invalid*, Boston, Clapp, 1895.
50. *Ibid.*
51. Victor Robinson, *The Story of Medicine*, New York, Boni, 1931, p. 475.
52. Jean Burton, *Lydia Pinkham Is Her Name*, New York, Farrar, Straus, 1949.
53. S. Weir Mitchell, "The Evolution of the Rest Treatment," *J. Nerv. & Ment. Dis.* 31:368, 1904.
54. G. M. Beard, "Neurasthenia or nervous exhaustion," *Medical and Surgical Journal*, 3:217, April 29, 1869.
55. E. H. Van Deusen, "Observations on a form of nervous prostration (neurasthenia) culminating in insanity," *J. Insanity*, April, 1869, p. 445. See also H. A. Bunker, in *One Hundred Years of American Psychiatry*, Am. Psychiat. A., New York, Columbia, 1944.
56. G. M. Beard, *A Practical Treatise on Nervous Exhaustion (Neurasthenia)*, New York, Wood, 1880.
57. Edward Cowles, "Progress in the case and treatment of the insane during the half-century," *Am. J. Insanity*, 51:10, 1894.
58. J. Wesley, *The Desideratum, or, Electricity Made Plain and Useful by a Lover of Mankind and of Common Sense*, London, 1759.

59. G. M. Beard and A. D. Rockwell, *Medical Use of Electricity,* New York, Wood, 1867; *Medical and Surgical Uses of Electricity,* ed. 8, New York, Wood, 1892.
60. "Neurotherapy," *Alienist and Neurologist,* 5:135, 1884.
61. M. Rosenthal, *A Clinical Treatise on Diseases of the Nervous System,* translated by L. Putzel, New York, Wood, 1879, Vol. II, pp. 51–52.
62. Victor Robinson, p. 424.
63. Oliver Wendell Holmes, *Medical Essays,* Boston, Houghton, 1895.
64. George M. Beard, "The Influence of the Mind in the Causation of Disease," *Trans. Am. Neur. Assn.* Vol. II, p. lx, 1877.
65. G. M. Beard, *Sexual Neurasthenia, Its Hygiene, Causes, Symptoms and Treatment,* edited by A. D. Rockwell, ed. 6, New York, Treat, 1905.
66. Comment on "Beard on Insanity," *Amer. J. Insanity,* Vol. 32, Oct. 1880, p. 229.
67. S. Weir Mitchell, *op. cit.*
68. Anna R. Burr, *Weir Mitchell, His Life and Letters,* New York, Duffield and Co., 1929, p. 151.
69. S. Weir Mitchell, *Fat and Blood, an Essay on the Treatment of Certain Forms of Neurasthenia and Hysteria,* Philadelphia, Lippincott, 1877–1905.
70. C. K. Mills, *The Nervous System and Its Diseases,* Philadelphia, Lippincott, 1898.
71. W. R. Gowers, *A Manual of Diseases of the Nervous System,* Vol. 2, London, Churchill, 1888.
72. H. Oppenheim, *Diseases of the Nervous System,* translated by E. E. Mayer (from 3rd German edition), Philadelphia, Lippincott, 1904.

6

The Lunatick and His Asylum

THOSE melancholics and frenzied patients who had been treated humanely in medieval monasteries were apparently persons of means and social standing. In contrast, indigent "simples" and lunaticks roamed the streets of towns and byways of the countryside without care. As their numbers grew, their behavior constituted a nuisance to the citizenry. Bethlehem Hospital in London, founded in 1257, began admitting lunaticks about the end of the fourteenth century.[1] Known as Bedlam, the hospital's reputation spread to Europe. Three centuries later, Lemnius, a Dutch physician, recognized "Bedlem madnesse" among his patients who showed "losse of right witte, feebleness of brayne, phrensie...."[2] Londoners knew Bedlamites to be lesser criminals, prostitutes, vagrants, beggars, and the feebleminded in addition to the insane. Bedlam was known as a place for punishment of ne'er-do-wells rather than a hospital offering help. Hogarth's famous portrayal of "The Rake's Progress" shows his descent to ultimate degradation in Bedlam. Unlike the quiet monasteries of earlier days, which cared for the insane in kindness and humility, Bedlam became a circus operated for the profit of the wardens. Londoners went of a Sunday afternoon to titter at the madmen for the payment of one shilling. Tickets that admitted a man and his guests cautioned that "no knives or Instruments of any kind be delivered to the Patients...."[3] For safety, "four Constables and four stout fellows [were to be] placed in each gallery...to suppress any riots...."

In time, voices raised against this public mockery of the insane led to investigations. Daniel Defoe, the writer, demanded Parliamentary control of private and public Mad-Houses.[4] Conditions at Bethlehem were not unlike those described by Robin of the Salpêtrière in Paris in 1787:

> Patients massed in fours or more in narrow cells; a dirty sack of straw, with vermin crawling through; rats running in troops by night, eating the clothes, the bread, and in time, the flesh of the patients...poisoned in their insanity worse than before...the more delicate perished in little heaps.[5]

The recommendations made by the Committee in London (1707) stated:

> That no Officer...shall beat or abuse any Lunatick...but upon absolute Necessity, for the better governing of them...That no Lunatick lie naked...without order of the Physician...That every Day [they be] provided with fresh and clean Straw...a convenient Bathing Place to cool and wash them...is of great Service in airing their Lunacy....

In spite of beatings, nakedness, and fetters in the management of the insane (madmen were generally considered to be insensible to pain and temperature changes), isolated areas in Europe maintained the humane tradition. The Valencia Asylum (1409), as an example, treated its charges with kindness rather than chains. Bassoe, an American neurologist, in studying old records, found that asylums in Zaragosa, Granada, and Barcelona managed their insane under the rational influences of Islamic tradition transmitted through Moorish doctors.[6] Ramon Sarro, a Spanish psychiatrist, stated that the first hospital "properly called psychiatric...in Spain...[was] not a reservoir for madmen but a humanistic institution."[7] He quoted a letter by a

Spanish Jew, one Benjamin de Tudela, describing a humane institution for the insane in the tenth century. Nor was this unknown to earlier psychiatrists; Pinel,[8] in the second edition of his famed *Traité médico-philosophique sur l'aliénation mentale* (1809), remarked: "We must look to a neighbor country for an example, not to England, or Germany but to Spain. . . ."

In Italy also Vincent Chiarugi at the Bonifazio Asylum in Florence, a few years before Pinel's epoch-making action in Paris, had organized, in the words of George Mora, an "all comprehensive and well-integrated approach to the treatment of the insane."[9]

Research has shown that "isolated" areas of humane treatment were more common than thought hitherto. George Mora has described[10] the work of Barone Pisani in Palermo, Italy in humanizing care of the mentally ill at the old Leprosy Hospital, organized in 1419. Indeed, during the Renaissance, St. Vincent de Paul founded the Maison de St. Lazarus in Paris (1632), and the dedication of Juan Vives, Spanish-born educator and reformer, all but transformed the management of the insane and paupers in France (circa 1530). His philosophic quarrel with St. Augustine won him the charge of heretic—"What the soul is, is of no concern to us. . . . What its manifestations are, is of great importance,"[11] but his organization of public relief won him acclaim. Noting that the insane and the poor tended to be herded together in workhouses, Vives, in a 1526 work called *De Subventione Pauperum* (The Support of Paupers), called attention to the need not only of their separation but of courteous treatment and the benefits of "enlightenment and instruction" for the insane.

It remained, however, for a shy, retiring physician, Philippe Pinel, to dramatize the therapeutic revolution in the midst of the turmoil of the French Revolution. In the second year of the French Revolution, Pinel called upon his friends, asking for support for a new project that would apply the practice of humaneness to the insane.[12] Thouret, Commissioner of Public Safety in 1793, and Cabanis, physician to Mirabeau, were staunchly in favor of enlightenment. But Thouret was a realist; earlier, acting for the Faculty of Medicine, he had upheld science in denouncing Franz Mesmer, who sought offical sanction for his "animal magnetism," by remarking that Mesmer's universal treatment was "an illusion which cannot be excused in an enlightened age."

Pinel, who had already read Cullen (whom he translated into French) and Baglivi (whom he translated from the Italian) and Colombier's treatise on treatment of the mad, wrote articles for the *Gazette de Santé* on mental disease and suicide. Study was his life—mathematics, physics, clinical medicine, philosophy. While working in Dr. Belhomme's private sanitarium in Paris, he conceived a new project—to apply to the insane the same benefits of Liberty and Equality about which Marat and Danton were thundering in the National Assembly. As a bespectacled, tongue-tied young student, Pinel had appeared before Thouret, prefect of the Faculty of Medicine, seeking the prize for an essay answering the question, "Give the best ways of effectively treating the insane." Apparently Cabanis and Thouret were impressed by Pinel's plan, for, in their role of Administrators of the Hospitals of Paris, they granted his request and appointed him physician to the lunatic asylum of the Bicêtre in August, 1793.[13]

On September 11, 1793, Pinel repaired to the old graystone house on the outskirts of Paris. Here was his chance to apply the theories that had been moiling in his mind for several years, the logical outcome of the new humanitarianism triumphant in France. After all, were not madmen men? Did not their afflictions rise from the same passions, intellect, and will as our own? Pinel, as he hurried to the asylum, thought of the zealous Jacobins, those extremists who were then controlling France, and of the tumult and the unleashed passions that filled the streets of Paris. "Yes," he murmured to himself, "they are like us, only more so."

He walked into the office of Couthon, the prison-commission member of the Paris Commune, and explained his proposal.[14]

Couthon, a hardened warden, belonged to the old school. He listened impatiently to the doctor. "Why not," he satirically suggested, "proceed to the *zoo* and liberate the lions and tigers?" Pinel persisted, and finally Couthon agreed and, partly out of curiosity, accompanied him to the scene of the great experiment. A ferocious little man, Couthon started to walk ahead as befitted his office, but at the sound of three hundred maniacs screaming and clanking their chains he drew back, his face white. "Citizen," he said to Pinel, "are not you yourself crazy that you would unchain these beasts?"[15] But Pinel lost no time; this was his opportunity. Quickly he entered the cell of an English captain who was believed to be particularly dangerous because he had once killed an attendant with a blow from his manacles. Pinel was alone. Outside, Couthon, by this time completely shaken, murmured: "Do as you will, but you will be sacrificed to this false sentiment." Pinel addressed the English captain: "Ah well, Captain, I will cause your chains to be taken off; you shall have liberty to walk in the court if you will promise to behave like a gentleman and offer no assault to those you meet." "I would promise," answered the old soul, "but you deride me; you are amusing yourself at my expense." Pinel called the attendants, and the fetters were struck off. The old man tried to walk; he could not. He had been in chains for forty years! After many attempts, he tottered from his dark cell to the corridor, where he could see the sky. "Ah," he cried, "how beautiful!" The second to be released was a drunkard who had been discharged from the French Guards, Chevigné by name. For ten years he had been in chains. His mind disordered, assaultive, and surly, he was considered incurable. Pinel went to him, took off the iron anklets and handcuffs. Behold a revelation! The vicious sot stood up, and with a courtly flourish bowed to Pinel. He became a model of good conduct and in time was released.

Pinel passed on among his newly acquired charges, encouraging this one and talking to another. He unleashed some from stone posts in which anklets and chains were riveted, removed patients from dungeons, some of whom had lain there on filthy straw mats for years. He gave them better food and forbade attendants to beat them. Pinel did what any humane administrator would have done in a modern institution, but he did more. He dosed his patients with a new kind of medicine mentioned nowhere in the textbooks that were read by doctors of the 1790s. This new drug was kindness. And strangely, it worked. Dazed lunatics, rubbing their eyes at their good fortune, talked for the first time in years, and became almost human again. Skeptical Couthon could not believe his eyes; it looked like a royalist plot. "Citizen," he said sharply to Pinel, "I will visit thee in the Bicêtre tomorrow and woe to thee if thou hast deceived us and concealed enemies of the people among thy madmen."

The success of his venture and the radical nature of his ideas attracted attention throughout Europe. When Pinel's *Treatise on Insanity*[16] was published in London in 1806, the translator, Dr. D. D. Davis, observed that, distinct from most treatises, which were "advertisements of lunatic establishments under the superintendence of their respective authors," Pinel's book was the work of an "enlightened foreigner."

The moral treatment was codified. For maniacal fury Pinel recommended the "bland arts of conciliation or the tone of irresistible authority pronouncing an irreversible mandate." Violence was absolutely forbidden. In its place Pinel substituted the burden of humane management on the shoulders of the physicians whose "many great qualities both of mind and body...are necessary in order to meet the endless difficulties and exigencies" of the maniac's situation.

The second edition of Pinel's *Treatise* stressed the extension of the moral treatment to the hospital as a human unit:

One of the principal rules in a well-regulated hospital is to have a central authority who shall decide without appeal, having the sole control over both domestics and patients, and being never interfered with either by any other officer or by the friends of the patients. I am opposed, for many reasons, to blows as a means of cure; which measure has been in constant use; . . . and which was used by a farmer in Scotland, who worked patients sent to him as beasts of burden, and who was famous for the cure of insanity. Blows are incompatible with the character of the French nation, and would rather suit those who had been always slaves.

Pinel's fame spread throughout France. He was elected a member of the Institute of France. Soon after he became Professor of Pathology at the School of Medicine. Honors multiplied. In 1803 when the Emperor Napoleon returned from Elba in a frenzy of popular admiration, he received his physician at a reception at the Institute with a question about the reputed increase of the number of the insane. Dr. Pinel answered in the negative; "but I thought to myself," he quipped afterwards, "that the superior geniuses and ambitious conquerors were not exempt from a trace of madness."

As a member of the Institute and France's foremost alienist, he was called upon by Napoleon to investigate the claims of Franz Gall, the craniologist. Pinel took Gall's technique to the Bicêtre and honestly tried to determine what type of skull showed a predisposition to insanity. The skulls of the insane did not match Gall's charts, and for this and another reason Pinel joined his fellow Academicians in denouncing Gall.

At the Salpêtrière, Pinel inspired all who came to hear him lecture on his moral treatment. Ferrus, Esquirol, and other men who became famous later were among his students. In a congenial atmosphere he labored for twenty years to bring medicine to the scientific level of other branches of natural history, but again he met with political difficulty. Suspected of having opposed the delivery to authorities of a great number of priests and emigrés whom fear had compelled to take refuge at the Bicêtre, Pinel was denied the return of his teaching post.

He accepted his decline philosophically. Under the cloud of suspicion of being a royalist, Pinel lived out his life in comparative destitution. Pinel was essentially a product of France, of French philosophy, enlightenment, and liberalism. Great as the man was, his times were greater. The private misfortunes of Pinel did not stem the tide of humane treatment of the insane.

During the early months of 1791, visitors to one Hannah Mills, a Quaker inmate of the Lunatick Asylum of old York, were denied admission by the overseer. No reason was given; a few days later, it was announced she had died. The relatives brought the story to William Tuke, a well-respected merchant of York. With his son Henry, William interested the Society of Friends, his personal acquaintances, and several town doctors of the need for a hospital for insane persons.[17] In preparation he quietly investigated other asylums; what he saw amazed and horrified him, and yet no one seemed to have bothered themselves about the poor unfortunates housed there. A visit to St. Luke's Hospital showed him how mental patients were coerced, hounded, or neglected as a matter of course. He saw one young woman chained to a wall, lying half-nude on some loose, filthy straw, her body crusted with excreta, her hair matted, a blank expression on her face. It was enough for the Quaker. Burning with indignation, Tuke told his friends what he had seen and how he intended to remedy the situation. "We shall have a place," cried Tuke, "in which the unhappy might obtain a refuge; a quiet haven in which the shattered bark might find the means of reparation, or of safety."

The initiation and the development of the York Retreat was a direct reflection of the Quaker conception of closeness to God, which meant unity with the brotherhood of man. The Society of Friends as a religious group was founded on a view of man's contact with the spirit of God as an immediate experience—a personal response to an Inner Light. The Quakers have been called "the most practical mystics the world has ever seen."[18] Yet William Tuke had considerable opposition to overcome in putting his ideas into action. His fellow members protested, and even Tuke's wife[19] pleaded with him against the project, saying, "William, thou hast had many children of thy brain, but this will prove an idiot."

The first report published by the York Retreat proclaimed that the hospital was not operated as a prison, as was the contemporary institution in London, Bedlam, but embodied the "idea of a rural farm." Not a physician himself, Tuke insisted that "bleeding, blisters, seatons, evacuants . . . appear too inefficacious to deserve the appellation as remedies." He observed "how much was to be done by moral means and how little by any known medical means" in the relief of mental patients. Physicians also noted that after the acute maniacal excitement was over in many of their cases, patients responded to a regimen of encouragement, kindliness, and routine work. William Tuke's work was carried on by his grandson, Samuel Tuke, author of a widely read book on the Retreat.[20] The York Retreat, supported, managed, and lived in by "the family," became a mecca for observers from the Continent and America.

In spite of the spirit of optimism reflected in enlightened treatment of madmen, medicine in Britain remained at a disgraceful level in the field of lunacy. Beyond that, confusion reigned throughout Europe generally regarding insanity, as witness Lichtenberg's witticism (1769):

> There are certainly just as many, if not more, people imaginatively sick as there are those who are really sick. There are just as many people, if not more, imaginatively sane as there are people, who are really sane.[21]

On the other hand, social uplift in general carried noncynics to a level of euphoria, as seen in a statement discovered in a church in Gotha, Germany (1784):

Our age occupies the happiest period of the eighteenth century. Emperors, kings, and princes humanely descend from their dreaded heights, despise pomp and splendor, become the fathers, friends, and confidants of their people. Religion rends its priestly garb and appears in its divine essence. Enlightenment makes great strides. Thousands of our brothers and sisters, who formerly lived in sanctified inactivity, are given back to the state. Sectarian hatred and persecution for conscience' sake are vanishing. Love of man and freedom of thought are gaining the supremacy.[22]

The confusion was confounded by the madness of King George III. The King's recurrent manic attacks, especially one that left England without a monarch during the winter of 1788-1789, roused the House of Commons. Guttmacher, in reviewing the debate over George's illness, comments: ". . . instead of being seated on his throne . . . [he] was much of the time confined in a strait-jacket."[23] Parliament was disturbed over the King's doctors and their methods. Unable to secure results from medication, Doctor Munro, an outstanding practitioner in the field of mental diseases in England, was summoned. Further consultations brought Sir George Baker and Dr. Heberden, who recommended blistering the King's shaved scalp. Advice poured in from the four corners of the world. One advocated "communicating the Itch" to the royal patient. Another recommended the ingestion of the blood of an ass, to which the brains of a ram were to be added.[24] Finally, Dr. Francis Willis, clergyman turned psychiatrist, was called in. From the first, Doctor Willis showed skill in handling his patient. He employed a combination of leniency and firmness for which he was deservedly renowned.

During the hearings in January, 1789, a bitter controversy broke out between mentors Warren and Willis as to the need for force in subduing the King during his delirious period. Warren made the statement that he would rather have persons of common sense, such as nurses, attend the King than men who purported to be mental specialists. Willis countered that his royal patient would recover, and that "as a rule" his patients recovered if they were brought to him within three months of the onset of illness. Parliament's investigating committee deemed that the report of the hearings "must be published immediately in the public interest."

The Parliamentary inquiry of 1815 opened up a hitherto unanswered question: Just what transpired in private madhouses? The Select Committee on Lunacy took testimony that shocked its members. An investigator of Bedlam reported:

> I saw in the female galleries, ten naked females, chained by one arm or leg to the wall...allowing them merely to stand up or sit down.... On the male side it had the complete appearance of a dog kennel. William Norris had a stout iron ring around his neck, fixed by a short chain to a horizontal bar.... [25]

More lurid stories came to light. At Dr. Warburton's Whitmore House, the male keepers were characterized by an observer as "fellows whose touch would taint putridity itself, and render it more abominable." What had been rumors and information leaks came into the open. A woman who had requested release from a private madhouse was "flogged with a rope, tied to her bedpost for a week, not permitted to retire for the purposes of nature, and the stench in her room was abominable."

Cruelties unearthed by the Parliamentary Committee were commonplace, but specialists themselves were in conflict as to the proper methods of handling madmen. Professor Cullen at Edinburgh, mentor of Benjamin Rush and other prominent physicians in Colonial America, taught that "Stripes and blows about the body" were advisable for maniacs. Another expert, John Battie, suggested that reliance be placed on the "sagacity of the physician." [26] If these failed, time-tested methods were relied on, as witness the advice, "Body pain may be excited to purpose and without the least danger. Beating is often serviceable." Battie prescribed "blisters and caustics and rough catharticks" in disturbed patients, to cause pain and discomfort, and hence reduction in excitement.

The therapeutic attitude of physicians and wardens alternated between the sadism of punishing treatment and the guilt of having used it. Like despairing parents, physicians did not know whether to apply censure or gentleness to their erring children. Each physician accused the other of ignorance. Battie became involved in several bitter controversies, particularly with Dr. John Monro, then medical superintendent of Bethlehem Hospital. In his treatise, Battie had deplored the fact that the public treatment of mental patients was in the hands of "quacks and certain gentlemen (wardens, etc.)." At the same time, Battie, who represented the private-hospital physician, had written a series of papers in which he outlined a very fanciful theory of treatment and management. Dr. Monro, as physician to Bedlam, took violent exception to his writings. In vigorous language, Monro objected to Battie's use of "bleeding, blisters, rough cathartics, the gum and foetid anti-hystericks, opium, mineral waters, cold bathing, vomits.... If these general methods are applied without judgement or discretion," he added, "common sense will at once join with madness and reject them too." While Monro and his fellow workers at Bedlam were beginning to see the need of training attendants to understand their charges, Monro insisted that he "never thought of reading lectures on a subject that could be understood no otherwise than by personal observations." Scornfully he pointed out that Battie's book contained "30 pages of medication, against two pages, which were adorned, on management."

Other routines recommended for raving maniacs were the scarifying and the bleeding of the scalp. The skin was blistered in order to overcome one of the basic causes of insanity, "over-determination of blood to the head." The apologetic apothecary of Bethlehem Hospital, Haslam, with a candor not restricted by medical tradition, reports of the practice of vomiting patients "frequently and severely: I am sorry that it is not in my power to speak of it favorably."[27] Haslam, for one, did not like the attitude of the gaping crowds who paid for an opportunity to see the howling madmen and chained idiots. He wrote of the need for human understanding of the patient and fair treatment: "It should be the object of the practitioner to remove ... disease rather than irritate and torment the sufferer." To Haslam, the idea that the mental patient should be beaten for whatever salutary effect it might have appeared ridiculous. "If the patient be so far deprived of understanding why he is punished, such correction, setting aside its cruelty, is manifestly absurd."

The controversy over treatment of lunatics in England, the writings of Pinel, the family Tuke's efforts in York, reached doctors in the Colonies. Lunatics were a not uncommon problem on the eastern seaboard. Benjamin Rush, America's first psychiatrist, commented on:

> ...[the increase of] apoplexies and true melancholy.... The excess passion for liberty, inflamed by the successful issue of the war, produced...a species of insanity which I shall take the liberty of distinguishing by the name of *Anarchia*.[28]

By 1817 a Friends Asylum had opened in Frankford, Pennsylvania, the McLean Asylum in Boston, and the Hartford Retreat in 1824.

There had been other facilities available for the insane. The Pennsylvania Hospital in Philadelphia, which opened in February, 1752, had maintained an "Insane department"[29] from the start as a prominent part of "this noble charity." In New York, in 1745, a building on the "precise spot where now stands City Hall"[30] received the sick, the indigent poor, and "the maniac." In company with the Pennsylvania Hospital,[31] the New York Hospital, in New York City, utilized its basement for the mentally ill until thirty years later (1821), when the trustees established the Bloomingdale Asylum as a separate institution for the insane. The first state (colonial) hospital for the insane was opened at Williamsburg, Virginia, in 1773.

These bald figures indicate little of the struggles that accompanied efforts to humanize treatment of madmen in the States. The story of Dr. Eli Todd, founder of the Hartford Retreat, as reconstructed by John Winkler, paints a vivid picture of this development.[32] A graduate of Yale, Dr. Todd made his rounds in rural Connecticut on horseback, encountering sights that stirred him—farmers who boarded up their insane in crates, imbeciles chained to a barn or outhouse, local halfwits jeered at by schoolboys on the village roads. Moving to Hartford in 1819, then a city of 4,000, Todd organized the Connecticut State Medical Society. One night in December, 1820, at a meeting of the Medical Society, he related what he knew of Pinel, concluding:

> Not only do the people of New England inherit the constitution of their ancestors...but other causes operate here with peculiar force.... Gentlemen, it is our duty as civilized men to attack this disease....[33]

The Society voted $400.00 to the cause; within two years, $12,000 had been collected from donations ranging from 12½ cents to a lottery and a small grant from the State of Connecticut. As director of the Hartford Retreat, Dr. Todd embarked on the "moral treatment" popularized by Pinel "to treat them [the patients]...as rational beings." At night, he walked, talked, and dined with his charges, placed ale and beer on the table, played the violin and flute for the patients, who called him "Father." The British traveler-author, Captain Basil Hall, discovered the self-effacing Todd on a trip in 1827. In his book, *Travels in America*, Captain Hall waxed ecstatic over the Retreat's management:

> Instead of showing them off as monsters [he] introduced us to each of them and encouraged conversation as if all the company had been in perfect health.[34]

Todd, who claimed 91.3% cures during the year 1826, became a celebrity. His success, as broadcast by Captain Hall, started what Albert Deutsch has called the Cult of Curability.[35]

In the Colonies, no less than in England and Europe generally, treatment of insanity rose in importance at the turn of the nineteenth century. Benjamin Rush, signer of the Declaration of Independence, a vigorous, embattled figure in medicine, the patron saint of American psychiatry, saw the need and met it. Rush, appointed to the Pennsylvania Hospital in Philadelphia in 1783, became impressed by the needs of "patients afflicted by madness." His insistence that the mad should be the "first objects" of the physician's attention pushed the legislature to appropriate $15,000 for a separate building for the Insane at the Hospital.[36]

Rush's fame rested on more than his interest in madmen. He was at once a political activist, espousing abolitionism[37] and organizing the Pennsylvania Society for Promoting the Abolition of Slavery (1787), a strong patriot, a professor of chemistry in the College of Philadelphia, a member of the American Philosophical Society (founded by Benjamin Franklin), medical hero of yellow fever epidemics in Philadelphia, and a voluminous writer.[38] His chief interest, man's mind in health and disease, culminated after fifty years in what is reputedly the first American treatise on psychiatry (1812).[39] In spite of Overholser's unearthing two volumes appearing in America before Rush's opus —namely, *View of the Nervous Temperament*, by Thomas Trotter, published in Troy, New York in 1808 and *Practical Observations on Insanity* by Joseph Mason Cox, Philadelphia, 1811[40]—Rush's *Medical Inquiries* stood as an American authority on mental diseases until the 1880s.

Rush's contribution to mental treatment methods matched his personality; in particular, his drastic therapy and the theory behind it irked some of his colleagues. Nor was he without an insistent moralistic strain, as witness a pamphlet, *Effects of Spiritous Liquors on the Human Body,* purchasable by the public at "4 d. single or 2½ d. by the dozen."[41] The high ethical tone in his work with patients, however, enabled Rush to diagnose individuals now known as sociopathic or psychopathic personalities. These disorders he called "MICRONOMIA, partial or weakened action of the moral faculty" or "ANOMIA...total absence of this faculty."[42] In the rhetoric of the times, he asked his colleagues:

> Why should it be thought impossible for medicines, to act...upon the moral faculty? May not the earth contain ...antidotes to our moral, as well as natural diseases?—Let those, who refute me...recollect, that moral evil was introduced into our minds—as well as natural evil into our bodies—by eating the apple.[43]

His chief weakness, and his strength, lay in espousing bloodletting based on the theory that "the cause of madness is seated primarily in the blood vessels of the brain."[44] Since "overcharging" the brain with blood was the cause of mental disease, relief was obtained by depleting the body of blood to the point of causing faintness and debility. Bleeding was carried out vigorously; an average of 20 to 40 ounces (600 to 1,200 cc.) of blood was let per treatment. Commenting on the technical problem of having the patient stand during bloodletting to induce fainting more quickly, Rush recommended keeping the patient in an erect posture for 24 hours at a time. Taking his cue from a method of taming refractory horses in England, "by first impounding them ...and then keeping them from lying down or sleeping by thrusting sharp pointed nails into their bodies for two or three days and nights," Rush saw the same advantages of keeping madmen awake in a standing posture "for four and twenty hours, but by different and more lenient means." This would fatigue the muscles and "the debility thus induced in those muscles would attract morbid excitement from the brain, and thereby relieve the disease." Having reduced the action of the blood vessels "to a par of debility of the nervous system," he proceeded in workmanlike fashion to stimulate the body with diet, alcoholic beverages, emetics, bitters, alkaline salts, asafetida, tar infused in water and garlic and the "noble" medicine, laudanum. This was followed by a routine of baths, massage, exercise, with perhaps blistering and cupping.

In Rush's hand the theory of depletion and stimulation was advanced with more vigor, though with no more persistence, than was common among good psychiatrists of the period. Many physicians had worked on the problem of mental stimulation for "torpid" cases. For example, Dr. Cox,[45] of London, secured mental stimulation through the action of a "rotator." This was an ingenious device consisting of a cage moved by a set of pulleys, which rotated the patient to the point of nausea and prostration. Cox reported a case of a furious maniac who was treated for eight days, rotation lasting six minutes each treatment. The first day the patient became pale and was carried to bed, where he slept. The next day rotation lasted four minutes, followed by prostration. The next day he refused to eat and was rotated four minutes again. "He had abundant vomiting," the notes read, but seemed more calm; after further treatment the patient was finally "reduced of his mania." Even Christian Reil[46] had invented a movable wheel which operated like a squirrel cage, "the least motion making the patient toss about," thus forcing him "to repose."

Rush's own machine, the gyrator, for "torpid madness," and the tranquilizing chair for maniacal states were simply applications of generally accepted principles. In common with Cox's "rotator"[47] the gyrator subjected the patient to rotary motion so as to give a centrifugal direction of the blood toward the brain until nausea, vertigo, and perspiration were produced. The tranquilizer was a chair in which the patient was strapped at the ankles, the wrist, across the chest and the abdomen, his head being confined in a wooden box. Rush invented the tranquilizing chair in reaction to the "mad shirt" or strait-waistcoat which did not allow for bleeding. In Rush's treatment, the patient in the tranquilizing chair was bled until his reason returned or his pulse diminished. The original description of the apparatus,[48] with line drawing, was accompanied by the report of case A. D., whose pulse was 96 strokes to the minute when he was placed in the tranquilizer:

Upon examining him an hour after I found the pulse diminished in frequency 6 strokes. Upon the 2nd hour the fullness diminished. By the 4th hour his pulse was nearly normal and the ferocious looks of the maniac were changed to an agreeable aspect.

Nevertheless, the need for humane management was not lost on Rush. In his lectures he urged that the attitude of the physician be fitted to the mood of the patient. In melancholia, one must be gentle. In mania, a different address was needed, for "the dread of the eye was early imposed on the beast in the field . . . tygre and mad bull all fly from it" and hence "a man deprived of his reason . . . is terrified or composed by the eye" of a sane man. [49] If a stern eye did not suffice, obedience could be secured by a firm voice and countenance of the physician, or through acts of justice or kindness. If this was not effective, pouring cold water under the coat sleeve, so that it might descend to the armpits and down the trunk of the body, was advised. If these methods of punishment "did not suffice," it would be proper to resort to the fear of death, and Rush quotes several cases in which fear of death was followed by mental improvement.

It was not uncommon in that period to resort to the "fear of death" or other humiliating experiences in dealing with stubborn mental cases. One statement of this theory, adapted by a phrenologist, was "to regulate the exercise of the different powers of the mind, so as not to leave those which are naturally in excess in undisturbed sway over the rest." [50] Driving morbid ideas from the patient's mind became a specific aim of psychiatric treatment; in the hands of some physicians, it consisted in a type of mental legerdemain calculated to outwit patients. A patient of Pinel who believed that his head had been cut off was cured after being forcibly exposed to view the head of one who had been guillotined. Rush recites the case of an opium addict treated by her physician, who

took a large snuff-box out of his pocket. She looked at it as if she wished for a pinch of snuff. The physician put it into her hands. Upon opening it, an artificial snake that had been coiled up in it, suddenly leaped upon her shoulder. She was convulsed with terror, and from that time left off the use of opium and rapidly recovered.[51]

The vigorous treatment of the first half of the nineteenth century did not abate, but was modified by earnest efforts to utilize the "moral" (which meant mental) treatment espoused by Pinel. Leuret, an ingenious French physician, employed a type of crude conditioning and forcibly repressed the expression of every insane or morbid idea by giving the patient a douche each time he uttered the delusion.[52] Leuret combated passions with passions; he would place himself face to face with the patient, struggling with the latter's ideas, behavior, and determination. If the patient was adamant, Leuret was doubly so. If the patient developed an ingenious delusional system, Leuret outdid him. He used pain as a "motive power" that banished evil and sought to replace morbid ideas by good. Convinced of Pinel and Esquirol's doctrine of acceptance and compassion for the insane, Leuret did not hesitate to enter into and combat the patient's inner mental struggle: "To passion, abuse and blows, oppose sangfroid and compassion." Leuret's premise, which he later modified, encompassed "the use of all methods that directly agitate the intelligence and emotions of the insane... without recourse to physical methods."[53] His work represented a courageous and premature attempt to enter the chaotic terrain of the insane mind.

Pinel's influence, however, remained the most pervasive. His *"traitement moral,"* carried forward by his student, Jean Etienne Dominique Esquirol, became the moving spirit of French psychiatry. Esquirol joined Pinel in condemning the "bath of surprise" and the abuse of bloodletting among the insane. Esquirol set the tone by stating, "One has to love the mentally sick in order to be worthy and capable of serving them." His text, *Des maladies mentales,* [54] appearing in 1838 with its calm, measured descriptions and recommendations for mental cases, contrasted with the drastic use of venesection, mechanical gyrators, and the like. Esquirol's sanity stood up well alongside Cox's rotator,[55] and the latter's vivid use of music therapy:

> (For) torpid patients—SCREECHES and YELLS, made in an apartment painted *Black* and *red* or *glaring* white... (for) an opposite state... patient to be placed in *airy* room, surrounded with *flowers breathing odours,* the walls colored green and the air agitated by softest harmony.[56]

Riese points out that Pinel's "moral treatment" went beyond kindness and sympathy for his patients; it involved acceptance of "the insane's symptoms as basic manifestations of human nature."[57] "The inner experiences of his patient in the all-human terms he used" stamps Pinel, in Riese's words, as a "pioneer and forerunner of *Individual Psychotherapy* of psychoses." At all events, it is safe to say that few physicians during the middle of the nineteenth century did not ponder a method to effectively influence the mad world of delusions and "morbid passions." Rush's recommendation to the managers of the Pennsylvania Hospital for a man "of education to superintend the Lunaticks... to walk with them, converse with them, etc. in order to awaken and regulate their minds"[58] bespoke his disaffection with the "penetrating eye" that would overwhelm the madman. Others also recognized the hopeless nature of dramatic methods. Haslam,[59] the perspicacious director at Bethlehem who carried the title of apothecary to the hospital, complained that "carrying no thunder in my voice, nor lightning in my eye," he had to rely on knowing his patient's history, on a mild manner and a real interest in his patient's problems. Haslam disbelieved in the arresting cure, the dramatic collapse of mania under the weight of a physician's personality. In 1835, Prichard[60] summarized the state of psychotherapy through moral means by stating the maxim that it is not well

> to direct the attention of patients to the subjects on which their illusions turn, or to oppose their unreasonable prejudices by argument, or contradiction.... It is better to excite interest in connection with things remote from the morbid train of thought.

It was a perplexing situation. The deliverance of mental patients from chains and fetters still left the problem of control and management a vital one. Translated into practical terms, although kindness was recognized as the patient's right, "obedience is the ground of the physicians' management."[61] What Heinroth, the German authority, stated in restrained terms, another German, Dr. Teschallener, of Tyrol, put more realistically: "Kindness...is my right hand, as earnestness and severity are my left."[62]

In spite of pious hopes, restraint in public institutions remained the mainstay: it was accomplished by means of iron rings on ankles and wrists. Patients chained to the floor were considered put "into treatment" for the day and left to wallow in excrement. Other patients were washed with a broom and doused with cold water in the open courtyard. Deaths were falsified in the annual reports. Implements resembling medieval armor were openly in use and condoned by authority. The commissioners investigating the Lincoln Asylum (England) in 1820 came upon

> padded iron collars, heavy, cumbrous leathern muffs, belts with manacles, solid iron wrist-locks, jointed iron leg-locks or hobbles and the quarter-boots of Dr. Charlesworth, a well-thought-of man in insanity, to keep feet secured to foot-board.

From Rush's tranquilizing chair to Dr. Charlesworth's quarter-boot to the Utica crib or Aubanel's restraining bed, the basic theory was relief of the patient from the destructive effects of his mania.[63]

Notes to Chapter 6

1. E. G. O'Donoghue, *The Story of Bethlehem Hospital from Its Foundation in 1247*, London, Unwin, 1914, and New York, Dutton, 1915.
2. Levinus Lemnius, *The Touchstone of Complexions... Englished by Thos. Newton*, London, 1576, quoted in Hunter and Macalpine, p. 23.
3. Committee Books, 1764–1779, *Bethlehem Hospital*, quoted in Hunter and Macalpine, p. 427.
4. Daniel Defoe, *An essay upon projects...*, quoted in Hunter and Macalpine, p. 265.
5. Robin, *Nouvelles de Médecin et de chirurgie, A Description of Salpêtrière*, 1787, p. 107.
6. Peter Bassoe, "Spain as the Cradle of Psychiatry," *Amer. Jour. Psych.*, Vol. 101, May 1945, p. 731.
7. Ramon Sarro, "Spain as the Cradle of Psychiatry," in *Centennial Papers*, St. Elizabeth Hosp. (1855–1955), ed. W. Overholser. Washington, D. C., 1956.
8. Philippe Pinel, *Traite Medico-philosophique sur l'alienation mentale* (1809), 2nd ed.
9. George Mora, "Bi-Centenary of the Birth of Vincenza Chiarugi (1747–1820), A Pioneer of the Modern Mental Hospital Treatment," *Am. J. Psych.* Vol. 116, Sept. 1959, p. 267.
10. George Mora, "Pietro Pisani and the Mental Hospital of Palermo in the Early 19th Century," *Bull. of Hist. of Med.* Vol. 33, May-June, 1959.
11. J. L. Vives, *Encyclopaedia Britannica*, ed. 13, 1945, Vol. 23, p. 227.
12. Louis Peze, *Les precurseurs de Pinel en France*, These de Paris, Paris, L. Arnette, 1922; Vives, "De Subventione Pauperum" (1526).
13. Rene Semelaigne, *Les grands alienists francais*, Paris, Stein & Neil, 1894, Vol. I, p. 31.
14. Louis Peze, p. 78.
15. Semelaigne, p. 42.
16. Philippe Pinel, *Op. Cit.*
17. Robert O. Rob Mennell, Woden Law, Kenley, Surrey, England. Personal Communication, 1943.
18. W. W. Comfort, *Just Among Friends, The Quaker Way of Life*, Philadelphia, Blakiston, 1945, p. 9.
19. *The Retreat, York, Addresses Given During the 150th Anniversary Celebrations*, William Sessions, York, Ebor Press, 1946.
20. Samuel Tuke, *Description of the Retreat in the Institution in York, for Insane Persons of the Society of Friends, Containing an Account of Its Origin and Progress and Means of Treatment and Statement of Cases*, York, England, 1813.
21. R. D. Loewenberg, "A review of Georg Christoph Lichtenberg," *ETC.* 1:102, 103, winter, 1943-1944.
22. J. H. Randall, Jr., *The Making of the Modern Mind, A Survey of the Intellectual Background of the Present Age*, rev. ed., Boston, Houghton, 1940, p. 384.

23. M. S. Guttmacher, *America's Last King*, New York, Scribner, 1941.
24. *Ibid.*, p. 188.
25. *Ibid.*, p. 205.
26. John Battie, *Treatise on Madness*, London, Whitson & White, 1758.
27. John Haslam, *Observations on Insanity, with Practical Remarks on the Disease, and an Account of the Morbid Appearances on Dissection*, London, 1798.
28. Benjamin Rush, "An account of the influence of the military and political events of the American Revolution upon the human body," in *Medical Inquiries and observations, upon Diseases of the Mind*, Phila., Kimber & Richardson, 1812.
29. T. S. Kirkbride, "A sketch of the history, buildings, and organizations of the Pennsylvania Hospital for the Insane," *Am. J. Insanity* 2:97, 1845.
30. Miscellaneous, *Am. J. Insanity* 1:287, 1845.
31. S. W. Hamilton, "The History of American Mental Hospitals," in *One Hundred Years of American Psychiatry*, New York, Columbia, 1944, p. 73 et seq.
32. John K. Winkler and Walter Bromberg, *Mind Explorers*, New York, Reynal & Hitchcock, 1939.
33. Winkler and Bromberg, p. 86.
34. Basil Hall, *Travels in North America in the Years 1827 and 1828*, Edinburgh, Cadell, 1829.
35. Albert Deutsch, *The Mentally Ill in America*, New York, Columbia Univ. Press, 2nd ed., 1949, Chap. 11.
36. N. G. Goodman, *Benjamin Rush, Physician and Citizen*, Philadelphia, Univ. of Penna. Press, 1934.
37. Betty L. Plummer, "Benjamin Rush and the Negro," *Am. J. Psych.* Vol. 127, Dec. 1970, p. 93.
38. Benjamin Rush, *Two Essays on the Mind. An Enquiry into the INFLUÈNCE of PHYSICAL CAUSES UPON THE MORAL FACULTY and on the INFLUENCE OF PHYSICAL CAUSES IN PROMOTING AN INCREASE IN STRENGTH AND ACTIVITY OF THE INTELLECTUAL FACULTIES OF MAN*. Reprinted from the original, 1799, Brunner/Mazel, New York, 1972. Intro. by Eric Carlson, M. D., p. v.
39. Benjamin Rush, *Medical Inquiries and Observations upon Diseases of the Mind*, Phila., Kimber & Richardson, 1812.
40. Winfred Overholser, *Cox and Trotter—Two Psychiatric Precursors of Benjamin Rush*, Vidonian Club Address, New York, Oct. 1951.
41. Benjamin Rush, *AN INQUIRY INTO THE EFFECTS OF SPIRITOUS LIQUORS on the Human Body, to which is added a MORAL and Physical THERMOMETER*. Advertisement in the *Massachusetts SPY or, the WORCESTER GAZETTE*, Worcester, Mass. Aug. 5, 1790.
42. Benjamin Rush, *Two Essays*, p. 16.
43. Benjamin Rush, *Two Essays*, p. 27.
44. Benjamin Rush, *Medical Inquiries*.
45. J. M. Cox, *Practical Observations on Insanity*, London, C & R. Baldwin, 1806.

46. J. M. Galt, *The Treatment of Insanity*, New York, Harper, 1846, p. 181.
47. Winfred Overholser, *Cox and Trotter—Two Psychiatric Precursors of Benjamin Rush*, Address, Vidonian Club, New York, October 27, 1951.
48. Benjamin Rush, *Essays, Literary, Moral and Philosophical*, ed. 2, Philadelphia, Bradford, 1806, p. 183.
49. *Ibid.*, p. 175.
50. Andrew Combe, *Observations on Mental Derangement, Being an Application of the Principles of Phrenology to the Elucidations of Causes, Symptoms, Nature and Treatment of Insanity*, Boston, Marsh, Capen & Lyons, 1834, p. 277.
51. Benjamin Rush, *Medical Inquiries and Observations upon the Diseases of the Mind*.
52. Francis Leuret, *Du traitement moral de la folie*, Paris, Bailliere, 1840.
53. Leuret, Biographical notice: A Brievre de Boismont gaz. Medicale de Paris, *Am. J. Insanity* 8:361, 1852.
54. J. E. D. Esquirol, *Mental Maladies, A Treatise on Insanity*, translated by E. K. Hunt, Philadelphia, Lea & Blanchard, 1845.
55. M. K. Amdur and E. Messinger, "Jean Etienne Dominique Esquirol," *Am. J. Psychiat.* 96: 129–135, 1939.
56. J. M. Cox, p. 61.
57. Walther Riese, "An Outline of a History of Ideas in Psychotherapy," *Bull. of Hist. of Med.* Vol. XXV, No. 5, Sept. 1951, p. 442.
58. Benjamin Rush, *The Autobiography, His Travels through Life together with his Commonplace Book*, ed. by G. W. Corner, Am. Philos. Soc., Princeton, 1948.
59. John Haslam, *Observation on Madness and Melacholia*, 2nd ed., London, J. Callow and G. Hayden, 1809.
60. J. C. Prichard, *A Treatise on Insanity and Other Disorders Affecting the Mind*, London, Sherwood, Gilbert and Piper, 1835.
61. Pliny Earle, "Institutions for the Insane in Prussia, Austria and Germany," *Am. J. Insanity*, Vol. 9, April, 1853.
62. *Ibid.*
63. S. W. Hamilton, "The History of American Mental Hospitals," in *One Hundred Years of American Psychiatry*, New York, Columbia, 1944, p. 107.

7

The Struggle Over Restraints:
The Asylum Comes of Age

THE object of Dr. Charlesworth's quarter-boot was "not punishment but security"; in the United States, the Utica crib, or Aubanel's restraining bed,[1] was a companion device. Dr. Charlesworth's mechanism held the patient's feet at the end of the bed in an upright position; it was used for the night hours, *after* the patient had been in restraint most of the day! Few asylum superintendents questioned the need for restraint. Yet stories leaked out of these institutions, telling of rat bites, amputations from frostbite, fettered lunatics continuously in iron collars and iron waistbands. Investigations followed, placing the evidence on record, but reforms were slow. Partly this was due to public apathy and partly due to conservatism among physicians. The editors of the *Lancet*[2] were outraged at the innovation of nonrestraint proposed by Dr. Gardner Hill of the Lincoln Asylum in London. Others critized Hill, who boldly claimed that "restraint is never justified for the insane" by writing, "[this] curious opinion...is more remarkable for its *rashness* even than its *boldness*." The Hillite system was denounced for being the "wild scheme of a philanthropic visionary," "an attempt for popular applause," a "breaking of the Sixth Commandment."

116

Who was this "raving" theoretician? Dr. Hill, house surgeon at the Lincoln Asylum in 1829,[3] came upon the "quarter-boot" of Dr. Charlesworth. From this and other observations he conceived the idea of "Total Abolition of Restraint," the first frank statement laid before the British public.[4] In nine years at the Lincoln Asylum he was able to reduce restraint hours from 20,423 per year to none! By 1840 every trace of restraint had been removed, with "All recent cases discharged... incurable cases discharged... no suicides... the inmates happy and comfortable...." As Hunter and Macalpine remarked, "So ended the old era in psychiatry."[5]

Opposition, however, was not quelled. The wall of defensiveness against admitting the insane person into the circle of human beings was not easily dissolved. The notion that the insane could not be treated without restraint was one with the idea that the insane belonged to another, perhaps lower, order of beings. For proof, it was pointed out that they required stronger doses of drugs, were insensible to pain and like the "mad bull," were susceptible of being stared into submission. The strength of this prejudice was reinforced by practical considerations. In many asylums there were not enough trustworthy attendants to be given the privilege of using manual restraint when necessary in place of mechanical restraint. Besides, there were suicidal patients who needed control; there was the general view that "moral restraint" was insufficient for "liberty-loving Americans," and so on. Dr. Isaac Ray[6] declined to abolish restraints on the grounds that "the abolition of mechanical restraint meant merely the substitution of another form of coercion— manual restraint' or force exercised at the hands of attendants—which was hardly more desirable."

Soon other asylum physicians followed Hill's example. In 1839, at the Hanwell Asylum,[7,8] Dr. John Conolly discarded mechanical restraints completely. And while the orthodox continued to mutter about Hill's "mania," and Moreau de Tours caustically remarked that it was "an idea entirely Britannic," and hence impractical, the more thoughtful physicians embraced Hill's and Conolly's techniques.

When locked doors were opened, complaints by conservative physicians were voiced. An editorial comment in the *American Journal of Insanity* stated, relating to the removal of locks from insane wards, "[it is] humane treatment but there must be some limit to the removal of restrictions on the insane."[9] As late as 1880, M. Christian, speaking at the Annual Medico-Psychological meeting in Paris, November, 1880, critized Conolly as not "confining himself within prudent limits." Where Pinel had done so, Christian complained, "Conolly... wished to invent a new system."[10] Conolly, who worked in larger institutions than had Hill (Middlesex County Lunatic Asylum), had indeed perpetuated a "new system"; he was revered as a "practical reformer" throughout Europe and the States.

The "new" theory that the insane were treatable encouraged the erection of many special institutions where the "curables" could be isolated from the "incurables." In Germany, under the leadership of Langermann, new asylums were built, or old ones remodeled, to accommodate the treatment needs of the "curables." During the first three decades of the century, public asylums in Saxony, Schleswig, Heidelberg, Prague, were built for new patients,[11] and older institutions were set aside for the incurable epileptics, idiots, and dements. Against the abstruse discussion of the philosophy of insanity, the morbid psychology of the soul, etc., which was the preoccupation of German psychiatrists, the "English practice" of using asylums for treatment made headway. Griesinger, in the second edition of his text, admitted that his inner wish for reform had been influenced by the "adverse opinions of German psychologists," but that he felt we could now "pursue the new system fearlessly."[12]

In spite of the reasonableness of the nonrestraint principle and the marked improvement in patients (which physicians using it could demonstrate), the question was intensively discussed in the medical literature for almost fifty years. In America, as an example, the problem exercised the Association of Medical Superintendents of American Institutions for the Insane (now the American Psychiatric Association) from their initial meeting in 1844, when a resolution was passed upholding the use of restraints. Thirty years later, at the meeting of 1874, discussion on the subject raged on.[13] The great majority of psychiatrists over this period recognized the occasional need for restraint, but in general practiced it sparingly. As late as 1885, Hack Tuke observed in his exhaustive survey of American institutions that American psychiatrists, such as Dr. John P. Gray, were "stout defenders of mechanical restraint, including the crib-bed," and that among British superintendents the teachings of Hill and Conolly were held rather as "pious opinion" than invariable rule.[14]

In the private hospitals of the period, particularly those that received their stimulus from the Quakers, the situation admittedly was different. On admission patients were immediately put "under treatment." This meant medication three times a day, purgatives and baths, sometimes outdoor recreation, frequently work, and amusements in the form of lectures or concerts in the evening. Under Dr. Kirkbride's aegis at the Pennsylvania Hospital for the Insane, a routine was established by waking the patients at a quarter after five in the winter and a quarter to five in the summer, the attendants unlocking the doors and giving "the patients a kind greeting."[15] After medicine was distributed, the patients breakfasted and the physician spoke to each patient.

Then there were walks in the garden, occupational activity and, after tea, reading, visits by the physicians, lectures, or entertainment. Restraint was still used for difficult patients, but the greatest reliance was placed on the presence and the kindliness of the physician, who acted as paterfamilias. Religious services were frequent, and occupational therapy in the form of suitable work was constantly advocated and pressed.

For all these improvements, the "new" attitude towards the insane was not reflected among the pauper insane. The disparity among asylums in various parts of the civilized world was great. A Canadian physician reported that until 1845, there had been "no attempts to treat insanity as a disease"![16] While at the New York State Lunatic Asylum in Utica, New York, the *Opal*, a monthly newspaper was published for the "exercise of the intellectual faculties of the patients... the first effort of this character."[17]

On a visit to an East Cambridge Jail in 1841, Miss Dorothea Dix came upon a few lunatics housed among the criminals. She protested to the jailor that no stoves were provided for the insane inmates on this blustery spring day. The jailor gave the stock answer that the insane were insensible to cold.[18] Her Puritan conscience aroused, Miss Dix vowed to investigate this shocking situation; systematically, she visited every jail and almshouse in Massachusetts during the next two years. As a commentator remarked, "The jailor who refused fire for patients thought he was dealing with a woman, not with destiny."[19] The horrors she witnessed moved her to dedicate herself to their alleviation:

> Cages, chains and whip, strong heavy chain [hanging] from an iron collar which invests neck... band of iron one inch wide around the neck with a six foot chain... hands restrained by clavis and belt of iron... and to each wrist united by a padlock in a cell six feet by eight feet by eight feet, patients were chained up all night.

As a result of this inspection, Miss Dix sent her famous memorial, a vivid memorandum, to the Massachusetts legislature.[20] It began: "I shall be obliged to speak with great plainness, and to reveal many things revolting to the taste and from which my woman's nature shrinks.... But truth is the highest consideration," and, after thirty pages of a report, painstakingly gathered, of revolting conditions that she had encountered, ended: "Gentlemen, I commit to you this sacred cause. Your action upon this subject will affect the present and future conditions of hundreds of thousands."

The Memorial produced a sensation in Boston; many attacked her, while others, including Dr. Luther V. Bell, of the McLean Asylum, came to her support. The result was the passage of a bill for relief of overcrowded conditions in the Worcester State Lunatic Hospital.

From New England Miss Dix traveled to New Jersey, and thence north and south and west, investigating and studying in minute detail the condition of patients. She badgered legislatures to appropriate money for state insane asylums. Through sheer will she battered the unwilling asylum superintendents into allowing her to inspect their buildings and, by direct appeal to state legislatures, forced them to give decent medical care to their charges. It was the influence of Dorothea Dix that added medical men to the staffs of many institutions in the States. By 1847 she had visited 18 penitentiaries, 300 county jails and houses of correction, and 500 almshouses. It was through her personal activity that she founded or enlarged 32 mental hospitals, among them the Government Hospital for the Insane at Washington, D. C., now St. Elizabeth's Hospital.[21]

Her success in state after state was phenomenal. Finally, in 1848, Miss Dix conceived the idea of urging the government to cede public land to the states, the sale of which was to be earmarked for improvement of the care of the insane. Her plan was encompassed in a bill that finally passed both houses of Congress, calling for the setting aside of 12,225,000 acres "from the many hundreds of millions of public lands."[22] So vigorously and successfully had Miss Dix fought that had it not been for President Pierce's veto on "constitutional and States' rights" grounds, the bill would have become law in 1850 and the revolutionary principle that the insane are "wards of the nation" would have become established. This inspired scheme was attacked in many quarters. The *Boston Medical and Surgical Journal* commented that "to create a mammoth hospital . . . would soon become an instrument with adroit, designing politicians for disturbing the peace of the country."[23] This was manifestly not her plan, but the complaint that the states might "slide off" their patients to the federal government was a compelling one. Nevertheless, psychiatrists recognized the vitality of her attack. As early as 1853 the Association of Superintendents resolved that "this association regards with continued admiration and unabated interest, the benevolent and unwaried efforts of Miss Dix."[24]

Increasing interest in psychiatry during the mid-century and the consecration of Miss Dix and other reformers began to puncture the verdict of the ages: "once insane, always insane." The entering point became a wedge, then an opened sluice gate and finally a torrent of optimism.

Physicians who dealt with mental troubles, called "psychiatrics" by Von Feuchtersleben (1840),[25] became known as "Psychological physicians" or "psychiatric practitioners." Books and journals devoted to mental disturbances appeared: the first, in 1805, was *Archiv für Gemüths und Nervenkrankheiten,* by A. S. Winkleman;[26] the second, established by Christian Reil in the same year, was *Magazin für psychische Heilkunde.* Other German journals appeared, such as the *Magazin für die philosophische, medizinische und gerichtliche Seelenkunde* (1829), which became the *Archiv für Psychologie für Ärzte und Juristen* (1883). The *Annales Medico-Legales in French* was published in 1842, and the *American Journal of Insanity* (predecessor of the *American Journal of Psychiatry*) was founded in 1844. English psychiatrists brought out the *Asylum Journal of Mental Science* in 1854.

Medical men, however, were interested in fevers and heart disease, in pneumonia and Bright's disease. They were intrigued by Laennec's stethoscope, fascinated by autopsies, involved in urine and blood analysis, animated by the controversy over the cause of puerperal (childbirth) fever—but toward insanity they were indifferent. Dr. Worthington of the Friends' Asylum, writing in the *Ameri-*

can Journal of Insanity in 1866,[27] castigated the "very stupid but very popular error" (on the part of physicians) to "skip" papers on insanity in medical journals. It was not until European physicians, building on the dominant cellular school of Virchow, began to see the relevance of pathology for mental diseases, that medicine slowly moved into psychiatry. The Germans particularly, working on the pathology of the brain and nervous system, glimpsed the vistas of bringing neurologic and medical knowledge into relation with psychotherapy. Van der Kolk's synthesis of pathology and therapeutics of nervous system disorders[28] was viewed on this side of the Atlantic as the beginning of a scientific study of the psyche. A few years earlier Griesinger, whose text on psychiatry appeared originally in 1845, stated, "The brain alone can be the seat of...abnormal mental action." As Sigerist remarks, the organic view of the German school developed "a psychiatry without psyche."[29]

Asylum superintendents and reformers meanwhile were flooded with optimism. Whereas insanity was commonly considered an "awful visitation from Heaven and that no human agency can reverse the judgement by which it was inflicted,"[30] the therapeutic approach now became positive. The contrast between Rush's statement in his *Treatise on the Mind* ("In entering upon the subject of the following Inquiries and Observations, I feel as if I were about to tread on consecrated ground") and Burrows' summary ("Few popular errors have been more prejudicial...than that insanity is commonly incurable"[31]), sounded the new note.

From the time that Dr. Willis, King George III's physician, claimed that "within three months after the attack, nine out of ten (of his patients) recovered" asylum physicians were reporting increasing successes. Burrows reported some years later (1820) on a series of figures collected from twenty-one asylums in Britain, 8 in France and 1 in Italy, and was "glad to note" that the recovery rate varied from 39 to 43 percent.[32] He demonstrated further that there was a yet higher proportion of recoveries of recent cases in "private lunatic houses." Agreeing that Willis' finding of "8 in 10, or even 6 in 7 recent cases credibly" reported recovered was sound, Burrows stated that 81 percent of patients in his own "House (verified under oath)" recovered, including those in a state of "fatuity, idiocy, and epilepsy." Considering recent cases only, he claimed 91 percent cured.

The remarkable assertion by Captain Hall contained in the Report of Visiting Physicians that Todd cured 91.3 percent of all recent cases during the year 1826 (21 out of 23 recent cases) was read with incredulity in England; especially Hall's further comment that "at two most ancient and celebrated institutions" of the same kind in Great Britain, the percentage of recent cases cured was 25.5 percent.[33] Until then, Todd and the Retreat had been practically unknown. Todd's figures of cures astounded the world, and all eyes turned toward Hartford, while every private institution in the United States set out to copy Todd's methods and improve his figures.

Turning to their records in an effort to emulate Dr. Todd's successful management, hospital superintendents discovered that they also could report high percentages of cures. Dr. Samuel Woodward, superintendent of the State Lunatic Hospital at Worcester, which opened in 1833, reported 82¼ percent recovered for the first year of operation.[34] Later reports showed increasing successes: in the 1836 report, 84 percent recoveries, and in 1837, 89 percent recoveries of "recent cases" were announced. In reviewing his cases for a five-year period, Dr. Woodward admitted that if the deaths and those cases left in the hospital (not yet cured) were subtracted, "we should increase the percentage to 94." The record established by Dr. Woodward of 91.42 percent of cures of recent cases (1840) was soon to be eclipsed by Dr. John M. Galt of the Eastern Asylum at Williamsburg, Virginia, who, in 1842, announced 92.3 percent recoveries. Finally, the following year, the ultimate of 100 percent recoveries was promulgated by Dr. William Awl, superintendent of the Ohio Lunatic Asylum at Columbus!

Enthusiasm mounted; insanity was under control! European authorities, such as Guislain in Belgium, reported that "of 227 offering probabilities of cure, 191 achieved notable improvement, or 84 per cent."[35] Men of stature of Luther V. Bell, of the McLean Asylum, wrote (1840 report) that "the records justify the declaration that *all cases*, certainly recent—recover under a fair trial." Arraignment of early psychiatrists for their "deficiency of modesty,"[36] as Earle put it, was not justified, but the onrush of sentiment favored the Cult of Curability. Dr. Amariah Brigham, eminent head of the Utica State Hospital and a *moderado* in Earle's opinion, stated "that no fact relating to insanity appears better established than the general certainty of curing it in its early stage." New hope for the cure of the insane, derived from mounting statistical successes, stimulated the building of more asylums. Convinced that the millennium had been reached, legislative committees urged the construction of more state hospitals,[37] and these, in turn, proved the thesis of curability by providing the material for more statistics.

The inevitable reaction set in. Gradually, the leading medical superintendents of the asylums in America began to modify their therapeutic optimism as their mathematical analyses improved. In a decade, the reported cures dropped to 48 percent (State Hospital, Maine, 1850), and within two decades, cures of recent cases tumbled to between 30 and 40 percent. Dr. Thurnam, of the York Retreat in England, summed up the situation in 1845 by concluding:

> In round numbers, of ten persons attacked by insanity, five recover, and five die, sooner or later during the attack. Of the five who recover, not more than two remain well during the rest of their lives: the other three sustain subsequent attacks.[38]

Analysis of the statistical difficulties culminated in a

series of studies by Pliny Earle, extending from 1876 to 1885, which effectively called a halt to the Cult of Curability. Earle pointed to cases that had been tabulated as "recovered" each time they had been readmitted to a given institution during one year. One patient had been recorded as recovered in one asylum or another as often as forty-six times during her lifetime! For example, he showed that of 92 recoveries of "repeaters" presented in a report of the Worcester Hospital, only four were permanent recoveries when followed some years later, and two of these were readmitted after his survey was completed.[39] No less serious were errors in criteria of recency of illness, of the "personal equation" (charitably called the observer's "own temperament") in favor of his own cases, and the practice of estimating percentages of cures based on those discharged to those admitted rather than to the total hospital population. One can readily side with Earle when he said of his work, "It is not presumptuous to claim that [my work] greatly modified the aspect of insanity as a curable condition."

The euphoria induced by the Cult of Curability, although markedly reduced by Dr. Earle's analysis, resulted in important changes in the medical and public attitude towards insanity. The condition, insanity, tended to be recognized earlier, and asylum resources were utilized with increasing frequency for hundreds of hitherto neglected patients. On one point, there was a general agreement: The earlier a person "attacked with insanity" was placed under treatment, the greater was the prospect of recovery. Another consequence was the determination of leading alienists throughout the world to establish a reliable method of calculating statistics of mental patients and the results of treatment. In 1867, the International Congress of Alienists appointed a committee to set up a reliable system, to be used by the various superintendents of asylums. The Commission was composed of distinguished men: Bucknill, of England; Falret, of Bicêtre; Griesinger, of Berlin;

Lombroso, of Pavia; Pujadas, of Spain; Tuke, of Great Britain, and so on. The report was prefaced by the statement that "It is no longer doubtful to anyone that the numeric method may be usefully applied to the study of mental diseases."[40] The growing experience of psychiatrists and the apparently growing number of insane created a salutary reciprocal reaction between the public and the profession. The result of this can best be gauged by a series of propositions, voted as resolutions by the Association of Medical Superintendents of American Institutions for the Insane at their annual meetings from 1844 to 1875. Written by Thomas Kirkbride and Isaac Ray, they represented a Magna Carta, whose basic tenets the modern hospital continues to observe as a guide:

1. Insanity is a disease—to which everyone is liable.
2. Properly and promptly treated, it is about as curable as most other serious diseases.
3. In a great majority of cases, it is better and more successfully treated in well-organized institutions than at home.
4. It is humanity, economy and expediency for every state to make ample and good provision for all its insane.
5. The best hospital—best built, best arranged and best managed—is always cheapest in the end.
6-9. Hospitals should be plain, in good taste and well ventilated.
10. A proper classification is indispensable.
11-13. Overcrowding is an evil of serious magnitude.
14. Abundant means for occupation and amusement should be provided.
15. As little restraint as possible should be used.
16. The insane should never be kept in almshouses or in penal institutions.
17. Insane criminals should not be treated in ordinary state hospitals.
18-20. There should be a qualified physician in undivided

charge of each hospital. He should be responsible to a board of trustees of high personal character and without political motives.[41]

In view of the increasing numbers of insane brought to asylums, medical superintendents faced practical problems. The recognition of the need for asylum for large numbers of insane still housed in county almshouses brought with it practical building problems. Construction became a subject of importance for medical superintendents the world over. One of the founders of the American Psychiatric Association, Dr. Thomas Kirkbride, was a pioneer in this important field.[42] His propositions for construction of hospitals embodied his plans. These later were published as a book, *On Hospitals,* which remained until recently the bible for architects of state institutions. Kirkbride worked out in the greatest detail the familiar central building with extended wings, ground location, ventilation, heating, air space, water supply, and so on. His plan to provide maximum air and sunshine for each patient, so commonplace now, was revolutionary then. Kirkbride put his whole philosophy of humane management of the insane into brick and stone, in plumbing, kitchens, fireproofing, water lines, and in constant attention to these details.

As cases hitherto domiciled in county almshouses moved into asylums, housekeeping, as much as treatment, became the immediate duty of state hospital heads. State care attained after a severe struggle enlarged the potentialities and the responsibilities of the state hospital and reduced the intrusion of politicians and legislators. Such innovations as the cottage system, a renascence of the colony plan in vogue at Gheel, Belgium, since the fourteenth century, had to be reconciled with Kirkbride's construction propositions which formed a "set of cast iron rules"[43] to which hospital men adhered. Questions as to the size of the asylums,[44] as to physical or chemical restraints, the type of assistants, custody versus treatment, cried for solution.[45]

As asylum practice attracted more public participation,

or at least more scrutiny, restraints were gradually eliminated. As Bucknill, an English authority, wrote in 1857, restraints were reduced due to the "altered state of feeling now prevalent among civilized nations, in regard to the infliction of pain on the insane...."[46]

The insane, now admitted to the family of man as sensitive creatures who could respond to heat, cold, pain, and emotional pressures, began to be studied for causes of their disease. Medical records spoke of "jealousy, abusive husband, disappointed love, novel reading, blasted prospects" (Kirkbride).[47] Confusion of cause and effect, of symptom and etiology, was noted in listing the causes of mental disease as "tight lacing." The events in the lives of patients were taken at their face value. In a Scottish asylum, reading "works of fancy," as well as "chagrin" and "politics," was considered one of "the apparent or supposed causes of insanity."[48] An English preacher "ascribed his insanity to the dull, flat and unvarying scenery of the neighborhood of Cambridge."[49] In 1879, Daniel Tuke, son of the enlightened Samuel Tuke, warned in his widely accepted textbook of the "haste of life" in "our railway age."[50] In a word, the vicissitudes of life appeared as causes of some mental conditions.

French psychiatrists had already begun to recognize, among their insane, distortions of basic aspects of human nature. Pinel, for example, saw "love, hatred, greed, arrogance and bigotry"[51] among his patients astonishingly similar to that found among normal persons. His successors, Esquirol and Falret[52] realized the impress of cultural factors, such as the competition of commerce, "with defeat inevitable for most of the competition," as responsible for insanity. Esquirol, following Pinel, stressed the nature of insanity as the response of human nature to life's injuries.[53] He pointed to the stress of the French Revolution, the changing life under the Industrial Revolution, etc., as the shaper of types of insanity. In the same vein Esquirol noted, "The English say, a republican or representative government, in giving play to all passions ought, other things

being equal, to be more favorable to production of sanity."
Place of origin seemed an undoubted factor; Great Britain
was acknowledged to be a fruitful site where derangements
of mind "may be considered almost endemical."[54] Recognition that mental illness represented a struggle of the
healthy versus the sick tendencies within the patient[55]
brought alienists closer, but not close enough, to the enig-
matic cause of mental illness.

A common problem was that of analyzing and classifying patients. Each alienist used different psychiatric standards in evaluating cases, depending on teaching. Before
the turn of the twentieth century, it was common for asylum physicians to view their cases as "either maniacal,
melancholic or demented."[56]

Clinical descriptions varied markedly: Frances Morel
described *demence précoce*, while Kahlbaum and Hecker, in
Germany, further differentiated such cases as catatonia and
hebephrenia. The English held to ideational insanity
(Maudsley), whereas the French followed Esquirol's classification of monomania (partial ideational insanity). Many
agreed with the diagnosis chronic mania, but some called it
chronic delusional insanity, or even chronic melancholia or
folie systematisée. Falret, in France, delimited circular insanity (*folie circulaire*) when mania alternated with melancholia,
while Maudsley complained that "there has been in France
an ambition to discover a new variety of insanity and to coin
a new name for it." The German authors brought hypo-
chondria and melancholia under depression, and acute
mania and monomania together under conditions of exaltation. In addition to this bewildering array of diagnostic entities, specific diseases, as phthisical, postconnubial,
anemic, diabetic insanities, were described.[57] The Italians
followed Morselli, who placed mania, melancholia, and
catatonia under phrenopathies, although Tanzi states that
they also adhered to Krafft-Ebing's classification of delusional insanity (monomania) under the psychical degenera-
tive states, while melancholia was classified under the
psychoneuroses!

By the end of the century, the tangled threads of psychiatric nosology were sorted out and arranged in orderly groups by Kraepelin. Adopting the "life-history" idea,[58] Kraepelin united the multifarious cross-sectional pictures of mental illnesses into meaningful concepts, which had a history, a course, and a prognosis, if not an etiology. His concepts of dementia praecox, manic-depressive insanity, organic states, morbid personalities, etc.,[59] provided a foundation for a clinical psychiatry. His diagnostic innovations were, as Zilboorg puts it, "the natural culmination of a generation of efforts in France and Germany."[60] Kraepelin's work, though not directly related to treatment theories or procedures, lightened the world of insanity, which until then, had been conceptually unwieldy.

Gradually Kraepelin's achievements strengthened the profession's grasp on the inchoate world of insanity. In 1883, Spitzka wrote that the "day is past when the asylum physician can content himself with such a classification as: mania, melancholia, amentia and general paresis." Although some diehards complained that Spitzka was a "weak echo of a class of modern crazy German pagans, who are trying... to break down all the safe guards of our Christian civilization" with their probing of every area of human mentality, psychiatry had indeed become a branch of established clinical medicine with the opening of the twentieth century.

Improvements in psychiatric diagnoses, chiefly under Kraepelinian influence, did not materially change treatment methods in the asylum. Neurologists who had been working with "neurasthenic and nervous exhaustion" patients in their offices, were brought a little closer to the insane by virtue of the "new" classification schemes. Cases of manic-depressive psychosis and dementia praecox were appearing in offices prior to being sent to state institutions or private asylums. The neurologist who followed his patient to the asylum or state hospital was appalled at the ignorance asylum physicians showed of the pathological and clinical information being amassed on all sides. The ivory-tower position of the medical superintendent and his staff irked conscientious physicians who had eagerly watched the progress of neuropsychiatry in European and American centers from 1870 to 1900. Criticism was rife: tension developed to the point that psychiatrists and neurologists maintained their individual factions: as Adolf Meyer commented in retrospect, "some of the best [were] hardly speaking to each other."[61]

Weir Mitchell, as dean of neurologists, sent out a questionnaire to 30 prominent physicians during the heat of the silent controversy, asking their opinion of asylum practices. Among those who answered, William Osler wrote (on a postcard):

> Needs are, (1) Emancipation from politics, (2) Separation of executive and professional functions, (3) Assistants to be trained in modern psychological and pathological methods.[62]

Mitchell gathered his questionnaires and marshalled his thoughts: the confrontation was not long in coming.

Invited to the May 1894 meeting of the American Medico-Psychological Association meeting as the main speaker, he unloosed an attack on the complacency of asylum doctors:

> [on] that which has been gravely enfeebling your value ... [your] tendency to isolation from the mass of the active profession...Your hospitals are not our hospitals...you live out of range of critical shot....[63]

His comments were caustic and vigorous.

> Where, we ask, are your annual reports of scientific study, of the psychology and pathology of your patients.... To compare your annual output with the great English or German work were hardly a pleasant thing to do...What is the matter?... You have immense opportunities, and, seriously, we ask you experts, what have you taught us of these 91,000 insane whom you see and treat?... Upon my word, I think asylum life is deadly to the insane.

Spokesmen for the hospital physicians arose in defense of Mitchell's "hissing cautery."[64] Walter Channing, a prominent asylum superintendent, replied in kind:

> ... [it is] useless to expect neurologists will make successful executive officers of insane hospitals...able men have not sat blind-folded, or played puss-in-the corner, or milked cows...it is not a question of knee-jerks, or ankle clonus or reaction-time...but how to house the already large number of insane.[65]

Out of this controversy grew recommendations for special wards or pavilions in general hospitals,[66] increased interest in neuropathology, general adoption of Kraepelinian psychiatry, an improved morale for staff physicians in state institutions. Adolf Meyer, then a pathologist in the Illinois Eastern Hospital, whose gigantic efforts to improve scientific work in asylums were a landmark, remarked that Mitchell's criticism was a "burst of vision...a spur" toward implementing the scientific attitude within state hospitals.[76]

Meyer's first laboratory was in the morgue,[68] a "most unhygienic place for a laboratory." There he worked out the pathology of cases of senile dementia, epilepsy, general paralysis, acute mania, demonstrating these to the staff. Under Illinois Governor Altgeld and Superintendent Clarke Gapen, Doctor Meyer's work seemed to give the lie to Mitchell's criticism of the asylum physician's unproductivity, for German authorities had sanctioned the view that the only legitimate research for the alienist was pathologic anatomy of the nervous system. But autopsies of insane patients proved disappointing; spectacular findings were absent, and often there were none at all to report. The findings of pathologic studies that caused Nissl, German student of neurosyphilis, to remark that

> as soon as we agree to see in all mental derangements the clinical expression of definite disease processes in the cortex, we remove the obstacle which makes possible agreement among alienists,[69]

did not obtain in functional psychoses. Meyer ventured to look behind the tissue slides and the chemical analyses. A true medical study of the insane "must begin before the patient is dead,"[70] he averred. In psychiatry this meant integration of a hospital about the patient as a person, his life story, aspirations and plans, home environment, mental and physical state; it meant that the scientific pathologist must enter a new field of leadership where young psychiatrists would be taught to unite the "medicine" of the patient with the story of the patient as a person.

The neuropathologist of Kankakee, Illinois (later of Worcester and Ward's Island, New York), was more impressed by the question a jury foreman asked after a report of an autopsy, "And what did you find on the mind?", than with the "quasi-intoxicants" and neuron theory of pathologists. When Meyer brought living patients for study to the Pathologic Institute of the New York State Hospitals, whose head he became in 1902, he united neurology with psychiatry. When this organization became known as the Psychiatric Institute of Ward's Island, the subtle change Meyer wrought became concretized in America as a living psychiatry.

Notes to Chapter 7

1. S. W. Hamilton, "The History of American Mental Hospitals," in *One Hundred Years of American Psychiatry*, New York, Columbia, 1944, p. 107.
2. Hunter and Macalpine, *op. cit.*
3. R. G. Hill, "Modern treatment of the insane" (letter), *Lancet*, Sept. 21, 1850, p. 355.
4. *Ibid.*
5. Hunter and Macalpine, *op. cit.*
6. Albert Deutsch, *The Mentally Ill in America*, ed. 2, chap. XI, New York, Columbia, 1949.
7. John Conolly, *An Inquiry Concerning the Indications of Insanity, With Suggestions for the Better Protection and Care of the Insane*, London, John Taylor, 1830.
8. John Conolly, *The Treatment of the Insane Without Mechanical Restraints*, London, Smith Elder, 1856.
9. Book review: *Amer. J. of Insanity*, vol. 32, July 1880, p. 95.

10. M. Christian, "On Non-Restraint," *Amer. J. of Insanity,* vol. 32, Jan. 1881, p. 307.
11. W. Griesinger, *Mental Pathology and Therapeutics,* translated by C. L. Robertson and J. Rutherford, ed. 2, New York, Wood, 1867 and 1882.
12. *Ibid.*
13. H. A. Bunker, in S. W. Hamilton, *One Hundred Years of American Psychiatry,* New York, Columbia, 1944, p. 201.
14. Hack Tuke, *The Insane in the United States and Canada,* London, Lewis, 1885.
15. E. D. Bond, *Dr. Kirkbridge and His Mental Hospital,* Philadelphia, Lippincott, 1947, p. 56.
16. Fremont, "Report on the Past and Present Condition of the Insane in Canada East," *Am. J. Insanity,* vol. 7, July 1850, p. 29.
17. Note, *Am. J. Insanity,* April 1851.
18. Francis Tiffany, *Life of Dorothea Lynde Dix,* Boston, Houghton, 1890.
19. S. C. Beach, *Daughters of the Puritans,* Boston, Am. Unitarian A., 1906, p. 142.
20. Dorothea L. Dix, "Memorial to the Legislature of Massachusetts on Behalf of the Insane." Old South Leaflets, vol. 6, no. 148, p. 489, Old South Meeting House, Boston, Directors of the Old South Work, 1843.
21. Winfred Overholser, "Dorothea Lynde Dix," a note, *Bull. Hist. Med.* 9:210, 1941.
22. Deutsch, *op. cit.,* Chap. 9, pp. 175 et seq.
23. Memorial of D. L. Dix, praying of Congress a grant of land for the relief and support of the indigent curable and incurable insane, *Am. J. Insanity* 5:286, 1849.
24. Association of Superintendents, "Resolution on Dorothea Dix," *Am. J. Insanity* 10:87, 1853.
25. Hunter and Macalpine, *op. cit.,* p. 952.
26. M. K. Amdur, "The dawn of psychiatric journalism," *Am. J. Psychiat.* 100:205, 1943.
27. Dr. Worthington, Comment, *Am. J. Insanity,* vol. 22, Jan. 1866, p. 413.
28. J. L. C. Schroeder Van der Kolk, *Die Pathologie und Therapie der Geisteskrankheiten auf Anatomisch-Physiologischer Grundlage.* Braunschweig, F. Vieweg u. Sohn, 1863. Trans. by J. Workman, *Am. J. Insanity,* Vol. 22, April 1866, p. 463.
29. H. E. Sigerist, "Psychiatry in Europe at the Middle of the Nineteenth Century," in *One Hundred Years of American Psychiatry,* New York, Columbia, 1944.
30. Deutsch, *op. cit.,* p. 137.
31. G. M. Burrows, *Commentaries on the Causes, Forms, Symptoms and Treatment, Moral and Medical of Insanity,* London, Underwood, 1828, p. 507.
32. Burrows, "An Inquiry into Certain Errors Relative to Insanity," in Rush, *op. cit.*
33. Capt. Basil Hall, *Travels in North America in the Years 1827 and 1828,* Edinburgh, Cadell, 1829.

34. Pliny Earle, *The Curability of Insanity, a Series of Studies*, Philadelphia, Lippincott, 1887, p. 22 *et. seq.*
35. J. Guislain, *Traité sur les phrénopathies, ou doctrine nouvelle des maladies mentales*, Bruxelles, Etablissment Encyclo., 1833, p. 352.
36. Pliny Earle, *op cit.*, p. 27.
37. Deutsch, *op cit.*, p. 193.
38. John Thurnam, *Observations and Essays on Statistics of Insanity*, York, 1845.
39. Pliny Earle, *op cit.*, p. 12.
40. "A project of a System of Statistics," *Am. J. Insanity*, 26: 49, 1869.
41. E. D. Bond, *op cit.*, pp. 107, 108. Collected from *Am. J. Insanity*, 1855–1876.
42. T. S. Kirkbride, "Remarks on the construction, organization and general arrangements of a hospital for the insane," *Am. J. Insanity*, 2:1, 1854.
43. Deutsch, *op cit.*, chaps. 12 and 13, gives full treatment of this historic development.
44. H. M. Hurd et al, *The Institutional Care of the Insane in the United States and Canada*, Baltimore, Johns Hopkins Press, 1916, Vol. I, p. 207.
45. Editorial: "Large and small asylums," *Lancet*, p. 163, Jan. 27, 1883.
46. J. C. Bucknill, Review of Conolly's *The Treatment of the Insane Without Mechanical Restraint*, *J. Ment. Sc.* 3:253, 1857.
47. Bond, *op. cit.*
48. *The Philosophy of Insanity, by a late inmate of the Glasgow Royal Asylum for Lunatics at Gartnavel*, with an introduction by Frieda Fromm-Reichmann, New York, Greenberg, 1947, pp. 62, 108.
49. "Psychological Gossip," *Asylum J. Ment. Sc.* 2:338, 1856.
50. D. H. Tuke, *Insanity in Ancient and Modern Life*, London, Macmillan, 1878, p. 182.
51. W. Reise, *op. cit.*
52. J. P. Falret, *Des maladies mentales et des asiles d'aliénés*, Paris, Baillière, 1864, p. xii.
53. J. E. Esquirol, *Mental Maladies, a Treatise on Insanity*, translated by E. K. Hunt, Philadelphia, Lea & Blanchard, 1845, p. 43.
54. J. C. Spurzheim, *Observations on the Deranged Manifestations of the Mind or Insanity*, Am. ed. 1, with appendix by A. Brigham, Boston, Marsh, Capen & Lyon, 1833, Eng. ed., London, 1817.
55. Falret, *op cit.*, p. liii.
56. F. A. White, *Forty Years of Psychiatry*, p. 17.
57. D. K. Henderson and R. D. Gillespie, "Classification," Chap. 2 in *A Text-Book of Psychiatry*, ed. 3, New York, Oxford, 1932.
58. S. E. Jelliffe, "Some historical phases of the manic-depressive synthesis," *A. Research Nerv. & Ment. Dis.* Annual Meeting, Dec. 1930.
59. A. R. Diefendorf, *Clinical Psychiatry*, abstracted and adapted from the seventh German edition of Kraepelin's *Lehrbuch der Psychiatrie*, ed. 2, New York, Macmillan, 1907.
60. Zilboorg and Henry, *A History of Medical Psychology*, New York, Norton, 1941, p. 458.

61. Adolf Meyer, *Collected Papers,* ed. Franklin Ebaugh, Johns Hopkins Press, Baltimore, 1951, Vol. III, p. 546.

62. Harvey Cushing, *Life of Sir William Osler,* London and New York, Oxford Univ. Press, 1940, p. 393.

63. Weir Mitchell, Address Before the Fiftieth Meeting of the American Medico-Psychological Association, *Proceedings,* p. 101, May 1894, p. 101.

64. Reviews, *Proc. Am. Med.-Psychol. Assn.,* Fiftieth Meeting, Philadelphia, 1894, *J. Ment. Sc.,* Vol. 42, Jan. 1896.

65. W. Channing, "Some Remarks on the Address Delivered at the American Medico-Psychological Association Meeting by Weir Mitchell, M. D., May 16, 1894," *Am. J. Insanity,* Vol. 51, Oct. 1894, p. 171.

66. Frederick Peterson, "Treatment of the Insane Outside of Asylums," *Am. J. Insanity,* Vol. 50, July 1893, p. 74.

67. Adolf Meyer, "Presidential Address: 35 years of psychiatry in the United States and our present outlook," *Am. J. Psychiat.* 85:1, 1928.

68. John P. Altgeld, Governor, Adolf Meyer, Pathologist, *Pathological Report,* Illinois Eastern Hospital for the Insane, Chicago, Blakely, 1896.

69. Quoted in Adolf Meyer, "A few trends in modern psychiatry," *Psychol. Bull.* I:217, 1904.

70. Adolf Meyer, *Collected Works,* edited by Eunice E. Winters, Baltimore, Johns Hopkins Press, 1951, Vol. 2, pp. 63, 78, 100.

8

Mesmerism, Hypnosis, and Psychotherapy

F RANZ Anton Mesmer belonged to a stirring era: social enlightenment and scientific progress vied for attention among the educated. The discovery that static electricity could be conducted (Gray, 1729), stored in the ingenious Leyden jar (Mussachenbroek, 1746), and plucked from the heavens to be discharged upon the earth (Franklin, 1752) caught the imagination of doctors and, as will be seen later, charlatans. For Mesmer, graduated in medicine from the Medical Faculty of Vienna in 1765, the magnetic influence of celestial bodies upon human beings via some subtle force answered a vague dream. His thesis presented at the time of graduation was titled *De Planetarum Influxu in Corpus Humanum.* Mesmer became a physician only a few years before Gall but mountains separated their methodology. Mesmer's experiments started with mysticism and tended toward science, Gall's work began in science and ended in mysticism.

As a young man, Mesmer lived the life of a cultured Viennese: music was his hobby; Gluck, Mozart, and Haydn his friends.[1] A note in the *Mozart Jahrbuch* indicates that Wolfgang Amadeus Mozart produced his opera *Bastien and Bastienne* in 1768 "at the private theatre of Dr. Mesmer." His life was otherwise uneventful until he witnessed Father Maximillian Hell, a Jesuit astronomer, treating a nervous patient by applying a magnet to the body. Mesmer tested Father Hell's cure on his first patient, Fräulein Oesterline, aged 29.[2] The outcome was so dramatic that it determined the course of his life: her convulsive illness of several years' standing showed instant improvement. His experience suggested the opportunity for proving the "flux and reflux" action of animal magnetism, which Mesmer had deduced theoretically. Mesmer applied a magnet over the stomach and to both of Fräulein Oesterline's feet. In a short time, she experienced "extraordinary sensations" and spasmodic pains moving through her body, due to a "subtle fluid" coursing in different directions, which finally passed out her lower extremities. For six hours thereafter, the patient was free of symptoms. Mesmer repeated the experiment the following day with the same success. "My observations," wrote Mesmer, "opened up a new horizon. . . . They taught me that another principle acted on the magnet, itself incapable of this action on the nerves." He concluded that the magnetic fluid, passing from the magnets, had revitalized the nervous tissues. Mesmer conceived the nature and the action of animal magnetism to be analogous to those of the magnet and electricity; further, that the body was susceptible of receiving this magnetic principle, that the (magnetic) fluid could penetrate everywhere and, like electricity, "could operate at a distance."[3]

Convinced of his findings, Mesmer hastened to invite Doctor Stoerck, president of the Viennese Faculty of Medicine, to witness his experiments. Baron Von Stoerck declined. Presently, Mesmer was able to induce Ingenhousze, a renowned botanist and inoculator of Vienna, to watch a demonstration on Fräulein Oesterline at Mesmer's house. The doubting Ingenhousze was asked to touch the patient. No movement resulted. Then Mesmer "magnetized" the botanist by touching his hands and bade him repeat the action. A convulsion resulted. They repeated the experiment many times, and each time, "to his great astonishment," Ingenhousze, when magnetized, obtained the same convulsive response. Subsequently he magnetized a porcelain cup with a like result. As a final demonstration to Ingenhousze, Mesmer showed how magnetism could be conveyed over a distance:

> I directed my finger toward the patient at a distance of eight steps; an instant after her body went into convulsion, to the point of rising from the bed.... I continued, in the same position, to direct my finger towards the patient, placing M. Ingenhousze between her and me; she experienced the same sensations. These experiments having been repeated to the satisfaction of M. Ingenhousze, I asked him if he were satisfied, and if he were convinced of the marvelous properties which I had announced to him.

The botanist appeared convinced but asked Mesmer not to communicate to the public what he had discovered to avoid the possible ridicule that would follow. A short time later the Faculty of Medicine in Vienna appointed a committee, of which Ingenhousze was a member, to investigate Mesmer's claims. After painstaking tests, it concluded that his cures were based on imagination and expelled him from the medical fraternity. Unwilling to drop his newfound science of magnetism, Mesmer set out for France, the land of enlightenment.

When Mesmer reached Paris in 1778, his reception was heartening. With the approval of Louis XVI, he addressed a statement to the Academy of Sciences, who informed him he could work with the sick, provided he was supervised by physicians.

Meanwhile, he had discarded the magnet, relying on the action of an "incomparably subtle fluid," which, joined to a "universal spirit," could influence the human body in disease[4]—a theory closely akin to that of Paracelsus three centuries earlier. This magnetic fluid passing from magnet to doctor brought the desired effect; thus Mesmer magnetized any object—the person, water, bread, silk, clothes—to achieve a healing effect. Mesmer believed a *rapport* needed to be established between physician and patient for the *fluidum* to be effective.

Mesmer set himself up in a house in the Place Vendome. Clients increased and he was forced to move to the Place de la Bourse, where he lived in a style designed to attract the best of pre-Revolutionary Parisian society. His salon was beautifully decorated with thick carpets and gorgeous wall hangings. A concealed band suffused the dimly lit atmosphere with subtle strains of music, catching the fancy of plumed and brocaded ladies, young blades and the best-dressed men about town that besieged Dr. Mesmer's clinic. They took their places around the *baquet*, a kind of great copper bath in the middle of the room, filled with bottles around which magnetized water flowed. From the cover of the *baquet* projected a variety of magnetized objects—metal rods, twists of wire, and other articles that could be grasped by the enchanted audience, convinced it was connected with a great reservoir of magnetized fluid. This magnetic fluid was the substance that connected the stars and planets with human beings. Patients sat around the vat while Mesmer gravely touched each with his previously magnetized iron wand. Soon signs of restlessness appeared as they twitched and trembled violently. Jerky movements of the hands and body muscles increased in tempo until, palpitating and convulsed, they achieved the *grand crisis*. With the patient's nervous system brought to a state of crisis, the cure was ensured, as was Mesmer's practice.

Critics were contemptuous. A contemporary spoke of the "copious leisure of rich fools of pre-Revolution Paris"[5] who gossiped about Mesmer and his wondrous magnetism. Yet, eyewitnesses were impressed. Deleuze, the librarian, recounts the picture:

> The patients then drew near to each other, touching hands, arms, knees or feet. The handsomest, youngest and most robust magnetizers held also an iron rod with which they touched dilatory or stubborn patients....
>
> The women, being the most easily affected, were almost

at once seized with fits of yawning and stretching; their eyes closed, their legs gave way and they seemed to suffocate.... Sardonic laughter, piteous moans and torrents of tears burst forth on all sides. Bodies were thrown back in spasmodic jerks.

Another room was padded and presented a different spectacle. There women beat their heads against padded walls or rolled on the cushion-covered floor. In the midst of this panting, quivering throng, Mesmer, dressed in a lilac coat, moved about, extending a magic wand...gazing steadily into their eyes, while he held both their hands in his, bringing the middle fingers in immediate contact, to establish the *communication*.[6]

Medical men who observed Mesmer's treatment were greatly disapproving. The chemist Berthollet stated:

I did not see anything in the convulsions, spasms, crises which are said to be produced by magnetic processes, that cannot be attributed to imagination or to the mechanical effect of friction on very nervous parts...or to the law of imitation.[7]

Mesmer's social and financial success did not satisfy him. He wished to receive the approbation of the French Academy; again and again he sought to interest the Academicians, but without success. Doggedly he submitted a paper composed of twenty-seven propositions, which theoretically explained his "animal magnetism." Against their inclination the Academicians examined the writings. Mesmer started with the premise that "a reciprocal influence exists between the heavenly bodies, the earth, and animated bodies" (Proposition 1). Proposition 2 stated, "A fluid universally diffused, so continuous as not to admit of a vacuum, incomparably subtle, and of its nature susceptible of receiving, propagating, and communicating all motor disturbances, is the means of this influence." He went on to elaborate vaguely the mechanism of this influence in Proposition 4, "Alternate results from this action, which may be considered to be a flux or a reflux," and concluded by, "The art of healing (through this method) reaches thus its final perfection."[8]

The doctors were outraged at this effrontery. Thouret, regent physician of the Faculty of Paris, wrote a book criticizing "animal magnetism," in which he accused Mesmer of fraud. The fact that certain diseases were not susceptible to magnetic action was a "resource contrived in order to account for failures...in certain cases." Thouret continued, "To pretend to the discovery of a means...a universal medicine, is an illusion which cannot be excused in an enlightened age."

Nevertheless, a commission from the Academy tested the effect of Mesmer's treatment on themselves. They reported that during the séances nothing was felt but a "slight nervous irritability and a pain in the hollow of the stomach" where the magnetizer had touched them. Their report admitted that peculiar effects were observed in the crises, but concluded that they were due to imagination in the subject. "Magnetism minus imagination is nothing." Since the patient's imagination was involved, there was nothing more to be said.

Alone of the prominent physicians in Paris, Charles d'Elson, professor in the Faculty of Medicine, gave credence to Mesmer. What if imagination had the greatest share in the effects of "animal magnetism"? If it helps, then it is a valuable "invention" for patients. This new agent, explained M. d'Elson, "might be none other than imagination itself, whose power is as extensive as it is little known." The Academicians were unmoved; they condemned Mesmer and his magnetism, and came close to expelling d'Elson also. Disillusioned, Mesmer left Paris.

Meanwhile d'Elson continued to experiment, and a group of enthusiastic followers organized the Society of Harmony for the Spread of Magnetic Ideas. The nobility took up Mesmer's struggle and pressed Louis XVI for an appeal to the Academy to consider magnetism once more.

In 1784, after several years of wrangling, the Academy

of Science and Faculty of Medicine appointed several illus-
trious men to investigate the situation. The commissioners
included Benjamin Franklin, the American Ambassador;
Lavoisier, who discovered oxygen; Doctor Guillotin, inventor of the instrument of death; Bailly; and others.[9] D'Elson
took an active part in the tests and proposed to show how
the fluid worked. Before the commissioners, d'Elson magnetized a tree in an orchard. Then he led a boy with ban-
daged eyes among the trees. As he approached the magnetic tree, and while still some feet away, the subject went into
a crisis, with limbs rigid and arms extended. The examiners
were sure that the patient was party to a preconceived plan.
They experimented with many other tests also, but concluded with a "unanimous voice that the presence of animal magnetism was not proven." The commission decided
against the usefulness of magnetism. They put the crisis
down to the three causes, "imagination, imitation and contact." Mere imagination had no place in science. The commission countered d'Elson's arguments:

> If then, M. d'Elson...says...these effects are to be as-
> cribed to the agency of a fluid which is communicated from
> one individual to another by touch...he cannot avoid con-
> ceding...that only one cause is requisite to one effect
> and...since the imagination is a sufficient cause, the sup-
> position of the magnetic fluid is useless.

At the same time, a secret report was rendered King
Louis showing the moral dangers of magnetism. "It is apparent," wrote the commissioners, "that the crisis occurs
more frequently in women than in men.... Women have,
as a rule, more mobile nerves; their imagination is more
lively and more easily excited." The Academicians, aroused
by the seductive nature of the crisis, were compelled to
denounce it in the interest of public morality. The women
who went for magnetization were, the commission observed, "not really ill; many came out of idleness or for
amusement." They retained "their senses unimpaired
and the sensitiveness of youth...their charms are such

as to affect the physician." The secret report closed with a warning:

> There is nothing to prevent the convulsions in this case also from becoming habitual from producing an epidemic, and from being transmitted to future generations; such practices and assemblies may also have an injurious affect upon morality.

> Signed: Franklin, de Bory, Lavoisier, Bailly,
> Majault, Sallin, d'Arcet, Guillotin, Le Roy.
> (Paris, August 11, 1784)

Mesmer took the report badly: his only recourse was to retire to his native Mersburg, embittered and empty-handed.[10] His claims, however, intrigued many.

Nor did the scientists let the matter rest: it was assumed that the magnetic fluid passed along the nerves to the peripheral organs in response to the operator's will.[11]

This hypothesis obviated Mesmer's universal-fluid theory, and competent medical men—Husson, at Hôtel Dieu, and Georget, at Salpêtrière—spoke less of magnetic "fluid" and more of the magnetizer's will in their reports. Nevertheless, Deleuze ironically counseled his magnetizing students to

> forget for a while all your knowledge of Physics and Metaphysics. Dismiss from your minds all objections that may occur. Have an active desire to do good, a firm belief in the power of Magnetism, and an entire confidence in employing it.... Be very credulous, be very persevering, reject all past experience and do not listen to reason.

At all events, a more naturalistic theory was being evolved when the Academy of Science's committee, in response to pressure from lay and medical groups, commenced its deliberations in February, 1826, on the "Magnetical Experiments."[12] This commission, authorized to re-study the subject, was composed of eminent physicians, including men like Itard, the father of the movement for training the feebleminded; Magendie, a pioneer in anatomy of the nervous system; Laennec; and others. In 1831, Husson, the secretary, presented the commission's report, which affirmed the existence of "animal magnetism" in a few cases, but declared that in many others, "weariness, monotony or the imagination" produced the phenomena observed. The commission affirmed that magnetism was a "therapeutic expedient" and as such had a place in medical science. They recommended that it be practiced by physicians only, and concluded, "The Committee has collected facts... to allow it to believe.... The Academy should encourage... researches on magnetism, as being a very curious branch of psychology and natural history."

The commission also had gone far enough in experimentation to indicate that the phenomenon of somnambulism and certain new faculties such as *clairvoyance* and *intuition* were, in their opinion, due to definite physiologic changes: "A certain number of phenomena... (were) produced by magnetism alone and could not be produced without it."[13] This report was read at a meeting of the Academy on the 21st of June, 1831, but was not accepted.

Medical officialdom, through the commission, had decreed that magnetism "ranked within the framework of medical knowledge" but physicians would have none of it. A few nonmedical magnetizers carried their art to other countries at public gatherings, on the lecture platform and in *conversazioni*, where the demonstrations were watched with awe. Often these peripatetic magnetizers healed patients, read diagnoses through their subjects made clairvoyant by magnetization, and gained followers for their art among laymen. One such was M. Poyen, whose demonstration in New England stimulated Quimby to embark on a career of mental healing; another was Richard Chenevix, who exhibited in London. At many of these *conversazioni* curious physicians were present, prepared to disprove the induced somnambulism that they witnessed and to prick the bubble of scientific romanticism that had infiltrated the social thinking of the day.

In 1829, Dr. John Elliotson, brilliant professor of medicine at University Hospital, London, became so impressed at Chenevix's séance that he commenced magnetizing at the hospital. A man of vision, Elliotson had already been marked a radical in medicine by discarding the knee breeches and the silk stockings, the orthodox dress of the physicians of that era. He espoused the use of the stethoscope recently invented by Laennec in Paris, insisted that the university or college be affiliated with a hospital, and improved standards of teaching to the point where his confreres' classes were relatively deserted by students. But his outright support of medical mesmerism could not be stomached: it won for Elliotson the strongest abuse by colleagues, culminating in a request for his resignation. The Council of the College had already ordained that "animal magnetism" or mesmerism be barred from the hospital (1837). Frustrated, Elliotson withdrew from organized medicine, bending his efforts and practice in the direction of mesmerism. Since the columns of the *Lancet* were closed to him, Elliotson organized and edited the *Zoist*, a magazine[14] dedicated to "truth though opposed by the philosophy of ages...physiological truths of incalculable value and importance...."[15]

In 1846 at the Harveian Lecture, Dr. Elliotson tried once more to interest his colleagues in a scientific appraisal of mesmerism, but was shouted down with cries of "Humbug!"

The contumely heaped on Elliotson was staggering: a London surgeon, one Mr. Wakely, said in 1842:

> Mesmerism is too gross a humbug to admit of further serious notice. We ought to regard its abettors as quacks and imposters. They ought to be hooted out of the professional society.[16]

In part, this was due to the fantastic theories of mesmerism and of clairvoyance promulgated during this period. Indeed, the explanations of the efficacy of mesmeric passes over the bodies of patients were extreme: a "quasi-electric chain"; a "transference" of thought from doctor to patient; a "mesmeric fluid... emanating from the active brain"; the "universal fluidum" of Mesmer himself. In the pages of the *Zoist* can be read descriptions of the vital principle, which appeared like a "halo... its color blue, like the electric spark, from lightest to deep violet."[17] The theory of odylic force, the luminosity emanating from "sensitives" under mesmerism, and the magnetoscope of Rutter,[18] which measured each individual's specific magnetic force, were persistent remnants of astrology invading mesmerism.

Parenthetically it may be remarked that overtones of the influence of metal on the body lingered in Charcot's acceptance of Burq's metalo therapy (1878)[19] as the scientific basis for hypnosis (transfer of anesthetic effects from copper to skin). Even later, in 1886, another French expert in hypnosis, Luys, placed hermetically sealed tubes containing iron and other metals under the head of the patient to obtain hypnotic effects. Nevertheless, crusty realists of the time could only sputter: "The parties concerned in the infamous publication [the *Zoist*]... bite and rail: The leper [sic] must be taken with his spots."[20]

But there was value in mesmerism in its anesthetic properties during surgical operations. Reports of major surgery done under mesmeric stupor had already been published sporadically in France, but Elliotson's espousal allowed Dr. James Esdaile to report in full his remarkable surgical results from a Calcutta hospital. Under induced trance Esdaile described a series of more than two hundred major operations.[21] Many recommended it in preference to ether and chloroform, then coming into common hospital use. The case reports were dramatic enough to compel attention from English surgeons. Though Esdaile could prove the authenticity of mesmeric anesthesia, his papers were not accepted for publication in England, save in the *Zoist*. His Indian experience with 261 major operations under mesmeric influence only served to make him, in his own words, "the best abused man in the world."[22] Such dramatic operations as the removal of a tumor of the eye "involving half the cheek" without the patient's knowledge or perception of pain under mesmerism, even "when nitric acid was used to clean the socket" postoperatively, were disbelieved. Esdaile's work in the Mesmeric Hospital in Calcutta, for a time under government auspices, was greeted by the ready cry of "Fraud!"

The flurry of accusations and counter-accusations continued; Dr. Copland at the Royal Medical and Chirurgical Society meeting in 1842 attacked mesmeric anesthesia, which removed the "agony during the operation" by declaiming, "pain is a wise provision of nature, and patients ought to suffer pain...."[23] Doctor Asburner, protesting vituperation upon *Zoist* contributors as "liars, imposters, satanic agency" wrote, "John Elliotson...[became] an object of mortal envy to a host of pismires...."[24]

Meanwhile Dr. James Braid of Manchester brought mesmerism to a level of physiological respectability.[25] Visiting a séance by M. Lafontaine in 1841, James Braid, a medical practitioner of Manchester, was impressed that the subject was unable to lift his eyelids during the mesmeric state. This he felt to be a physiologic effect neither imaginary, magnetic, nor magical. It represented a weakened function of certain muscles, perhaps due to excessive fatigue. Doctor Braid proceeded to test out his theory on a young friend, a Mr. Walker, and upon Mrs. Braid. To his amazement, when Walker looked fixedly at a bright object—Braid used his metallic lancet case—he almost immediately fell into a trancelike state. Braid had proved that "animal magnetism" was not essential in acquiring the mesmeric state of stupor. The subject had merely to fix his gaze on a bright object for a short time, induce pathologic fatigue of the eye muscles, and forthwith he passed into a stupor.

At the end of a six-month period Braid had already written a paper, entitled "Practical Essay on the Curative Agency of Neuro-Hypnotism," which he proposed to offer before the British Medical Association at its annual congress in 1842. He was anxious to demonstrate the scientific validity of the condition he called *hypnotism* as a curative power. By this time he had amassed a large series of cases in which striking improvements had been accomplished through hypnotism in rheumatism, paralysis, pharyngitis, spasmodic torticollis (wry neck), migraine, spinal irritation, epilepsy, valvular heart disease, frontal-bone abscess, deafness, nearsightedness and strabismus. The program committee of the British Medical Association was not impressed. Caustically they replied to his offer that they were "pleased to decline entertaining the subject."

Braid continued his therapeutic experiments. Using his lancet case, he had his patients look fixedly at it until they fell asleep. Awaking from the hypnotic state, they had no memory of what had happened. The effects of the hypnosis itself were sufficient to cause improvement in the patient's symptoms. Doctor Braid stressed relaxation, "absolute repose of body, fixed attention and suppressed respiration." Braid freely professed that he did not understand the reason for the overpowering reaction that occurred in his patients; nor was he willing to ascribe hypnosis to any personal power in himself.

For a time Braid's results met with the usual objections and censure. The rebuff of the British Medical Association irritated him not a little, especially since he desired to subject his method to the most careful scientific scrutiny.

His claims of *Neurypnology,* which discounted *magnetism,* aroused Dr. Elliotson. The letter complained that "a man, a most vain and swaggering mechanic of a surgeon, named Braid, at Manchester" declared he could induce all the phenomena of mesmerism by merely having his patient fix his eyes on a light suspended before him. Indeed, in his book, *Neurypnology, or, The Rationale of Nervous Sleep,*[26] he established the subjective nature of hypnotism. Like Abbé Faria and Bertrand several decades before, Braid called for a study of the patient rather than of the magnetizing fluid, remarking that patients became susceptible "according to their expectation or belief," by which was meant suggestibility.[27] In this paper he wrote, "I adopted the term 'hypnotism' to prevent my being confounded with those who have extreme notions...of exoteric influence being the cause of sleep." It is apparent that Braid was an excellent observer, and, within limits of the psychology of the times, perceptive to the emotional influence of doctor on patient, as witness the statement:

> It is well known, however, that so long ago as December, 1841, I particularly pointed out the remarkable docility of patients during hypnotism, which made them most anxious to comply with every proper request or supposed wish of others.

The Braidian theory that hypnosis followed upon concentration of attention on an idea, so-called *monoideism*, was an early concept, modified later to encompass hypnosis as an "artificial condition created by suggestion."[28] The problem of memory alterations also concerned Braid. The "extraordinary revivification of memory,"[29] of things long forgotten, under hypnosis brought him to the notion that a "double consciousness" existed, a circumstance that offered a naturalistic explanation for clairvoyance. "The mesmeric intuition [clairvoyance?] very probably is nothing more than extraordinary memory referred to."[30] Rather than being "old fashioned and a believer in phrenology,"[31] as Zilboorg concludes, Braid was a careful investigator, physiologically oriented and alert to artifacts of thinking.

Indeed, the "swaggering mechanic of a surgeon" had brought hypnosis back to physiology sufficiently so that Professor Velpeau could reopen the question at the French Academy of Medicine meeting in 1860. Azam's paper on surgery under hypnotic anesthesia[32] made Braid's name synonymous with hypnosis (*braidism*) on the Continent, and, as contemporaries remarked, "distinguished physicians were now anxious to study these phenomena, without fear of compromising themselves."[33]

The pivotal figure around which hypnosis underwent its scientific renascence was Jean Martin Charcot. The authority of Charcot, which was in the main that of French neurology, and the serious approach of his students to the effects of hypnosis, conferred an enduring sanction upon hypnosis as a legitimate medical technique. An associate, Dr. Charles Richet, in 1875 took the problem to Charcot, who by now had literally carved a clinical science of neurology from the motley group of syphilitics, chronic invalids, and paralytics who thronged the halls of the Salpêtrière. Charcot set himself the task of unraveling the nosologic position of hypnosis among abnormalities of the nervous system. With the same unremitting observation and patience with which he had studied multiple sclerosis, muscular atrophies, tabes dorsalis, and other poorly understood neurological conditions, Charcot applied scientific method to the demonstration of the reality of a "special state of the nervous system." On the whole, interest at the Salpêtrière was concentrated more in method and experiment than in therapeutics.[34] Painstaking tests of sensibility under metallic contact of anesthesia, catalepsy, the effect of scalp stimulation by galvanic electricity, neuromuscular excitability under hypnosis, the occurrence of contractures, reflex changes under hypnosis, production of hysterical stigmata, etc., formed the basis of Charcot's classic nosologic description of the hypnotic state. This encompassed the states of lethargy, catalepsy, and somnambulism representing levels of hypnotic effect in hysterical subjects. Charcot's summation[35] of the clinical limits of hypnosis established both himself and his subject within the *Academie des Sciences.*

Jean Martin Charcot graduated in medicine in 1853 and became an interne at the Salpêtrière in 1862. His early interest was in art; it colored his life and personality. Charcot's early sketches were witty caricatures of Parisian types done with a fine enthusiasm for bodily motion. It may have been this feeling for art in motion that attracted him to an analysis of muscular and nervous deformities. Many accused him of flamboyance in the famous Tuesday morning clinics. His work, however, was meticulous; his observations of patients prolonged; his dedication to clinical medicine complete. Charcot's lectures on hypnosis were both a milestone in medical history and a landmark in the life of Paris. The penetrating perception of hysterical neuromuscular patterns, Charcot's gifts as a lecturer, his feeling for the poetry of distorted movement in hysterics, for the meaningfulness of postural changes as reflections of intense emotional states, soon led to charges of theatricality. Clinicians elsewhere could duplicate neither the three phases of hypnotic action (lethargy, catalepsy, somnambulism) nor the grotesque contractures of Salpêtrière patients. The apperception of tonic distortions, which Charcot identified both in the demoniacs of medievalism and in hysterical seizures and contractures, in his study of medieval art,[36] were considered the evidence of mass suggestion, possibly peculiar to the Gallic psyche. Bernheim[37] remarked that only once did he see the three stages of hypnosis reproduced in his Nancy clinic, and that in "a girl who had spent three years at the Salpêtrière." Dubois noted that Charcot's patients acted like "marionettes or like circus horses."[38] German clinicians treated these dramatic demonstrations with disdain, pointing to the decadence of the Latin race. Ernest Jones,[39] Freud's biographer, notes that when Freud was in Paris in 1886, Charcot's teaching sanctioned a more scientific attitude towards hysteria in French medical circles but "had little effect on the Continent and only a negative one in Anglo-Saxon countries." Nevertheless, Charcot's demonstrations of *les états hyster-ique* at his Tuesday morning clinics were so unique in medical circles as to merit an eyewitness's report of the 1890s:

> The lecture hall, holding an audience of nearly six hundred is filled with doctors in frock coats, foreigners carrying note books, elegantly gownèd women. There is a muted feeling as in a theatre before the curtain rises. Precisely at 11:00 A.M., Dr. Charcot walks in, starts to talk without gestures or inflection.
>
> "It is my duty to lecture you, because we have...a truly remarkable collection of patients which we can study together."
>
> The Maître nods to his assistants; the patient is brought

in. He relates the history of the patient, a woman of twenty-eight, describing her symptoms, her nervous spasms, twists of the arm, flutter of the eyes, and sudden falling spells. He announces that he will show that hypnosis will bring out these symptoms, proving that they are truly hysterical. She stands uncertainly, body bent backward, her eyes fixed on the ceiling, her breast heaving. With a quick look Charcot signals her guards to loosen their hold. She sinks into a chair. The silence is intense. One can hear the half-suppressed gasps of the audience.

The patient sits in a chair, her eyes half closed, in a state of repose or lethargy. With a few words he puts the patient into hypnosis. Charcot looks questioningly at Dr. Pitres, his first assistant, who has many times hypnotized the patient on the wards; the latter nods in affirmation. The skin is pinched, again the patient does not move. Anesthesia of the skin has been produced under hypnosis. Charcot goes over the patient, and with a few more words puts her into a deeper state, somnambulism. He raises her arm in an awkward position and removes his supporting hand. The arm does not come down. He says a few words quietly into her ear and suddenly her body becomes rigid.

This is the stage of catalepsy. The assistants bring in chairs. They are placed back to back, about five feet apart. The attendants place the woman with her heels on one chair, and the nape of her neck on the back of another. She lies in that position immobile without slipping or falling. It is like the trick of a magician. Charcot looks at Dr. Richet and then at the audience. There is no question that she is completely cataleptic. He brings out other instruments, electrical devices, metal disks, testing her responses. He puts cold and warm substances repeatedly on her arms; she remains immobile and inactive. After a time the chairs are removed and Dr. Charcot releases her from the hypnotic trance. She rests for a while, then, calmly and obediently, walks toward the door. The demonstration is over. Doctors turn reflectively in their chairs. One asks a question; it is answered precisely and courteously. In a few moments there is a separation of the group: the neurologists and serious-minded students gather around Charcot who leads them to the wards; the nonmedical audience goes away.

The doctors follow him in clumps, discussing quietly what they have seen. The first stop is a small clinic room where there are two male patients. Here Charcot explains briefly that he can bring out the same symptoms in men as in women and that the old theory that hysteria as a prerogative of women is not entirely according to fact. He tells them he has been able to put his male patients through the same steps of lethargy, somnambulism, and catalepsy. "We must no longer think that hysteria is limited to the female sex. It is merely an evidence of the special hysterical personality," says Charcot.[40]

Neurologists practising hypnosis did not dispute its effectiveness; their interest centered upon whether it was a physiologic or psychologic phenomenon. The chief criticism of the theory that certain persons (hysterics) were "selectively responsive" came from Hippolyte Bernheim, of Nancy. Convinced by Liebault, a fellow townsman of Nancy, whose quiet work over a decade proved that the trance-state was possible because of a "side-tracking" of attention, Bernheim became the spokesman for the Suggestion School. As early as 1864, Liebault, an unassuming country doctor, magnetized his patients with marked success through the simple suggestion that they sleep. His book,[41] contending that magnetism and somnambulism represented no more than the obedience of one person to the suggestion of another, received scant attention until Bernheim, as a young physician recently graduated from the Salpêtrière, joined him. Bernheim was impressed by Liebault's theory of hypnosis: "The concentration of attention causes the isolation of the senses, the cessation of muscular movement and the rapport between the somnambulist and the hypnotizer."

Liebault's technique was on a nontheatrical but personal level. He placed the patient in a recumbent position, requested him to fix his eyes on a glittering object, then suggested in a soothing voice: "You are sleeping; your breathing is slow and deep; you are becoming calm and relaxed; your body is warm; you are getting sleepy; now go to sleep!" With this technique, Liebault had asserted that one fifth of his patients could be placed in a state of somnambulism; Bernheim insisted that 90 percent of all persons could be hypnotized. The contentions of the Salpêtrière group were exposed as inadequate by the new theory. To Bernheim, hypnotism was an intensification of normal suggestion. Due to restriction of attention, the patient became an automaton, in a state of "helpless obedience." The demonstration of anesthesia induced by copper plates placed on the skin of hysterics, called *Aestheogenism* by Charcot, was clearly unnecessary: "There is no hypnotism; it is all suggestion." Bernheim considered it gratuitous to define the hypnotic state as a hysterical neurosis; sleep and somnambulism were identical conditions. How could sleep be considered pathologic, asked Bernheim; how could hypnosis be a disease?

General adoption of Bernheim's[42] ideas led to a widening of the area of hypnotic usage. Treatment was extended to alcoholic, neurasthenic, medical problems of every description, and hypnosis was regarded as an adjuvant to a rationalistic medical therapy. Moreover, the simplification of hypnosis lent itself to pedagogy and treatment even of "vicious and degenerate children."[43] Suggestion is a force, said Bernheim, which is close to daily life.[44] It is used in everyday affairs. Suggestion is used by the mother on her child, by the teacher on his pupil, by the state on its citizens. Indeed, suggestion is an essential part of education and provides the encouragement that causes people to control the old and try the new.

The area of suggestive therapy extended to schools and prisons; a single hypnotic séance in the public schools of Nancy was reported to have converted lazy children into children of industrious habits. The press carried accounts of idiotic children being taught reading and writing in two months' time under the efforts of hypnotists:

> Stupid children are made gifted by this discovery of hypnotism with mere verbal suggestion and instruction. By this

process children become mere machines, and their studies may be directed the way their parents incline.... The confirmed bad habits of years' standing are now also cured by hypnotism. It is claimed that in fifty years more such a thing as a chronic drunkard will be unknown.[45]

The psychologic world, with its intense interest in hypnotism, began to take sides with Bernheim. Mark Baldwin, an American psychologist writing from Paris in 1892, mirrored the distrust of Charcot's hypnotism:

Prof. Janet has another patient, a hysterical woman, in whom the stages of Charcot are very marked.... Nothing could be more definite than the lapse into lethargy... when the proper button is pushed.... But one cannot rid himself of that suspicion that it is all acquired machinery, that the magic "suggestion" works through sub-consciousness....[46]

Baldwin's impressions were confirmed when he visited Bernheim at Nancy. There he witnessed an "authoritative and imperative" operator:

His first and last word to the patient is "Dors, dors, absolument!" He closes the eyes with his hands, then doubles up the patient's fists...revolving them round each other in front of the patient's face.... Then the proper suggestion is made; "Your head is well." "Your back shall never ache again." "Your legs are as sound as mine.", iterated and re-iterated....[47]

Reasoning from suggestion, the notion of auto-suggestion, advanced by Wetterstand, a Swedish psychotherapist, asked why hysterics could not be helped by a "firmly rooted autosuggestion."[48] In the hands of Coué, some years later, autosuggestion moved into the arena of quasi-faith healing (see chapter 10) but at the moment moral questions arose. Could a subject be swayed to act criminally on a posthypnotic suggestion? Could a Svengali or a Rasputin, in the guise of a hypnotist, cause a patient to act against his or her ethical convictions? Laymen worried lest "hypnotism... used as a moral remedy to correct evil habits... or evil inclinations"[49] could have the reverse effect. Physicians insisted no one could be forced to desert his customary ethical standards but laymen still prayed "that scientific investigators stop... lest we learn too much of the secrets of the nervous system."[50]

In spite of opposition, even ridicule, hypnosis finally had arrived at the level of a moderately predictable therapeutic technique. If not the mainstay of mental healing, it was at least an acceptable adjunct.

Notes to Chapter 8

1. Von Otto E. Deutsch, *Die Mesmers und die Mozarts*, in *Mozart Jahrbuch*, Salzburg, 1955, p. 54.
2. F. A. Mesmer, *Mémoire sur la découverte du magnétisme animal*, Geneva and Paris, Didot, 1779, p. 12.
3. Mesmer, p. 23.
4. Van Helmont, quoted in Alexandre Bertrand, *Du magnétisme animal en France*, Paris, Baillière, 1826, p. 8.
5. L. Mercier, *The Waiting City*, p. 68.
6. Foveau DeCourmelles, *Hypnotism*, translated by Laura Enser, London, Routledge, 1891, p. 8.
7. Alexandre Bertrand, *Du magnétisme animal en France*, Paris, Baillière, 1826, p. 62.
8. Mesmer: p. 74.
9. *Rapport des commissaires chargés par le roi, de l'examen du magnétisme animal*, Paris, L'imprimerie royale, 1784.
10. F. A. Mesmer, *Lettre à messieurs les auteurs du Journal de Paris*, 1784.
11. Alexandre Bertrand, p. 303.
12. Husson, *Report of the Magnetical Experiments Made by the Commission of the Royal Academy of Medicine*, Paris, June 21 and 28, 1831, translated by Charles Poyen, St. Sauveur, Boston, Hitchcock, 1836.
13. *Ibid.*, p. 165.
14. George Newbold, Famous names in hypnotism: John Elliotson (1791–1868), *Brit. J. M. Hypnotism* 1:2, 1950.
15. *The Zoist*, 7:4, no. 25, London, Baillière, April, 1849.
16. *The Zoist*, no. 25, p. 4.
17. *The Zoist*, no. 27, p. 231.
18. John Ashburner, *Notes and Studies of Animal Magnetism and Spiritualism*, London, Baillière, 1867.
19. Foveau DeCourmelles, p. 29.
20. Editorial, *Lancet*, July 31, 1847.
21. James Esdaile, *The Zoist*, no. 26, p. 125.
22. James Esdaile, *Natural and Mesmeric Clairvoyance with the Practical*

Application of Mesmerism in Surgery and Medicine, London, Baillière, 1852.

23. J. Milne Bramwell, *Hypnotism, Its History, Practice and Theory,* London, Grant Richards, 1903.

24. Ashburner, Chap. 5.

25. Bramwell, p. 22.

26. James Braid, *Neurypnology, or, The Rationale of Nervous Sleep Considered in Relation with Animal Magnetism, illustrated by numerous cases of its successful application in the relief and cure of disease,* London, Churchill, 1843.

27. James Braid, "On hypnotism," *Lancet* 1:627, 1845.

28. Bramwell, p. 294.

29. James Braid, "Observations on mesmeric and hypnotic phenomena," *M. Times,* London 10:31, 1844.

30. *Ibid,* p. 47.

31. Gregory Zilboorg and G. W. Henry, *A History of Medical Psychology,* New York, Norton, 1941, p. 356.

32. Azam, Note sur le nerveux ou hypnotisme, *Arch. gén. méd.* 1:1, January, 1860.

33. Alfred Binet and Charles Fere, *Animal Magnetism,* New York, Appleton, 1889, p. 78.

34. J. M. Charcot, *Oeuvres complètes,* Vol. 9, Paris, Lecroshier & Babé, 1890.

35. J. M. Charcot, Essai d'une distinction nosographique des divers états compris sous le nom d'hypnotisme, *Compt. rend. Acad. sc.,* Vol. 44, 1882.

36. J. M. Charcot and Paul Richer, *Les difformes et les malades dans l'art,* Paris, Lecroshier & Babé, 1889.

37. H. Bernheim, *Suggestive Therapeutics, A Treatise on the Nature and Uses of Hypnotism,* translated by C. A. Herter, New York, Putnam, 1889, p. 90.

38. Paul Dubois, *The Psychic Treatment of Nervous Disorders,* translated and edited by S. E. Jelliffe and W. A. White, New York, Funk, 1909, p. 16.

39. Ernest Jones, *The Life and Works of Sigmund Freud,* New York, Basic Books, 1953, Vol. I, p. 226.

40. Dr. J. Muir, Personal communication, New York, 1935.

41. A. A. Liebault, *Du Sommeil and des états analogues considérés surtout au point due vue de l'action du moral sur le physique,* Paris, Masson, 1866.

42. Bernheim, *Suggestive Therapeutics,* p. 138.

43. Berillon, editor, *Rev. hypnotisme et psychol. physiol.* 14:255, February, 1900.

44. Bernheim, *Suggestive Therapeutics,* p. 159.

45. "Hypnotism," *New York Sun,* June, 1890.

46. J. Mark Baldwin, "Among the Psychologists of Paris," *The Nation,* vol. 55, July 28, 1892, p. 68.

47. J. Mark Baldwin, "With Bernheim at Nancy," *The Nation,* vol. 55, August 11, 1892, p. 101.

48. O. G. Wetterstrand, *Hypnotism and Its Application to Practical*

Medicine, translated from the German edition by H. G. Petersen, New York, Putnam, 1897, p. 52.

49. Clark Bell, quoted in "Hypnotism," Proc. Med-legal Soc., New York, *J.A.M.A.* 12:247, February 15, 1890.

50. G. M. Beard, "Current delusions relating to hypnotism," *Alienist & Neurologist* 3:57, 1882.

9

Faith, Occultism, and Beyond

WHILE the mental sciences were proceeding toward objectivity in mental and nervous ills, magic and faith healing continued unabated. Indeed, there never was a time when mental healing through faith—whether at a religious shrine, at the hands of a self-confessed "divine," a wise woman, a shaman, or an inspired evangelist—did not produce unexplained successes. Faith healers were rampant during the medieval days and earlier; they took on a new vigor during the eighteenth century, flowered in the nineteenth century, and recently (1970s) have returned via Eastern Mysticism and religious fervor.

When Jesus said, "Thy faith has made thee whole," he spoke for the human race, for faith knows neither boundaries nor limitations to one group of humans. The "human reality of faith," states Tillich, "is the promise of ultimate fulfillment,"[1] a statement that accurately describes what supplicants, clients, or patients expect from faith healers.

Every period of history has chosen its own modality for faith. The vehicles for faith healing in early eras have been described in previous chapters. For the eighteenth century, the discovery of static electricity was the stimulus for a new modality: Electricity was to the Age of Reason what alchemy was to the Middle Ages.

Mesmer was one of a company of scientific magicians who purveyed to the credulity of the eighteenth century public. Ironically, in his case, mysticism paved the way for a scientific psychotherapy generations later. Advances in magnetism, optics, and mechanics of the eighteenth century became grist for the charlatan's mill. Men like Cagliostro,[2] who prescribed "extract of Saturn"; Weisleder, the "Moon Doctor"; Schuppach, the Swiss "mountain doctor" who shocked his patients with electricity; and Perkins with his metallic tractors—all charmed the throngs of aristocracy and the third estate. A mythology surrounded magnetism and electricity, and Mesmer, Graham, Perkins, and Cagliostro became its divinities. While Wiegleb[3] attacked the forces of superstition in twenty volumes, and Franklin said "Quacks were the greatest liars in the world, except their patients,"[4] thousands used Elisha Perkins' "tractoration" for their distressing pain.

Inspired by the famous observation of Professor Galvani that a muscular twitch occurred in a frog's leg when touched with a piece of metal, Doctor Perkins concluded that two such pieces of metal could be used to cure bodily pain. Doctor Perkins, a founder of the Connecticut Medical Society,[5] announced his discovery in 1796. Traveling through the eastern states, he introduced his patented tractors, one iron, the other copper, which drew pain from limbs with miraculous ease. In the same year, the Connecticut Medical Society voted that the doctor whose methods were "gleaned up from the miserable remains of 'animal magnetism' " be expelled from the Society. But Perkins' magnets, now made of gold and silver, spread in popularity. George Washington bought one for family use. The tractors were obtainable in a "neat Red Morocco Case . . . for five guineas the set."[6] Doctor Perkins died believing he had come upon a great natural secret. His son, Benjamin, a graduate of Yale, carried on his work in London at the Perkinean Institute with the condemnation of the Royal Medical Society ringing in his ears.

The practice of tractoration spread to the Continent. Its adherents, including physicians who obtained marvelous cures with the tractors, prophesied that they would displace the family physician, make medicine unnecessary, and revolutionize the art of healing. Surgeon Rafn, in Germany, reported his personal experience with intractable rheumatic pain:

> I determined to try the effects of Dr. Perkins Metallic Tractors. The application was made...at a time when my pain was very violent. After having operated with them for 5 or 6 minutes...the pain disappeared entirely, and I have not felt any since.[7]

Eventually, it was proved by Dr. Haygarth,[8] in England, that tractors made of wood or lead or tobacco pipe produced the same miraculous cures as were accomplished through the gold and the silver tractors sold by Perkins. The boom collapsed. Perkinism, as Holmes wrote, "perished by an easy and natural process."

The public, taught by the Age of Enlightenment to deride witchcraft, was intrigued by electricity and "animal magnetism." From this fascination with magnetism, quacks like James Graham drew their sustenance. As a youth, Graham—bold and a rogue by any measure—had studied at Edinburgh University, leaving by common agreement between his professors and himself, long before taking his degree. When he met the stimulating Franklin in Paris, Graham conceived the idea from Franklin's experiments with lightning that electrical stimulation could cure disease. Styling himself John Graham, O.W.L. (O Wonderful Love!), he opened his Temple of Health in London in 1779. In this gaudy showplace he held forth, promising to "dissipate melancholy and mitigate extravagant gaiety" with "electricity communicated by magnetized baths." In this Templum Aesculapium Sacrum, adorned with magnets and electrical devices, set upon forty pillars of glass, flanked by marble statues, bathed by intoxicating incense, the Celestial Magnetica-Electrico Bed held out a promise of rejuvenation to the jaded coxcombs of London. Graham, the Barnum of his time, thundered: "In this tremendous edifice, are combined or singly dispensed the irresistible, and salubrious influences of electricity."

One of the consequences of Mesmer's "animal magnetism" was a fascination with *clairvoyance,* which was exhibited by mesmerized patients. Romanticists recognized in somnambulism and clairvoyance the entrance to a new world of sensationalism. Mesmerism was pitched to new heights, claiming what Gall claimed for phrenology, "Truth though opposed by the philosophy of Ages."[9] Lay magnetizers, spirits, and mediums reaffirmed that somnambulists during the crisis could penetrate to "the furthest horizons of life." In Europe and America, magnetizers, table-turners, and somnambulists were rampant; magnetism was almost universally accepted. The Vatican, in a letter from the Holy Office (June, 1840),[10] condoned the use of magnetism, "provided it does not tend to an illicit end or one which may be evil." But as spiritism and clairvoyance threatened to get out of bounds, the Vatican interdicted the use of magnetism (1847) and condemned as heretical "those who profess to see things which are invisible...or apply purely physical principles to things which are in reality supernatural." Finally, in 1856, an Encyclical letter warned the clergy of the errors and the dangers of magnetism.

Just as the scientific spirit of the Age of Reason colored the techniques of healers by faith, so studies of the brain, which were beginning to reach the literate public, intrigued many in the Romantic period. Gall's phrenology had already reached psychological and metaphysical levels (see Chapter 5) and his disciple Spurzheim was to go further. Literature reflected this preoccupation with the nervous system and emotional fervor: the vastness of mind and soul impressed itself alike on De Quincey, author of *Confessions of an English Opium Eater,* the poet Tennyson, and Edgar Allan Poe. Fitz Hugh Ludlow, an American journalist hailed as a "minor De Quincey,"[11] was inspired, after smoking hashish, to write:

> ... The sublime avenues in spiritual life, at whose gates the soul in its ordinary state is forever blindly groping are opened widely by hasheesh....

Romanticism, feeding on the science of the time, joined spirituality with cranial anatomy and brain function.

It seemed natural then for Spurzheim, when he left Gall in Paris, to shake off the last remnants of scientific restraint. In Britain, sensing the need for an English translation of Gall's work, he wrote seven volumes (1815) claiming Gall's discoveries as his own. In England and Scotland, Spurzheim became the toast of the intellectuals. Shakespeare's immortal characters were subjected to phrenological analysis. "I feel sure," wrote George Eliot, "that Hamlet had a square anterior lobe... the necessary organic concomitant of a temperament sufficiently developed to see ghosts."[12]

Spurzheim sailed to the States in 1832; here he found fertile ground: New York, Philadelphia, Boston welcomed him as a prophet. Dr. Capen, President of the American Phrenological Society, described Spurzheim: "He was a feasting presence...full of light...six feet in height...a picture of vigor...." After his death in 1832,[13] Boston Brahmins mourned his passing as evidenced in a speech by Dr. Bartlett:

> Worthily did he fulfill the great mission.... Singlehearted seeker after truth.... Compassionate mourner over all human perversity and ill.... Peace be to thy ashes....

Combe and others took up Spurzheim's mantle: Education experts extolled phrenology as the "greatest advance in psychology in years." The trustees of the Albany Female Academy resolved in 1843 that phrenology as taught by Mr. Grimes...is destined to improve our race, remodel the present mode of education, become useful in legislation...."[14]

Publishers in the 1840s reaped a harvest from popular books on phrenology. Fowler and Wells,[15] from their publishing house on East 21st Street, New York, spewed out books and journals until 1881. Americans of the last century were a hardheaded, earthy group, eminently practical yet capable of deep spirituality. The genius of Early America resided in its capacity for physical hardship and a simultaneous seeking for things of the spirit.

Revivalism was in the ascendancy in the 1820s. In part, it was a reaction to the Age of Reason, the repressive puritanism of Colonial America, and the need of intellectual and emotional nutriment for hungry minds. Frontiersmen were as eager for the rough country evangelists as were the Brahmins of Boston for the transcendental philosophy of Emerson and the Concord group. The spiritual revival that passed over into spiritualism was vigorous and gusty. Emotional strivings, brought to a "high plane of experience"[16] by Evangelist Charles Finney, self-styled "Brigadier-General of Jesus Christ," resulted in trance states as he exhorted his audiences to "Agonize, I tell you!"

On a more contained level these emotional upheavings were channeled into numerous reform movements. The Abolitionists were clamoring for the end of slavery; temperance societies demanded the prohibition of alcohol and tobacco; the Oneida Colony, established by John Noyes the Perfectionist, strove for a practical embodiment of the communist plan of life; and socialism, imported from France through Fourier, was to be based on "The Principles of a True Organization of Society." Everywhere the "crust of Puritanism broke, and from its fiery core came new idealisms and strange fantastic religions."[17] In 1840, Emerson wrote: "We are all a little wild here, with numberless projects of social reform. Not a reading man but has a draft of a new community in his waistcoat pocket."[18]

In the glow of the Romantic era, it is not surprising that "magnetic influences, clairvoyance, antagonization, mental telepathy, Christian Science..."[19] entranced some of the American public. As Van Wyck Brooks reconstructs the scene:

> ...spiritualists held camp-meetings, trance speakers addressed the crowd...mediums gave exhibitions of self-expansion and self-compression, and mesmerists and faith-healers waved their wands...since the [Civil] war the vogue of phrenology, hypnotism, astrology, galvanism ...study of astral forms had grown immensely.[20]

Even William James was loath to cast phrenology completely out of psychology. In his famous text *The Principles of Psychology,* he agreed that although phrenology did not satisfy scientific criteria, it still had empirical value: "A hook nose and a firm jaw are signs of practical energy.... Prominent eyes is a sign of power over language and a bull-neck a sign of sensuality."[21] With or without scientific approval, faith healers continued their spiritualistic and neo-religious activities. To transform houses of common clay in which they dwelt into divine habitations became the guiding principle of New Thought, theosophy, and numerous shades of religious healing groups. Borrowing from Buddhism, the proponents of New Thought propounded, "All that we are is the result of what we have thought!" And Emerson exclaimed, "Never name sickness!"[22] In this state of intoxication, diseases became immaterial, pathology a chimera, emotions a dross of an unspiritual intellect, and psychological science unnecessary.

Faith healers, riding the tide, rediscovered mind cures through hypnotism and the magic of spiritualistic séances. The Fox Sisters of Rochester, New York, for example, had startled the country with their "spirit rappings." Communicating with the great spirits of the ages through these rappings, they obtained directions for healing their clients of obscure or chronic illnesses. Cases that had passed through the hands of physicians unbenefited went to the

Fox Sisters. The new movement started by them enveloped the country. Sober-minded folk were alarmed at the shift toward spiritualism. Mary D. Wellcome, in 1860, in a tract exposing the spiritualism of Dods and Davis, noted that there were already 1,537,000 persons who were spiritualists in the United States alone, and that 150,000 "are from our own loved Maine."

At another point in the spectrum of latter-day faith healers came self-appointed healers who sought to represent within themselves the healing power of divine faith. Among the garish examples of this group were Dowie and Schlatter, messiahs and prophets. The Rev. John Alexander Dowie, an Australian, received the revelation that he was the reincarnation of the Prophet Elijah. Arriving in the United States in 1888,[23] he traveled through the country preaching the advent of salvation. Organizing the Christian Catholic Church in Zion City, Illinois, he developed a community along theocratic lines, which, among other things, prohibited the presence of physicians. Besides the title of a second Elijah, Dowie claimed the power of healing through prayer and the laying on of hands. Well organized and lashed by his domination, Dowie's hosts, in 1903, moved on to New York to convert and heal the unenlightened millions of the metropolis. His blatant manner cost him followers, and an ensuing scandal soon dissolved Dowie's kingdom.

Francis Schlatter belonged to the same tragicomic group of inspired healers who traveled along the Mississippi and through the Southwest as public healers a half century ago. He appeared in Denver, reporting that he had undergone a forty-day fast and was the carrier of the divine power of healing by touch, transmitted from Jesus through the sovereigns of Europe to him. Thousands flocked to him. Schlatter conceived the idea of extending his operations by sending out through the mail, to those who needed aid, handkerchiefs that had been touched by him. The federal postal authorities felt that the extension of his power through the mails was fraudulent and summarily acted on this decision.

Inspired healers rose and fell, taking their places in a never-ending stream of psychologists, physiologists, health experts, and seers. Some ephemeral healers utilized a newly discovered physiologic fact, as in the case of Horace Fletcher, the food faddist. Fletcher pinned his faith on the healing properties of uncooked cellulose in raw vegetables, espousing vegetarianism, which was advanced as a reaction to the heavy consumption of meat during Victorian days. He developed the idea that slow, thorough mastication added enormous value and energy to food. If chewed properly, Fletcher claimed, only one twentieth of what was ordinarily consumed was needed. From nature's storehouse a new source of energy was available, which he claimed would be reflected in mental and physical well-being. Fletcherism became a household word, almost a new creed. William James, the psychologist, tried it for three months and gave it up because "it nearly killed me."

And preceding Fletcher was Dr. Sylvester Graham, promoter of vegetarianism, open windows and cold baths. Young men like Horace Greeley, the crusading editor of the *New York Tribune*, who lived at Dr. Graham's "Diet-Reform" hotel on Chatham Street, New York, during his youth,[24] succumbed to the new reform. Similar psychotherapeutic systems attached themselves to other dietary ideas; during the middle of the century bread pills enjoyed high repute because of their curative power. The healing power of the sun shining through blue glass, in the hands of General Pleasanton, became a powerful and popular curative method about 1870. Thousands sat exposed to the sun with blue glass interposed; physicians prescribed it for debilitated patients, not daring to resist the pressure of socially approved magic. Each year witnessed a new "psychic" science, arising like the phoenix from the ashes of the last. The transcendental philosophy of nineteenth-century America was practical. When Thoreau wrote, "The fickle person is he ... who has not an ancient wisdom for a lifetime but a new prudence every hour,"[25] he meant seriously to find a way for salvation of the individual, for a better use of his life. A sense of practicalness, an American confidence that all religious truths were not exhausted and "the distrust of the expert, rationalized into a democratic axiom during the Jacksonian era...deeply ingrained in the American character,"[26] were the factors that stimulated the flood of religious-philosophic healing systems during the nineteenth century.

Systems like John Bunyon Campbell's "Spirit Vitapathy" or Edward's "Christolution" drew thousands of adherents while clergymen and physicians fumed. Of the new class of "Christopaths," a neurologist wrote: "the Christopath evolves... [from] a brain strained by the trials of life or disease... insomnia, neuratrophia, cerebrasthenia...."[27] Nevertheless, mind-cure systems spiraled into neo-religions: from theosophy to Christian Science, quasi-religions moved into healing, achieving dignity and maturity as the century progressed.[28]

Of the schools of mental healing derived indirectly from transcendentalism, Christian Science, founded by Mrs. Mary Baker Eddy, far eclipsed the others in attaining a continued success. Mrs. Eddy was a product of the spiritualistic and pious atmosphere of New England. Attuned by a sensitive personality to receive benefits of magnetism from Phineas Quimby, she transformed his "Science of Health" into a religion, a cosmology, and a method of psychotherapy.

The origins of Christian Science differ according to the sources of its history. Disciples of Mary Baker Eddy indicate that after the first meeting between Mrs. Eddy and Quimby, a mesmerist of Portland, Maine, the former interpreted the cure of her nervous symptoms as the result of her "endowing him with her faith."[29] The cure was due to "Quimby's mediatorship between herself and God." Quimby, on the other hand, finding that magnetism was unnecessary, had discovered that his cures resulted from showing the patient his "deranged state of mind." In a word, Quimby perceived, through his discoveries, how Christ had healed.

His methods were simplistic; with some head-stroking, he would intone:

> If I (as a typical doctor) tell you that you have congestion of the lungs I impart my belief to you by a deposit of matter in the form of words.... If you eat my belief it goes to form a disease.... Like its author, my belief grows, comes forth and at last takes the form of a pressure across the chest. All this is very simple when you know what caused it.[30]

Mrs. Eddy's biographer, who claimed Quimby's manuscript to be "absolutely hypothetical," insisted that Mrs. Eddy explained to Quimby, "It is not magnetism that does this work...it is your understanding of the truth which Christ brought into this world and which has been lost for ages."[31] Some considered Quimby a quack, but few could deny his sincerity of purpose and success. His political creed was unassailable; as pointed out by the *Portland Advertiser* in 1860, "Dr. Quimby is a strong union man; as soon cure a sick rattlesnake as a sick rebel."[32] Some hailed him with such fervor that Quimby at one time published an essay called "A Defense Against Making Myself Equal with Christ." His perceptions were remarkable: "A person may perceive feelings of another by simply sitting near by and rendering himself receptive—no mesmerism necessary. Higher spirit—is God spirit and healing is Christ's method." As he grew older, Quimby, imbued with the idea that he had rediscovered the universal technique for healing disease, pressed his son George and a Mrs. Dresser into service as disciples to carry on his works and spread his doctrines; but overshadowing these was the vigor of his pupil, then Mrs. Patterson.

Mary Baker Glover Patterson Eddy, born in 1821, was a poetic, moody—some said hysterical—child,[33] intellectually precocious. The thought she carried in the recesses of her mind was that she was predestined for a noble mission. The affair of the "Rochester rappings" by the Fox sisters stimulated Mrs. Glover (she had been married now) to interest herself in spiritualism, a subject for which she had always had a penchant. She discovered that she possessed considerable ability as a spiritualistic medium. But it was not until 1862 that her psychic predilections abruptly became a cogent philosophic system. For several years after her contact with Quimby she contemplated the influence of Christ's teachings, conducting her "solitary research"[34] and trying to understand Quimby's method, "the self-taught man walking wisdom's ways." Revelation attended Mrs. Patterson, for in 1866 she "discovered the Christ Science of divine laws of Life, Truth and Love and named my discovery Christian Science."[35]

By 1872, literally driven by want and a compulsiveness to communicate her discoveries, she had written notes and Bible commentaries called "The Science of Man by which the Sick are Healed, Embracing Questions and Answers in Moral Science, Arranged for the Learner by Mrs. Mary Baker Glover." During this period her manuscripts were changing through many laborious rewritings, so what was at first called "Extracts of Dr. P. P. Quimby's writings" became "Christian Science Mind Healing," and, in 1875, "Science and Health, with Key to the Scriptures."

The basis for Mrs. Eddy's therapeutic effectiveness resided in attaining the belief that if the concept of matter could be dispensed with as an illusion of "false materiality," disease would also vanish. "If the Scientist reaches his patient through divine love, the healing work will be accomplished at one visit, and the disease will vanish into its native nothingness like dew before the morning sunshine."[36] All other types of psychotherapy, indeed medical therapy, as mind cure, hypnotism, materia medica, etc., belonged to "mortal mind" and hence inherently "error." Particularly hypnotism (magnetism) earned Mrs. Eddy's condemnation, for while she was evolving the principles of Christian Science he had found herself "hampered by the theories of Quimby"[37] and the effects of "malicious animal magnetism." Freeing herself from this unseen power, which was equated with evil, allowed Mrs. Eddy to expunge manipulation from her healing system in 1872 and denounce it as without a scientific foundation, criminal, subtle, ubiquitous, and enslaving.

In 1881, she moved to Boston and established the Massachusetts Metaphysical College, in which "pathology, ontology, therapeutics, moral science, metaphysics, in their application to treatment of disease" were taught. Students, intoxicated with her doctrines, went there for instruction in metaphysical "obstetrics" and moral science. Her success grew; students propagated her methods throughout the world. Practitioners of Christian Science healing were located in many cities of Europe and the Orient. Some astonishing cures were reported through Mrs. Eddy's teachings. One such case, said to have been related by Mrs. Eddy to her classes, concerned a cripple whom she had healed merely by putting out her hand as he came to the side of a carriage in which she rode.[38]

The period from 1890 to 1910 witnessed the growth of the Christian Science Church numerically, politically, economically, financially. Its critics multiplied as anxiety covering the Christian Science "Trust" spread. Mark Twain, writing in 1899, feared for the nation's future as the popularity of Christian Science reached its apogee:

> It is a reasonably safe guess that in America in 1920 there will be ten million Christian Scientists... that this will be trebled in 1930.... In 1920, the Christian Scientists will be a political force, in 1930, politically formidable—to remain that permanently.[39]

Orthodox religious leaders and medical lobbies became alarmed at the spread of the religion. Psychologists and clergymen studied its cases and theories. Public leaders were disturbed by its monetary power. Mark Twain, scornful of this financial interest, remarked:

> The Dollar is hunted down in all sorts of ways; the Christian Science Mother-Church and Bargain Counter in Boston peddles all kinds of spiritual wares to the faithful, on one condition... cash, cash in advance.[40]

Support and derision echoed and reechoed in the press and family magazines about Mrs. Eddy and her Science. But her power and the acumen of her supporters, as well as the therapeutic results obtained, have become fixed in the institution of Christian Science. A critic in the early part of this century wrote:

> [from] Animal Magnetism, the fertile matrix of a shadowy brood of latter-day mysticism, Theosophy, Spiritualism, Christian Science . . . [the] practice of healing once again is inseparably connected with the practice of religion. . . .[41]

An official spokesman, Emily Ramsay, avers that Mrs. Eddy "has furnished a key by which we may enter into the heart of the Gospel teaching."[42] The principles that Mrs. Eddy intuitively divined—"the sick are terrified by their sick beliefs"—combined with faith in a personal helpful God, as mediated through Jesus' example, to form the basis for effective therapy.

Underlying this practical application of faith ran a wider feeling during the last half of the nineteenth century. It was that the old theology was too binding, that a liberal Christianity[43] had something to offer in the direction of practical help. This attitude was at the bottom of such movements as New Thought, Unity, and Christian Science. The period of 1880 onward witnessed a sweep toward readjustments in Christianity. As Atkins noted, people were requesting "illumination and spiritual deliverance along other than accepted lines of Christian redemption."[44] Protest against the "old school medicine," the challenge of a psychology that recognized power in the "subconscious" mind, the influence of evolution and the "lure of the short cut,"[45] all combined to push the quest for religious aid against an engulfing national disease—neurasthenia. Christian Science, New Thought, mind-cure, "mental science" (dubbed the "Boston Craze"[46] in 1882), were movements that spread to include Oriental mysticism at one extremity and transcendentalism at the other. From Quimby's work in the 1860s, which denied the validity of disease except as a projection of men's ungodlike thinking, to the teachings of Unity and theosophy that man through God is divine in essence and can claim his freedom by thought, there lies the irregular evolutionary growth of a new attitude toward human mental frailty.

Mind-cure groups gradually diverged into two main streams: Those that clung to spirituality as their chief therapeutic weapon, and those that sought the aid of neurologic scientists who were studying personality dissociation as this phenomenon demonstrated the function of the subconscious mind. The former group encompassed New Thought, Theosophy, Unity, and the Baha'i movements. These religiophilosophic systems do not practice mental healing directly, but are supportive of faith healing as it arose from a sharing of perfection with a perpetually perfect Divine Universal Spirit. The latter group was exemplified by the Emmanuel movement, a religiopsychological healing method, the work of two clergymen and a psychiatrist. It was this branch of mind-cure that became the precursor of modern pastoral psychiatry.

The New Thought movement, developed by a Boston minister, Elwood Worcester and his associate, Rev. McComb, represented a sincere use of spiritual participation for therapeutic purposes. Stirred by Weir Mitchell, Rev. Worcester sought to introduce the healing ministry of Jesus[47] through suggestion, which was proving so effective in medical practice. Why, he asked, could not the reputable method of suggestion be combined with faith healing without "hurt to intelligent Christianity or to scientific medicine?" If a higher form of spiritual reality existed, why not harness it for healing?[48] Moreover, the clergymen had the backing of the influential Prof. James at Harvard, who felt the mind-cure movement was real, although it incurred the "enmity of the trades union wing" of the medical profession. During his periodic depressions James himself was benefited by mind-curers. For this melancholia he felt:

> It is barely possible that the recovery may be due to a mind curer with whom I tried eighteen sittings.... I should like to get this woman into a lunatic asylum for two months, and have every case of chronic delusional insanity in the house tried by her. That would be a real test.[49]

As a "metaphysical hypothesis of first importance," James thought mind-cure provided an experimental approach to supernaturalistic faith. But there were other views of this amalgam of suggestive psychotherapy and spiritual faith. A British theologian insisted that "moral therapeutics" for neurotics lay on a different level than faith cures.[50] Healing through Christ, e.g., miracles, was inexplicable through psychology; they were "unique," depending on the "Unique Person of Christ." An orthodox theologian found fault with the pragmatism underlying modern mind healing; by emphasizing the health of the body, it left no room for "the necessity of a spiritual life."[51] In answer, the proponents of New Thought and neo-Christianity exclaimed:

> Many are figuratively looking back over their collars to some ancient mountain to hear what God said to the race in its childhood, instead of looking up...to hear what God will say to the race in its manhood.[52]

While the controversy smoldered, the real problems of reconciling religion and psychiatry in their common therapeutic goals engaged more and more attention from exponents in both fields. Both disciplines[53] taught methods for attaining serenity and peace of mind; both charged themselves with the task of resolving basic concepts of psychotherapy with correlative ones from the Christian doctrine of redemption and the Judaic concept of the "revelation of God's working in history."[54,55]

Clergymen, following Worcester, worked with psychiatrists in a clinical team or used clinical concepts in their counseling. A pioneer in this field, John Rathbone Oliver, an Episcopalian priest, had studied medicine and psychiatry to "diversify the spiritual reactions"[56] in his patient-petitioners who suffered from emotional problems. The field of pastoral counseling is distinct from faith healing in its pure form. The particular function of pastoral psychiatry, which has developed in the last several decades, is to apply whatever remedial and preventive measures ministers of the gospel can contribute as they arise from a simultaneous use of the perceptions of modern psychiatry and the values of religious solace. These include instruction, prayer, confession, persuasion, assurance, encouragement and suggestion.[57] The method discussed by the Rev. Mr. Stolz starts with a series of relaxation treatments, as developed by Edmund Jacobson, which release muscular and nervous tension. It is then suggested that a survey be made of the possibilities of aid through God, a God who is "a partner in our fortunes," a living reality. Finally, specific problems are thought through and a plan is developed to cope with them. More recently, some clergymen have carried their counseling to the level of a psychoanalytically oriented procedure, with its roots in the use of faith as a therapeutic measure.[58]

During the 1940s pastoral counseling employed psychoanalytic procedures, as in the church clinic at New York's Marble Collegiate Church,[59] where neurotic, unhappy individuals are seen first by a psychiatrist, who evaluates the specific problem presented by the client. The client is referred to a psychologically oriented clergyman who uses prayer and Scriptures most suited to the psychic state to be treated. Working as a team, the psychiatrist demonstrates to the patient what his symptoms mean in terms of his emotional life, and the minister shows how prayer and faith taken from "the great medicine chest of the Christian faith" can restore balance to the patient's life. As Dr. Blanton writes:

> Religion wells from the unconscious mind. It was and it remains an emotional experience; ordinary reason cannot be applied to it. Even the power of prayer depends to a large extent on the deep unconscious mind.[60]

Dr. Norman Vincent Peale, with whom Dr. Blanton worked, went beyond the Emmanuel movement in attempting to remove the anxiety that prevented faith from being effective. Although he spoke from a pulpit, at the venerable St. Marks-in-the Bouwerie, in New York City, illumined by two crisscrossing shafts of bluish light,[61] Dr. Peale and Dr. Blanton worked in consonance with psychotherapeutic principles; rationalizations were singled out, denials were confronted, and symptoms were interpreted. The patient-client then faced his shortcomings "able to receive the healing power of God."[62]

Through the mind-cure swell ran the need to strengthen the will, a facet of treatment borrowing heavily from Jamesian strong-mindedness. Moreover, emphasis on the will reflected the Puritan influence of our country's pioneers. "The education of the will is the object of our existence," said Emerson. New Thought adopted this stance: "Perfuse the patient's mind with the desire, the *will* to be well," they wrote. Faith provided an aura of invincibility, a "sense of the transforming power of spiritual feeling" that spread like a wave, regenerating the life of an individual.[63]

The group of mind-curers who depended essentially on a religio-philosophical basis for healing asked less for psychopathologic guidance than for esoteric philosophies and Oriental mysticism. One of the main schools in New Thought was theosophy, built upon a doctrine espoused by a brotherhood of Mahatmas (Tibet).[64] This was an expression of Oriental philosophy, which considered the body a "ductile instrument of intelligence" amenable to control through thought as it participated in the essence of divinity. From this general spiritualistic doctrine, theosophists dipped into the mystic explanations of Madame Blavatsky and Annie Besant. The latter described the effects of mental healing wherein the "irregular vibrations of the diseased person are so worked . . . as to accord with the regular vibrations of the healthy operator."[65]

Though occultism, as a vehicle of faith, often strains credulity to the utmost, its practitioners and adherents are eternally active. In recent years Lee Steiner[66] has tracked down many of these psychotherapists in their counseling chambers, on the radio, and on the lecture platform. She estimated in the 1940s that from fifteen to twenty million Americans were influenced by irregular practitioners of the healing art, and Seabrook's statement that "half the literate white population in the world today believe in witchcraft"[67] seems to be borne out by one reverend gentleman whom the author heard on the radio in 1970. As this man sold hallowed handkerchiefs to be sent through the mail, he claimed: "I lay hands on a cloth. . . . The healing power of God which I received four years ago is passed on to the cloth which I send to you."

As the findings of psychology and psychoanalysis seeped into the religio-philosophic mind healers' verbiage and techniques, "personality development" became the central theme. Speakers and writers extolled their methods of extending the personality with its concomitant gains in health, vibrancy, and business success. Haddock's book, *The Personal Atmosphere*, Carson's *Vital Science System*, Clark's *Power and Force*, Norris's *Winning Personality*, Fear's *Voice and Personality*, Carnegie's *How to Win Friends and Influence People*, and a hundred others flooded the book stalls. The Cult of Personality swung away from faith healing per se into a generalized antidepressant therapy aiming chiefly at subduing an "inferiority complex" and building the personality to emerge as a social and financial success. There is no record of countless thousands who read these books or embarked on lecture courses to improve their personalities, but these enthusiasts unwittingly treated a vast number of neurotic and inadequate-feeling individuals.

The economic Depression of the 1930s had the effect of dampening the ardor of "applied psychologists," but the religio-philosophical movement was not stemmed.[68] Divine Science, Universal Science, Life Science, Jewish Science, and later Scientology, served thousands. Evangelists with the "healing touch"—Billy Sunday, Father Divine— were the prototypes that brought, and bring today, a healing force through faith in Christ's transmitted power. The radio, and later television, broadened the horizon of healing. The democratization of psychological knowledge, as will be seen in chapter 14, is reflected in an insistence in applying this knowledge to the human condition and its frailties. In this drive for amelioration, the universal power that resides in religion can be harnessed by some as a healing force.

Notes to Chapter 9

1. Paul Tillich, *The Dynamics of Faith*. World Perspectives, Vol. 10, New York, Harper & Brothers, 1957.
2. Grete de Francesco, *The Power of the Charlatan*, translated from the German by Miriam Beard, New Haven, Conn., Yale, 1939, p. 188 *et seq.*
3. *Ibid.*, p. 234.
4. Carl Van Doren, *Benjamin Franklin*, New York, Viking, 1938, p. 770.
5. Elisha Perkins, *Dictionary of American Biography*, Vol. 14, p. 466.
6. Perkins' Patent Metallic Tractors, London, George Cooke, 1800.
7. B. D. Perkins, *Experiments with the Metallic Tractors in... Various Topical Diseases*, translated by Charles Kampfmuller, London, Herboldt & Rafn, 1799.
8. O. W. Holmes, *Medical Essays, Homeopathy and Its Kindred Delusions*, Boston, Houghton, 1895.
9. *The Zoist, a journal devoted to cerebral physiology and mesmerism*, London, 1843.
10. Georges Surbled, "Hypnotism," *Catholic Encyclopedia*, Vol. VII, p. 609.
11. Fitz Hugh Ludlow, "The Hasheesh Eater," *Putnam's Monthly Magazine*, Vol. 8, July 1856, p. 625.
12. Winkler and Bromberg, *op cit.*, p. 29.
13. Winkler and Bromberg, p. 32.
14. S. J. Grimes, *The Mysteries of the Head and Heart Explained, An Improved System of Phrenology*, Chicago, W. B. Keen, Cooke & Co., 1875, p. 355.
15. O. S. Fowler, *Matrimony or Phrenology and Physiology Applied to the Selection of Companions for Life*, New York, Fowler & Wells, 1847.
16. C. G. Finney, *Dictionary of American Biography*, Vol. VI, p. 394.
17. H. S. Canby, *Thoreau*, Boston, Houghton, 1939, p. xiv.
18. Emerson, *Works*, Vol. X.

19. Van Wyck Brooks, *New England: Indian Summer,* New York, E. P. Dutton & Co., 1940, p. 335.
20. Brooks, p. 331.
21. R. B. Perry, *op cit.*
22. Van Wyck Brooks, p. 335.
23. J. A. Dowie, *Dictionary of American Biography,* Vol. V, p. 413.
24. W. H. Hale, *op. cit.,* p. 126.
25. Quoted in Canby, p. 186.
26. H. S. Commager, *The American Mind,* New Haven, Conn., Yale, 1950, p. 12.
27. C. H. Hughes, "Christopathy and Christian Science (so called)," *Alienist & Neurologist* 20:611, 1899.
28. Annie Besant, *Esoteric Christianity, or, The Lesser Mysteries,* New York, John Lane, 1901.
29. Sibyl Wilbur, *The Life of Mary Baker Eddy,* ed. 4, Boston, Christian Science Publishing Society, 1938, p. 87.
30. P. P. Quimby, *The Quimby Manuscripts, Showing the Discovery of Spiritual Healing and the Origin of Christian Science,* edited by H. W. Dresser, New York, Crowell, 1921, p. 31.
31. Wilbur, *op cit.,* p. 88.
32. Quimby, p. 96.
33. E. F. Dakin, *Mrs. Eddy; The Biography of a Virginal Mind,* New York, Scribner, 1929, p. 9.
34. Mary Baker Eddy, *Science and Health, with Key to the Scriptures.* From authorized version of 1875. Boston, Stewart, 1917, p. 109.
35. *Ibid.,* p. 107.
36. *Ibid.,* p. 365.
37. L. P. Powell, *Mary Baker Eddy, A Life-Size Portrait,* New York, Macmillan, 1950, p. 109.
38. Dakin, p. 148.
39. Mark Twain, *Christian Science,* New York, Harper, 1907, p. 72.
40. *Ibid.,* p. 68.
41. Frank Podmore, *Mesmerism and Christian Science, A Short History of Mental Healing,* Philadelphia, George W. Jacobs, 1909.
42. E. M. Ramsay, *Christian Science and Its Discoverer,* Boston, Christian Science Publishing Society, 1923, p. 111.
43. H. W. Dresser, *A History of the New Thought Movement,* New York, Crowell, 1919, p. 153.
44. G. G. Atkins, *Modern Religious Cults and Movements,* New York, Revell, 1923.
45. *Ibid.*
46. Dresser, p. 132.
47. L. P. Powell, *The Emmanuel Movement in a New England Town,* New York, Putnam, 1909, p. 6.
48. Elwood Worcester and Samuel McComb, *Body, Mind and Spirit,* Boston, Jones, Marshall, 1931.
49. R. B. Perry, *op. cit.*
50. C. J. Wright, "Christianity and Healing Miracles," *Quarterly Rev.,* London, Apr. 1922, p. 161.

51. A. M. Bellwald, *Christian Science and the Catholic Faith*, New York, Macmillan, 1922.
52. *The Emmanuel Press* 1:12, April 12, 1912.
53. Casey *et al*.: Faith and Psychopathology; A Symposium, Washington, D. C., American Psychiatric A. Meeting, May 18, 1948.
54. J. L. Liebman, *Peace of Mind*, New York, Simon and Schuster, Inc., 1946.
55. Roberts, *op. cit.*
56. J. R. Oliver, *Psychiatry and Mental Health*, New York, Scribner, 1932, p. 298.
57. K. R. Stolz, *Pastoral Psychology*, rev. ed., New York, Abingdon-Cokesbury, 1941, p. 255.
58. *Pastoral Psychology*, Great Neck, N. Y., Pulpit Digest Pub. Co., 1952.
59. Smiley Blanton and N. V. Peale, *Faith is the Answer*, New York, Prentice-Hall, 1941.
60. *Ibid.*, p. 48.
61. Personal observation, New York, 1939.
62. N. V. Peale and Smiley Blanton, *The Art of Real Happiness*, New York, Prentice-Hall, 1950.
63. *The Emmanuel Press, A Magazine Devoted to the Fine Art of Being Well*, Berkeley, Calif., T. P. Boyd, August 12, 1912, p. 4.
64. Theosophy, Theosophical Societies, 1875 (started by Madame H. P. Blavatsky), in *Encyclopaedia Britannica*, Vol. 22, p. 69.
65. Annie Besant, *op. cit.*, p. 339.
66. L. R. Steiner, *Where Do People Take Their Troubles*, New York, Internat. Univ. Press, 1945.
67. William Seabrook, *Witchcraft, Its Power in the World Today*, New York, Harcourt, 1940.
68. Morris Fishbein, *Fads and Quackery in Healing*, New York, Blue Ribbon Books, 1932.

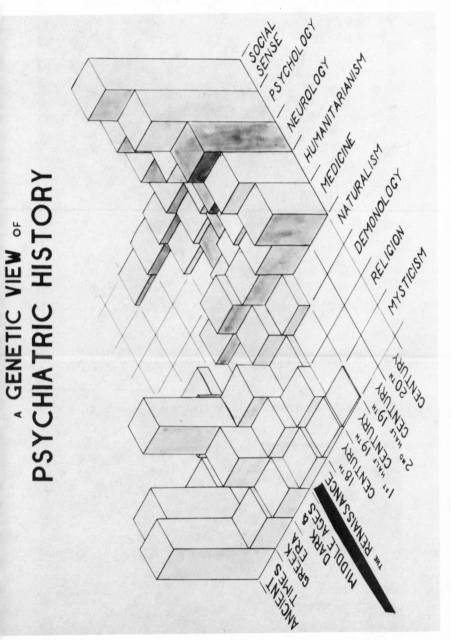

A GENETIC VIEW OF PSYCHIATRIC HISTORY

SOCIAL SENSE
PSYCHOLOGY
NEUROLOGY
HUMANITARIANISM
MEDICINE
NATURALISM
DEMONOLOGY
RELIGION
MYSTICISM

ANCIENT TIMES
GREEK ERA
DARK AGES
THE RENAISSANCE
18TH CENTURY
1ST HALF 19TH CENTURY
2ND HALF 19TH CENTURY
20TH CENTURY

A Genetic View of Psychiatric Evolution

Greek Psychotherapy—Religion and Naturalism

Mysticism—Potent Forces in the Dark and Middle Ages

Witchcraft—Sexual Psychopathology of the Middle Ages

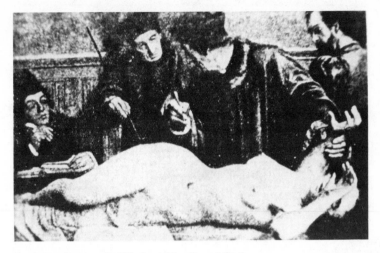

Demonology—A Clinical Medieval Science

fter þ we haue bi helpe
of god ended the treaty
se of the propretees of
thynges that comforte
and helpe and socour &
kepe and saue mannes
... We shall speke of thynges that
... to man arens kynde/ The thin
gys þt greue mannes kynde. cause of sykes
... sykenes and accydent that folowe
... Of the cause of sykenes
... euyll & vnkynde dyspolycyon in
... bodyes of euyl complexcyon. other to
... repleccyon other to grete abstynence
... þe defaute of vertue other chaungyng
... repletes & dyssolucion & departyng ge
... All thyse bey cause other
... of sykenes/ So sayth þ by syk

nes the body is greued and nored.
by feuers and postumes and suche ot
Accydent is a thynge þ foloweth t
se passyons þ cometh & is brought in
the body. whether it be arens kynde
not. as heed ache in Cephanica other i
arens kynde. as periplesimora. the
kes were redde. Good dyspolycion
body is callyd hele by the whiche m
nes body in complexyon & composicion is
suche state þ he may freely & perfytly
his werkes & dedes/ And yet kynde
deth oute of this temperature. & falls
... to euyll & sykenes. for of dystempe
... unce & benynis of humours euyll b
... of one maner passyon. as feuers & D
... pelse & suche other/ And of euyll orde
... ticion of membres cometh euyll pas

Monastic Medicine—
Humane Treatment

The Manner of His Majesties Curing the Disease
CALLED THE
KINGS-EVIL.

Passage of Priestly Power to Kings

Greatrakes—
The Commoner as Therapist

Irregular Practitioners

MÉMOIRE
SUR LA DÉCOUVERTE
DU
MAGNÉTISME
ANIMAL;
Par M. MESMER, Docteur en Médecine
de la Faculté de Vienne.

A GENEVE;
Et se trouve
A PARIS,
Chez P. Fr. DIDOT le jeune, Libraire-
Imprimeur de MONSIEUR, quai
des Augustins.

M. DCC. LXXIX.

Mesmer—Eighteenth-Century Mysticism and Science

Mesmer's Baquet—Magnetism in the Mode

Confusion of
Eighteenth-Century Therapy

Isaac Ray—
Psychiatric Leader

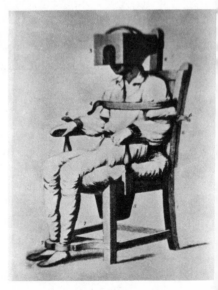

Benjamin Rush—
Assays into Social Medicine

Benjamin Rush—
The Clinician Deals with Insanity

Charcot—Hypnosis Comes of Age

Weir Mitchell—Neurologists
and the "Nervous Breakdown"

Freud—Evolution
of Dynamic Psychiatry

Adolf Meyer—
Common Sense in Psychiatry

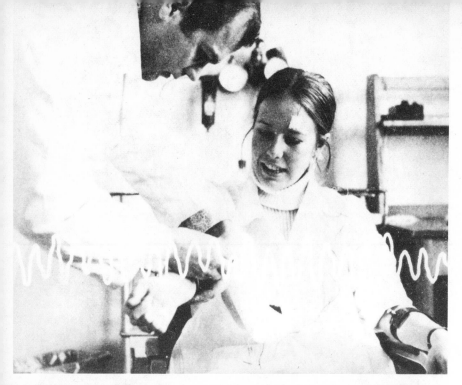

Biofeedback—The Return of Neuro-Science

James Braid—
Physiology Displaces Magnetism

10

A Psychologic Psychotherapy
Emerges

THE rationale for what is now called dynamic psychotherapy lies in the notion that the main function of the personality (self or ego) is in its adaptation to its environment. The environment is conceived totally as the individual's early family interactions, the cultural and social matrices in which the person developed, and the physical environment. This formulation, so easily stated now, required experiments, observations, and analyses lasting almost a century. Our current concept of the ego as an adaptive organ depended basically on Darwin's evolutionary theories, to which was added an analysis of nervous system function by psychologists, neurologists, and physiologists. Stanley Hall, President of Clark University and a vivid spirit in psychology, stated the general position some three quarters of a century ago:

> ...there are just as many rudiments and vestiges in our psychic activities...as in our bodies...a product of slow evolutionary tendencies.[1]

The formulation that the ego adapts to a complex biological and psychologic environment pushed psychotherapy into a new direction. Simply stated, it read: If deviations in the mind and emotions were essentially dynamic, i.e., reactive to stresses of the environment, they were treatable; if symptoms were the products of nerve deterioration (as exhaustion or organic changes), they were in the main untreatable. It is the former view that underlies the philosophy of psychoanalysis and today's dynamic psychotherapy. This dynamic notion allowed a new therapeutic optimism but its growth was devious, consuming the better part of a half century.

The scientific reputation of Charcot and his associates underwrote the accepted theory that hypnosis was effective because of the peculiar nervous system of the hysteric. But questions arose: Was the hypnotic effect due to a magical property of the operator able to elicit the "stages" of hypnosis—lethargy, catalepsy, somnambulism—or was it simply due to the patient's suggestibility? Bernheim, who led the attack, claimed, "There is no hypnosis; it is all suggestion," and he was echoed by Dubois, a Swiss physician, who used *persuasion*[2] on his patients. He spoke in direct, intimate terms, denying that suggestion was needed. Life problems were discussed in ordinary terms by the ebullient Swiss therapist in trying to persuade his patients to give up their troubles. Persuasion, combined with an optimistic outlook, a "rosy view of life," and the force of authority were the main tools with which Dubois worked. He treated people as a doctor, giving them advice on the routine of their lives, on food and rest—a therapy closer to the Mitchell Rest Cure than to hypnosis. To a tuberculous patient, Dubois said:

> "You cannot put on weight unless you take your food properly.... A consumptive who is losing weight is on the downward path; but it is a happy augury when such a patient puts on flesh." The patient answers: "I'll try to eat, doctor." "Try! What's the use of that? The word 'try' conveys a doubt of the result, and the doubt will not fail to reduce your impetus. What you must say to yourself is, 'I am going to eat!' "

The "paternal spirit," to which Dubois readily admitted, aroused opposition among Dubois' colleagues. Forel, a Swiss authority on hypnosis, claimed "Professor Dubois slangs hypnotism and suggestion, while in reality he practices suggestion from alpha to omega."[3] Others complained of the hortatory and inspirational type of psychotherapy used by the affable Swiss doctor. Janet joined others in noting that Dubois' methods were antipsychological and antiscientific. "Too much exaltation," too close to faith healing, Janet remarked, while across the Atlantic Prof. William James was talking of "unlocking our mental energies," of striving to overcome our weaknesses. The Dubois method, which saw energizing of the will as the key to success with various neurotic symptoms, was tacitly pragmatic in tone. It spoke in terms of action: "Pass a sponge over [your] past and wipe out [your] phobias," he told his patients.

In spite of professional opposition, suggestion as a method of treatment spread. In the 1920s, Emile Coué, a modest, quiet-spoken apothecary of Nancy, used suggestive therapy on his "patients." From individuals, he proceeded to groups, never mentioning disease but merely the contrary state of health. Coué's quiet personality, his kindliness, his forceful yet dignified manner, contributed to the success of his method. He did not indulge in theoretical explanations to his patients; scientific theory was quite secondary with him. Only occasionally did he present the result of his work to a psychological congress. Light, humorous, "sometimes firm, sometimes gently bantering," varying his tone to suit the temperament of his patient, he taught his autosuggestive therapy[4] to his patients. The first exercise was a demonstration of the power of implanted ideas over the will by a simple experiment. The patient, his hands clasped together, was instructed to think, "I cannot open them"; contrary to an order to open them, the patient could not do so. The subject was then ordered to think, "I *can* open them," and immediately the cramped hands were loosed. So with the various diseased and nervous states presented to him, with kindly persistence and vigorous suggestion, Coué insisted that these patients "will" to move a stiff joint or exercise palsied legs. His patients were to carry away with them the idea that day by day they were able to *will* their bodies to be healthy and straight. "Go home and will that *tous les jours, a tous points de vue, je vais de mieux en mieux*" (Day by day, in every way, I am getting better and better), he suggested.

The practical benefits of hypnosis and suggestive therapy had been established, but the physiological and psychological mechanisms operative therein remained an open question. The *rapport* between physician and patient that brought about improvement defied understanding. One intriguing possibility was the notion of a "double consciousness" (the *Doppel Ich,* double ego, of Desoir) or more specifically the "unconscious cerebration" of Carpenter. The latter, during the 1870s, had observed that a large part of our intellectual activity was automatic, due, he thought, to the "reflex action of the Cerebrum." Dr. W. B. Carpenter, an English neurologist,[5] surmised that ideas and emotional states that appeared out of nowhere—the reappearance of forgotten ideas—were held in the "unconscious." Oliver Wendell Holmes expressed the same notion in more dramatic form:

> We wish to remember something.... No effort of the will can reach it.... Presently, some minutes later the idea we are in search of comes all at once into the mind, delivered like a prepaid bundle, laid at the door of consciousness, like a foundling in a basket.[6]

Indeed the idea of an unconscious had been part of German metaphysics from the time of Leibnitz; as witness, Eduard von Hartmann (1868) had written three heavy volumes about physiologic and mental phenomena in which inductive reasoning established the validity of an unconscious.[7] The oft-repeated theory of consciousness as merely the tip of the iceberg was phrased by Schopenhauer "as a sheet of water of some depth...the whole process of our thought seldom lies on the surface."[8] Long-forgotten memories, brought to awareness through hypnosis, emphasized the probability of another kind of consciousness. Especially conclusive were studies in multiple personalities, elicited by hypnosis, where a few ideas, at first forced into the unconscious, were "incubated and after synthesizing became egocentric systems on their own."[9] Cases of double or multiple personalities, the Beauchamp case (Prince), the Hanna case (Sidis),[10] and others, proved that emotional shock, actual trauma, or even "voluntary repression" could produce a dissociation of the personality entirely analogous to that evoked through hypnosis.

The concept of double personality was reinforced by Morton Prince,[11] in his study of Sally Beauchamp, the girl who lived in four different worlds with speech and behavior peculiar to each. His investigation of the dissociated personality was mirrored in Robert Louis Stevenson's celebrated story, *Dr. Jekyll and Mr. Hyde*, and a host of unexplained spiritistic experiences. It also made the idea of a "dissociated personality" and an "unconscious" more palatable, not only for the profession but also for the public. Phrases like "subconscious," "dual personality," and "Jekyll and Hyde" personality were bandied about. In one sense, this acquaintance with another or "subliminal" aspect of our minds prepared the way for acceptance of theories of mental healing during the early decades of this century.[12] The unconscious was conceded to exert a tremendous, hitherto undreamed of, influence on human behavior and thinking.

Pierre Janet, Professor at the University of Paris and Charcot's successor, accepted the notion of dissociation of personality in hysteric states but argued that it rested on an *enfeeblement* of consciousness due often to psychic exhaustion. The difficulty then lay in the disordered physiology of the nervous system, which permitted dissociation under stress. As early as 1889, Janet spoke of emotional trauma's causing a dissociation in hysterical subjects in which certain fixed ideas pushed into subconsciousness caused a "psychological disaggregation," resulting in symptoms.[13] The split-off idea was "emancipated," pursuing its own course into a system of symptoms, e.g., convulsions, paralysis, etc. Later, this mechanism was extended to account for obsessions, impulsions, and phobias where a fixed idea[14] (sexual or emotional trauma, dread of loneliness, need to be loved, etc.) forced the dissociation of consciousness through a weakened nervous system.

As pathological examinations of the brain tissue were becoming more precise (Golgi, Cajal, etc.), explanations of the dissociation phenomenon were couched in terms of the neuron theory. Energy in the neuron, *neurokyme*, was released for any psychologic activity; the potential energy in the nerve tissue became kinetic when discharged, i.e., when thinking or feeling were engaged in. If this discharging energy was blocked by some resistance, or if it were too high, a hysterical reaction ensued. This, in brief, was the "intracerebral tonic excitation" theory which Breuer and Freud used in their early studies on hysteria.[15]

Hypnosis, at the beginning of the century, was practised as a medical specialty, albeit not without some uneasiness on the part of doctors uncomfortable with the aura of mysticism still clinging to it. Professional and lay writers hid their anxiety under an insistence that some organic basis must exist. Wrote one critic of hypnotism:

> I do not deny the physical fact of hypnosis...[it is] mental and purely subjective but there must be a pathological coefficient on which the susceptibility of the patients...depends.[16]

Others were more caustic. An unnamed commentator noted:

> As hysteria develops...some phases of it are mildly immoral because they represent in an insane way...[the] conscientious business of degenerating. A woman will go into a

chronic state of martyrdom . . . she thinks her husband does not "understand" her . . . she longs to "pour out her soul" to somebody. . . . [17]

Nevertheless, the theory of dissociation, the split-off traumatic ideas or emotions emerging as symptoms, gained a solid foothold in the search for a satisfactory explanation of hysteria. The problem of the mechanism of dissociation concerned many, including Sigmund Freud, who on returning from his four months' sojourn at Charcot's clinic in Paris, tried hypnosis on several patients. He was struck, as he uncovered traumatic events in the patient's early life, by the direct connection between these recalled events and the hysterical symptom under treatment. When the pressure of emotion accompanying the recall of these memories was released, the hysterical symptom disappeared. In company with Dr. Josef Breuer, a well-established Viennese physician, Freud published a paper in 1893,[18] which concluded that the "splitting of consciousness . . . the tendency to this dissociation . . . exists rudimentarily in every hysteria." Their success in removing paralyses, anesthesias, and neuralgias was gratifying, and the paper ended with the careful statement that the authors had "advanced our knowledge in the mechanisms of hysterical symptoms and not in the subjective causes of hysteria. . . ." Janet, who read the paper, remarked archly, "We are glad to find . . . Messrs. Breuer and Freud have recently verified our interpretations, already somewhat old, of subconscious ideas with hystericals."[19]

During the next few years, Dr. Breuer and Dr. Freud treated several hysterical cases with hypnotism; they found in each case a confirmation of their theory—awakening of significant memories with accompanying emotion resulted in disappearance of the symptoms.[20] The historic cases of Anna O., Emmy von N., and others were gathered into a book, *Studies in Hysteria* (1895), where Dr. Breuer's "talking cure" (as Anna O. humorously dubbed it) was outlined in detail. As the cathartic method of relief of hysterical symptoms developed, Freud decided to treat other neuroses with Breuer's method, modified to the extent that he "ordered the patient to . . . shut his eyes so as to concentrate his mind."[21] The result was emergence of reminiscences without hypnosis. But other problems arose; not every patient could be hypnotized. Apparently, a *resistance* was present against the "unbearable" idea, which "crowded it out of consciousness." As the mechanism of defense against unacceptable (predominantly sexual) ideas became clearer in his cases, Freud settled on a therapeutic technique that dispensed with hypnosis and, to some extent, with the "talking" abreaction as the primary tool of treatment. The psychic force that had to be overcome in uncovering amnesias for significant emotion-laden events in the life of the patient proved to be the same force that initially *repressed* the affect, turning it into symptoms. Recognition of repression as a hidden psychic activity provided the dynamic accent that started psychoanalysis as an independent therapeutic system.

At this point a brief digression is in order to comment on the frequency with which the concept of "force" has been invoked throughout the history of psychotherapy. Apparently, it has always been tacitly assumed that a superior force was required to overcome mental symptoms. Examples jump to mind: Electricity, electroshock, lobotomy, suggestion, even "moral persuasion," all involve force. Ancient man's conception of *mana*, a supernatural force that grew crops and healed the sick; the religionists' belief in the Supreme Power of God; Mesmer's magnetism, a force borrowed from the stars; the use of physical punishment of the mad during the seventeenth and eighteenth centuries, all speak for this general proposition. Even the moral treatment of Leuret, which combatted delusions with superior reasoning, and the hypnotic techniques of today impose a foreign force on the patient in the hope of ridding the latter of symptoms. Psychological systems are no exception; mental healers work with energy forces, however conceived.

It was natural, then, that Freud, living in an era when neurophysiology conceived the nervous system to be formed of neurons carrying charges of energy, should develop the notion of *cathexis*, or charge of psychic energy. In his *Project for a Scientific Psychology,* written in 1895,[22] Freud described the ego as an "organism distinguished by the possession of a constant cathexis of energy." This quantity of energy, attached to emotionally charged ideas that could not be discharged, became the link for Freud between disordered cerebral function and the neurosis. Psychic energy from an unacceptable or "hostile" memory trace could be deflected by a "counter-energy" or "counter-cathexis" (resistance), thus causing the emergence of a symptom. This general theory, which Kris[23] called the "cornerstone of the psycho-analytic theory of psychical structure," made the Freudian method of treatment plausible. The counter-force was analyzed and interpreted, i.e., the unconscious resistance to recognizing the patient's uncontrollable impulses, and the original psychic force causing the symptom was vanquished. This complex theory fitted well into Freud's idea of the ego structure and formed the basis for his method of analyzing the defenses which the ego put up against conflicts waging within it. Certain it was, that Freud had come closer than anyone else to a picture of what went on below the surface in the tormented, neurotic ego of the patient.

In a letter unearthed by Oberndorf,[24] Breuer expressed himself as aware, as far back as 1880, that in the study of hysteria "a glimpse was being offered into deeper layers of psycho-pathologic processes." As Freud developed the basically sexual nature motivating this repressing force, Breuer apparently deemed it wise not to pursue investigations further. A gradual deviation occurred between the two men as Freud demonstrated to his satisfaction that sexual elements lay behind the rapport (transference) of patient and physician, and announced the sexual etiology of the neurosis in later papers. The disbanding of the joint investigation was spurred, Freud notes, by Breuer's dislike of the sexual connotation. Simmel put it more positively in saying that Breuer was a "slave to conventional beliefs."[25] At any rate, Breuer "stopped his investigations right there."[26] Breuer had fixed psychotherapy on a dynamic level, and Freud carried it to its clinical and metapsychological conclusion. As Freudian psychology deepened, in the words of Bernard Hart, "it left the phenomenal plane and ascended to the conceptual."[27]

The development of Freud's ideas during the next decade has been traced in minute detail by his biographer, Dr. Ernest Jones.[28] Freud's early neurologic studies on spinal cord nuclei in the medulla,[29] his valuable clinical report on cerebral diplegia in children,[30] his discovery of cocaine as an anesthetic (later developed as novocaine), his profound interest in evolutionary physiology,[31] have been outlined as indicators of a "genius-given gift."[32] Freud's impact on other areas of psychologic life has been tremendous. His illumination of cultural anthropology and religion, his analysis of literary and historical figures, his discussions of such global problems as war and civilization, although contested by some, have spread his insights into every area of human concern. These efforts belong to the history of ideas rather than to techniques of mental healing. They covered a span of fifty-four years of intense intellectual work and thought. In and through these years, a research method, a philosophy of the mind, and a method of treatment developed. To his new science, Freud gave the name *psychoanalysis* in 1896. It became the root of a dynamic psychotherapy, which transformed the practice of mental healing.

For a decade following publication of *Studien Uber Hysterie*, Freud worked alone at 19 Berggasse, Vienna, developing his dream theory, theories on obsessions and phobias, delineation of the sexual life of the child, and the vital concepts of repression and regression. Abandoning a growing practice in nervous diseases, he became intensely absorbed in his work. From many descriptions and innumerable reports of personal contact with Freud, the picture emerges of a man of immense power of concentration, scientific honesty, and meticulous concern with clinical detail that illustrated, rather than obscured, his fundamental hypotheses. As his small circle of pupils increased, he lectured and expounded his views before a privately organized Vienna Psycho-Analytic Society. It was a matter of ten years before Freud's ideas on the significance of the unconscious were appreciated. Meanwhile, he lived through the bitterness and the beauty of the "heroic era,"[33] fortified against the "slings of outrageous fortune" by an inner sense of confidence in the overwhelming significance of the psychological world he was unearthing.

The period from 1900 to 1910 became roughly an incubation period during which Freudian ideas of the unconscious, the analysis of obsessive and phobic cases, the libido theory, Oedipus complex, the pleasure principle, and the mechanisms observed in the dream were digested, pondered over, reported and rereported. By 1906, the circle of men devoted to psychoanalysis included Rank, Abraham, Ferenczi, Jung, and Jones.[34] The small circle of followers around Freud in Vienna helped to build a theoretical structure of the instinct life to explain not only neuroses and psychoses, but also social institutions such as religion and the man-made arts.

As practitioners of psychiatry from outside Vienna were attracted to Freud's theories and his accent on the sexual basis of the neurosis, opposition became vociferous. Some called them "foolish conclusions."[35] Critics in Europe were shocked at Freud's intrepid entrance into the inner lives of his patients and his methods.[36] "It [psychoanalysis] is a criminal investigation which aims at the discovery of a culprit in the unearthing of past happening. ... It is more the work of a detective than a psychiatrist." American psychiatrists, stung by the irrationality of Freud's unconscious psychology, opined that "it would not hold my attention except for its astonishing standpoint and novelty. The whole book reminds one much of the thinking of primitive minds, of persons with unscientific, uncritical systemization of ideas."[37] To attacks of licentiousness, scientific frivolity, or worse, Freud had an answer, "I do not see what we shall gain by being ashamed of sexuality."[38]

His technique of treatment was altered by now. He dispensed with hypnosis or the "pressure procedure" in which the patient was urged to recall forgotten events, aided by the doctor's firm hand placed on the former's forehead.[39] Placing the patient on a couch out of sight of the doctor, he requested him to talk freely without regard for coherence or the amenities of polite conversations. This always led, after evasions and tortuous ramblings, to the patient's hidden problems. Freud was able to show his patients how their unconscious was deceiving them, and they could see after days and months of this psychological work something of the emotional drives that caused their symptoms. These drives came mostly from childhood influences and had been forgotten (that is, repressed) by the patient. Since much of the trouble commenced in childhood, where sexual play or talk is suppressed, Freud in his patients' life stories stumbled upon the totally undiscovered sexual life of the child.

In general, Freud's theories of the cause of neuroses excited more attention than did his therapeutic methods. Invasion of the sacred precincts of childhood aroused revulsion; reactions in Viennese society (circa 1900) were pointed: "It was considered bad taste to bring up Freud's name in the presence of ladies." The publication of his monograph on sexuality in childhood[40] was the signal for a fresh barrage of criticism, especially in America. Morris Fishbein, editor of the official *Journal of the American Medical Association*, scorned psychoanalysis in these words: "One ritual demands that the patient lie upon a couch in a dimly darkened office. There she—and the words fall naturally, for it is usually a feminine patient—begins her long autobiography and there the psychoanalyst sits—we hope— listening and stimulating ever more and more juicy revelations." The academic psychological world was more elegant in its deprecation. Professor Pillsbury of the University of Michigan, contemptuous of Freud's lack of university connections, wrote: "He brought in a few friends in a back room. There they worked out psychoanalysis."

Two Swiss, whose names became significant in psychiatry, C. G. Jung and Eugen Bleuler, joined the Viennese group. Dr. Jung had experimented with the word association test,[41] wherein the reaction to key words, chosen out of a random sample, indicated an emotional, unconscious significance to the individual tested. The time of response to the word was noted, and a delay in association, an unusual emotional response, a failure to respond or a superficial reaction, indicated a blocking or a repression of the idea related to the word, i.e., a complex. Although Freud later noted[42] that the association experiments offered no essential contribution to the technique of treatment, it brought psychology into relation with psychoanalysis and popularized the concept of "complex" in the literate world and the world of literature.

The analysis of neurotic symptoms as well as dreams and occurrences in everyday life involved a search for unconscious motives and resistance in random associations uttered by the patient. Psychoanalytic therapy during the early period followed the theory of sexual etiology of the neurosis.[43] This stated in brief that "no neurosis is possible with a normal *vita sexualis*."[44] Freud early had found that anxiety rested on dammed-up sexual outlets (so-called "free floating libido"), with consequent inadequate sexual gratification, dependent upon coitus interruptus, abstinence, frustrated sexual activity, etc. To cases of anxiety neurosis due to dammed-up libido, Freud applied the term *actual neurosis* in contradistinction to neurasthenia and to the *psychoneuroses*, wherein emotionally involved ideas, split off from consciousness, caused the symptoms. Further study showed that these unconscious ideas were also related to sexual disturbances, often fantasied and deriving from an infantile period. Analysis provided "incontestable" proof that psychoneurotic symptoms represented repressed and defended-against perverse sexual components, which assumed a tortuous path into consciousness. The aim of treatment, then, was the release of unconscious sexual elements, infantile and perverse in nature, through free association and interpretation, and brought to the patient's consciousness against his resistances. Thus repression of traumatic events (or fantasied ones) was undone, the unconscious made conscious and the morbid condition removed.

The ingenuity of Freud's method and its basis in an unexplored area of human feeling attracted the attention of psychologists in this country. The lectures by Freud arranged by President G. Stanley Hall at the twentieth anniversary of Clark University were regarded as a respectable success among scientific men. Even the American press treated Freud with regard. An article appearing in the magazine section of a Boston paper in 1909 was captioned "Prof. Sigmund Freud, the Eminent Vienna Psychotherapist, The Founder of a Most Successful School Interviewed." A. Albrecht, a reporter on the *Boston Evening Transcript*, described Freud as follows: "One sees at a glance that he is a man of refinement, of intellect, and of many-sided interests. His sharp, yet kind, clear eyes suggest at once the doctor. His high forehead with the large bump of observation and his beautiful energetic hands are very striking. He speaks clearly, weighing his words carefully, but unfortunately never of himself."[45] Professor William James was somewhat less complimentary. At the time of Freud's visit to America in 1909, he stated:

> I hope that Freud and his pupils will push their ideas to their utmost limits so that we may learn what they are. They can't fail to throw light on human nature; but I confess that he made on me personally the impression of a man obsessed with fixed ideas....[46]

In turn, Freud voiced a deprecating attitude toward the United States. Years after his American trip, Hans Sachs reported Freud's reflection: "America is the most grandiose experiment the world has seen, but I am afraid it is not going to be a success."[47]

The Freudian era was marked by much acrimony, chiefly because of the shock reaction to Freud's sexual theories on the part of professionals and laymen alike. Moreover, the politics within the psychoanalytic profession, especially in the early days of the "dissenters"—Jung, Adler, Rank, and others—had occupied Freud and his followers to an unusual extent. Partly this was due to the uncompromising attitude of Freud himself toward those who in his judgment had lapsed from intellectual honesty.[48] Partly it was due to differing orientations of co-workers. As a working scientist in mental fields, Freud's interest was fastened as much on an integrated theory of mental function as on a technique for treatment of neurosis. Indeed, his position, late in his career, is summed up in the statement:

> We do not want to see psychoanalysis swallowed up by medicine, and then to find its last resting place in textbooks on psychiatry—in the chapter headed "Therapy" next to procedures such as hypnotic suggestion, autosuggestion, and persuasion, which were created out of our ignorance, and owe their short-lived effectiveness to the laziness and cowardice of the mass of mankind.[49]

Notes to Chapter 10

1. G. S. Hall, *Adolescence, Its Psychology and Its Relation to Physiology, Anthropology, Sociology, Sex, Crime, Religion and Education*, New York, Appleton, 1904.
2. Paul Dubois, *The Psychic Treatment of Nervous Disorders*, translated and edited by S. E. Jelliffe and W. A. White, New York, Funk, 1909, p. 16.
3. Auguste Forel, *Hypnotism, or, Suggestion and Psychotherapy, a Study of the Psychological, Psychophysiological and Therapeutic Aspects of Hypnotism*, translated by H. W. Armit, New York, Rebman, 1907.
4. Emile Coué, *How to Practice Suggestion and Autosuggestion*, New York, Am. Lib. Service, 1923.
5. W. B. Carpenter, *Principles of Mental Physiology With Their Applications*

to the *Training and Discipline of the Mind and Study of its Morbid Conditions*, New York, Appleton, 1874.

6. Oliver Wendell Holmes, *Mechanism in Thought and Morals*, Boston, James R. Osgood & Co., 1871, p. 38.
7. Eduard von Hartmann, *Philosophy of the Unconscious*, translated by W. C. Coupland, ed. 9, New York, Macmillan, 1884.
8. Edward Margetts, "The concept of the unconscious in the history of medical psychology," *Psychiat. Quart.* 27:126, 1953.
9. Morton Prince, "Clinical and Experimental Studies in Personality," Cambridge, Massachusetts, *Sc.-Art. Pub.*, 1929, p. 130.
10. Boris Sidis and S. P. Goodhart, *Multiple Personality, an Experimental Investigation into the Nature of Human Individuality*, New York, Appleton, 1905, p. 83.
11. Morton Prince in *J. (and Proc.) Soc. for Psychical Res.*, London, July-Oct., 1952.
12. W. F. Prince, and J. H. Hyslop, "The Doris case of multiple personalities," *Proc. Am. Soc. for Psychical Res.*, vols. 9, 10, and 11, York, Pa., York Printing Co., 1915 and 1917.
13. Boris Sidis and S. P. Goodhart, p. 191.
14. Pierre Janet, *Psychological Healing, a Historical and Clinical Study*, translated by E. and C. Hall, New York, Macmillan, 1925, p. 596.
15. Josef Breuer and Sigmund Freud, *Studies in Hysteria*, translated by A. A. Brill, New York, Nerv. & Ment. Dis. Monographs, 1936.
16. Ernest Hart, "The Eternal Gullible, with confessions of a professional hypnotist," *Century Magazine*, vol. 48, October 1894, p. 833.
17. Ernest Hart, *The Independent*, vol. 58, Mar. 30, 1905, p. 736.
18. Sigmund Freud and Josef Breuer, "On the psychical mechanism of hysterical phenomena," *Neurolog. Zentralbl.*, 1893, translated by J. Rickman, in *Collected Papers*, vol. 1, p. 24, New York and London, Internat. Psychoanal. Press, 1924.
19. Pierre Janet, *op. cit.*, "Mental State of Hystericals," p. 195.
20. Josef Breuer and Sigmund Freud, *Studies in Hysteria*.
21. Sigmund Freud, *The Origins of Psychoanalysis (1887–1902)*, translated by E. Mosbacher and J. Strachey, New York, Basic Books, 1954, p. 358.
22. *Ibid.*
23. Ernst Kris, notes in Freud, *The Origins of Psychoanalysis, op. cit.*, p. 26.
24. Josef Breuer, *Autobiography*, edited and trans. by C. P. Oberndorf, *Internat. J. Psycho-analysis* 39:64, 1953.
25. Ernst Simmel, "Sigmund Freud, the man and his work," *Psychoanal. Quar.* 9:170, 1940.
26. Sigmund Freud, "A History of the Psychoanalytic Movement," in *The Basic Writings of Sigmund Freud*, trans. by A. A. Brill, New York, Modern Library, 1938, p. 936.
27. Bernard Hart, H. Munsterberg, *et al. Subconscious Phenomena, A Symposium*, Boston, Badger, 1910, p. 131.

28. Siegfried Bernfeld, "Sigmund Freud, M. D., 1882–1885," *Internat. J. Psychoanalysis* 32:204, 1951.

29. S. E. Jelliffe, "Sigmund Freud as neurologist," *J. Nerv. & Ment. Dis.* 85:696–711, 1937.

30. Siegfried Bernfeld, "Freud's scientific beginnings," *Am. Imago* 6:3, 1949.

31. Alexander and Selesnick, *op. cit.*, chap. 13, p. 203 *et seq.*

32. Helene Deutsch, "Freud and His Pupils, a footnote to the history of the psychoanalytic movement," *Psychoanal. Quart.* 9:184, 1940.

33. Sigmund Freud, "A History of the Psychoanalytic Movement," in *The Basic Writings of Sigmund Freud.*

34. Jones, *op. cit.*, vol. 2, p. 35.

35. Editorial: "Sigmund Freud's foolish conclusion," *Alienist & Neurologist* 20:113, 1899.

36. Pierre Janet, *Psychological Healing*, p. 610.

37. Meyer Solomon, "Psychopathology of everyday life, a critical review of Dr. Sigmund Freud's theories," *J. Abnormal Psychol.*, April 1916, p. 23 et seq.

38. Breuer and Freud, *op. cit.*, p. 109.

39. Max Graf, "Reminiscences of Professor Sigmund Freud," *Psychoanalyt. Quart.* 11:465, 1942.

40. Sigmund Freud, "Three Contributions to the Theory of Sex," *Nerv. & Ment. Dis. Pub. Co.*, 1910.

41. C. G. Jung, *Studies in Word-Association. Experiments in the Diagnosis of Psychopathological Conditions Carried Out at the Psychiatric Clinic of the University of Zurich*, translated by M. D. Eder, New York, Moffat, 1919.

42. Freud, *Autobiography*, translated by James Strachey, New York, Norton, 1935.

43. Freud, "My Views on the Part Played by Sexuality in the Aetiology of the Neurosis," in *Collected Papers*, London, Internat. Psycho-analytic Press, 1924; Vol. I, p. 272.

44. Freud, "Freud's Psychoanalytic Method," in *Collected Papers*, Vol. I, 264.

45. A. Albrecht, *Boston Evening Transcript*, 1909.

46. R. B. Perry, *op. cit.*

47. Hans Sachs, *Freud, Master and Friend*, London, Imago, 1946.

48. Sachs, p. 121.

49. Freud, *The Question of Lay Analysis*, translated by Nancy Procter-Gregg, New York, Norton, 1950, p. 121.

11

Mental Hygiene—
Psychotherapy's Catalyst

O F all the factors promoting acceptance of psychotherapy among the public, the mental hygiene movement was the main energizer, the catalyst of this enterprise. Essentially an American idea, the mental hygiene movement used salesmanship and the techniques of public relations to demonstrate the need for better mental health. Retaining its social idealism, the movement flourished in a democratic atmosphere. Although public exposure of intimate matters like one's mental peculiarities was involved—brash in contrast to the nineteenth century's emphasis on suppression of "dirty linen washed in public"—the notion was eminently practical.

The movement arose in the mind of one man—Clifford W. Beers of Connecticut—but its practical idealism, in time, caught the imagination of much of the world. Whether Beers appreciated the power that exposure of his mental illness and mistreatment in an asylum generated is doubtful, but it helped start the present century's sociopsychological revolution. Historian Commager's construct that

> the decade of the nineties is the watershed of American history...on one side lies an America predominantly agricultural...on the other side lies the modern America....[1]

can be applied to the mental hygiene movement: it was

indeed the watershed of mental healing.

In 1900 the man in the street knew little about psychiatry, except as the insanity of a relative brought his attention to the red-bricked asylums or to the electrical machines and tonics of neurologists. The term "alienist" was better known than "psychiatrist" and, although psychology assumed a respectable position in the university curriculum, it was generally recognized as a deep and somewhat impractical subject. Concerning insanity and its treatment, the citizen was content to stand by the dictum, "once insane, always insane." True, his reading in magazines[2] and the press touched on discovery of the "subconscious" region of the mind, on the neuron theory of the brain tissue, on hypnosis and psychic experiments. Men and women read long articles on the "backward races" of man in Africa and the South Pacific in family magazines.[3] Eugenics was widely discussed, but the concept of freeing the insane from neglect and indifference remained a Utopian dream. The dark history of psychiatry, illuminated by the gentleness of Pinel, the persistence of Dorothea Dix, the penetration of Freud, the industry of Charcot, was an unopened, even unwritten book to the vast majority.

Still, social projects concerning hygiene were far from unknown. The National Association for the Study and Prevention of Tuberculosis was established in 1904; the American Association for the Study and Prevention of Infant Mortality was organized in 1909, thus adding to such older movements for social betterment as the American Public Association (1872), the Charity Organization Society (1877), etc.[4] Physical hygiene, compounded of physiology and moral preachments, exposed the evils of alcohol, tobacco, excessive eating, tight corsets (the wasp waist), and lack of exercise to the young generation. Schools emphasized "deep breathing" before open windows; young men's institutes encouraged Indian club calisthenics, bicycling, and marathon running; books on hygiene deplored tobacco and other unmentionable habits:

> Many boys are throwing away their manly strength and dwarfing their minds, by the use of tobacco.[5]

Another educator wrote:

> Bad habits...sooner or later wear out the nervous machinery.[6]

Medical men ventured to discuss "wholesome habits" and health in general terms but went no further for the layman into the mysteries of mental abnormalities. Among professionals, a "hygiene of the mind" had been cautiously mentioned: Albert Deutsch found the first use of the phrase "mental hygiene" in Sweetster's book, *Mental Hygiene, an Examination of the Intellect and Passions, Designed to Illustrate Their Influence on Health and Duration of Life,* published in 1843.[7] Isaac Ray, dean of American Psychiatry, published a book in 1863 titled *Mental Hygiene.*[8] From the 1870s onward, the term "mental hygiene" passed into general use, concentrated initially in movements concerned with the civil rights of the insane and their mistreatment by restraint. As recounted in stirring detail by Deutsch, the running controversy between neurologists in practice and physicians in the asylums resulted in the formation of a National Association for the Protection of the Insane and the Prevention of Insanity, organized in 1880. The association succumbed within a few years because of professional jealousy and a too narrow base of public support. The concept, "mental hygiene," was therefore not unfamiliar to alienists when Clifford Beers, Connecticut Yankee, burst upon the world with his book, *A Mind That Found Itself.*[9]

Beers, a Yale graduate and young businessman, suffered his first mental breakdown at the age of twenty-four years. Committed to the Hartford Retreat, he went through depressive and manic phases. His elated periods earned him confinement in a straightjacket and padded cell—once for twenty-one days. Talkative, obstreperous, unmanageable, Beers proved to be a troublesome patient. Years later he recalled his wild behavior:

> I refused to open the door [which I barricaded] until the Governor of the State and the Judge who committed me came...the door once opened, in rushed the doctor and four attendants...I was thrown on the bed with two or three of the attacking force on top of me. Again I was choked, this time by the doctor....[10]

For the next six years he was in and out of hospitals. The "grandiose" idea to write a book exposing "existing evils in the care of the mentally ill" reasserted itself in his manic phases. Exalted in mood, full of energy, he overwrote his story and that of many mistreated patients he had seen; words poured out on paper to be mercifully deleted by his wife—"superfluous pages...that would have plagued the reader later."

Finally, *A Mind That Found Itself* was finished. Beers approached Professor William James at Harvard with a draft of the manuscript. The professor pointed to a pile of manuscripts on his desk, commenting that he was the "target for all sorts of cranks and dreamers." Nevertheless, James read it with growing astonishment. "It sounds like fiction but it is not fiction," he wrote in the introduction to the first edition. It was more than that, it was a clarion call. James wrote:

> ...what should be regarded as a common functional disease is handled as a social stigma. It is he [Beers] who has convinced us that the hour for doing something—not merely feeling and wishing—has struck.[11]

Recognizing that he needed psychiatric as well as psychological support, Beers went to Doctor Adolf Meyer, the Director of the New York Psychiatric Institute, for support. Doctor Meyer approached the volume, published in 1908, soberly. His reaction: "It looks at last as if we had what we need...a man for a cause." Meyer himself suggested the name "mental hygiene" for the movement Beers organized, first in Connecticut, then, with the aid of philanthropists Andrew Carnegie and John Rockefeller, in other states and eventually nationally. By 1909 the National

Committee for Mental Hygiene was organized in New York and in 1912, Doctor Thomas Salmon became Medical Director.

The problems that faced Doctor Salmon were staggering. The insane needed legal protection, for many were committed to state institutions on a criminal charge, after exposure to a jury. Brutality and abuses required attention and relief. Detention in jails for those insane awaiting commitment called for new laws. Where to begin? First, how many insane and mental defectives were abroad in the country? Statistics on these matters did not yet exist when Doctor Salmon started his investigations. Some of his finding rivalled the "Snake Pit" image. In a County Poor Farm in a Southern state he reported in 1917:

> I found a "yard man," formerly a trolley car conductor taking care of the insane... three or four remained in cages all day, on stone floors instead of on green grass.... [12]

In more sophisticated areas, mental patients' domiciles were less primitive. When the present author started his career at the Manhattan State Hospital on Ward's Island, New York, in 1928, dungeons, then unused, where maniacal patients were placed for safety, still occupied the basements of massive buildings housing hundreds of patients. A brief description of a hospital of an admittedly higher grade than greeted Doctor Salmon, and of a decade later, will illustrate the problems that faced the early mental hygienists.

The main structures of the Manhattan State Hospital, fronting the East River, were replicas of those designed by Kirkbride in the 1850s. Spacious high-ceilinged halls surrounded by wards and single rooms, a sitting room lined with wooden chairs, a nurses' station and office near the entrance, constituted the approved plan. The buildings that housed the "back wards," including the Inebriate Asylum, built in 1854, appeared more antiquated as one moved away from the Administration Building. Here patients of all varieties, cases of dementia praecox, melancholias, manics, whiled away their years. The more disturbed were ordered to sit in straightback chairs while those more compliant pushed a heavy wooden block across the hall for the obvious purpose of polishing an overpolished floor. There was no communication between patients and little with the nursing staff; some argued with imaginary foes outside the windows; some sat in Rodinesque immobility; some giggled foolishly. During the nonwork hours, the halls looked like an old Hogarth print. Occasionally a cackling laugh issued from an upstairs window or a grunt from a restrained manic broke the empty hum.

In the morning, long lines of rag-tag patients filed from the halls under attendant-guards, en route to menial jobs in the laundry or on the grounds. The men dressed in ill-fitting drab clothes, a cloth cap set at an idiotic angle, talked and gesticulated to themselves. The women patients, in clumsy shoes and dun-colored dresses, giggled or mumbled to the morning air. Occasionally one would depart from the file to emphasize a point to an imaginary persecutor or lunge at a vexing enemy. The scene was dreary, hopeless, eternal.

Such were the situations that faced Doctor Salmon. Earnestly he set to work but World War I intervened. The head of the American Expeditionary Forces in France, General Jack Pershing, sent an urgent message to the War Department requesting psychiatric aid. In brief it said:

> Prevalence of mental disorders in replacement troops
> ... suggests urgent importance [of] eliminating unfit.... [13]

There was one man for the job, Doctor Salmon. Elevated to the rank of Lieutenant Colonel in the Medical Corps, Salmon was sent to France. He so successfully organized the neuropsychiatric services in base hospitals that he practically forced a new hygiene attitude in the military. From France he wrote:

> I have seen guards armed with a rifle and fixed bayonet in an observation ward but since ... the clinical supervision of

all mental cases has been placed in our hands...such a thing is as impossible as it would be in a pneumonia ward.[14]

From 1918 onwards, the impetus carried on by Beers and an increasing number of psychiatrists flowered into a national and international movement. The aim of the organization, under the leadership of Doctor Salmon and Doctor Frankwood Williams, was to spread an attitude that befriended the insane, that made mental illness no more blameworthy than contracting the measles. A spirit of euphoria was in the air. Doctor Williams, after visiting Soviet Russia just after the revolution, said on his return, "I have seen the future and it works." (Lincoln Steffens, the journalist, said it first.)

An extensive educational program was initiated. The public should know the results of scientific study of mental disease as they had been educated in the new knowledge of tuberculosis or diet. Pamphlets written in nontechnical words and sold at low prices were broadcast such as "Suicide," "Sex Education," "The Job of a Parent," "The Problem of Bed-wetting," etc. By the 1920s the fiery efforts of Beers had spurred the Association to deal with prevention, with social symptoms as well as individual complaints. The mass euphoria of the period (1928), coinciding with the pre-stock market crash exhilaration, pushed mental hygiene to propagandized heights. An official spokesman for the Mental Hygiene Association said:

> Mental hygiene presents wide aspects... [it] has a message also for those who consider themselves normal, for by its aims, the man who is fifty per cent efficient can make himself seventy per cent efficient; the man seventy per cent, perhaps eighty per cent; and so on.

The euphoria itself was a spinoff of the conscientious work being done by psychiatrists through the National Committee for Mental Hygiene. The strands that energized the movement had many origins. In 1908, Doctor Henry Goddard of the Vineland, New Jersey, Institution for the Feeble Minded had introduced the Binet-Simon Psychologic Test, which had recently been used in calculating the Mental Age (M.A.) of children in the Paris schools. The idea of a measure of intelligence was revolutionary; no longer would the blanket term "imbecility" or "idiocy" cover all grades of defectiveness. Clinical psychologists, administering the Army Alpha Psychological Test to Army recruits in 1917, became important members of the team that opened the mental capacities of Americans to investigation. On many sides the neurotic and psychotic were being given attention; psychopathic hospitals in the cities—Ann Arbor, Michigan, Bellevue Hospital in New York, Boston Psychopathic Hospital, the Albany (New York) Psychopathic Pavilion—were being established.

And still Beers and his associates maintained the pressure to enlighten the public in recognizing the human basis of mental illness. In 1919, Beers conceived the idea of an international congress of Mental Hygiene, resulting in the first International Congress in Washington, D. C., in 1930. Meanwhile, Freud had been lecturing at Clark University in 1909 and, more significantly, A. A. Brill had translated Freud's *Outlines of Psychoanalysis*, opening up new vistas for the eager group of oncoming psychiatrists. Books were appearing that explained Freudian ideas; in 1916 Bernard Hart wrote a luminous work on the *Psychology of Insanity*, which was widely read by the profession. The converging streams of psychologic and psychiatric interest lay behind the Mental Hygiene movement, but the organizing force, as Doctor Julius Schreiber expressed it some years later, lay in the "validity of an idea."

The bulldog courage and luminous idealism of Clifford Beers were undoubtedly the main forces in the development of the Mental Hygiene movement. Years after his exposé of asylum conditions had been published, Beers received an honorary degree from Yale University. On the occasion of the twenty-fifth anniversary of the Mental Hygiene movement, Doctor G. Adler Blumer, himself a pioneer at the Butler Hospital in Providence, Rhode Island, said of Beers:

> His eagerness, intensity, pertinacity, untiring energy, ease of approach . . . have stood him and his evangel in good stead . . . No "push" for Clifford Beers, . . . save his own ardent spirit; no "pull" save that of might and main to fulfill his humane vision.

Yet other influences were at work to soften the ground upon which the seeds of Mental Hygiene fell. One remote factor was the vigor of Theodore Roosevelt with his trustbusting activities. Another was the growing trade union movement and still another, the general feeling of optimism and "bullishness" that pervaded the land. More particularly, the psychology of William James with its accent on pragmatism, of utilizing every bit of our mental energy, which had occupied the literate world's thinking after his *Principles of Psychology* had been widely read, coincided with Beer's activism. The practical value of "doing" filtered down through Professor James' writings; in his lectures to teachers, James espoused the virtue of the will and habit. He wrote:

> Let us make our nervous system our ally instead of our enemy . . . the aim of education is to fund and capitalize our acquisitions and live at ease upon the interest of the fund . . . habit was the basis for mental growth.[15]

It is to the credit of Jamesian psychology that the view of mental illness as alien to the ordinary individual was softened by his interest in emotional problems. Himself plagued by depressions, "philosophical pessimism" was James's own description of his melancholic periods; he endorsed any method that brought psychological truths to the public. He wanted psychology to get close to life: pragmatism, an "attitude of utility," a way of thinking that *worked*, was his answer. James offered remedies to his fellow Americans:

> When a decision is reached, dismiss all responsibility and care about the outcome. *Unclamp* your intellectual and practical machinery. . . .

A less obvious influence on mental health as a movement affecting the American scene was that of John Dewey, University of Chicago philosopher. His emphasis on learning through experiment and practice stimulated the progressive school movement and with it the basis of a democratic society that leaned towards self-help. The "shirtsleeve psychology" of Dewey, as Boring has phrased it, did away with the "mystery of inner experience," substituting faith in progress, away from old "absolute," rule-of-thumb methods.

These excursions from the academic field exerted a strong influence on opening the citizen's mind to the world of the "mental." But this general up-spading of the public mind was not enough to implant the ideas of mental hygiene. Nourishment in the form of careful dosages of psychiatric principles was a needed fertilizer. Doctor Meyer's *Principles of Psychobiology* provided it. It stated in essence that a commonsense view of the patient's life from cradle to grave, which painted him as a psychobiologic *unit*, made abnormal behavior less mysterious, less shrouded in technical terms. While Beers was spilling out his story in feverish haste, Meyer was calmly teaching the importance of a life story in his mental patients.

A neurologist by training, Meyer lived through the period that regarded insanity exclusively as a "brain disease." Wherever his studies took him in Europe, the dictum that mental disorder must have a corresponding brain lesion was honored. Accordingly, he plunged into neuropathology with dissecting knife and microscope, seeking the elusive cause of insanity. Negative results disillusioned him, but more disenchanting was the absence of interest in the patient as a human being. When called from Illinois to the Worcester Lunatic Hospital in Massachusetts in 1895, he complained in a letter to President Stanley Hall of Clark University that physician assistants in the Illinois asylum had brought him many brains to dissect but had little interest in the patients.

[their] notes...full of reports of queer and "interesting" delusions, of terms like "disturbed," "noisy,"..."untidy" ...usually given in pseudomedical jargon which physicians use with laymen.[16]

Irked by the avoidance of a living clinical approach to the insane on the part of asylum physicians, Meyer evolved the psychobiology of the individual: "...man undissected is more real and important than a divided individual," he wrote. By the time his message was recognized at the New York State Institute and later at Johns Hopkins Hospital, his influence had set the basic tone for American psychiatry in a period when it was still unleavened by psychoanalysis.

Seeing the patient as a person brought another innovation. Doctor Meyer sent his wife, then his social worker staff, to the patient's home in New York City to observe the milieu of the illness, to learn about the patient's emotional history and pre-psychotic behavior. These visits were perhaps the first field studies of the as yet unformed profession of psychiatric social work. As it developed, the profession spearheaded by Mary C. Jarrett and Doctor E. E. Southard, Director of the Boston Psychopathic Hospital, pushed mental hygiene ideas before a large segment of the population in hospitals, clinics, and in the field. One observer at the National Conference of Social Work (1920) stated that social workers proved to be a "landslide for psychiatry."[17]

But ideas do not come out of a void. Other influences were at work in the emergence of Mental Hygiene. For one, the child was receiving attention as a creature entitled to "self-development." As early as 1909 a Swedish feminist, Ellen Key,[18] called for the emancipation of the child from the tyranny of both the factory and the docility of the Little Lord Fauntleroy image. The "seen but not heard" doctrine for children was overwhelmed by an onslaught of developmental studies of children, of concern for their emotional life, and of careful screening of parental emotion. Watson, the behaviorist, advised the "modern" parent to "learn not to talk to children in coddling terms." Neurosis begins with the parents:

> Mother love is a dangerous instrument, an instrument which may inflict a never-healed wound. [19]

Abolition of child labor was followed by an enthronement of children as the first step in universal mental hygiene. Among many others, Gesell and Ilg, at the Yale Clinic of Child Development, studied the behavior of children from early ages, transforming grandmother's knowledge of "what's good for a child" to scientific programs. Child Study Associations and the Child Guidance movement became one of the entering wedges of Mental Hygiene into the public consciousness.

Child guidance became involved with juvenile delinquency; psychologically informed ideas replaced punishment or hortatory lectures by parents, clergymen, or teachers. Doctor William Healy in Chicago, serving the Juvenile Court in that city (1899), began making psychiatric evaluations of youthful behavior disturbances—lying, stealing, truancy, sexual misconduct, vandalism, assaults. Healy's pioneer work in the Juvenile Psychopathic Institute (1909) transferred to the Judge Baker Guidance Clinic in Boston, became the keystone of the new mental hygiene attack on delinquency. [20] Children's crimes, regarded as a reflection of slum poverty and "depravity" of parents, were now found to rest on the basis of neglect, ignorance, and the suppression of normal "instinctive urges." The sting of criminal prosecution was replaced by a calm, inquiring attitude seeking for the emotional causes of delinquency.

Healy, with his wife, Augusta Bronner, developed the "team" concept of handling juvenile offenders—combining the talents and skills of psychiatrists, social workers, psychologists—in his clinic. From this evolved the essential structure of the child guidance movement, and Orthopsychiatry as a discipline. An Institute for Child Guidance, founded by Doctors Lawson Lowry and David Levy in New York, trained workers and doctors for the "team approach." School problems, phobias, compulsive habits, tics, enuresis, and the myriad troubles that parents expected children to "outgrow" became the material for analysis and treatment. The Commonwealth Fund, uniting with the National Committee, proposed a five-year program in 1921 to develop the child guidance movement with the ultimate aim of preventing juvenile delinquency.

If children commit crimes out of emotional frustration and rejection, was it possible that adult criminals could be approached in the same way? The law's attitude towards criminals stood on the solid ground that convicts were "evil," or mentally defective or physically inferior. Had not Lombroso shown that "moral imbecility, epilepsy and the born criminal belong to the same natural family"? Did not an American penologist, Henry Boies, state, "The cause of crime is the moral depravity of the criminal..."? It required two decades of this century to prove Lombroso wrong. Charles Goring in England in 1913[21] proved that the signs of degeneracy—"the outstanding ears, voluminous jaw, thin upperlip...the low brow..." did not characterize British convicts; and Bernard Glueck,[22] examining prisoners in New York's Sing Sing (1918), determined that mental defectiveness was *not* a major finding among convicts. Doctor Glueck turned his attention to personality distortions and neurotic tendencies as the cause of crime. Clearly, the answer to the prevention of crime lay in guiding the child and removing emotional distortions among youth.

But many did not take to psychiatry (or rehabilitation) for prisoners so readily. A West Virginia judge, at the turn of the century, upheld the rule of punishment for crime:

> The morality of our laws is the morality of the Mosaic interpretation of the Ten Commandments, modified only as to the degree and kind of punishment.[23]

An editorial in *Scientific American* in 1912 lamented the new tendency to soften penal punishment:

... there is a tendency to make prisons so comfortable that one is puzzled why those against whom indictments have finally been secured, do not immediately enter these luxurious institutions, instead of wasting so much of the time of jurymen... there is constant agitation for the substitution of trepanning for hanging... of optometry for trial by jury or treatment by a nose and throat specialist, or by the adjustment of proper spectacles... may nevertheless, by the exercise of a little consideration, yield to deep breathing, or the rest cure, or the hot air apparatus, and the like.[24]

Such carpings meant little to active mental hygienists. Opportunities in schools for improving behavior spread to colleges and high schools. Investigators moved into fields previously held to be the domain of fate or God. The problem of unemployables, of prostitution, of illegitimacy, of suicide, even of industrial conflict or inefficiency were discussed in the official journal *Mental Hygiene*. E. E. Southard of Harvard, writing in that journal, stated prophetically in 1920: "Industrial medicine exists; industrial psychiatry ought to exist." World War I proved the vulnerability of men under fire; a decade of study of social problems indicated the vulnerability of children and adults alike under stress. Enough of psychoanalysis was known by the public to alert them to the tremendous implications of modern methods of understanding man's emotions. A dozen authors explained psychoanalysis to the lay public, dozens more popularized psychology in bowdlerized versions. The Overstreets wrote a book titled *The Mature Mind* (1949), which met with great success, and Doctor Karl Menninger, co-founder of the Menninger Clinic in Topeka, Kansas, summarized what laymen should know in an immensely readable book, *The Human Mind* (1930). Even the Great Depression of 1929 and the '30s did not stay the progress of mental hygiene as an accepted movement in American as well as in European life.

The decade 1940–1950 witnessed an even more spectacular spread of mental hygiene attitudes. Competent publicists, Albert Deutsch, Albert Q. Maisel and others, familiarized the public with psychologic and psychiatric contributions to mental hygiene in journals, books, the press and radio. Mental hygiene moved into a permanent place in our national format by the passage of the Vocational Rehabilitation Act in 1942 to which provisions for psychiatric disabilities were added.[25] The National Mental Health Act, passed in 1946 by the Congress of the United States, expanded training of personnel as well as research and improvement in mental health services under the guidance of the United States Public Health Service. Congressional and state legislation followed as the enormity of the mental health problem was borne home by the war and its aftermath. The Hill-Burton Act of 1946 increased the psychiatric facilities in general hospitals throughout the land; and finally the establishment of the National Institute of Mental Health (1949) fixed concern with mental problems as an ineradicable duty for our government.

The World Federation for Mental Health, cooperating with the World Health Organization, under the United Nations, held their first meeting in London in 1948. The program transcended mental illness and reached out to include, in the words of Brock Chisholm, Executive Secretary of the Interim Commission of the World Health Organization, "responsibility, [among] mental hygienists, for a co-ordinated attack on world problems of inter-relationships."[26] The representatives of the Western nations, of Asia, North America, the Soviet Union and its satellites, sat in congress in London, asking profound questions:

> Can catastrophe of a third world war be averted? Can the people of the world learn to co-operate for the good of all?[27]

and the answer given was, "Perhaps the most important contribution of Social Sciences in their joint approach ... is the recognition of the plasticity of human behavior."

A half century of mental hygiene effort convinced many that human behavior could indeed be modified. In the process, what had been considered "personal" and the concern of parents, clergymen, and law enforcement agents, now became the substances of mental health programs. The tradition of privacy between patient and doctor gradually dissolved as Social Psychiatry, analogous to Public Health, evolved. Psychiatrists talked of dealing with "social realities,"[28] a harbinger of Community Psychiatry—the minority problem, housing, youth work, integration, social welfare, senior citizens, etc.

An early start in Community Psychiatry was initiated by a study of state and private hospitals for the mentally ill. It was questioned whether therapeutic procedures really reflected the needs of patients, whether the "milieu," the world in which hospitalized patients lived, was aimed towards their betterment or followed the needs of doctors and administrators.[29] Under a grant from the National Institute of Mental Health, Stanton and Schwartz started a trend resulting in moving mental patients back to the community where they originated to better serve their emotional needs. Community treatment, in place of state hospitalization, progressed rapidly throughout the 1960s, when halfway houses, community residences, and mental health centers were utilized to serve patients in a more homelike and less institutionalized atmosphere. Legislatures of the leading states—New York, California, Massachusetts, Minnesota, etc.—enacted statutes [30] that ended the "inappropriate, indefinite and involuntary commitment of mentally disordered persons" under the philosophy that "mentally handicapped persons...are entitled to normal residential surroundings...provided in the local community...or in general hospitals" (California Mental Health Services Act).[31]

The net effect of community treatment of mentally ill persons has been virtually to empty the state hospitals and stimulate medical and psychiatric treatment in the areas where the patients resided. As McGarry and Kaplan pointed out, "we have come full circle" from the time when private "mad-houses" and asylums housed those who could afford treatment and the almshouses and jails domiciled those who could not. More significantly, the right to treatment for the underprivileged and those in institutions has been written into the law by court decisions (Wyatt *v.* Stickney, Alabama Federal District Court, 1971). In fact, the "open door" policy in mental health facilities across the land has given help to many who would not ordinarily request psychologic aid for help with their problems in living.

One of the areas invaded by Community Psychiatry is that of delinquency and crime. The original notion expounded by Doctors E. E. Southard and Mary Jarett in their book *The Kingdom of Evils,* that "social maladjustments" should be regarded in a clinical light,[32] stimulated the Healys and others to treat juvenile delinquents as juvenile (neurotic) behavior problems. Under the stimulus of an expanding use of psychotherapy in social problems, a few pioneers attempted to treat adult offenders (felons) in penal institutions and probation clinics. In the late 1930s and 1940s, Robert Lindner[33] analyzed a chronic burglar in a federal penitentiary with deep hypnosis. Ben Karpman[34] at St. Elizabeth's Hospital used psychoanalytic methods (principly following Stekel) on numerous major criminals, notably psychopaths. Arthur Foxe[35] coined the term "criminosis" to show the relation between neurosis and criminality as an aid to treatment concepts. The present author treated a few felons on probation in New York County Courts in the 1930s. Following the World War II experience, a group of dedicated psychiatrists (Guttmacher, Schmeideberg, Banay, Brancale, and others) in penal institutions and clinics began the tedious task of applying psychotherapeutic principles to criminal offenders. In these situations the thorny problem of treating psychopaths and professional criminals who had little motivation for becoming better adjusted, blocked treatment efforts.[36] Still, psychiatrists with psychoanalytic leanings plunged into this disheartening work as the issue of whether psychopathic personalities were treatable or not[37] continued to be debated in the literature.

The basic tenet in this attempt to therapeutize criminals lay in the attitude that crime represents *misbehavior* rather than *evil* per se. The offender, viewed as one with a neurosis or character defect (the *criminosis* of Foxe), acts out his psychologic conflicts on his victim in contradistinction to the "neurotic" whose symptoms caused him or her to suffer. The therapeutic problem involved is to convince the offender that his acts were caused by neurotic conflicts and are thus susceptible to analysis, hypnosis, or other type of counseling. Although the semantic change from *evil* propensities to *neurotically directed* misbehavior may have sounded trifling to some, it does involve tremendous attitudinal changes of the kind the mental hygiene movement fostered. Though combated as an indication of "mollycoddling" criminals, and though criticized as irrelevant by sociologists who insisted crime is purely social and cultural in origin, the psychological treatment of offenders (juvenile and adult) has crept on since the 1940s: many penal institutions attempt treatment programs and many individuals on probation are seen in clinics and private offices.

It must be admitted, in view of the increase in crime both in its incidence and in its spread to affluent or middle-class groups in our society, that early psychoanalytic interpretations of crime no longer hold. It was Freud who offered the suggestion of a "criminality from a sense of guilt" but later studies have not corroborated this hypothesis. Aggression in crime has its own life, untouched by guilt and considered in our present social climate as a human right.[38] This changed attitude, especially among young adults, has led to the idea that the most effective treatment for crime with potential offenders—the oncoming generation—would be through a vast educational program via that new breeder of attitudes, television.

It is here that mental health propaganda could possibly make its message both effective and viable.

The spread of mental health concepts has been so vast and all-inclusive that *Mental Hygiene,* a journal that published articles for the profession for fifty years, has changed its name and format in 1970 to *M. H.,* "designed for policy-makers—both lay and professional—in the mental health field." The aim of the editors is to involve the "growing number of citizens faced with major policy decisions" in public situations that affect mental health. These can be population control, abortions, ecology, civil rights, pollution, and social planning of many descriptions. The Community Mental Health Services Act of 1963 opened up areas far beyond traditional clinical practice, areas that call for the viewpoints and knowledge of sociologists, attorneys, legislators, and administrators.

So mental hygiene, the catalyst that brought about vast changes in public attitudes towards the mentally ill, moved to the position of an active participant in mental healing on a grand scale. The movement that started as a stimulus to improved care of hospital patients evolved into a process of emotional education and ultimately a form of social action. While modern psychology and psychiatry were aborning, mental hygiene catapulted them into vigorous adulthood. The mental sciences, given the pragmatic test, were as predicted by Adolf Meyer in 1928—"assimilated in the common sense of tomorrow."[39]

Notes to Chapter 11

1. H. S. Commager, *The American Mind,* New Haven, Yale Press, 1950, p. 41.
2. *Harper's Magazine:* Vol. 99-105, New York, 1900–1905.
3. *Macmillan Magazine:* Vol. 82-93, London, 1900–1905.
4. Albert Deutsch, *The Mentally Ill in America,* 2d ed., rev., New York, Columbia Univ. Press, p. 301 *et seq.*
5. Thayer Smith, *The Human Body and Its Health, A Text Book for Schools, Having Special Reference to the Effects of Stimulants and Narcotics on the Human System,* New York, American Book Company, 1884, p. 154.

6. E. B. Hoag, *Health Studies, Applied Physiology and Hygiene*. Boston, Heath, 1909, p. 52.
7. A. Deutsch, p. 310.
8. Isaac Ray, *Mental Hygiene*, Boston, Ticknor & Fields, 1863.
9. W. C. Beers, *A Mind That Found Itself*, ed. 2, New York, Longmans, 1910.
10. J. K. Winkler and W. Bromberg, *Mind Explorers*, New York, Reynal & Hitchcock, 1939, Chapters 8 and 12.
11. Ralph B. Perry, *The Thought and Character of William James*, Cambridge, Harvard University Press, 1948, p. 250.
12. Thomas W. Salmon, "A County Poor Farm," *Mental Hygiene*, No. 1, Jan. 1917, p. 25.
13. Nina Ridenour, *Mental Hygiene in the United States: A Fifty Year History*, Cambridge, Harvard University Press, 1961.
14. E. D. Bond, *Thomas Salmon, Psychiatrist*, New York, Norton, 1950, p. 104.
15. William James, *The Energies of Man*, New York, Holt, 1916.
16. Adolf Meyer, *The Worcester Plan, A Holograph Letter to Stanley Hall*, Roche Co., 1895.
17. Jessie Taft, "The New Impulse in Mental Hygiene," *Pub. Health Nurse*, Oct. 1919.
18. Ellen Key, *The Century of the Child*, trans. by M. Franzos, New York, Putnam, 1909.
19. J. B. Watson and R. R. Watson, *Psychological Care of Infant and Child*, New York, Norton, p. 87.
20. William Healy and Augusta Bronner, *Delinquents and Criminals*, New York, Macmillan Co., 1926.
21. Charles Goring, *The English Convict*, London, His Majesty's Statery Office, 1913.
22. Bernard Glueck, "A Study of 608 Admissions to Sing Sing Prison," *Mental Hygiene*, Vol. 2, Jan. 1918, p. 881.
23. Moore v. Stickling: W. Va. 515:33:S.E. 274, Court of Appeals. Apr. 1899.
24. Editorial, "Lunacy and Morals," *Scientific American*, July 1912, p. 22.
25. "The Vocational Rehabilitation Act Amendment, 1943," *J.A.M.A.* 123:572, 1943.
26. Brock Chisholm, "Organization for World Health," *Ment. Hygiene*, Vol. 32, 364:1948.
27. H. K. Lewis, International Preparatory Commission, Intern. Congress of Mental Health, London, Aug. 1945, p. 5.
28. Sol W. Ginsburg, "Mental Health and Social Issues of Our Time," *Jour. of Orthopsychiatry*, Vol. 20, Apr. 1950, p. 267.
29. Alfred H. Stanton and Morris S. Schwartz, *The Mental Hospital: A Study of Institutional Participation in Psychiatric Illness and Treatment*, New York, Basic Books, Inc., 1954.
30. Louis McGarry and Honora Kaplan, "Overview: Current Trends in Mental Health Laws," *J. Psych.*, Vol. 130, June 1973, p. 621.
31. Community Mental Health Services: Lanterman-Petris-Short Act,

Amended by Stats. 1968. Governor's Re-organization Plan, No. 1, 1970.

32. E. E. Southard and Mary Jarett, *The Kingdom of Evils*, New York, Macmillan, 1922.

33. Robert Lindner, *Rebel Without A Cause: The Hypnoanalysis of a Criminal Psychopath*, New York, Grune & Stratton, 1944.

34. Ben Karpman, *The Sexual Offender and His Offenses*, New York, Julian Press, 1954.

35. Arthur Foxe, "Classification of the Criminotic Individual," in *Handbook of Correctional Psychology*, ed. by Robt. Lindner and Robert Seliger, New York, Philosophical Library, 1947.

36. Hervey Cleckley, *The Mask of Sanity*, 2nd ed., St. Louis, C. V. Mosby Co., 1950.

37. Walter Bromberg, "The Treatability of the Psychopath," *Amer. J. of Psychiatry*, Vol. 110, No. 8, Feb. 1954, p. 604.

38. Walter Bromberg, "Is Punishment Dead?" *Am. J. Psych.*, Vol. 127, Aug. 1970, p. 163.

39. Adolf Meyer, "The 'Complaint' as the Center of Genetic-Dynamic and Nosological Teaching in Psychiatry," *New Engl. J. of Med.*, Vol. 199, 1928.

The Freudian Reign—Dissenters and Champions

W HEN Freud's *Introductory Lectures* reached the English-speaking public in 1916, his discoveries of the unconscious and of the hidden sexual life and its influence on nervous ailments literally overturned the psychiatric world. This eventuality, however, was slow in developing its full impact. Meanwhile, a small band of psychiatrists in New York, studying Freud's writings in German, met in private to report their experiences with the new methods. The New York Psychoanalytic Society, organized in 1909, discussed cases analyzed by men like A. A. Brill, Clarence Oberndorf, Trigant Burrow, and Adolph Stern. About the same time interest in psychoanalysis had been stimulated by a few psychiatrists in Boston and Washington, D.C.

With the end of World War I, communications between Europe and this country increased and with it a flow of publications on Freudian methods of treatment. In the 1920s there were still too few who understood Freudian psychology and were equipped to enter this complex field. But the imagination of neurologists and psychiatrists had been captured: Their indifferent results with routine bromides, static electricity, and placebos impelled them to enter this new field without adequate training. Equipped with a few ideas and several hours of free associations, they proceeded to inform their patients of the complexes unearthed, whereupon the "analysis" was then considered completed. "Cures" reported by physicians who indulged in "wild" analysis were commonly reported. Ferenczi characterized such extravagant claims of treatment as due to the "blissful mood into which acquaintance with the unconscious transports one." He recognized (1919) the "honeymooning months" of analysis as the period when the patient flourished on the permissivity and the understanding of the therapist.[1]

In America especially, "wild analysis" grew in association with the psychoanalytic invasion of literature.[2] In the decade 1912 to 1922, stimulated by James Joyce's appropriation of symbolism and unconscious motivation in literature (*Ulysses*, 1922), writers and playwrights adopted Freudianism as their guide. The adoption of Freudian thinking amounted to no less than a literary revolution. Writers varied in their attitudes: Bernard DeVoto wrote: "[Freudianism]... was one of the fads that periodically rage through the antechambers and subbasements of literature."[3] In 1923 Gilbert Chesterton, author and Catholic apologist, unloosed his blasts at the "Freudian intellectual bullies... with their monomania of sex,..." He continued:

> Psychoanalysis can no longer be dismissed as a fad; it has risen to the dignity of a fashion.... It stands now in the open street, visible to the man in the street like some florid and magnificent tailor's dummy outside a tailor's shop. And...as a humble passer-by, it is time that somebody knocked the stuffing out of it....[4]

A more thoughtful analysis of psychoanalysis as it affected the layman was given by Walter Lippmann. Acknowledging that a layman could not properly assess Freud's researches, Lippmann pointed out that "Freud has a way of revealing corners of the soul which we believed were safe from anybody's knowledge."[5] This eminent essayist caught the pitch of public reaction: "This uncanny wisdom [of psychoanalysis] is to most people both fascinating and horrible. They can neither take hold nor let go."

As noted, the availability of Freud's *Introductory Lectures* in English together with Brill's translation of Freud's papers, opened the floodgates to the medical and general public. The greatest attraction undoubtedly was Freud's freedom with psychosexuality and its repression as the key to the formation of neurosis. For many, investigation of the sexual life and the place of the unconscious in our psychic lives produced a sense of liberation, a sense of excitement difficult to describe. It was as if a veil had been lifted on an area of life many had speculated on but few dared to explore. The author's first contact occurred, as an undergraduate at the University of Cincinnati, when the Leopold-Loeb case in Chicago (1922) was directing attention to dynamic psychiatry. Famous alienists like Drs. Jelliffe, Bernard Glueck, and William White, in testifying at the trial, openly discussed homosexuality and other obscure tendencies among young men. While the professors in the Psychology Department at the University were wary of admitting Freud's ideas to *academe*, the students became instant psychoanalysts, recognizing phallic symbols in church steeples, complexes in their associates, the Oedipus situation in hitherto prosaic friends.

Meanwhile, American analysts were journeying to Vienna to be treated and instructed by Freud himself. Dr. Abram Kardiner started treatment in 1919; others followed. Years later (1974) Kardiner related his experiences in Vienna: "In analysis, Freud made a beeline for the Oedipal conflict. His favorite way of resolving this syndrome was in terms of 'unconscious homosexual conflicts.'"[6] With the spread of psychoanalytic treatment and teaching, some of the irritation produced by Freud's theories decreased. Rivers, an English psychiatrist, remarked in 1919 on how "great an extent the psychoneurosis of warfare supported the views of Freud."[7] And a religionist, some ten years later, writing on psychoanalysis as the only subject, aside from religion, "provocative of such violent and contradictory opinion today," agreed that the psychoanalyst "can do much to help in individual reconstruction."[8] When the King of Critics, H. L. Mencken, placed his imprimatur on Freudianism as "the twentieth century's version of man's struggle against fate, in a new form,"[9] the profound insights of "depth psychology" became a fixed aspect of the sophisticated literary and psychologic scenes.

There was, however, still an underground swell of opposition towards accepting Freudian principles among neurologists and medical men in the late 1920s. The defections of Jung, Adler, and Rank still irritated some American analysts. A meeting at the New York Academy of Medicine, arranged in the interests of amity among Jungian and Freudian analysts, illustrates this point. Dr. Esther Harding, a Jungian, was invited by several New York analysts, among them Drs. Brill, Jelliffe, and Oberndorf, to sit down in conference to reconcile their differences. After a polite skirmish, Dr. Harding reported an involved dream of a patient she had analyzed in terms of archetypal and collective unconscious elements. As she wove ancient symbols and veiled *anima* and *animus* figures through her dream interpretations, Dr. Brill tensed, glancing at the impatient Jelliffe and the gentlemanly Oberndorf. Finally, after an hour, Dr. Brill, unable to contain himself, burst out: "This has nothing to do with analysis...I can do nothing with these symbols."[10]

Neurologists objected to capitulating to distorted sexual impulses in explanation of complicated clinical problems. The florid language of analysis in common currency among psychoanalytically trained physicians—organ inferiority, penis envy, dammed libido, anal erotism, clitoral orgasm, Oedipus and Electra complexes—raised the hackles of the older group.

For the younger generation of psychiatrists, criticism fell on deaf ears. The younger men were delighted with this new linguistic equipment: It provided a passport to the higher realm of understanding human frailties. The dissension among psychiatric leaders lighted, rather than dimmed, appreciation of the new era. Adler's homespun simplicity contrasted with the impressive mastery of mythological and classical learning of Jelliffe and the earthy observations of Brill. The factors pushing young psychiatrists towards psychoanalysis as the most significant form of treatment were the glamor of the new profession with its esoteric language, freedom in investigating sexual matters, and the intellectual pleasure of dealing with convoluted thinking. The Talmudic preoccupation with intricate suppositions was, in the idiom of the day, a "natural" for the intellectual doctor.

As a resident neurologist at the Mount Sinai Hospital in New York a few years later, the author, along with his colleagues, fell under the sway of Dr. Brill, the acknowledged stimulus for the American psychoanalytic movement. With his pale blue eyes, scraggly Van Dyke beard, and a trace of Austrian accent, he lectured to medical audiences on the psychopathology of everyday life. There were few psychiatric congresses that did not hear Dr. Brill, in or out of the meeting halls, expound his contact with Dr. Jung at Burgholzli in the early days; his analysis on the basis of anal erotism of Abraham Lincoln's mordant humor; his handling of analytic patients. His informality, charm and directness provided the window through which the "crepuscular light of psychoanalysis"[11] first filtered to a generation of eager young psychiatrists.

State hospitals where most young psychiatrists received their training reflected this enthusiasm. At the Manhattan State Hospital on Ward's Island, New York, preoccupation with the "new" dynamic views introduced by psychoanalysis divided the staff into the old-line descriptive psychiatrists and the inspired neophytes.[12] But probing the depths of libidinal displacements in dementia praecox or paranoid cases was not the same as analytic treatment of neurotics. A didactic analysis was necessary to expose the unconscious difficulties within the analyst himself. The euphoria that attended the neophytes' entry into training at the New York Psychoanalytic Institute (and elsewhere) lay upon the assumption that psychoanalysis represented a truly scientific, i.e., predictive, psychotherapy. As a candidate, the author underwent a didactic analysis by Dr. Abram Kardiner and later by Dr. Adolph Stern. Both had been trained by Freud in Vienna. In effect the author became, figuratively speaking, a grandson of Professor Freud. From the 1930s onward, psychoanalytic thinking and technique were tacitly assumed to be the basis of any meaningful psychotherapy in the major centers throughout the eastern United States.

Psychoanalysis as a method of treatment had been fairly well codified by the 1920s. For the layman, books describing the basic ideas, summaries of summaries, and popular articles appeared in great numbers. For the profession, Ernest Jones' summary (1913)[13] of treatment procedure was set down as (a) a recital of the patient's life story with careful notation of amnesias, (b) the word association test of Jung to find clues for further analysis, (c) analysis of slips of the tongue, dreams, symbolic movements, and free associations. One of the earliest manuals for the student analyst was *Glover's Technique of Psycho-Analysis*,[14] published for the *International Journal of Psycho-Analysis*. It contained a thorough and much more sophisticated account of transference, counter-transference, defense analysis, terminal phase and "active" treatment. As the technique evolved, publications increased in geometric proportions. The *Psychoanalytic Review* had been established in 1913 by White and Jelliffe, and the *International Journal of Psychoanalysis*, published in London, appeared soon after; meanwhile, many psychology journals featured articles on the subject.

To detail the technique of psychoanalytic treatment would stretch beyond the confines of this book. Many competent texts and summarizations exist for professional and lay readers, which are authoritative and complete. For present purposes it will be sufficient to point to some of the major problems facing psychoanalytic practitioners 40 years ago. These related to resistance, defense mechanisms, and the transference.

Resistance of the patient to uncovering buried material led to the problem of the *transference,* in which painful, repressed memories and impulses were transferred to the doctor. Thus unconscious love and hate feelings derived from the patient's early experiences with parents were lived out in the analysis.[15] The transference-relationship became the fulcrum around which the patient accepted the analyst's interpretation of unconscious findings; it allowed assimilation into the personality of uncovered wishes and drives through the authority and the influence of the therapist.

The unexpected depth of relationship between neurotic patient and analyst, the complex expression of resistances within the patient, forced the necessity of an analysis of the analyst in order that the therapist might become acquainted with his own blind spots. Investigators of the unconscious "subjected themselves...to the same sort of searching character-analysis to which their patients were being subjected at their hands."[16] This preparation, now a regular feature of the psychoanalyst's training, was further stimulated by the uncovering of counter-transference, a reciprocal re-experiencing of the analyst's unconscious wishes and attitudes in and through the patient. The eternal vigilance of analysts to their own unconscious trends represents the first occasion on which the human instrument of psychotherapy—the therapist himself—was subjected to analysis.

As experience accumulated, the living out of the patient's early feelings on the analyst, i.e., the transference with interpretations of the unconscious meaning of his behavior, was found to be insufficient for a permanent cure.

It required a "working through" of those infantile feelings and impulses that shaped the patient's neurosis and life pattern. Psychoanalysis did not seek to impart ethical teachings or superimpose the physician's attitude on the patient; it sought to "release the individual from the domination of regressive tendencies and infantile fixations," which appeared as neurotic symptoms. Treatment was an emotional experience, not an intellectual one, which required a "living through" of the infantile neurosis in the analysis, with all its frustrations, deprivations, rejections, denials, pleasure-seeking, and hostilities.[17]

The expectation that uncovering unconscious wishes, making conscious the unconscious, would suffice to remove the symptoms met with dissatisfaction in some quarters. The "essential remodeling" was left to the patient, when the ego had been "weaned" from its infantile libidinal attachments. It was assumed the ego, once more in control of instinctual impulses, could then adapt itself to demands of reality in conformance with social rules and mores. The patient would be free to work, love, and relate himself to others unhampered by infantile, regressive tendencies. Although analysis exposed the basic forces at work in the conflict, what of *synthesis*? This was a question many asked. How could the mobilized infantile fixations be aided in their assimilation into the personality? Did the filling of gaps, restitution of distortions in the history of the patient's libido development, complete the therapeutic work?

Some psychotherapists had begun to question whether the synthesizing element in analytic treatment was not a separate factor. Morton Prince,[18] for example, felt that "repersonalization," a process of integration occurring within the personality, as seen in the merging of multiple personalities within one ego after hypnosis, was the active force involved. And Jung departed from Freudian psychoanalysis in part on the issue of a need for active synthesis in a patient through the "therapist's ultimate conviction... and search of those religio-philosophic conceptions which correspond to the emotional state of the patient."[19]

This attempt to synthesize the elements analyzed out, engendered one of the first dissensions. Theoretical differences between Freud and Jung were great enough to divorce Jung's analytical psychology from psychoanalysis as a system of therapy. Disagreement occurred early regarding the concept of libido, the biologic instinctive force whose repressions and displacements during childhood were considered as the cause of neurosis. Jung viewed libido as a deeper force than implied by Freud; it was part of the creative energy, *elan vital*, common to the race of man. Hence Jung's analyses[20] searched for racial images and archetypes represented in the *racial* or *collective unconscious* shared by each individual. His therapy called upon the creative force, one aspect of which represented spiritual yearning.

Here lay a real difference of opinion. In its application, the difference would appear thus: For Jung, the explanation of night terrors in children lay in a revival of ancient racial fears; for Freud, it connoted the anxiety arising from the revival of the child's unconscious fear of its father (Oedipus complex) displaced and symbolized in some terrorizing dream figure such as an animal. The archetype of the racial mother was of greater importance to Jung than was the father-image to Freud. The mother, Jung concluded, lay deep in the consciousness of human beings; the first instincts of the child and the last thoughts of man are toward the mother.

Treatment of the Jungian school aims to analyze the patient into the archetypes we have described, then direct the patient's life along the line of his innate tendencies. As the analysis proceeds, the patient is able to see how the attitudes responsible for his symptoms developed. The patient sees that he or she is fixating on impossible or undesirable objects, reaching back to racial and primitive levels for satisfaction. As this interpretation of dreams goes on, the patient is shown that his tendencies are those of universal mankind, and gradually the patient develops a feeling of "oneness" with all humanity. It is obvious that Freudian analysis and Jungian psychology were as mutually exclusive as their philosophic bases were divergent.

As the implications of Jung's metapsychology extended to mystic symbolism and to a wider horizon of human spirituality, the gulf increased. Glover, an English analyst, threw down the gauntlet to Jungians:

> ...the key to the riddle of Jung's psychology is that Jung is a conscious psychologist;...indeed his whole system is based on conscious and descriptive criteria.... His psychology...has little or no relation to Freudian psychology. The mostly implicit but often explicit tendency of his theories is to prove that Freud's discovery of the unconscious and of the laws that regulate its functions is either inaccurate, totally false, or totally unnecessary. Whether he knows it or not, this is Jung's consuming passion.[21]

The gulf, now an impassable chasm, represented the earliest "separatist" schism from the Freudian movement. Glover's barrage included an attack on the "reactionary" eclectic who obstructs the progress of clinical psychology by seeing some value in Jung's ideas as well as in others. Perhaps a clearer view of Jungian psychology in its comparative and practical aspect is given in Crichton-Miller's paradigm: "That Freud's psychology is most intricate, evading subjective (spiritual) difficulties in its objective approach, and hence most appealing to intellectuals and Jews; that Jung's psychology is most profound, congenial to limited groups, as mystics and introverts; that Adler's psychology is most practical, superficial and sociologic."[22]

The name of Alfred Adler brings forth another dissident who sought to supply what he considered a deficiency in the early libido theory, namely, the problem of the "character" of the neurotic individual. Just as Jung was intent on supplying a *Weltanschauung* for the patient to aid in synthesizing the ego after analysis, and as Horney later sought to remedy the lack of sociologic orientation, so Adler, starting with compensations for organic inferiorities, developed a therapy based on the total directiveness of the personality—the *life-plan*.[23] Treatment by Adler's Individual Psychology, accordingly, is not so deep as in orthodox psychoanalysis. It aims in a practical way to satisfy the desire common to neurotics and nonneurotics to achieve satisfaction from life. The patient's life is searched for evidences of the struggle between superiority and inferiority that run from childhood onward.

For Adler, the moving factor in the emotional life of people, neurotic or otherwise, was the will to dominate.[24] The philosophy behind Adler's school of Individual Psychology was readily understandable; for this reason Adler's theories were accepted, without much resistance, in Europe and in this country. The aim of the Adlerians was to bring the message of Individual Psychology to the people, and the writings of his disciples deal as much with the problems of the unhappy, unfulfilled, but not actually ill, groups of persons as with definite cases of neurosis. These developments, in addition to the denial of the sexual doctrines of Freud, gave the Adlerian psychology a popular appeal that was lacking in the orthodox psychoanalytic school. Adler's emphasis had been on therapy primarily. The most important thing in life is the goal toward which each individual strives. It is unformed and undifferentiated in childhood, but more specific and recognizable in adult life. It is, indeed, a *life-plan*. Deserting the unconscious, and the essentially sexual theory of the neurosis, Adler, as did Jung, moved to another level of psychologic treatment.

As psychoanalytic procedures became refined, it became important to define the part played in the patient's ego by the forces labelled as "id" (the reservoir of primitive, infantile impulses of which the patient is unaware). On rethinking the libido theory, so called, Freud in 1922 published *The Ego and the Id*,[25] which reorganized his psychoanalytic theory and the direction of treatment. In it he recognized the id and superego (conscience) as unconscious forces with which the ego contended. Treatment was enlarged to include the ego defenses against these unconscious, and neurosis-stimulating, forces in other than hysterical neuroses.[26] The new "ego psychology" broadened the scope of therapy to include borderline states: depression, schizoid characters and, later, psychoses, in addition to hysteria, anxiety neurosis, obsessions, and phobias. Treatment manifestly required more time, two years or more of intensive work for patient and therapist. The goals of treatment were more clearly delineated, the "phases" of the analysis defined within limits and crucial technical problems of the transference worked out to the point at which they could be taught to students and practitioners of psychoanalysis.[27] Recognized earlier by Freud as an artificial situation, the "transference neurosis" now formed a vital aspect of the treatment process.

Knowledge of the uniqueness of the transference situation placed the analysis of neurotic patients on a more certain basis. The task of therapy could now be stated:

> Generally stated, [it] is to *mobilize* the energies of the id, to make the super-ego more tolerant, and to help the ego regain its synthetic and sublimating faculties as well as its own function of undisturbed perception and purposeful action. Through this change in the id, ego and super-ego, the neurotic will lose his anxiety caused by the danger which seems to accompany his instinct-demands, and will learn to react to them adequately and without fear. The task of therapy is therefore very complicated.[28]

With organization of analytic technique and a fairly satisfactory metapsychological theory, psychoanalysis had advanced in the 1930s to the position of a vast body of illuminating clinical knowledge, an intricate and time-consuming therapeutic procedure. The mainstream of psychoanalysts still consider psychoanalysis as (a) a body of knowledge of the ego and its unconscious elements, (b) a method of research into abnormalities and normalities of personality function, (c) a theoretical system covering behavior, feeling, and thinking of human beings of genetic and dynamic type, and (d) a technique of treatment of mental and emotional disturbances.

The tremendous body of literature on the practice and theory of psychoanalysis that accumulated between 1930 and 1950 cannot be summarized in a large volume, much less in a paragraph. (It should be added that writings on psychoanalysis and its modifications, including brief therapies, have reached gigantic proportions by the 1970s.) Still, Fenichel's text on *The Psychoanalytic Theory of the Neurosis* (1945)[29] signified a stability to analysis of which he could say, "There are many ways to treat neurotics but only one way to understand them." The circle had become complete; in 1900 Nissl had stated, "We see in all mental derangements the clinical expression of definite disease processes in the cortex,"[30] while in 1954 Stengel wrote, "Dynamic psychiatry is a psychiatry informed by psychoanalysis... in which psychological factors have largely taken the place previously held by heredity or hypothetical organic causes."[31]

The stability of psychoanalytic doctrine, as evolved by Freud and added to by many workers, seemed secure. Jung had developed his own *Analytic Psychology,* Adler his *Individual Psychology,* and Freud, *Psychoanalysis.* The new ego-psychology permitted analysts to enlarge the patient-types they treated. Freud in his *New Introductory Lectures* (1933) commented that patients requested treatment not only for hysteria and obsessions but for depression, dissatisfaction with their lives, loss of efficiency in work, and generalized anxiety. The uses of psychoanalysis extended to what Rieff called "moral pedagogy."[32] Not only personality problems, e.g., character neurosis, but somatic conditions like hypertension and ulcerative colitis were treated analytically by Alexander and his associates at the Chicago Psychoanalytic Institute.[33] Extension to psychosomatic illnesses brought analysis closer to medicine, while it simultaneously called for a somewhat modified technique. In patients without the emotional urgency of the hysteric, progress could be slow. The bland noninterfering attitude of the psychoanalyst seemed to enhance the patient's dependence on the father-figure or increase his hostility.

To interrupt this stagnation, Ferenczi[34] proposed, in accordance with Freud's basic view, that since neurosis originated in frustration, its treatment should be continued in an atmosphere of abstinence. The patient was therefore prohibited from activities that might interfere with exposure of unconscious libido during the analysis. Thus phobic patients were ordered to face their phobias, sexual activities that drained off unconscious gratification were prohibited, and symptomatic acts were curtailed. The meaning of these prohibitions was to have the patient face his inner fears without recourse to his symptomatic defenses. In addition, a time limit was set for the termination of the analysis.[35] The activity proposed by Ferenczi and seconded by Otto Rank added to the notion of shortening the duration of analytic treatment, but it led eventually to Rank's defection from the ranks of orthodox analysts.

Rank's departure from the fold arose from his consideration that anxiety represented the psychic experience of being born into the world. Although common to all mankind, the process of birth, for the neurotic-to-be, involved a basic anxiety situation, which reappeared in the treatment process as a disinclination to leave the protective atmosphere of the analyst. Rank proposed to move directly to this anxiety-provoking situation in the treatment, work it through, and liberate the patient from his "basic" anxiety. For this reason he proposed a time limit for the treatment (the rebirth itself, so to speak). From this premise, Rank considered the transference of patient to physician to be essentially a "duel of wills," the patient desiring to remain in the blissful state of womb-life, resisting efforts of the analyst to be psychologically weaned.[36] The trauma of birth, the fact of being born, Rank insisted, was the precursor of anxiety, which pervades all neuroses. The patient must be freed of his fear to leave the mother so he may develop his own "creative self." For this his "will" required strengthening so that "in the end phase [of psychotherapy] the therapist is to be given up as a leaning post."[37]

The method proposed by Rank (who had a doctorate in anthropology), with its accent on the positive, was readily utilized by psychiatric counselors, especially psychiatric social workers.[38] Freud agreed that the theories of his lieutenant—for Rank stood high with the founder of psychoanalysis—were "bold and ingenious" but not suited for psychoanalysis. The emphasis on birth trauma as the key to anxiety later in life went beyond therapy. For example, one recommendation of the Rankian group was to bring children into the world through Caesarean section to avoid the psychic trauma of natural birth. This and other improvisations aimed to shorten treatment were rejected by Freudians. Stekel, another of Freud's early associates, proposed, for example, that dream analysis be shortened by attending mainly to what the patient reported, i.e., the manifest content, the "microcosm" of the patient's conflict.[39] Rank's and Stekel's innovations alike were disposed of by Freud's comment that "the best way to shorten analysis is to carry it out correctly." Treating the transference as a struggle of wills was, to Freud, the wish to "accelerate the tempo of analytic therapy to suit the rush of American life." By 1937 the final verdict on Rank was handed down: "The theory of and practice of Rank's experiment are now things of the past—no less than American 'prosperity' itself."[40]

In spite of Rank's defection, his ideas made an imprint on psychoanalysis, particularly his interest in anxiety. To Freud, the problem of anxiety was far wider than its involvement with birth trauma. Rethinking the entire crucial question of anxiety, Freud revised his earlier notions in 1926.[41] He now conceived anxiety rather as a function of the ego than as the result of a dammed-up libido. Anxiety was a signal to the ego of an unknown fear. Whereas objective anxiety represented fear of a known danger, as of an accident, neurotic anxiety signified fear of an unknown force. His formulation that anxiety was the response of the ego to pressure from unconscious id and superego forces was assimilated into the instinct theory,[42] moulding the aims of psychoanalytic technique. Anxiety, the prototype of the original helplessness of infantile life, was experienced repetitively by the ego when new dangers arose. Repeated acquaintance with and control over these forces enabled the ego to master this fear. Treatment then could help master anxiety by a process of reeducation of the ego after reviving unconscious traumatic memories.

The issue of anxiety, what caused it, and how it was to be alleviated became a central issue in analytic treatment. During the last half century it also was the concern of philosophers, theologians, and psychologists. Rollo May has demonstrated how, during the nineteenth century, through the efforts of the Danish philosopher Kierkegaard and, later, Freud, anxiety has "emerged as an unavoidable problem"[43] in the psychological life of the individual. Present-day existentialists, following Kierkegaard, have postulated anxiety as a natural state of man when he confronts the possibility of freedom of action in his world. The problem of anxiety merges into the concerns of philosophy and religion. Christian philosophers see anxiety as deriving from man's finiteness in nature in contrast with his potential freedom. A Catholic psychologist, Rudolf Allers, puts the paradox succinctly in *The New Psychologies*: "Anxiety, like guilt, springs from the attitude of revolt against man's limited nature" in contrast with God's. That which has occupied theologians for centuries as a general problem of man became an explicit one for psychotherapists.

The decade 1930 to 1940 witnessed many modifications in the orthodox psychoanalytic school. The issue of anxiety brought divergences from classical analytic techniques.

Karen Horney, trained in Freudian analysis in Berlin, and transplanted to Chicago in 1932, introduced the concept that "basic anxiety" was conditioned by social life.[44] Differing from Freud, who saw anxiety as the result of pressure from intolerable instinctual drives, Horney showed how the child, in a hostile world, develops anxiety because of a "pervading feeling of being lonely and helpless." Thus, basic anxiety was considered a protective device rather than a symptom. Horney's treatment, therefore, helped the patient identify the causes of his anxiety and resolve it by assuming responsibility for his life. Her emphasis was away from rooting out primitive instinctual drives; in fact, she was accused of being antibiological because she questioned some of Freud's sexual accents. Horney tried to show how the culture with its hypocritical values (brotherly love versus dog-eat-dog competition) was the main source of neurotic anxiety. She insisted that real-life problems were more important than a reconstructed history of the patient's childhood emotions. As a female analyst, Horney was criticized for denigrating the sexual basis of the libido theory with its implied masculine bias. As Alexander put it: "Horney tried to create the effigy of a one-sided biologically oriented Freud. Then, in order to destroy this effigy, she became extremely one-sided in the opposite direction."[45]

One significant change in psychoanalytic practice was foreshadowed by Dr. Horney's attack on the neutral, passive attitude of the analyst. The therapeutic goal, to show the patient how he developed his or her neurotic anxiety, required more than the "mirror" attitude of the orthodox analyst. It called for a *constructive friendliness* in which the "whole person" of the therapist participated in the treatment contact. Hence, Horney took a more direct position in conducting the analysis, trying to understand the patient as a social being, not a bundle of primitive impulses, ego resistances, and superego punitive pressures.[46]

Criticism directed against Horney's methods linked her work to that of Alfred Adler, whose emphasis on the social conditioning of neuroses had a long history. The impact of social factors on the growing personality of the child, which Adler urged at the time of his break with Freud, was a believable concept. Moreover, it shortened the time of therapy since the traditional couch was avoided, the treatment being carried on as a *dialogue* between equals. The main emphasis was on pressures in the social environment under which the patient had suffered from childhood. The aim of Adlerian therapy focused on the patient's *life style*, [47] his release from the neurotic "safeguards" he erected to protect himself from inferiority feelings or fears of failure. The stress on the child's smallness in a terrifying world of large adults tended to place the neurotic conflict in the patient on an understandable level of his life experiences.

Adler's Individual Psychology, although submerged by the brilliance of Freudian developments, met with considerably warmer feelings in this country than did Jung's concepts. The former's recognition that women showed neurotic symptoms ("masculine protest") because they were forced into an inferior position in a male-dominated society, his emphasis on aggression as part of the individual's striving to overcome inferiority feelings, Adler's warmth and activity towards the patient, kept Individual Psychology alive on the American scene. [48] Indeed, Adler held the first American Chair of Medical Psychology at the Long Island College of Medicine, Brooklyn, New York, in 1932. (Dr. Franz Alexander was appointed to the first Chair of Psychoanalysis in America at the University of Chicago in 1930.)

Freudian original tenets were opposed in other ways, both theoretically and practically. Amendments and modifications of the practice of classical psychoanalysis increased in number and complexity as the century advanced. One significant change led to analysis of the character structure of the patient rather than to specific symptoms. Wilhelm Reich, a Viennese analyst, concerned with the resistance patients showed on recovering uncon-

scious material, directed his attention to the character structure, the "protecting armor," which shielded the analysand
from uncovering his neurotic pattern.[49] Reich's contribution had the effect of enlarging the field of treatment to
include borderline psychotic states, psychopathic personalities and the like, a group of patients early analysts felt
to be out of the range of psychoanalysis.

Spurred on by a drive to find the basic physical unit of
energy to replace Freud's "libido," Reich discovered the
"orgone...a visible, measurable (unit) of psychic energy of
cosmic nature,"[50] which he felt energized the nervous system, including the genital apparatus. Seeking a way to
measure the basic energy of life—the orgone—Reich developed various electrical devices, including the "orgone
energy accumulator" or "orgone box." At this point his
psychoanalytic colleagues vigorously disowned him. In
1934 Reich was charged with being "in the service of Communist ideology" and broke with organized psychoanalysis. His treatment of orgone deficiency with the orgone box brought him into conflict with federal law in the
State of Maine. Convicted, cut adrift by his colleagues as
paranoid, he died in prison (1957). Reich's life was capped
by a "distressing denouement, the spectacle of a major
system of mental healing seemingly gone mad," but as
this recent commentator pointed out, "paradoxically
Reich's influence has grown in the counter-culture" of
today.[51]

A more practical development in improving the efficiency of analytic treatment was initiated by Franz Alexander, whose principle of flexibility ushered in a new era in
psychoanalytic treatment. Alexander, a transplanted
Berlin-trained analyst, whose work in criminology and in
psychosomatic medicine were milestones in the progress of
dynamic psychiatry, initiated the "brief" analysis, which,
among other innovations, brought the time consumed by
treatment into manageable proportions. Like Oberndorf,[52]
who had questioned "the permanency of results" in relation to the length of treatment, Alexander courageously

asked whether the *ritual* of analytic technique was the same as the *essence* of the analytic process. Bringing the patient's unconscious motivations into awareness in the transference constituted the essence of psychoanalytic practice. Hence, the frequency of visits should be curtailed and interruptions in treatment arranged, to discourage the patient's dependency upon the analyst.[53] Further, Alexander pointed to the "corrective emotional experience" as the vital factor in analytic cure, not insight or knowledge gained of the unconscious. Short-term psychotherapy so modified psychoanalytic technique that it formed the "core of our present-day concepts"[54] of psychodynamic psychotherapy.

The subtle alteration of the therapist's position vis-a-vis the patient from a silent observer sitting out of sight of the patient neither exerting pressure nor giving advice, to a real person with values and attitudes, softened the isolation of the patient. The newer methods leaned towards therapy as a learning process.[55] The ego, equipped with some basic (instinctual) "inherited reflexes," "adapts" itself to the environment by learning what is self-preservative and what is harmful.[56] Learning theory as applied to psychoanalysis broadened its base to include psychological developments, which will be dealt with in a subsequent chapter. Simultaneously, analysts like Kardiner[57] and Fromm[58] explored the effect of cultural and mass pressures on the individual neurosis. For example, Kardiner, who studied veterans of World War I, victims of "shell shock," found the trauma of war to be a direct cause of traumatic neurosis, wherein the affront was not on the sexual instincts but on life-preservative ones.[59] Harry Stack Sullivan, treating schizophrenic individuals, reformulated the treatment situation to the end that persons entered analysis, not as inert subjects waiting for the magic skill of the analyst wielding his wonders, but as participants in an "expert-client" situation.[60]

The main elements of Freud's discoveries were not discarded in these developments, but new aspects of the doctor-patient relationship inevitably resulted in modified treatment techniques. Psychoanalysts adhering closely to the "classic analysis" attitude were not unmindful of the need to refine their instruments. Among these was Paul Federn,[61] who painstakingly enlarged the technique, originally suggested by Ferenczi, by "nourishing the transference through sincerity and kindness," avoiding free association and watching the reality relationship which lay behind the unconscious material. One of Federn's helpful innovations consisted in supplying a female assistant to the male analyst to strengthen the trust of sensitive, especially schizoid, patients. Empathic sensitivity of the therapist and the freedom to express his or her personality in a warm, "motherly" way toward the patient mitigated some of the desolate loneliness of the schizophrenic. Gertrude Schwing, a Viennese worker, carried this instinctive "motherliness" to her patients to the point of offering them fruit or candy, combing their hair or indulging infantile longings for attention and love.[62]

It became apparent that the donor of treatment—the physician—required consideration as well as the recipient of treatment—the patient. A sense of security within the analyst was an important element in the therapeutic transaction, as Frieda Fromm-Reichman[63] so clearly demonstrated in her treatment of schizophrenics. Recognition that the warmth of the analyst's personality, especially in the treatment of schizophrenic or borderline neurotic cases, and his or her more natural attitude towards the patient were effective tools gradually humanized the practice of psychoanalysis. Beyond this, forces were building to practically reorient the practice of psychotherapy and to compete with, but not displace, the enduring foundations Sigmund Freud had constructed.

Notes to Chapter 12

1. Sandor Ferenczi, *Further Contributions to the Theory and Technique of Psychoanalysis*, translated by J. I. Suttie *et al.*, New York, Boni & Liveright, 1927, p. 177.

2. C. P. Oberndorf, *A History of Psychoanalysis in America,* New York, Grune, 1953, p. 129.
3. Bernard De Voto, "Freud in American Literature," *Psychoanalyt. Quart.* 9:236, 1940.
4. Gilbert K. Chesterton, "The Game of Psychoanalysis," *Century Magazine,* Vol. 106, May 1923.
5. Walter Lippmann, "Freud and the Layman," *New Republic,* vol. 2, suppl. 9, April 17, 1915.
6. A. Kardiner, American Academy of Psychoanalysis, Meeting, 1974; *Frontiers of Psychology,* Roche Report, Feb. 1, 1974.
7. W. H. Rivers, "Psychiatry and the War," *Science,* vol. 49, April 1919.
8. S. T., "A Modern's Search in Science. The Priest Becomes the Physician and the Physician the Priest," *Century Magazine,* vol. 118, May 1929, p. 90.
9. H. L. Mencken, Editorial, *American Mercury,* vol. 11, July 1927, p. 288.
10. Personal observation, New York, 1935.
11. Breuer and Freud, *Studies in Hysteria.* Introduction by Brill, p. vii.
12. Personal observations, 1928–30.
13. Ernest Jones, *Summary of Treatment Procedure,* 1913.
14. Edward Glover, *The Technique of Psycho-Analysis,* Paris, Bailliere, London, Tindall & Cox, 1928.
15. Freud, "The Dynamics of the Transference," in *Collected Papers,* Internat. Psycho-analytic Press, 1924, Vol. II, p. 312.
16. J. J. Putnam, *On Freud's Psycho-analytic Method and Its Evolution,* Harvey Lectures, Philadelphia, Lippincott, 1912.
17. S. Ferenczi and Otto Rank, *The Development of Psychoanalysis,* translated by C. Newton, Washington, Nerv. & Ment. Dis. Pub. Co., 1925, p. 19.
18. Morton Prince, "Suggestive repersonalization," *Arch. Neurol. & Psychiat.,* 18:159, 1927.
19. C. G. Jung, "Psychotherapy and a Philosophy of Life," in *Essays on Contemporary Events,* translated by Elizabeth Welsh, Barbara Hannah and Mary Briner, London, Routledge, 1947, p. 41.
20. Jung, *Modern Man in Search of a Soul,* translated by Dell and Baynes, New York, Harcourt, 1933. Contributions to Analytical Psychology, translated by H. G. and C. F. Baynes, New York, The Bollingen Foundation, 1928.
21. Edward Glover, *Freud or Jung,* New York, Norton, London, Allen & Unwin, 1950.
22. Hugh Crichton-Miller, *Psycho-analysis and Its Derivatives,* p. 241.
23. Alfred Adler, *The Practice and Theory of Individual Psychology,* New York, Harcourt, 1924, p. 4.
24. Adler, *Understanding Human Nature,* translated by W. B. Wolfe, New York, Greenberg, 1927.
25. Freud, *The Ego and the Id,* translated by J. Rivière, London, Hogarth, 1927.
26. Franz Alexander, *The Psychoanalysis of the Total Personality; the Application of Freud's Theory of the Ego to Neuroses,* translated by B. Glueck and B. D. Lewin, New York, Nerv. & Ment. Dis. Pub. Co., 1930.

27. Edward Glover, *op. cit.*

28. Herman Nunberg, "The Theoretical Basis of Psycho-analytic Therapy," in *Psycho-analysis Today, Its Scope and Function,* edited by A. S. Lorand, New York, Covici Friede, 1933, p. 56.

29. Otto Fenichel, *The Psychoanalytic Theory of the Neurosis,* New York, W. W. Norton Co., 1945, p. 554.

30. Franz Nissl, quoted in Adolf Meyer, "A Few Trends in Modern Psychiatry," *Psychol. Bull.,* 1:217, 1904.

31. Erwin Stengel, "The Origins and Status of Dynamic Psychiatry," *Brit. J. of Medical Psychology,* 27:193, 1954.

32. Philip Rieff, *Freud: The Mind of the Moralist,* New York, Viking Press, 1959, p. 304.

33. F. Alexander and T. M. French, *Studies in Psychosomatic Medicine,* New York, Ronald Press, 1948.

34. Sandor Ferenczi, "The Further Development of an Active Therapy in Psychoanalysis (1920)," in *Further Contributions to the Theory and Technique of Psychoanalysis,* p. 198.

35. Freud, "Analysis Terminable and Interminable," in *Collected Papers,* edited by J. Strachey, London, Hogarth, 1950, Vol. V, p. 317.

36. Otto Rank, *Will Therapy* and *Truth and Reality,* translated by Jessie Taft, New York, Knopf, 1945.

37. Rank, *op. cit.,* p. 183.

38. V. P. Robinson, *Changing Psychology in Social Case Work,* Chapel Hill, N. C., Univ. North Carolina Press, 1930.

39. Wilhelm Stekel, *The Interpretation of Dreams,* translated by Eden and Cedar Paul, New York, Liveright, 1943, Vol. I.

40. Freud, "Analysis Terminable and Interminable," in *Collected Papers,* edited by J. Strachey, London, Hogarth, 1950, Vol. V, p. 317.

41. Freud, *Inhibitions, Symptoms and Anxiety,* London, Hogarth, 1925.

42. Freud, *New Introductory Lectures on Psycho-analysis,* translated by W. J. H. Sprott, New York, Norton, 1933.

43. Rollo May, *The Meaning of Anxiety,* New York, Ronald, 1950, p. 29.

44. Karen Horney, *The Neurotic Personality of Our Time,* New York, Norton, 1937, p. 89.

45. F. Alexander and S. T. Selesnick, *The History of Psychiatry,* New York, Harper & Row, 1966, p. 366.

46. Karen Horney, *New Ways in Psychoanalysis,* New York, W. W. Norton, 1939.

47. Alfred Adler, *The Neurotic Constitution,* translated by B. Glueck and John Lind, New York, Moffat, Yard & Co., 1917.

48. Alexandra Adler, "Present-Day Adlerian Psychiatric Practice," *Jour. Ind. Psychol.,* vol. 27, 1971.

49. Wilhelm Reich, "On Character Analysis (1928)," translated by R. Fliess, in *The Psychoanalytic Reader,* New York, Internat. Univ. Press, 1948, Vol. I.

50. Wilhelm Reich, "Orgonomic Diagnosis of Cancer Biopathy," *Orgone Inst. Press,* 14:78, No. 2, Orgonon, Maine, April 1952.

51. John Wykert, "Wilhelm Reich—The Abandoned Apostle," *Psychiatric News,* A. P. A., May 16, 1973.

52. Oberndorf, "Factors in psychoanalytic therapy," *Am. J. Psychiat.* 98:570, 1942; "Considerations of results with psychoanalytic therapy," *Am. J. Psychiat.* 99:374, 1942.

53. Franz Alexander *et al.: Psychoanalytic Therapy; Principles and Application,* New York, Ronald, 1946.

54. Judd Marmor, *The Contributions of Franz Alexander to Modern Psychotherapy,* Nutley, New Jersey, Hoffman, LaRoche Co., 1972.

55. John Dollard and N. E. Miller, *Personality and Psychotherapy, An Analysis of Learning, Thinking and Culture,* New York, McGraw-Hill, 1950.

56. Franz Alexander, *Psychoanalysis and Psychotherapy,* New York, W. W. Norton, 1956.

57. Abraham Kardiner, *The Individual and His Society; The Psycho-dynamics of Primitive Social Organization,* New York, Columbia, 1939.

58. Erich Fromm, *Escape from Freedom,* New York, Rinehart & Co., 1941.

59. Abraham Kardiner, *The Traumatic Neuroses of War,* sponsored by National Research Council, New York, Harper, 1941.

60. M. J. White, "Sullivan and Treatment," in *The Contributions of Harry Stack Sullivan,* edited by Patrick Mullahy, New York, Hermitage House, 1952.

61. Paul Federn, "Psychoanalysis of psychoses," *Psychiatric Quart.* 17:3, 246, 470, 1943.

62. E. B. Brody, "Treatment of Schizophrenia," in *Psychotherapy with Schizophrenics,* edited by E. B. Brody and F. C. Redlich, New York, Internat. Univ. Press, 1952, p. 46.

63. Frieda Fromm-Reichman, *Principles of Intensive Psychotherapy,* Chicago, Univ. of Chicago Press, 1950.

13

The Breadth of Psychotherapy

THE far-going influence of psychoanalysis on the entire psychotherapeutic field stimulated new techniques, new answers to old questions, new theories to explain clinical findings. But it did more. By enlivening psychiatry as a dynamic enterprise, it brought psychotherapy out of the consulting room into hospitals, clinics, schools, self-help groups, and counseling centers. The need for psychological guidance and help ballooned into a veritable obsession with the mind of man and its distortions. The result was a *democratization* of psychological knowledge in which a good proportion of the literate population sought out the discoveries of professional mind healers or entered into processes of self-discovery. Although fascination among laymen with the vagaries of the mind was not new, an opening wedge had been provided by the profession, achieving in effect the first break in the long line of priest-supplicant, shaman-recipient, physician-patient associations. As indicated in the last chapter, scrutiny of the therapist's own personality as participant in the therapeutic transaction altered the traditional doctor-patient dyad, i.e., the one-to-one relationship. In time, it represented one giant step to a broadened psychotherapy.

The subtle progress of democratization was aided by

psychiatrists, notably Paul F. Schilder, Harry Stack Sullivan, and Jacob L. Moreno, two with a Viennese background, the other an indigenous American, who understood the impact of society on the patient suffering from mental disturbance. Schilder, who came to Johns Hopkins and then to Bellevue Psychiatric Hospital in 1932, contributed a viewpoint growing out of his profound knowledge of neurophysiology, philosophy (phenomenology) and psychoanalysis. His first work to reach this country, *Medical Psychology* [1] (written in 1924), was more theoretical than clinical, but it pointed the way to the concept that all behavior is geared to a real, i.e., a social world. What this meant was that the instincts and the unconscious motives that Freud stressed as the causes of neurotic symptoms were also subject to the current life experience of the patient. The view espoused by Schilder was derived theoretically, but its import to therapy was great. For Schilder insisted that the basic problems each person must face and master—his body image, impulses for aggression and submission, self-concepts of masculinity and femininity, sex and love—were related to his real-life experience.[2] The psychologist, McDougall, had similarly found a "purposiveness in life strivings,"[3] as had Adler with his "life-plan" idea, notions that moved therapy away from Freud's ego psychology to the relevance of the patient's symptoms in his social life. As Schilder wrote, "The body image belongs to the community.... There is a continual interchange between our own body images and the body images of others."[4] To put it tersely, the Schilderian and Sullivanian concepts broadened therapy away from a "group of two," preparing the way for the evolution of group therapy.

Sullivan, in a slightly different direction, emphasized that therapy was a complex social situation "expressing the interactions of numerous individuals and of a cultural matrix beyond."[5] Thus he entered into the private world of the patient as a "participant observer" through communication by words and gestures and the bald fact of his presence, inviting a "togetherness" through which the patient could face his realities. The distinction between the older psychoanalytic treatment frame of reference and the newer one has been summarized by Murphy and Cattell:

> ...when clinical psychiatry appeared as an entity...the disease was inside the patient...with Freud the...transference made it embarrassingly clear that two persons were involved in every symptom...with Sullivan...we really see and deal with a career line of interactions between individuals....[6]

The conviction that the psychiatrist deals with the living, that the therapeutic situation is a "relationship," not a working of one person on another, placed an obligation on the therapist to use "pressure and education"[7] in assisting the patient to move from neurotic infantilism to social satisfaction. Sullivan's model of therapy involved a new set of concepts and a confusing terminology. He spoke of "marginal thoughts" rather than free association, "significant others" rather than parental surrogates, "parataxic phenomena" in place of transference.[8] In spite of the complexities of Sullivanian language, some important aspects of the therapeutic arose, notably a more careful regard for the tone of voice of the therapist, his facial expressions, his inner feelings toward the patient.[9]

The effect of Schilderian and Sullivanian views was reflected partly in the eclecticism that brought forth criticism from classical psychoanalysts. Glover in another connection wrote:

> The psychologic eclectic is accustomed to defend his hotch-potch of theories on the ground that...believing there must be at least two sides to any question, he finds it hard to conceive that one side may rest on total error.[10]

A reviewer in a psychoanalytic journal commented caustically on "...this twilight of eclecticism based on three-fourths rejection and infinitesimal acceptance of Freudian concepts...."[11] Not only professionals but literary men became alarmed at the opening breach in psychoanalytic practice. Lionel Trilling in a review of Horney's book *Self-Analysis* wrote:

> ...her denial...of Freud's concepts is the response to the wishes of an intellectual class which always found Freud's ideas cogent but too stringent and too dark.... Her protest is always that Freud sets gloomy bounds to man's nature...without faith. Faith means the belief that man is "free" and "good"—she has revived those old, absolute simplicities of eighteenth century liberalism.[12]

Nevertheless, the process of democratization had begun—with the analyst's examination of himself. Within two decades the process was to extend itself in a florid growth of encounter, sensitivity training, and group therapy.

One consequence of the dynamic era in psychotherapy was the appreciation that psychiatric methods fell into two distinct classes, expressive and suppressive therapy. The former delved into those emotional conflicts, usually unknown to the patient, which underlay his or her symptoms. The latter used inspirational or ego-strengthening measures with less interest in analyzing the problems than in giving emotional support. Overlapping naturally occurred in both groups. Expressive psychotherapy, borrowing from psychoanalysis, explored the patient's life to elucidate the "denied instincts" and then to release the "fettering hold" of infantile habits.[13] This type of reeducative technique was developed further at the Austin Riggs Foundation in Stockbridge, Massachusetts,[14] to readjust the patient to full social usefulness. Depth psychology, although comprehended, was eschewed in favor of developing an attitude of "living in the present." This form of psychotherapy, originating in New England, seemed to share the intellectualistic bent and common sense spirit of this region. It accepted the presence of unconscious conflict in the formation of neurosis, but insisted on the need for a philosophy of life that would permit the patient to view his symptoms in proper perspective.[15]

Later treatment at the Riggs Foundation included psychoanalytic contributions. Broadly conceived, the theory employed in recent years[16] does not necessarily always aim to "lift unconscious conflicts into full scrutiny," but the insights given to psychoanalytic therapists helps them guide patients to mental health. Terhune, summarizing this "eclectic" psychotherapy, to which group Riggs' work belonged, spoke of it as an "intensive method employing analytic technique without deep analysis."[17]

Accent on the living environment of the patient, past and current, brought up the question of intervention in life activities or even alteration in the patients' environment. Contrary to classical psychoanalytic technique, the patient is encouraged to assume, and "at times he is actually charged with," responsibility for attaining a total adjustment. He may even be "instructed" as to the general pace of life most compatible with his emotional capacities. This realistic relationship of therapist to patient obviates an analysis of the transference. Billings remarks in this connection, "In my experience, it is not necessary to work toward creating any special type of...transference situation."[18] More commonly, these derivative groups seek to evaluate and use situational factors equally with emotional ones. For example, Herzberg, who worked with the usual "uncovering" analytic technique, then directed his patient by imposing tasks calculated to "re-shape impulses and remove obstacles."[19] Others stressed participation of the therapist in the treatment process,[20] even to the point of advice and occasional attempts to influence, but not coerce, what now becomes the client.

Variants of therapeutic relationships, for example, that of Karpman,[21] reduced the sessions in number, requiring the patient to write an objective account of his life, which was then analyzed with the patient. The interviews were limited to ten minutes but much time was spent by the patient on his autobiography. The "objective psychotherapy" of Karpman related, in at least one respect, to "counseling," an approach developed by Rogers[22] and his associates, which was initially tried with college students in need of adjustment services. Since this type of therapeutic relationship was conceived primarily by psychologists, its frame of reference is nonauthoritarian and, by implication, nonmedical. The recipient of counseling is called a "client," and the method, "nondirective." Treatment is more accurately described as a nice variety of noncommittal guidance. It is focused on a concern with the client's own attitudes as he developed them under counseling, and not on the transference situation. Stress was placed on the immediate situation; "[Past history] for therapy to take place,... is not necessarily important.... When there is no probing for the 'facts' of the history, a better picture of the dynamic development of the individual often emerges."[23]

Briefly stated, the postulates of nondirective therapy are (a) that every individual has a drive toward growth, health, and adjustment, (b) that emotional blocks to integration of knowledge require removal, (c) that the immediate rather than the past situation is stressed, and (d) that counseling is change, not a preparation for change: "The therapeutic relationship itself is a growth experience." The contribution of Rogers has been essentially to allow the client to explore his own situation and behavior, and to accept responsibility for the forward movement of his escape from an emotionally blocked situation. The counselor is entirely permissive, neither interpreting nor directing the client, serving as a growth catalyst rather than a "doctor" in the ordinary sense, allowing and aiding the client to mature under his own self-scrutiny. The fundamental direction of counseling is opposite that of "doctoring"; neither dependence nor resistance is encountered, for, being "client-centered," the therapeutic process occurs within the client, who is helped to face his own problems and to make independent choices of solution.[24]

Psychologists working with this technique have made many experimental observations purporting to show how the forces of growth were released in the individual as the counseling proceeded. In fact, it was Rogers' hope that scientific investigation of therapeutic technique, through use of an electrical wire recording of an entire series of sessions, would put an end to "cultism in psychotherapy," substituting controlled measurement of therapeutic results for unsubstantiated claims.[25]

The issue of removing or reducing the "directiveness" of the therapist gained support from the social caseworkers, who handled many problems during the war years of the 1940s and later. The growing casework field received its chief stimulus in technique from Rogers' "client-centered" therapy. Handling personal problems developing out of disturbed familial situations brought the need to scrutinize the reality setting where the client's problems were enmeshed in family tensions. This type of social-work activity[26] was called *functional,* in that it did not imitate psychological analysis or indulge in "traditional concrete service of the family agency," but dealt with the question of how people could be helped to solve stated or unstated social-psychological troubles. Developed at the University of Pennsylvania Social Work School, this type of social casework involved an application of Otto Rank's ideas, especially the psychology of accepting help and the neglected problem of the "will." The essential feature of this "functional" casework attitude lay in the client's freedom, with help, to become himself. Rather than being a patient, the client was regarded as a person asking for a specific piece of social-psychological service.

As social workers moved more deeply into treatment areas, it became evident that individuals presenting personality deviations required some direction.[27] The type of therapeutic approach employed required modification, an amalgamation of nondirective and directive plans.[28] With the growth of psychiatric social work, the problem of distributing responsibilities and outlining the scope of work became apparent. A summary of opinions in the field in

1948[29] considered that psychiatric social workers engaged in both direct and indirect types of therapy, and that essentially there was a difference between interrelationship techniques implicit in psychotherapy and in casework. So rapid has been the development of this field, however, that the same group, which summarized opinions as to the caseworker's therapeutic area two years later,[30] pointed out how the range of therapeutic application of the caseworker became wider than that of the psychotherapist.

With the change from a nondirective to an expressive, or psychoanalytically oriented, type of therapy, the psychiatric social worker began to emancipate herself (or himself) from the traditional pattern of social work. Patients who had been treated in state or private psychiatric hospitals required more than medical treatment on their release. Social "weaning" of the state hospital patient became a new therapeutic goal. The concept of the "half-step home," in which patients ready for discharge from a state hospital were taken to live with a social worker or psychiatric attendant, was one step in the adjustment process. In this development, the accent was directive and educational, but applied with full knowledge of the psychopathology of the patient involved. The field of social-psychologic management was broadening.

Aided by the impetus from World War II and the corollary stimulation of the mental hygiene movement, the physician in general practice enlisted his viewpoint and talents in the field of psychotherapy. Social workers had already shown how the interview itself was an opening wedge for therapy, and physicians found that they were already in an advantageous position to utilize their consultations for psychotherapeutic purposes. The primary notion to assist "the patient to express feelings," which would otherwise be masked under the usually perfunctory relationship of a medical examination, was stressed.[31] Following Carl Rogers' indirect approach, the medical practitioner was encouraged to be a passive mirror of the patient's emotions toward his family and work situation. Interview therapy was the name dignifying an attitude employed by competent family physicians for years. A "folksy" approach, adapted to physicians distant from psychiatric centers in large cities, aimed at providing the practitioner with the "gist of what modern psychiatry has to say about human personality and the way it works."[32]

The development of the "therapeutic team" utilizing psychiatrists, psychologists, social workers, and psychiatric nurses grew out of the stirrings mentioned above. It extended to the state hospital, where Myerson[33] espoused the "total push" method for chronic mental cases. Abraham Myerson, a Boston psychiatrist, concluded that deterioration was not a necessary product of schizophrenia. Building on the basic principle that activity tends to dissolve patterns of withdrawal, his method emphasized the use of every known general medical measure, plus diet, exercises, games, and an accent on personal attention to patients, no matter how emotionally flattened and deteriorated. Its aim encompassed no more than the wish to stave off the dreaded deterioration of "backward" patients. The phrase and the technique, formulated by Myerson, have come to represent the personalized activities of all good hospital technicians and ward psychiatrists, and are widely used in many psychiatric facilities. Earlier, Bryan,[34] Superintendent of the Danvers State Hospital in Massachusetts, had used this principle, claiming improvements but no cures. Not the least result has been a "tonic effect" on the spirit and energy of technicians, nurses, and physicians who handle this discouraging type of human material. Weir Mitchell's epigram that psychiatry is "an art with assistive sciences," is virtually lived out in the concept of the teamwork approach to the rehabilitation of chronic patients. Each member of the team contributes a therapeutic atmosphere, in addition to his personal effort with individual patients; combined with group therapy, this became the standard for acute and chronic psychiatric facilities. It grew during the decade of the 1950s to become a "therapeutic community"[35] involving "milieu therapy," an ordering of the hospital to deal indirectly with the patient's mental troubles.[36] From Maxwell Jones' original idea of a therapeutic community, the tendency to involve patients in their own fate evolved into "patient government,"[37] social clubs,[38] and Abraham Low's Recovery Incorporated,[39] a club organized and operating in the community for discharged patients.

Reduction in importance of the authoritarian-subject system, implicit in the medical model of treatment, opened the door to many types of group action ranging from church groups under a pastoral psychiatrist[40] to the autonomous Alcoholics Anonymous organization.[41] A new face was put on psychotherapy in that the chasm of impersonality between doctor and patient was largely dissolving. Group therapy represented an outstanding result of the new alignment.

Dealing with hospital patients in a group setting immersed the therapist in the world in which patients lived and suffered, rather than seating him on the periphery. The beginnings of this enlarging area of psychotherapy can be traced to Dr. Joseph Pratt's handling of tuberculous patients in a "class" in 1905. Dr. Richard Cabot's introduction of medical social service at the Massachusetts General Hospital stimulated Doctor Pratt to gather "home-bound" consumptives into a class to instruct them in measures of physical hygiene and the newly discovered outdoor treatment of tuberculosis.[42] In so doing, Pratt discovered the "mental uplift" experienced by his tuberculous patients during his lectures on the proper care for this devastating illness. This line of endeavor, of distinctly medical social-service origin, was continued in classes for diabetics (Doctor Joslin) and other chronic sufferers.

As psychoanalytic principles pervaded psychiatry, group therapy began to achieve more than casual notice. Working with psychotic patients at St. Elizabeth's Hospital in Washington, D. C., Dr. Edward Lazell, about 1919, started lecture classes for mental patients. His lectures dealt with the dynamic meaning of such symptoms as delusions, hallucinations, inferiority feelings, and sexual perversion.[43] The accent was patently psychoanalytic, as Lazell adapted his lectures to members of his audience as individuals.

Another psychoanalytically oriented type of group therapy developed out of Trigant Burrow's reexamination of the neurosis as the product of social tensions arising within the individual. Burrow's groups were small in number, devoted mainly to the theory of *phyloanalysis*, the study of conflict between the self-image of one person as it interacted with the self-image of another within the group. In his group treatment Burrow made no interpretations,[44] but tried to divert attention in patients from their "symbolic psychological adaptation" in the thinking process to the organism's true physiologic function.

Less theoretical was Louis Wender's informal discussion of mental mechanisms among patients at the Hillside Hospital in New York.[45] His group discussions touched on emotional relations occurring in the hospital—sibling rivalries, patient-to-patient transference reactions, jealousies, envy, etc. Wender's benign and understanding attitude welded the group into a family unit, which made analysis of current emotional trends possible, a veritable "catharsis-in-the-family." Analytic group therapy attained prominence rather slowly; psychiatrists were wary of personal involvements with their patients. Incidentally, the same professional disinclination to get close to patients in an everyday manner also appeared later in the nonacceptance of psychodrama.

The results Wender obtained, and Paul Schilder's energetic espousal of group therapy in a clinic setting, did much to give this form of treatment a status of respectability in psychiatric circles before World War II. Schilder, at the Bellevue Psychiatric Hospital in New York, worked with patients who had previously been treated individually. With these he found that group work illuminated problems that did not arise in individual psychotherapy, particularly neurotic symptoms centering in attitudes toward the body, toward family ideals and social "ideologies." Using psychoanalysis "in a spirit of complete inner freedom,"[46] Schilder, before the group, uncovered material from patients that touched on their unconscious derivative attitudes toward sexuality; the expected shame dissolved in freedom. Schilder's group therapy technique was psychoanalytic in nature; interpretations were made; material developed through free association; and general remarks or discussions carried out with and by the patients.

It was significant that Schilder used psychoanalytic concepts freely in his group (and individual) therapy without the "codifications of the psychoanalytic school" that were prescribed in the period in which he worked. For example, he did not believe the rigid rule that the psychotherapist should not examine his patients physically if he planned to treat them analytically. Another innovation was his faith in, and perception of, the learning process implied in every psychotherapeutic contact, undeniably so in group therapy. The respect for the social world realities of the patient that Schilder contributed induced many workers to relax some of their professional caution in their therapeutic relations with patients. Activity and freedom were the watchwords of his therapeutic role.

A strong force in the burgeoning of group therapy arose from the natural tendency to handle disturbed children in groups. This activity was recognized in the field of child therapy,[47] but Slavson's consistent experimentation with behavioral problems, at the Jewish Board of Guardians in New York, exerted a strong influence on group therapy as a method. The early groups Slavson conducted (1934) emphasized diagnosis. When he allowed children free activity in groups, Slavson noted the transition from an infantile to a group superego. Misbehavior, habit difficulties, and neurotic traits within the group took on a different character.[48] Allowing the group complete permissivity, giving them "unconditional love," transformed problem children's behavior. Slavson's interpretation of the changes wrought in the children was based on the transference reactions of children to the therapist-figure. Extended to adolescents and adults, Slavson's *activity group* became an "analytic group" wherein the unrestricted activity permitted the children under a permissive, comfortable parent-figure to give way to the encouragement of verbalization. Group therapy became identical in technique with individual psychotherapy on a Freudian basis.[49]

All observers agreed that group therapy was a real experience for the patient, a sense of vivid reliving through role playing and "play acting."[50] On the other hand, some workers[51] felt that translation of group dynamics into terms of psychoanalytic ego psychology is "fraught with complication," while others agreed, with fewer qualms, that the primary aim of establishing insight into psychoneurotic mechanisms was not the function of group therapy. Its function, as conceived by Cotton,[52] was an attempt to "reinforce and strengthen the individual's defences against anxiety by identification with...and support from the group," to which formulation many workers added: "[The doctor] is the strongest single influence on the functioning of the group. He sets the aims and mores of the group and determines the...therapeutic effectiveness of the relationships formed among the members."[53]

The transition from analytic groups to action-oriented group therapy represented a step that had important consequences for the field of community psychiatry. The main contribution, made by J. L. Moreno, had its origins in the Theatre of Spontaneity,[54] in which, using random actors from an audience of the curious, he developed plays that spontaneously enacted scenes and dramatic content from the "private worlds" of the actors. Thus, his *psychodrama* owed more to drama than to psychotherapy. The actor,

Moreno found, tended spontaneously to create plays mirroring "his private world, his personal problems, his own conflicts, defeats and dreams." In the course of this work, which was actually part of the experimental theater movement initiated in Russia and Germany (1922–1925), which sought to free the drama from its traditional formalism (Stanislavsky), Moreno gradually recognized the therapeutic value of his "impromptu theatre." The emotional catharsis, which the actor achieved through spontaneous dramatic action, moved to the audience as the audience member automatically placed himself in the role of the actor. When the director reversed roles on the stage, the actor saw himself portrayed by another actor, enabling the former to visualize aspects of his own personality not ordinarily accessible or perceptible.

Action methods in group therapy led to new horizons; the spontaneous drama unfolded by the patients released "living creative forces" and an emotional catharsis, much as the Greek Chorus in ancient Grecian plays allowed emotional release of the audience. When the therapeutic possibilities of this form of group activity became apparent, Moreno recognized that he had stumbled upon a treatment method for the nontransference groups, namely children and psychotics, notoriously difficult to analyze, "by systematically developing play as a therapeutic principle."[55] The basic notion in psychodrama is reliving in dramatic action and counteraction the "unrealistic patterns of neurotic and psychotic patients,"[56] a concept that stands opposed to psychoanalytic or individual methods where acting-out is discouraged in favor of verbalizations of fantasies and impulses. In psychodrama, the primary data are the acts and the feelings of the actors, whereas in psychoanalytic treatment the primary data are recollections of emotion-laden events in the past. In psychodrama the aim is to understand conflict in its current form, its *status nascendi*, whereas in analysis the goal is the reconstruction of "bygone or regressive" acts and feelings. Hence psychodramatists felt that a reconstructive analysis does not have the truth that action "of the moment" entails. Rehearsed emotional relations were distorted, Moreno claimed, being removed in time from their *locus* of occurrence.

The intuitive and artistic aspects of psychodrama brought action methods closer to the daily problems of the patient. In the psychodramatic session, after a period of "warming up" in which intellectual interest passed into a kind of emotional arousal, action started when a patient became the protagonist for his own drama. The therapist or a trained staff member then portrayed persons vital to the patient's world—parent, wife or husband, friends, employer, etc., the so-called auxiliary egos. The action was spontaneous, yet sooner or later it moved to a central problem within the patient. By changing the cast of characters, the auxiliary egos, by giving the patient a "double," a reflection of himself, a "mirror" image, or suddenly reversing the roles of patient and staff members, a remarkably clear picture of the patient in a conflictful situation emerged.[57] The sudden placing of an individual in a role to which he was not accustomed, frequently a completely novel experience in life, itself a basic technique of Moreno's, was often productive of a startlingly new view of one's self. As the spontaneous play developed, the therapist and the staff withdrew gradually and became less participators than observers, more catalysts than direct therapists. The free use of acting-out and acting-in psychodrama brought forth criticism as Moreno extended his ideas to the "normal" community. The so-called *third* psychiatric revolution, according to Moreno,[58] rested not on the "minority" of the mentally ill but on the *"normal* group . . . responsible for general social and moral decay." Treatment of the normal community, therefore, by psychodrama should have reached out to mental hygiene clinics, prisons, schools, governmental agencies, and the like. The theoretical position of psychodramas, as noted, ran counter to analytic principles. Free movement on the psycho-dramatic stage contrasted markedly with the position of the patient on the analytic couch. Moreover, gestures, body movements, facial grimaces, besides being the currency of ordinary social life, were meaningful to the patient in the special social setting of the psychodrama.[59]

Those who opposed Moreno's views of the third psychiatric revolution debated his verdict that it represented "the passing of the psychoanalytic system."[60] Another critic[61] warned against the "coequal relationship between therapist and patient" on the grounds that the therapist has been "trained to understand emotional disorders, whereas the patient is not." The view of many professionals in the field coincided with Dr. Blake's dictum: "The concept of therapy is reserved to mean treatment or reduction of defect." Nevertheless, group therapy in its activity, whether analytic or psychodramatic in form, grew to become the basic format of therapy from the 1930s to the present.

While the mushrooming spread of group therapies, sensitivity training, and encounter groups continued (see Chapter 14), hypnosis, once controversial but now accepted, assumed its position as a viable technique. During the period that dynamic psychotherapy was in the ascendency, hypnosis held a minor position in medical therapy. True, there were always stage demonstrations of hypnosis, but from the 1920s to World War II—except for its occasional use in stubborn tics, chronic alcoholism, or hysterical symptoms—hypnosis was regarded with faint uneasiness by many psychiatrists. It was generally conceded that hypnosis, followed by suggestion, touched only the surface of the patient's emotional problems. However, partly growing out of the war experience, hypnosis was revived during the 1940s as a method to unearth unconscious material, to facilitate free associations,[62] and to remove resistances during the course of intensive psychotherapy.

The background of this extended use was Dr. Kardiner's observation, regarding World War I veterans suffering from "shell shock," that hypnosis could "cut the patient's escape from endless resistance." Drs. Grinker and Spiegel had further observed in the North Africa campaign of World War II that war neurosis among flyers could be abreacted by hypnosis combined with sodium pentothal. Using a *narcosynthesis* technique,[63] these psychiatrists found that "every war neurosis... [was based]... on an old unsolved conflict in the past." This method was extended into civilian practice, notably by Wolberg.[64] Combining hypnosis with a psychoanalytic approach, Wolberg achieved an abbreviated form of depth therapy by regressing patients to a childhood level, reliving traumatic experiences of infancy, and so on. Since it was accepted that hypnosis depended on the patient's trust and faith in the hypnotist, a replica of his or her childhood dependence upon the all-powerful parents, the modern hypnotist experimented with ways to utilize that patient-feeling to his betterment. Milton Erickson, Lewis Wolberg, and Jacob Conn of Baltimore had gone beyond simple suggestion to maneuvers like automatic writing, crystal gazing, suggested dreams (analyzed later), symptom substitution, and age-regression to evoke emotional abreactions. The trance state through which these situations were performed represented simply an altered state of consciousness, the "product of cumulative suggestions."[65] During this state the subject participated emotionally in the interpersonal relation. The knowledge that hypnotism constitutes a type of transference enables the modern hypnotist to deal with emotional problems that would absorb much more time in ordinary depth psychotherapy.

The uses of hypnosis in medical cases, for intractable pain in cancer, for arthritis, in dentistry, childbirth, and almost every type of medical ailment, have grown to the point where it is standard procedure for many physicians. The American Medical Association[66] approved its use for anesthesia, in addition to the medical problems mentioned, thus giving hypnotic psychotherapy the imprimatur of organized medicine. Indeed, the relaxation methods employed in behavior modification for states of tension and the like are simply a less intense hypnoid state in which resistance to suggestion or instruction is reduced. Hypnosis is psychologically akin to sleep, a state in which critical judgment is suspended but the mental functions remain intact.

The details of hypnosis induction, varied types of posthypnotic suggestion, and regression can be found in the large literature that has grown up around the subject and in courses of instruction by qualified specialists. Suffice it to say that the return of hypnosis to respectability has enlarged its therapeutic value in such diverse conditions as warts and insomnia, hysterical fugues and amnesias, headaches and anxiety states.

Psychotherapy in its breadth went further; it spilled over into writings covering every aspect of personal mental health. For the past four decades, the stream of books written for the public by physicians, psychologists, and medical journalists has grown from a trickle to a flood. At first explanatory with case histories and technical discussions, these tomes moved into the area of self-help for readers. Their availability increased; readers absorbed them, fascinated with the vagaries of the mind. Books like *Be Glad You're Neurotic, Outwitting Your Nerves, Release from Nervous Tension, Peace from Suffering, Guide for the Troubled Sleeper, Peace of Mind, Peace of Soul, Faith is the Answer, Games People Play, Everything You Always Wanted to Know* . . . and countless others swirled from the presses and are still swirling to bathe the public in advice and reassuring homilies.

In consonance with this democratizing tendency, psychiatrists writing theoretical treatises gradually shifted their viewpoint to practical expositions with the accent on self-help. Dr. William Glasser's *Reality Therapy* and Dr. Eric Berne's *Games People Play* spelled progress in bringing psychotherapy into contact with everyday life. An important element in this development was the use of "gut" words of common currency. Berne, borrowing colloquialisms from his patients and from the semantic shortcuts we all use to express complex emotional reactions, plunged into terms whose impact was unmistakable. Phrases like "Ain't it awful," "Now I've got you, you son-of-a-bitch," "See what you made me do!", "Schlemiel," expressed the helplessness, covert aggression, projected blame, and passive hostility commonly hidden in trite phrases.

Psychotherapists in their accounts of group or other sessions reported patients' use of expletives as a sign of anger, contempt, or aggression. The use of sexual terms on the street or in the privacy of the home, when occurring in therapeutic transactions, indicated how close they were to early experiences. Appearance in print of emotion-laden words showed the closeness of "gut" words to the *Muttersprache* (mother tongue), frowned on in polite speech. Pressure to evade this suppression has been constant since Elizabethan times, when the lid was clamped on the use of Anglo-Saxon words in print. Four-letter words embody too strong an emotional investment to be permitted free expression in print. A recent opinion from the field of law, a field where tastes change slowly, makes this statement about obscene written material:

> [it] . . . tends to promote lust and impure thoughts. . . . The correct test is the effect on sexual thoughts and desires, not of the "young" or "immature" but on the average, normal adult person.[67]

However the law may be, free expression of taboo words during group or individual therapies has found a place in books on recent treatment methods. Perls, the Gestalt therapist, introduced the term "mind-fucking" to indicate intellectual recounting of ideas in the service of resistance. Polster relates his interpretation of a woman patient "who takes me too seriously," in writing: "She is afraid that if she played with me, she too, would fuck me and go crazy...like her mother who seduced and fucked and went crazy."[68] In one sense expletives have lost their obscene connotation: "Shit" is an expression of disgust or frustration; "fuck it" and "bullshit" are frequently used to express rejection of artificiality or angry annoyance. As Humpty Dumpty says in *Alice in Wonderland,* "When I use a word, it means just what I choose it to mean...." The feelings expressed in Anglo-Saxon words have surfaced in psychotherapeutic writings as they have and do in life situations.

The therapeutic revolution has found its way in expressing feelings through the core of our language. What these innovations in popular psychiatric publications and in everyday group activity mean, is the entrance of a new *style* in therapeutic practice, a style that replaces defensive language with honesty, obscure phrases with plain speech. As will be seen in succeeding chapters, the democratization of therapy foreseen by early leaders in the field has outdistanced their prophecies. One consequence of this in the healing profession is that elitism is threatened by the common touch.

Notes to Chapter 13

1. Paul Schilder, *Medical Psychology,* translated and edited by David Rappaport, New York, International University Press, 1953.
2. Paul Schilder, *Goals and Desires of Man,* New York, Columbia, 1942.
3. William McDougall, *The Energies of Man,* New York, Scribner, 1933.
4. Paul Schilder, *Psychoanalysis, Man and Society,* New York, W. W. Norton Co., 1951, p. 12.
5. Gardiner and Cattell Murphy, "Sullivan and Field Theory," in *The Contributions of Harry Stack Sullivan,* ed. by Patrick Mullahy. Copyright, William Alanson White, Institute of Psychiatry, Psychoanalysis and Psychology. Published by Hermitage, New York, 1952.
6. *Ibid.*
7. P. Wagner, in *The Contributions of Harry Stack Sullivan.*
8. H. S. Sullivan, *Conceptions of Modern Psychiatry,* New York, Norton, 1953, p. 8.
9. H. S. Sullivan, *The Theory of Anxiety and the Nature of Psychotherapy.*
10. Edward Glover, "Symposium on the Theory of Therapeutic Results in Psychoanalysis," *Internat. J. of Psychoanal.* 18:127, 1937.

11. Review of Frieda Fromm-Reichmann, *Psychoanalyt. Quart.* 24:834, 1950.
12. Lionel Trilling, "The Progressive Psyche," *The Nation* 155:215, Sept. 1942.
13. J. A. Jackson and H. M. Salisbury, *Outwitting Our Nerves; A Primer of Psychotherapy*, New York, Century, 1921.
14. A. F. Riggs, "The psychoneuroses; their nature and treatment," *Am. J. Psychiat.* 3:91, 1923.
15. D. A. Thom, "Psychotherapy in private practice," *Am. J. Psychiat.* 13:77, 1933.
16. Austin Riggs Center, Inc., An Informational Report, Stockbridge, Mass., 1953, p. 6.
17. W. B. Terhune, "Advances in Individual Therapy, Emphasizing Brief Psychotherapy," Delivered at World Congress on Mental Health, London, August, 1948.
18. E. G. Billings, "General principles of psychotherapy in general practice," *J. Indiana M. A.* 42:1243, 1949.
19. Alexander Herzberg, *Active Psychotherapy*, New York, Grune, 1945.
20. Walter Bonime, "Some principles of brief psychotherapy," *Psychiatric Quart.* 27:1, 1953.
21. Ben Karpman, "Objective psychotherapy; principles, methods and results," *J. Clin. Psychol.* Monograph No. 6, Suppl., July, 1948.
22. C. R. Rogers, *Counseling and Psychotherapy; Newer Concepts in Practice*, Boston, Houghton, 1942.
23. *Ibid.*, p. 30.
24. C. A. Curran, *Personality Factors in Counseling*, New York, Grune, 1945.
25. C. R. Rogers, "Recent research in nondirective therapy and its implications," *Am. J. Orthopsychiat.* 16:581, 1946.
26. Jessie Taft, "Family Case Work and Counseling," in *A Functional Approach to Family Case Work*, edited by J. Taft, pp. 8, 301, Philadelphia, Univ. of Penna. Press, 1944.
27. Annette Garrett, "The worker-client relationship," *Am. J. Orthopsychiat.* 19:224, 1949.
28. L. G. Lowrey, "Trends in orthopsychiatric therapy; general developments and trends," *Am. J. Orthopsychiat.* 18:381, 1948.
29. Committee on Psychiatric Social Work, Group for Advancement of Psychiatry, Report No. 2, January, 1948.
30. Committee on Psychiatric Social Work, Group for Advancement of Psychiatry, Report No. 16, September, 1950.
31. S. G. Law, *Therapy Through Interview*, New York, McGraw-Hill, 1948.
32. Geddes Smith, Psychotherapy in General Medicine; Report of an Experimental Postgraduate Course, New York, Commonwealth Fund, 1946.
33. Abraham Myerson, "Theory and principles of the 'total push' method in the treatment of chronic schizophrenia," *Am. J. Psychiat.* 95:1197, 1939.
34. W. A. Bryan, "Re-education of demented patients," *Am. J. Psychiat.* 77:99, 1920.

35. Maxwell Jones, *The Therapeutic Community, A New Treatment Method in Psychiatry*, New York, Rinehart (Basic Books), 1953.
36. W. C. Menninger, "Psychiatric hospital therapy designed to meet unconscious needs," *Am. J. Psychiat.* 93:347, 1936.
37. R. W. Hyde and H. C. Solomon, "Patient government: a new form of group therapy," *Digest Neurol. & Psychiat.* 18:207, 1950.
38. E. B. Strauss, R. Ström-Olsen, and J. Bierer, "A memorandum on therapeutic social clubs in psychiatry," *Brit. M. J.* 2:861, 1944.
39. Abraham Low, *Mental Health Through Will Training*, Boston, Christopher Publ. House, 16th ed., 1950.
40. R. C. Leslie, "Pastoral group psychotherapy," *Group Psychotherapy 3:* No. 1, 1950.
41. *Medicine Looks at Alcoholic Anonymous* (reprints of papers presented to the Medical Society of the State of New York and the American Psychiatric Assoc.), New York, Alcoholic Foundation, 1944.
42. J. H. Pratt, "The class method of treating consumption in the homes of the poor," *J.A.M.A.* 49:755, 1907.
43. E. W. Lazell, "The group treatment of dementia praecox," *Psychoanalyt. Rev.* 8:168, 1921.
44. Trigant Burrow, "The group method of analysis," *Psychoanalyt. Rev.* 14:268, 1927.
45. Louis Wender, "Group psychotherapy: a study of its application," *Psychiatric Quart.* 14:708, 1940.
46. Paul Schilder, *Psychotherapy* (rev. ed. by L. Bender), New York, Norton, 1951.
47. Lauretta Bender, "Group activities on a children's ward as methods of psychotherapy, *Am. J. Psychiat.* 93:1151, 1937.
48. S. R. Slavson, *An Introduction to Group Therapy*, New York, Commonwealth Fund, 1943.
49. S. R. Slavson, *Analytic Group Psychotherapy; with Children, Adolescents and Adults*, New York, Columbia, 1950.
50. Walter Bromberg and G. H. Franklin, "The treatment of sexual deviates with group psychodrama," *Group Psychotherapy*, Vol. 4, No. 4, March, 1952, p. 274.
51. N. W. Ackerman, "Psychoanalysis and group psychotherapy," *Group Psychotherapy* 3:204, 1950.
52. J. M. Cotton, "Group Psychotherapy; An Appraisal," in *Failures in Psychiatric Treatment*, edited by P. H. Hoch, New York, Grune, 1948, p. 121.
53. Florence Powdermaker and J. D. Frank, "Group psychotherapy with neurotics," *Am. J. Psychiat.* 105: 449, 1948.
54. J. L. Moreno, *Das Stegreiftheater*, 1923 [The Theatre of Spontaneity], translated by the author, New York, Beacon House, 1947.
55. J. L. Moreno, *Psychodrama*, New York, Beacon House, 1946, Vol. 1, p. 6.
56. W. C. Hulse, "The social meaning of current methods in group psychotherapy," *Group Psychotherapy* 3:1, 1950.

57. J. L. Moreno, "Psychodramatic production techniques," *Group Psychotherapy* 4:243, 1952.
58. J. L. Moreno (with Z. T. Moreno), *Psychodrama, Foundations of Psychotherapy*, Vol. 2, New York, Beacon House, 1959, p. 104.
59. Walter Bromberg, "Acting and Acting Out," *Amer. J. of Psychotherapy* 12:264, April, 1958.
60. Jules Masserman, Discussion, "Functions of the Unconscious," in Moreno, *Psychodrama, Foundations of Psychotherapy*, Vol. 2, p. 60.
61. J. B. Wheelright and Robert Blake, Discussion in Moreno, pp. 77, 116.
62. Abram Kardiner, *The Traumatic Neurosis of War*, New York, Harper & Bro., 1941.
63. R. R. Grinker and John P. Spiegel, *Men Under Stress*, Philadelphia, Blakiston, 1945.
64. Lewis R. Wolberg, *Hypnoanalysis*, New York, Grove Press, Inc., 1945.
65. Jacob Conn, "Hypnosis in General Practice," *Medical Opinion & Review*, June 1969, p. 120.
66. John Watkin, "Hypnosis in the U.S.A.," in *Hypnosis Throughout the World*, Springfield, Illinois, Charles Thomas, 1964.
67. United States Court of Appeals, *U.S. v. Roth*, 237 F 2nd and 796 (2nd Cir. 1956); U.S. 476, L. Ed., 2nd, 1498 (1957).
68. Erving Polster and Miriam Polster, *Gestalt Therapy Integrated*, New York, Brunner-Mazel, 1973, p. 100.

14

Therapy and the Expanded Psyche

The third psychiatric revolution, which Moreno foresaw, had come to pass during the 1950s and 1960s. The form it assumed was that of a revolt against the medical model; in the case of psychotherapy, against the so-called dyadic or one-to-one model. The initiative for this development arose from several sources; from clinical psychologists, dissatisfied with the narrow field of psychometric testing; from social workers in contact with masses of untreated neurotics and personality problems and sociologists alert to the larger implications of therapy. A further source was from pressures of a public eager to benefit from a much publicized accumulation of psychological knowledge. An Age of Therapeutics[1] had arrived. Successful propaganda by the mental hygiene movement, an increase in easily obtainable psychological literature, the accent on a *full life* in an unstable and inflationary economy, spilled over the bounds of conventional psychotherapy. Business and industrial relations, family living, and the dynamics of society itself became grist for the therapeutic mill. Group therapy proliferated, sensitivity training techniques caught the public imagination, and the here-and-now therapy became an insistent theme.

Many of these new schools of psychotherapy, although

originated by psychologists and psychiatrists, conveyed a sociological flavor. Dr. Howard Rome, in his Presidential Address before the American Psychiatric Association in 1966, agreed that "Psychiatry is now in the arena of social change, in the community, part of the social action movement."[2] The total forces at work included philosophic considerations. The revolt against the medical model, colored by social concerns, was tinctured by phenomenology and existentialism. Transactional Analysis, for example, the product of Eric Berne's work,[3] emphasized the phenomenology of social transactions, which took the form of accepted rituals, pastimes, and games programmed into our social life. In these games, Berne distinguished Parental, Adult, and Child ego states, states that reflected the patient's programmed action at different times. Thus, when a person is in the Adult role, he or she is objective, autonomous, making mature decisions. When a Parent, the patient is authoritarian, strict, and fault-finding; when a Child, helpless, dependent, self-centered. The three stages of ego were analyzed as that of the Parent, Adult, and Child within himself and within others with whom he is interacting. Transactional Analysis developed on the basis of this formulation.

Dr. Berne's early work concentrated on the psychology of human relationships. His analysis of *Games People Play*[4] touched on such common ploys as "See What You Made Me Do," "Let's You and Him Fight," "Rapo," and other defensive "games which clutter up social intercourse." As with all therapeutic innovations, a new terminology developed, closer to the gut-level words used by people at large. Transactional Analysis as a treatment method used such terms as "stroking" for giving affection or love, "I'm Not OK—You're OK" for lowered self-esteem, "hooked" for involved, "plug in your Adult," to maintain a mature observer's attitude, and so on.[5] Actually, the Parent, Adult, and Child of Transactional Analysis corresponds to the Superego, Ego, and Id of Freudian nomenclature.

Transactional Analysis is essentially a teaching-learning process and as such acts as a conditioning modality through repeated exposure and working through of the Parent, Adult, and Child ego levels. Thomas Harris added to Berne's description of "Games" a euphoric atmosphere in transactional group therapy; the effectiveness of the leader "rests on his enthusiasm and ability as a teacher and his alertness in keeping abreast of every communication or signal in the group, verbal or otherwise."[6]

Emphasis on communication and programming is reflected in the terms used, e.g., *data processing, injunctions,* and *life script.* Programming forced into the child persists as patterns of behavior, so that the adolescent or adult patient reacts according to the early injunctions of his parents; e.g., "Don't grow; Don't be important; Don't be you," or the converse, "Be successful." When these injunctions are exposed, brought into the open and discarded, the Adult (or reasonable ego in psychoanalytic terms) can grapple with life's problems and exert its autonomy. Being educational in essence, Transactional Analysis enlarged to include treatment of delinquency and behavior problems among children. The simple concepts employed were easily understood by young children.[7] Others,[8] working with adults, have added Gestalt techniques to Transactional Analysis, which bypass theory in favor of direct expression or here-and-now experience. For example, patients face their parents in fantasy, expressing what they had been unable to voice. This expansion of one's "bounded sense of self,"[9] the feeling of having broken through a hitherto sacred wall, releases resistance towards perceiving the influence of the Parent or Child in the patient's mental world. This type of "encounter" led to other new therapies.

The notion of the *encounter* is solidly based on existential philosophy. Briefly stated, it is the "grasping of the being of the other person."[10] In this sense, an encounter is not the common experience of one person meeting another, of learning the banal aspects of his or her life, but a "decisive inner experience,"[11] which occurs in both individuals. Simply put, the bond between two persons, the "fact of the reality of two individuals in a room" involves an attachment that is the essence of the human relationship. In a therapeutic setting, this bond includes a *caring* of one person for another, an understanding by the analyst for the patient being-in-his-world, and hence a fundamental basis for therapy.

This special type of psychoanalysis, i.e., existential psychoanalysis,[12] practiced by a few, has been greatly expanded in other directions at the Esalen Institute in Big Sur, California. Founded by Michael Murphy, a Stanford psychologist, and William Schutz, Esalen took the form of a free university where teachers and students were undistinguished from each other—the former called "resource people," the latter, "free learners." The seminars and workshops included interpersonal encounter, Gestalt awareness training, psychosynthesis, structural integration, transpersonal or mystical experience, and the human body. Of these categories, interpersonal encounter is the one most readily identified with Esalen. Utilizing techniques such as sensory awareness, massage, fantasy, psychodrama, role-playing, video-tape playback, structured risk taking, concentration on the here and now, communication games, feedback, and symbolic charades, the encounter groups attempted to elicit latent emotions and channel them into interpersonal encounters or confrontations. The focus is on the experience of feelings and perceptions in the here and now, rather than theory and discussions, and on acting out feelings rather than talking about them.

Freedom at Esalen in encouraging any psychologic or physiologic measure[13] that would "emphasize the potentialities and values of human existence" aroused much curiosity among psychological sophisticates. It also stimulated ridicule, prurient interest, and irritation. A reporter in *Time* characterized Esalen activities as:

> ...a staff of uninhibited social scientists...engaged in the new sensitivity training. Their aim is to make business execu-

tives, doctors, lawyers, Peace Corpsmen, and assorted self-searching women more aware of... their "authentic" relations with others through sensual and physical rather than verbal experiences. [14]

Other lay commentators were contemptuous: "Esalen offers paths that lead to new ways of lying, sitting, breathing and moving... secret paths that wind into inner imagery and the language of contemplation." [15] U.S. Representative John Rarick opined in the *Congressional Record:* "Organized thought control and behavior programming... a perversion of group therapy that makes healthy minds sick," while the American Psychiatric Association spokesman described encounter groups as a "social oasis in which societal norms are explicitly shed.... The group offers intimacy, albeit sometimes a pseudo-intimacy... which has no commitment to permanence." [16] The sensational aspect of Esalen techniques did not escape notice. One reporter wrote: "People touch, hold hands, kiss, throw each other in the air, fight, use all the dirty words, tell each other cruel truths...."

Under the stimulus of the new encounter practice, human growth centers mushroomed throughout the country. As with "wild analysis" of the early psychoanalytic days (see Chapter 12), groups like the G.R.O.W. (Group Relations Ongoing Workshops) and Center for the Whole Person practiced elements of encounter and Gestalt therapy with little professional help. Wildcat encounter groups arising throughout the United States of America alarmed professional psychologists who asked: "Does the encounter cult provide a beneficial form of therapy or is it just a lot of (occasionally dangerous) fun and games?" [17]

What was the "growth movement" and where did it originate? It appears to have started in nonpsychiatric circles in the establishment of the National Training Laboratory for Group Development in 1947.

The basic notion of the Training Laboratory [18] pointed towards a democratic system for problem-solving among groups and in the community at large. The Carnegie Corporation in New York underwrote the first three-week laboratory session in Bethel, Maine. From its inception, the training program was a success; in 1947, one hundred paying participants or "delegates" attended the laboratory. By 1966 the laboratory served more than 1,300 delegates, to become "trainers" in turn. The total thrust of the program, now called "T-Groups" and later "Sensitivity Training" groups, was to utilize the latest psychological developments in handling a vast number of interpersonal relations problems arising from our complex technological society. In a democratic society, immature management decisions contributed to a crippling insecurity among workers, communities, even nations. Leaders equipped with human relations *skills* were needed to communicate knowledge of group dynamics and to study the processes of group thinking and group action.

One of the pressing problems was that of race relations. The Connecticut State Interracial Commission had already (1946) investigated the early work of Lewin, Bradford, and others on small group behavior, feeling that Lewin's formulations could be of value in a troubled society. Simply put, Lewin's researches found that small task-oriented groups functioned both more efficiently and more pleasantly if conducted in a democratic, leaderless manner than if autocratically organized[19] (the town hall meetings in colonial and later New England had learned the same lesson in democracy).

Kurt Lewin introduced concepts that had little to do, initially, with psychotherapy. As a sociologist he was interested in social situations, how groups operated collectively, what the "energy field" did to behavior—in short, how the group dynamics influenced the individual's psychology.[20] Borrowing from scientists—Maxwell, Einstein—Lewin formed a "field theory," speaking in terms of life-space, vectors, person-environment, and intra-environment. It led in time to methods of manipulation and communication within the group, reward-giving (positive valences) and punishment (negative valences) and how these factors made for group spirit and group motivation. During the struggle of ethnic minorities to gain their fair share of economic and social benefits (Detroit, Watts, Washington, D.C. riots), the findings of Lewin and his students[21] were applied. Leaders attempted to minimize *progress-preventing* and maximize *progress-conducive* forces to the end that group decision-making and problem-solving in American life could proceed without fear, frustration, or anxiety.

These considerations of a theoretical sociologist, almost mathematical in form, were directly applied to training groups. They so impressed governmental and industrial personnel that the Human Rights Commission, Standard Oil of New Jersey, and other giant organizations sent their upper-level managers to sensitivity and training laboratory sessions. Training awareness, or "diagnostic sensitivity," became the watchword for a host of leaders in areas where psychotherapy was never explicit—schools, industry, community affairs where ethnic groups clashed with the establishment, politics, situations where hostilities needed to be eased and decisions made to benefit all. Sensitivity training worked against preconceived expectations and prejudices.

The new idea of group manipulation to cure intolerance and to induce group self-evaluation increasingly impressed social psychiatrists; it dovetailed with the growth of group therapy and the sophistication of the patient-public. Notions like "feedback," examination of "immediate data," "role playing" infiltrated management thinking and group therapy alike. Sensitivity training focused on the self-observing process, on open discussion of intimacies, on confrontation of each member of the group with his or her biases or blind spots, distortions, and values. As such, it signaled the invasion of psychotherapy by sociologists who were thus enabled to evade the intricacies of Freudian metapsychology.

The step from sensitivity training for community living

and interpersonal relations in industrial life, to a freeing of the self among basically normal people, was the contribution of the Esalen Institute. Drifting away from psychotherapy as conceived by psychiatrists, Esalen leaders explored insights into mystical and "peak" experiences, parapsychological phenomena, and altered states of consciousness. Such disciplines as *aikido, hypnosis, meditation, yoga, biofeedback* (monitoring brain waves, which provided positive reinforcement for certain brain patterns corresponding to those encountered in sleep), were fostered. The contemplation of *mythical symbols, guided fantasy, Sufi* and *Taoist* disciplines, and energy awareness were added to provide modern men and women with a glimpse of what Abraham Maslow has referred to as the "farther reaches of human nature."

A technique of direct muscle manipulation (Rolfing), which realigned the body posture in such a way as to release excessive physical and psychological tensions, was used. The theory behind Rolfing, named for its originator, Ida Rolf, was Reich's insight that unconscious emotional stresses resulted in a typical characterological posture. The structural integration technique sought to release the affect trapped in this posture by working on the muscles underlying posture, rather than by conventional psychiatric means. Although it was called massage, structural integration was excruciatingly painful. Assumed to result in improved physical balance and emotional freedom, it was often combined with Gestalt awareness training and a post-integration instruction in proper "structural patterning."

Innovations introduced at Esalen were numerous; its founder, Michael Murphy, said, "We only knew that a forum was needed for all these new ideas...a University without academic trapping...combining the best of Western humanistic psychology and Eastern thought...."[22] Beyond structural integration, or "Rolfing," Eastern dance-yoga as well as the sensory awareness of Charlotte Selver and Bernard Gunther, which bore the improper appellation of "sensitivity training" in the popular press, were used. Sensory awareness included techniques for the cultivation of intellectual quietude; enhanced experience of the five senses (especially touch), spontaneous physical expression and activity and nonverbal communication.

The guiding genius behind the expansion of psychology into Humanist Psychology was Abraham Maslow, psychologist and philosopher, who transformed existential philosophy into a base for psychotherapy. Maslow's idea of "actualizing [the person's] potentialities... close to the core of his Being,"[23] a condition occurring among healthy, creative people, made the integration of the Self the most important therapeutic aim. His interest was in psychologic health, nor neurosis, hence he spoke in terms of the ability to love, to achieve identity and peak experience. Maslow would rather work with positive values and assets than with repressions and defenses. The assets Maslow invoked were, and are, already part of the human personality: "The transcendence... the very highest and most inclusive or holistic... levels of human consciousness."[24] Techniques for developing this inner core were of relatively little importance to Maslow; recognition of the transcendent experience, that the "sacred is *in* the ordinary [life]... in one's neighbors, friends, family and in one's back yard," brought its own techniques in train. It was Maslow's inspiriting message that therapists of the "expansionist schools" picked up and molded into several types of psychotherapy; his message went beyond analysis, even beyond synthesis, to an explication of their inner selves— in fact, to *self-actualization*.

In consonance with the humanist growth theme that "the mind, emotions and body of man is a single dynamic unity," that "joy rather than despair is the... natural condition of man" (George Leonard), encounter techniques led to marathon group therapy. The "ancient understanding that the *community*, set in a framework of honesty, openness and responsibility, is enlivening and healing"[25] set the tone for the marathon.[26] The marathon group therapy, "no longer for the diseased" but for those living a "full range of experiences — trauma, confrontation, intimacy" — carried groups beyond hours ordinarily set for psychotherapy (forty-five minutes to an hour) to a twelve-hour, forty-eight hour, or longer continuous session. The content of marathon sessions varied with the predilections of the leader. Esalen leaders combined various games and exercises to promote sensory awareness: physical maneuvers like the "flip-out," in which a person is held firmly on the floor until in desperation and panic he fights his way out; group hugging to promote security feelings, Indian wrestling and pillow fights to break rigid body boundaries that inhibit contact, etc.

Other proponents used forced fantasies to evoke a resisted event into present actuality;[27] some experimented with simple bodily exercises to put the patient in "touch with" his or her self.[28] Albert Ellis[29] in his marathon sessions lasting a weekend, among other reality therapy measures, asked members of the group to choose someone with whom they would like a love experience. This is permitted to continue for five minutes inside or outside the group room and is then discussed openly as an "entree to problem areas" and to "open up the participants to themselves and others."

Other activities in marathon sessions involve the unique dream analysis initiated by Fritz Perls and the "hot seat" technique. The dream analysis, carried out without interpretation, brings the elements of the dream to the light of day; they are then dealt with according to the patient's emotional relation to the symbols therein. For example, a patient dreams of sitting on a mountainside that begins to slide. He awakes in fright. The patient is asked to *be* the mountain, then the sliding debris and the base of the mountain. During this period of imaginative personalizing of dream symbols, they become clear as figures in his daily life to which he reacts with emotion. Similarly, in the "hot seat" technique developed by Perls, the patient faces an empty chair, peopled, in his imagination, with parents or other protagonists and antagonists in his life scene.[30] While on the "hot seat" his true feelings are evoked, expressed, and lived through in all their turmoil and tears, rather than simply recounted and interpreted. The techniques introduced by Perls to enrich marathon therapy arose from his espousal of Gestalt therapy, an important development in itself.

Dr. Perls, trained in psychoanalysis by Reich, Fenichel, and Karen Horney in Berlin, departed from orthodox analysis during his peregrinations following the Nazi explosion. Living and working as an analyst in Holland, Israel, South Africa, and finally this country, Perls evolved the Gestalt therapy, based in large part on the principles enunciated by Gestalt psychologists. His emphasis was on experience in the "now" and on the intensity and excitement of the *contact* between the self and the environment, on the Gestalt *closure* principle (the human disinclination to leave unfinished business), the figure-ground alternation in perception ("only one event can occupy the foreground of attention"), on perception of the whole ("we do not see three isolated points but make a triangle out of them").[31] From these principles, in the congenial atmosphere of Esalen, Perls developed a viewpoint opposed to Freudian psychology, an insistence that experience had to be lived through rather than interpreted, that sensory awareness expanded the boundary of the self, that encounter was needed to extend the body-boundaries. His language often earthy, his zest for life and "aware" experiences clearly visible in his life style, Fritz Perls influenced many therapists to open feeling-doors among their group patients, rarely met before in therapy. Marathon groups, when combined with Gestalt techniques, psychodrama, simple understanding and empathy, unraveling of *body language* and body image distortions,[32] proved to be effective therapy for many types of problems.

Before continuing with the amazing proliferation of

new therapies, it is worthy of note that with certain exceptions, many innovations were born and flourished in California. The general air of informality and the abandonment of rigid codified behavior patterns, both of which are characteristic of the West Coast subculture, combined with the activist movement of youth to demand a more immediate experiencing of the self in action. The strains that fed this attitude during the 1960s—protest against the hypocrisy of the Vietnam War, need for social progress, struggle against an engulfing technology—met in the doctrine of the "Now Ethos" (Polsters). This new perspective coincided with the freedom at Esalen to nurture new therapeutic approaches and to counter the alienation that many considered the chief psychologic-social evil of the time. For Perls and his associates, Esalen had "become the symbol . . . for the humanistic-existential revolution" where "the mystic, the esoteric, the supernatural and extrasensory perception seems to fit into the spirit of the place."[33]

Criticism of such a Utopian therapeutic center, which had spread to the East Coast within a few months, arose quickly. Doctor Joseph English, former head of the Health Services in the Department of Health, Education, and Welfare, noted that the human potential movement had "been oversold to an unaware public." Professor George Steiner of Cambridge University commented: "What's the point of self-discovery if there is nothing . . . to discover?" Psychiatric critics maintained that the Esalen techniques (encounter, marathon, personality growth, etc.) were medically irresponsible, anti-intellectual, and "smacked of anarchy, communism or at least 'Californiaism.' " Still, Carl Rogers, the psychologist, called the new group movement "the most significant social invention of this century."[34]

Interest in group dynamics led to the natural matrix of many nervous and mental conditions—the family. The notion of working with the spouse or parent of a patient, a sporadic occurrence among a few analysts (Oberndorf, Mittelman) until the 1960s, developed rapidly into family therapy. An outgrowth of early contacts with families of schizophrenic patients, Jackson and Bateson developed the notion of a *double bind*.[35] Here the patient received conflicting messages from the parents: thus assertions of love were countered by nonverbal communications indicating the opposite. Family therapy examined the *system* of familial interpersonal relations with its communicated nonverbal clues. A family organized around the patient who adopts the "sick role" places other members in a special status, requiring treatment of all the members in their intimate interrelations. Close attention was paid then to the hidden messages passing between members of the family, nonverbal commands, calls for help, unexpressed hostilities, and so on. Many have contributed to the present status of family therapy[36] (Carl Whitaker, Virginia Satir, J. Haley), where the therapist sitting with three or more members of the family constellation acts as "go-between," mediator, or "side-taker" to intervene in destructive relationships he may observe within the family.

The technique grew out of conferences between patients, often an adolescent or child but lately including partners in marital disharmony. In the hands of Nathan Ackerman,[37] the "organizational pattern of family life" was opened, the emotional climate examined, the roles of each member with the prevailing communication pattern exposed, to reduce the "defensive barricades among family members." Hostility, expressed or hidden, rebelliousness, injunctions to fail, passed as secret messages between parent and child, all came in for scrutiny. The family therapist balances these emotional forces, tries to redistribute hostilities and love within the very community that is the basis of our social life—the family.

The flowering of the humanist movement, its accent on body awareness, spread in directions remote from traditional psychotherapy. Workshops and seminars devoted to an expanded psyche, an appreciation of "personal and collective human energy... to experience ways to a full life... recharge, rediscover, refuel, recycle, rejoice..."[38] remained on a therapeutic level, while in other areas political Utopianism, combined with a "broadened horizon," stressed education, i.e., therapy, for the coming Revolution; here a Dialectic Psychology based on Marxism offered therapy "beyond psychoanalysis."[39] The woods were full of whirring birds of passage on the way to Nirvana. Psychoanalysis as conceived by Freud and his followers had been left far behind. One psychotherapist in Florida resurrected what he called a "lost art in India": he announced it to be *affectionism*, a guaranteed method to "bring out the most loving characteristics in human beings."[40] Workshops "releasing and extending... those deeper layers of ourselves..."[41] concentrated on union of body and mind to the end of involving what Anais Nin called "the cities of the interior." Others, capitalizing on Perls' dream analysis, offered seminars where "psycholytic psychodrama" enabled participants to "explore previously unknown parts of themselves."[42] The goals of "self-actualization: Peak experiences; Creativity training; Depth imagery; Personal growth" proliferated, extinguishing boundaries, crossing from professional to nonprofessional lines, passing beyond neurosis to the borders of unhappiness, mild dissatisfaction, and a general feeling of not being "in."[43]

In spite of the melange of psychic expansion techniques, the long-felt need to implement the results of psychological analysis in a positive direction came to expression in *psychosynthesis*. Originating with Roberto Assagioli, an Italian physician, psychosynthesis sought to amalgamate all schools of psychologic analysis with the spirit of man to form a total therapeutic approach.[44] Nominating the unifying spirit of man as a *Superconscious*, in distinction to the unconscious of psychoanalytic formulations, Assagioli sought to bring together the "truths of psychoanalysis of Freud, behavior therapy of Pavlov...during therapy of the Space Age...as a unified system of brain-mind equivalence...."

In effect, the Psychosynthesis School utilized Western psychologic discoveries combined with overtones of Eastern nonmaterial philosophy. Followers of Assagioli regarded psychosynthesis as a "way of looking at being human," rather than a type of psychotherapy.[45] The technique designed to "release energies of the Self" starts with a written autobiography, an assessment of the patient's traits, his "subpersonalities," the "origin of traits," tests of psychological type, which are then combined with "catharsis, introspection, meditation, intuition, relaxation, superconsciousness, will exercises," and so on. The essential aspect of Assagioli's therapy, however, is development of the will; the exercises he prescribes are simple. Starting with the question of "Who Am I?" the patient permits whatever image comes to his mind to govern his feelings, thus reaching "his true center of identity."

The superconsciousness of psychosynthesis is related philosophically to Doctor Frankl's *Logotherapy*,[46] which stresses the need to give a meaning to life. Frankl, a German psychiatrist who suffered through the destructive, degrading experiences of a Nazi concentration camp, found a new purpose in life expressed as a *will-to-meaning*. *Logotherapy* speaks to those deep wells of spiritual strength that emerge when neurotic or distraught persons seek to combat the emptiness of life in situations that seem hopeless. A trained psychoanalyst, the German-born Doctor Frankl, as a result of his trying experiences in concentration camps, recognized how psychotherapy had neglected such anguished circumstances. "The freedom of the spirit has been overlooked," he wrote. "Yet it is this freedom that truly constitutes the essence of man." Frankl's *Logotherapy* lies close to existential analysis wherein the meaning of the symptom in the neurotic patient's life is exposed and his attitude towards it reversed.

A simple technique, which Frankl called *paradoxical intention*,[47] is used, in which the symptom is accentuated to show its usefulness in the patient's life; the latter can then "detach himself from his painful problem." It amounts to an actualization by the patient of the symptom and its relation to his life. (Doctor Frankl dealt chiefly with obsessive-compulsive neurotics.) An example he quoted was that of a woman whose fear of dirt and germs (mysophobia) practically incapacitated her. Getting down on his knees, scrubbing the lecture hall floor, Doctor Frankl, caricaturing his patient, invited her to do likewise. "You see," Doctor Frankl said, "I cannot get dirty enough; I cannot find any bacteria." The patient, on repeating this procedure, broke through her phobias.

Techniques for self-realization take many forms. Since finding a place in one's world depends on one's body-image, Doctor Maxwell Maltz, a plastic surgeon whose work changed many persons' outlook on themselves, conceived the idea of changing the "self-image" through imagination. A negative self-image acts like a scar, he reasoned, and relaxation of "negative tensions" might improve the image. Finding a parallel with human personality function in the science of cybernetics (Norbert Weiner), where automatic servomechanisms (feedback) guide the machine towards its goal and negative feedback causes the machine to correct its course, Maltz worked on patients with inhibitions and disturbing tensions. In his book *Psycho-Cybernetics*,[48] he pursued the analogy, instructing his readers to use their imagination in modifying the course of their inhibiting feelings. To "take corrective action" towards one's negative self-image leads to positive ways of feeling and thinking, Doctor Maltz asserted. His system of self-help, paralleling the cybernetic model, moved in the direction of will therapy, habit training, and "programming" of success patterns.

The intriguing notion that early patterns in the brain are programmed, whether on a biochemical or electrical basis, in the way a high-fidelity recorder functions, has led to startling applications in psychotherapy. One of these was Ron Hubbard's *Dianetics*, presented in 1950, later burgeoning into *Scientology*, where "clearing the mind" of infantile experiences through an "auditing process" was claimed to result in mature behavior. The notion of "engrams," or latent memory images that might be revived, was originally advanced by neurologists to explain memory traces. In Janov's *Primal Scream* therapy,[49] memory traces of infantile anguish are obtained by a three-day period of frustrating isolation, followed by an experiencing of "that moment of icy, cosmic loneliness... when [the patient] discovers that he is not loved for what he is and will not be." This earliest evidence of psychic pain is expressed in a writhing, convulsive, sobbing, screaming episode during which the prostrate subject "feels" the excruciating experience from his past. In Janov's hands, the Primal Scream is not only claimed to be a tension-relieving technique, but a "curative agent." With this technique, interpretation, explanations, and insight are disregarded; *experiencing* the horror of that moment of psychic nakedness suffices to cure the patient.

Freeing the body of its straightjacket of imprisoned emotions, but without the drama of Janov's *Primal Scream*, has been developed by Alex Lowen in his system of *bioenergetics*.[50] Agreeing that the musculature of the body reflects emotional rigidity (especially in schizoid characters), Lowen exercises his patients, at first passively, then actively, to bring the individual into contact with his body. The exercises, starting with deep breathing, progress to striking, kicking, flailing of the arms and legs on a couch to the end that the patient is enabled to break through his characteristic rigidity. The therapist in bioenergetics encourages the patient to use his body to express feelings long buried in a habitual postural mold. The duration and details of Lowen's exercises vary with the needs of the patient and are combined with other measures of a liberating type.

The dream of relating measurable electric rhythms in the brain to mental control has become a reality in the last decade with the development of the biofeedback technique. Solidly based on observation of brain waves projected by the electroencephalograph, Doctor Neal Miller (with laboratory animals) and Doctor Kamiya (with humans) were able to train subjects to recognize alpha waves, and by a system of conditioning control, reduce or "tone" them down. The subject through a feedback arrangement recognized when alpha waves appeared and then consciously tried to reduce blood pressure or heart rate, thus proving that functions of the body governed by the autonomic nervous system (sympathetic and parasympathetic nerves) could be altered through training. Experiments in many university laboratories[51] have concentrated on vascular tone and heart action, on muscle relaxation, migraine, and paralyses in which the patient can, with training, influence his autonomic nerves and muscles to function as he wishes. Biofeedback is being developed in many areas for physical diseases and disability apart from nervous tension states.

The use of biofeedback in emotional and mental conditions opened up a vista that challenges the imagination. From combating anxiety to increasing mental power, the biofeedback techniques have attracted many regular and irregular practitioners. Feedback subjects, "connoisseurs of our inner world,"[52] have been taught to achieve relaxation deep enough to be recognized as the "blank mind state" characteristic of Zen and Yoga achievements. Preliminarily, they are taught to recognize their alpha waves over a period of weeks; then with a temperature-sensitive electrode on the forehead and hand, the subject through "mental power" is trained to increase the temperature of the hand (observed through a temperature trainer meter) and later to achieve relaxation of the head, neck, and body.

In the hands of scientific workers (Doctor Elmer Green at the Menninger Foundation, Doctor Bernard Glueck and Doctor Charles Stroebel at the Institute for

Living), the biofeedback technique has produced relaxation in patients beyond that provided by psychotropic drugs. About twenty sessions[53] are required to train the subjects to recognize their alpha waves, to learn the feelings associated with this experience, and hence to reproduce it at will. The feedback consists, usually, in a tone that issues via a microphone indicating that alpha waves are being registered on an electroencephalograph machine. When the patient achieves the alpha state, the tone is turned off. Thus, patients have a direct responsibility for their relaxation, and ultimately for their well-being. Current experiments are combined with Transcendental Meditation (see Chapter 17).

Notes to Chapter 14

1. Philip Rieff, *The Triumph of the Therapeutic; Uses of Faith After Freud*, New York, Harper & Row, 1966.
2. Howard P. Rome, "Psychiatry and Social Change, circa 1966," in *New Directions in American Psychiatry, 1933–1968*. Washington, D. C., American Psychiatric Association, May 1969, p. 317.
3. Eric Berne, *Transactional Analysis in Psychotherapy*, New York, Grove Press, 1961.
4. Eric Berne, *Games People Play*, New York, Grove Press, 1964.
5. Thomas A. Harris, *I'm OK—You're OK; a Practical Guide to Transactional Analysis*, New York, Harper & Row, 1969.
6. Harris, p. 207.
7. Alvyn Freed, *T. A. for Tots and Other Prinzes*, Sacramento, California, Jalmar Press, Inc., 1973.
8. Robert Goulding, Personal Observation. Mount Madonna, Watsonville, California, 1970–1971.
9. Erving and Miriam Polster, *Gestalt Therapy Integrated*. New York, Brunner/Mazel, 1973.
10. Rollo May, "Contributions of Existential Psychotherapy," in *Existence*, New York, Basic Books, 1958.
11. Henri F. Ellenberger, "A Clinical Introduction to Psychiatric Phenomenology and Existential Analysis," in *Existence*, p. 119.
12. Antonia Wenkart, *Existential Psychotherapy; its Theory and Practice*, Nutley, New Jersey, Hoffman-La Roche, Inc., 1972.
13. William Schutz, *Joy*, New York, Grove Press, 1967.
14. *Time:* Learning, "Schools for the Senses," Sept. 29, 1967.
15. Severin and Peggy Peterson, "Something New for Your Peace of Mind," *Ladies Home Journal*, February, 1968.
16. *Time:* Behavior, "Human Potential: The Revolution in Feeling," November 9, 1970.

17. Bruce L. Maliver, "Encounter Groupers Up Against the Wall," *New York Times Magazine,* January 3, 1971.
18. National Training Laboratories: Selected Readings Series. Washington, D. C., 1961.
19. Kurt Lewin, *Resolving Social Conflicts,* edited by Gertrude Lewin. New York, Harper & Row, 1948.
20. Calvin Hall and Gardner Lindsey, *Theories of Personality,* 2nd ed, New York, John Wiley & Sons, 1970.
21. "Where Executives Tear Off Their Masks—National Training Laboratories," *Business Week,* September 3, 1966, p. 76.
22. *Time,* November 9, 1970.
23. Abraham H. Maslow, *Toward a Psychology of Being,* 2nd ed. New York, Van Nostrand, Reinhold Co., 1968.
24. Abraham H. Maslow, *The Farther Reaches of Human Nature,* New York, The Viking Press, 1971.
25. Arthur Burton, in *Encounter,* San Francisco, California, Jossey-Bass Inc., 1970, p. 2.
26. George Bach, "The Marathon Group; Intensive Practice of Intimate Interaction," *Psychol. Reports,* vol. 18, p. 995, 1966.
27. Erving and Miriam Polster, *Gestalt Therapy Integrated,* New York, Brunner/Mazel, 1973, p. 356.
28. Frederick Perls, Ralph Hefferline, and Paul Goodman, *Gestalt Therapy,* New York, Dell Publishing Co., 1951.
29. Albert Ellis, "A Weekend of Rational Encounter," in *Encounter,* p. 113.
30. Frederick S. Perls, *Gestalt Therapy Verbatim,* Lafayette, California, Real People Press, 1969.
31. Frederick Perls, *In and Out the Garbage Pail,* Moab, Utah, Real People Press, 1969.
32. Walter Bromberg and Sara Hutchison, Center for Dynamic Therapy, Sacramento, California, 1970–1973.
33. Perls, *Garbage Pail,* p. 102.
34. *Time,* November 9, 1970.
35. Gregory Bateson and J. Ruesch, *Communication, The Social Matrix of Psychiatry,* New York, W. W. Norton, 1951.
36. Gerald Zuk, *Family Therapy,* New York, Behavioral Publishers, 1971.
37. Nathan W. Ackerman, *Psychodynamics of Family Life,* New York, Basic Books, 1958; *Treating the Troubled Family,* New York, Basic Books, 1966.
38. Association for Humanistic Psychology, San Francisco, 1972.
39. Center for Change, Manhattan Center, New York, 1974.
40. Syd Skolsky, *Affectionism.* South Miami, Florida, Earth Publishing Co., 1974.
41. Mann Ranch Seminars. Jungian and Transpersonal Psychology. Ukiah, California, 1974.
42. Explorations Institute, Berkeley, California, 1974.
43. *Personal Growth: A Magazine That Will Expand Your Awareness...* Berkeley, California, 1974.

44. Roberto Assagioli, *Dynamic Psychology and Psychosynthesis*, New York, Psychosynthesis Research Foundation, 1959.
45. Werner Mendel, "The Therapeutic Consequences of a Point of View," *World Journal of Psychosynthesis*, 4 (April) 1972.
46. Viktor E. Frankl, *The Doctor and the Soul; From Psychotherapy to Logotherapy*, translated by Richard and Clara Winston, New York, Bantam Books, 1955.
47. Frankl, p. 186.
48. Maxwell Maltz, *Psycho-Cybernetics*, New York, Prentice-Hall, 1960.
49. Arthur Janov, *The Primal Scream; Primal Therapy: The Cure for Neurosis*, New York, Dell Publishing Co., 1970.
50. Alex Lowen, *The Betrayal of the Body*, New York, Macmillan Co., 1967.
51. "Bio-Feedback in Action," *Medical World News* (March 9, 1973), p. 47.
52. Marvin Karlins and Lewis M. Andrews, *Bio-Feedback: Turning on the Power of Your Mind*, Philadelphia, J. B. Lippincott, 1972.
53. Alpha Bio-Feedback. Special Report, Frontiers of Psychiatry, Roche Report, Nutley, New Jersey, vol. 4, January 1974.

15

Shock, Drugs, and Mental Healing

MENTAL healing can be defined simply as that which modifies a person's ideas, emotions, attitudes, and behavior. But when one asks the question, "What effects these modifications?" the answer is shrouded in complexity. Is the agent that causes changes in a number of influences an ordered or quixotic combination, or one single influence? Is it psychologic, physical, chemical, or an ineffable spiritual feeling? We know that physical agents—electroshock therapy or tranquilizer drugs—change moods, minimize delusions, and modify behavior; it is equally undeniable that psychological methods—hypnosis, depth analysis, or faith healing—can influence bodily processes. This interchange between physical and mental techniques and their effect on mental and physical symptoms, makes it almost impossible to define "mental healing" precisely. Nevertheless, it is generally accepted that any maneuver, whether physical or mental, that affects a patient, client, or consumer of therapeutic service to his or her betterment, falls within the category of healing by mental means.

As has been implied in these pages, the search for a system of therapy that bestows *enduring* improvement or cure on a patient has never slackened over the centuries.

One method, based on accidental discovery, a hunch or intuition, reasoned thought or experiment, is superseded by another. Each new method is, after a period, equipped with a theory, always satisfactory for the moment, but soon frustrating in its incompleteness or inability to cover all cases, and then abandoned. Subsequently, a new cycle of empiricism and theorizing is set in motion. Meanwhile science—psychology, physiology, chemistry, electronics—advances by minute steps. New concepts arising therefrom lead to new experiments and empirical methods of treatment, which are again fitted with hypotheses. What the author called the "Use-Explanation-Cycle"[1] continues on its wavelike motion while the search for the Holy Grail of a final therapy grinds on. For therapy is the *raison d'être* of medicine in general and psychiatry in particular.

Medication and physical methods have never been absent from the physician's armamentarium. When it was believed that nervous troubles depended on depleted nerve cells in the brain and spinal cord, narcotics, sedatives, diet, hydrotherapy, tonics, and stimulants were prescribed, accompanied by a feeling of medical security. The notion of cellular function damage held sway for decades, passing from medical practice into folklore. It was reflected in the advice of Dr. Kellogg (of Battle Creek fame) to his patients and those who read his widely circulated books: "Don't worry; take a neural bath at bedtime, eat biologically, abjure tea and coffee, move the bowels three times a day and cheer UP."[2] Dr. Walter Alvarez, a respected physician of Chicago, based his counsel of patients suffering from nervous disorders on a similar theory: "the effects of emotion...from an overactive brain...nervous illness...the price of civilization."[3] Yet, in spite of the accent on traditional medical practice, the new view of the psychological basis of nervous disorders was making headway. Logan Clendening's popular book, *The Human Body* (1928),[4] inveighed against the methods of Rest Cure, baths, nerve tonics, and diet, saying they were "thoroughly stupid."

But the pathological basis for mental illnesses was not disregarded so easily. Cells and connective tissue in the brain did show, with improved methods of staining and microscopic examination, changes ranging from scar tissue to cell deterioration. The breakthrough discovery, by Noguchi and Moore (1913), that the dreaded General Paresis resulted from invasion of the syphilitic spirillum into brain tissue, led to treatment by salvarsan, mercurials, and finally the malarial treatment of Wagner von Jauregg.[5] Von Jauregg's discovery of the beneficial effects on General Paresis by inoculation with a strain of tertian malaria was hailed as a great advance in treatment of an invariably fatal disease; it won him a Nobel Prize. The malaria method, brought to St. Elizabeth's Hospital in Washington, D. C., in 1922 and to the New York Psychiatric Institute a year later, showed how a direct action on microorganisms in the brain (fever therapy) did cure some mental diseases.[6]

This finding led to other methods calculated to affect brain cells—fever production by baths and electric cabinets,[7] injection of sterile horse serum or other foreign protein (typhoid) vaccines. The production of an inflammatory reaction in the brain and spinal cord, causing an aseptic meningitis, was thought by Carroll and his fellow workers[8] to be useful in dementia praecox cases on the grounds that "perchance dementia praecox might prove a food-chemical deprivation, . . ." a view that returned in the 1970s as "megavitamin" therapy.

Search for a method to directly influence the brain was pursued on all fronts. Ether, hormones, refrigeration (lowering the patient's body temperature), nitrogen, and CO_2 inhalation were all tried with stubborn schizophrenic and neurotic cases but abandoned when the results were equivocal.[9] Various other chemical methods were tried—amphetamines, histamines, tolserol, glutamic acid (to improve intellectual capacity), vitamins, amytal, and penthothal. Chemicals resorted to for their influence on cortical functions were chiefly a means to an end, the ventilation of psychological conflicts lying behind psychoses and neuroses. In the hands of Bleckwenn and Lorenz in Wisconsin, it developed in narcoanalysis; simultaneously, Sargent in England[10] used pentothal narcosis in London during the bombing raids of World War II for quick relief of acute war hysterias. Later, "drug analytic" methods were expanded as a "shortcut" therapy and for investigative purposes in amnesias following civil traumatic conditions.

A type of sleep therapy developed by German physicians placed the patient in a state of semi-coma for hours to days following the use of barbiturates or opium derivatives. The direct effect on cortical functions by the drugs (Somnifene, by Klasi, 1922, and Luminal by Oberholzer, 1925)[11] reduced excitement in catatonic patients to the end that ventilation of psychological conflicts could then be attempted. This type of narcosis gave good results. Negativistic and catatonic patients began to eat under the influence of the sleep state, and chronic patients were reported to be much improved; eighty percent cures were reported in one series of cases. Modifications were introduced in the sedative drug employed (particularly Amytal),[12] with the general finding that such narcosis had a profound effect not only in reducing agitation of manics and catatonics but in decreasing self-absorption and increasing the possibility of friendly contact. In seriously disturbed patients, "a period of normal existence" followed administration of the drug. The net results were encouraging enough for narcosis treatment to gain adherents in this country.[13]

Sleep treatment, renamed the "twilight state" by the Germans (Dämmerzustand), was extended by the utilization of CO_2 gas, oxygen, or nitrogen. In this instance it was hoped that anoxia, a decrease in oxygen available for brain-cell metabolism, would reverse and possibly modify brain function and hence mental activity. Experimentation with gases, originated by Loevenhart[14] and Langenstrass,[15] resulted in direct but temporary improvement among stuporous schizophrenics or other types of inaccessible patients. For this reason, psychotherapeutic suggestions were added, treating the patient as if he were in "a transient state of hypnosis." For induction, nitrogen in the form of nitrous oxide was substituted.[16] This treatment was soon extended to neurotic patients[17] in addition to stuporous cases, on the general theory that a "shock" effect would produce disinhibition of rigid and inaccessible individuals.[18] Treatment of the "hyperventilation syndrome," a frequent finding among hysteria and anxiety patients, utilized the same principles as gas narcosis. Rebreathing into a paper sack decreased the symptoms of lightheadedness, anxiety, and panic consequent upon alkalosis by increasing the carbon dioxide[19] content of the blood and, ultimately, of the brain.

Medical measures calculated to influence mental symptoms have been legion. At one extreme were attempts such as that of Petit, who injected intravenously radioactive substances (thorium) in cases of dementia praecox or melancholia,[20] while at the other was the use of a salt-free diet in the treatment of insomnia.[21] Allied to these therapeutic assays into the unknown was the fascinating field of artificial psychoses produced by various drugs, on the supposition that the synthetic formation of mental states might lead to discovery of rational measures for their treatment. Psychopathologic changes induced by such drugs as mescaline and *Cannabis indica* (hashish, marijuana) in their action on the mid-brain, the cortex, and the basal ganglia, resembling schizophrenic reactions, have been amply studied.[22]

The question of sedation has occupied the major attention of physicians in the therapy of mental disorders from the days of Hippocrates. From opium to hellebore and nepenthe, bromides and chloral, to the infinite array of barbiturate compounds of today, sedation has been the mainstay of physicians in dealing with nervous afflictions. Coincidentally, from the patient's point of view, the vast power imputed to sedatives far outweighs all other methods of therapy. Indeed, there is a continuous subterranean struggle between the layman's wish for a blanket drug to still his anxieties and tensions and the physician's aim to alter these emotional disturbances through his technical means.

To return to the diversity of medical methods employed during the second and third decade of this century, ductless glands were exploited because of their relation to emotional states through the autonomous (sympathetic) nervous system. Thyroid extract,[23] known for a century as a substance the body requires for mental stability, was employed with depressions and involutional melancholias, with later additions of ovarian and testicular hormones.[24] The Aschner treatment, which resurrected some of the older methods of drastic purging, also utilized thyroid and corpus luteum glandular preparations in depressions among women.[25] During the period of enthusiasm for glandular treatment in medicine generally, the "misbehaving ductless glands"[26] were looked to for solution of many of the secrets of nervous disorders. Although no magical relationships were discovered between ovarian, testicular, pituitary, thyroid, or adrenal gland extracts and a wide variety of mental disturbances, the substances, refined and concentrated, continue to be used, particularly in depressive conditions. In the same sense of substitutive therapy, vitamin E has been experimented with in various neuropsychiatric conditions.[27]

The removal of focal infections, a recently discovered source of hidden infection in the teeth, tonsils, gall bladder, genital organs, and intestines, became in the 1920s the basis for a new approach to mental disease and a new theory of etiology of these conditions. Dr. Henry Cotton at the New Jersey State Hospital in Trenton[28] reported eighty percent cures in patients in whom foci of infection were removed. The success of his work induced Cotton to reevaluate the functional psychoses as disturbances "arising from circulating toxins originating in chronic foci of infection." Indeed, mental illness itself was considered merely a symptom of a "toxemia which acts directly on the brain." Although removal of focal infections did improve the general health of some patients, a careful analysis at the New York Institute[29] disproved the causal relation of body infection to mental disease in a controlled group of patients and relegated the treatment to a medical routine adopted by every well-run mental institution.

The various methods of physical treatment sketched in these pages were soon to be eclipsed by new sources of mental treatment, insulin shock and electroshock, aimed directly at the disordered brain metabolism thought to be at the base of mental disease. Dr. Manfred Sakel, a Viennese physician, had observed a beneficial emotional effect on certain schizoid drug addicts whom he had treated with insulin. The hypoglycemia thus produced diminished the addicts' withdrawal symptoms as well as improving their mental alertness. He reasoned that an increase in insulin dosage might result in major personality changes among schizophrenic patients.[30] Experiments were initiated in bringing these patients to a state of coma, induced by lowered blood sugar following large doses of insulin. Profound physical changes, sweating, convulsive movements, pallor, coma, and epileptic seizures resulted. When patients regained consciousness following administration of sugar to overcome the insulin effect, they showed mental clarity and relief from many of their delusional experiences. Sakel's method was recognized immediately as a most significant development, since a change in the chemical environment of the brain cells evoked definite observable alterations in mentation and mood in patients brought back from the hypoglycemic state. The treatment results were so striking among patients hitherto inaccessible that Sakel's method was hailed as a great advance and put into practice in many clinics throughout the world. Original work done by Sakel at the University of Vienna Clinic was continued in this country in various psychiatric and state hospitals, particularly at Bellevue in New York, in association with Joseph Wortis. By 1937, at the Congress of the Swiss Psychiatric Association,[31] representatives of European countries reported their already extensive experiences with insulin and other shock-producing methods.

The insulin treatment led to a new rise in therapeutic optimism. Early reports of the therapy indicated a level of from seventy to eighty-eight percent cures in cases recently ill.[32] When schizophrenic patients whose illness lasted more than a year were treated, the rate of remission of the illness after insulin therapy dropped to from forty to fifty percent. Early experiences pointed toward insulin shock treatment as a specific for schizophrenia, and the press gave prominence to a new treatment in their science reports. *Time* put it in layman's language: "The Sakel cure is complicated, difficult and dangerous because the patient must die of insulin shock several times before he can collect and use his wits like a normal human being."[33] Follow-up studies indicated less satisfactory results over a period of years than originally reported, but the indications were clear that schizophrenic patients showed gratifying immediate responses to treatment and were more quickly released from the hospital following treatment.[34]

The hypoglycemic treatment of schizophrenics reached a peak just prior to and during World War II. Meanwhile, a method of obtaining convulsions without the dangers of insulin coma had been advanced by von Meduna,[35] a Hungarian psychiatrist, in 1935. Using the stimulant Metrazol, he achieved a convulsion in the patient within a few seconds of the drug's injection. Whereas Sakel's origination of insulin was a clinical empirical procedure, von Meduna introduced Cardiazol (Metrazol) therapy on the deductive basis of antagonism between epilepsy and schizophrenia. The drug Metrazol was injected into the bloodstream, whereas the technique of electric shock depended on the designing of a compact machine that would deliver a variable but safely tolerated quantity of electric current through the patient's brain. Insulin treatment required a hospital setting, nursing service, and at least five hours of close supervision per treatment; Metrazol and electroshock called for briefer care and less extensive preparation and less supervision of the patient. After much clinical experimentation, the chemical method of shock production (Metrazol) originated by von Meduna was rejected in favor of electric-shock treatment for cogent reasons, namely, the initial anxiety experienced by the patient, the possibility of fractures following the convulsion, and the unpredictability of convulsion.

The production of an artificial convulsion, the so-called electric-convulsive therapy, had a long history starting with Leduc's experiments (1902) on "electric sleep," which occurred on passage of an electric current through the brains of animals. The Italian originators, Bini and Cerletti,[36] made a series of careful experiments with dogs before they extended the technique to human beings. Improvements with electrical apparatus and the lack of anxiety produced in the patient made electric-convulsive therapy most feasible and effective for many unmanageable or self-absorbed patients, particularly in the affective group—depression, melancholia, neurotic tension states. The moderate dangers of electric shock, namely, the accident of fractures after convulsions, have been mitigated by the use of curare[37] and the introduction of the glissando method of induction.[38]

The success of convulsive shock methods seemed assured even though it was acknowledged that these methods reduced depressions and mitigated agitation, but did not cure the disease. As experience accumulated, it became evident that the improvement was often temporary. After twenty years or more, shock therapy became standard. As with insulin coma treatment, some psychiatrists gave patients enormous numbers of shock treatments, reaching from 50 to 100 over a few months. The effects, though dramatic, were not predictable. One young patient with paranoid ideation was treated with 120 electroshock treatments in a state hospital with surprisingly little effect on her mental capacity; she subsequently achieved a doctorate degree in a large Eastern university.[39] The severity of the treatment, particularly on the patient's memory and the reciprocal uneasiness in the physician, combined to reduce drastically the number of treatments given. In recent years, electroshock is rarely extended beyond twelve treatments (more often four to eight) to reduce agitation or quiet extreme depressions. In a summary, Robitscher reported that an accredited hospital (The Pennsylvania Institute) gave shock treatment to only 7.5 percent of its patients during 1970 and 1971, whereas a comparative private hospital used electroshock in sixty to seventy percent of its cases.[40]

With the vast use of electroshock therapy, much speculation has been advanced as to the mechanisms involved. Cerletti, the originator, theorized that a substance, which he called *agonine*, formed in the brain and altered the chemistry of that tissue; whereas Schilder put his explanation of the success of shock therapy more dramatically by calling it a "Victory over the death threat."[41] Other suggestions, that the electric current stimulated the vegetative centers in the diencephalon, thus "re-establishing hemostasis" between the soma and the psyche, were countered by psychological explanations, i.e., the authority of a superior force (electricity) on the patient's ego.[42]

Reasoning from the possibility of altering the psychology and/or pathology of the brain physically, it was inevitable that some intrepid investigator would seek to enlist surgery. Experience has shown how neurotic and psychotic symptoms seem to share a "circular" form; could not these repetitive symptoms lie on the basis of a fixed *misarrangement* of cell connections in the brain? Destruction of these abnormal "circuits" from the frontal lobe to the thalamus might well interrupt symptom cycles.[43] So fantasized the creative genius Edward Bellamy, in a novel published in 1880 in which the heroine sought to extirpate the obsessive "pang of conscience" by a surgical operation. The "mental physician," speaking through the author, remarks that in "Twenty years . . . merely a question of mechanical difficulties to be overcome . . . a nice problem in surgery . . . we will be able to extract a specific recollection from the memory as readily as a dentist pulls a tooth."[44] And so reasoned Dr. Egas Moniz, a neurologist of Lisbon, Portugal, a half century later.

With understandable trepidation, Moniz, in association with Almeida Lima, a Portuguese surgeon (1936), initiated the operation of leukotomy in a group of patients by cutting the fibers in the motor areas of the frontal lobe. Their chronic patients demonstrated improvement in behavior but there was no real change in intellectual capacity. Other brain surgeons followed Moniz cautiously, although Furtado remarks that it was not until Freeman popularized the procedure that much attention was given leukotomy, even in Portugal.[45]

Since the fibers connecting the frontal lobe and the thalamus were chosen to be severed, Dr. Walter Freeman, of Washington, D. C., devised an operation of less complexity. He plunged a sharp pointed instrument, commonly called an "ice pick," directly into the underside of the frontal lobe through the orbital plate above the eye. The results were often melodramatic in two directions: the patients ceased their unmanageable behavior forthwith, or became conscienceless, zombie-like creatures with poor ethical judgement.[46]

A few neurosurgeons used a more refined technique by the approved trephining method, with careful cutting of the fronto-thalamic fibers. In the main, reactions to leukotomy, especially Freeman's crude surgery, were strong. Neurosurgeons in general were aghast at the technique employed, including the repeated electroshocks given to achieve anesthesia in Freeman's operation. As a consequence, lobotomy faded as a treatment of choice for schizophrenics. Recently, however, it has been revived as a means to modify behavior patterns, particularly among hardened criminals and psychopathic personalities. Drs. Sweet and Mark of Boston[47] suggested psychosurgery for those committing "senseless" crimes against the person while others decried surgical methods as politically and humanely indefensible (Dr. Peter Breggin).

The appearance of tranquilizers and antidepressant drugs in the 1950s gave rise to a wave of therapeutic optimism among psychiatrists that has not yet crested. The faintly resigned attitude of older physicians who doled out bromides and opium derivatives (laudanum) to mentally disturbed patients was replaced by a new confidence, born of a more exact knowledge of nervous system chemistry. The introduction of the barbiturates (Veronal, 1904, phenobarbital, 1912) and more than 2,500 derivatives of barbituric acid led to so wide a use that by the end of the 1930s "an estimated billion grains of sedatives" were consumed each year in the United States.[48] The enormous use of sedatives for anxiety, tension, and insomnia, whether prescribed by physicians or self-administered, outstripped bromides, the standby of "nerve doctors" of the early part of this century. These medications performed their function of quieting nervous symptoms among neurotics but had the adverse effect of clouding consciousness to a degree. Moreover, their effect on psychotic patients was minimal. But the rediscovery of *Rauwolfia*, extracted from the snake root plant in the 1950s, started the trend toward a more specific treatment of schizophrenics and anxiety neuroses.

Rauwolfia, named for its German discoverer, had been known and used by Hindu physicians for centuries. Marketed under the names Reserpine, Serpasil, etc., it initiated the tranquilizing era for many patients and for hypertensives with nervous complaints. In 1952, two French psychiatrists, Delay and Deniker, noted the antihistamine effect of Promethazine, from which Thorazine and kindred products evolved; the drugs reduced motor activity, slowed response to external stimuli, and improved the atmosphere of the hospital where treated psychotics were held. Within two years, the phenothiazines, as the class of drugs was generally known, were introduced, and adopted in this country to the point where they largely replaced Reserpine.[49] Indeed, it is estimated that fifty million patients were treated with drugs of this group and more than ten thousand articles written about their use. The fact that these antipsychotic drugs did not influence consciousness as they subdued excited patients, lessened resistance to psychotherapy, and replaced incoherence with responsive speech lent a touch of magic to the phenothiazines. Joseph Wortis, who helped bring insulin coma therapy to Bellevue Hospital in New York from Vienna, was able to write in 1954, "[the] Autonomous sedatives [Thorazine and Serpasil] are in the forefront of public and psychiatric attention." He noted parenthetically in the same review that "insulin coma treatment stands up well in Vienna."[50]

Within a few years the pharmaceutical industry stimulated their researchers into developing new varieties of phenothiazines (Sparine, Compazine, Thorazine, Vesprin, and later Mellaril, Prolixin, Trilafon, Stelazine) and the derivatives of the thioxanthene group (Navane,[51] Torecan, etc.). The main effect of the various groups was to reduce agitation and excitement and to improve the withdrawn, apathetic patient. In time, these drugs, plus a host of others (Haldol, Valium, Librium, meprobamate [Miltown]) were prescribed for anxiety and minor neurotic conditions. The frequency of depressions with the threat of suicide or suicidal attempts stimulated the pharmacological industry to develop a group of drugs commonly called "mood elevators." For the "masked depression" hiding under a varied group of vague physical symptoms, drugs like Elavil, Tofranil, Norpramine, Ritalin, and Sinequan were marketed. These and their predecessors—Marplan, Nardil, and the amphetamines (Benzedrine)—were effective in removing the sharp edge of anguish in depressions.[52] For mania, the mineral Lithium, introduced by Cade in 1949, is remininiscent of the minerals Paracelsus introduced into medicine five hundred years ago. The effect of Lithium in reducing excitement among manic patients and maintaining them at a close-to-normal level over a long period has been striking at times.

The development of new drugs proceeds at an accelerated pace. Advertising by mail, in the medical literature, through grants for research, programs of medical education, and personal solicitation by "detail men" have made the pharmaceutical profession virtually the partner of the practicing psychiatrist. Advertising campaigns, which have assumed the level of opulent, artistic productions, flood the doctor's mail with reviews of medical interest, soft-sell propaganda; incidentally, they have made medical journalism a well-founded specialty. Wortis, in his early review of psychologic treatments in the *American Journal of Psychiatry* (1960), commented that his task was "to help the bewildered psychiatrist" organize his information about the "vast and growing literature of psychopharmacology."[53]

Widespread use of tranquilizer drugs practically revolutionized the hospital treatment of psychotic cases. Moreover, it improved the hospital milieu and decreased the census, permitting chronic patients to attempt adaptation to a home environment through the "halfway house," but simultaneously increased the admission rates.[54] Reliance on tranquilizer drugs has so altered traditional treatment of nervous and mental disorders that critical studies determining the place of drugs with or without psychotherapy were instituted. These double-blind studies, wherein neither the treating doctors nor the patients were aware of the type of medication given, produced equivocal results. The National Institute of Mental Health, in a recent summary of drug versus psychotherapeutic efforts with schizophrenics, concluded that "drugs alone are the single most powerful and economical treatment for schizophrenics within one or two year time limits."[55] In fact, their survey of research reports indicates that psychotherapy without drugs provided "evidence neither for its effectiveness nor its helpfulness." Other comparison studies with psychotherapy alone or with tranquilizers (Stevenson) agreed that such comparisons "failed to demonstrate the efficacy of psychotherapy."[56]

Nevertheless, the march of drugs has been so irresistible that Stancer was able to write, in 1973, "it is now in the realm of ancient history to describe the 1950s when the exciting discovery was made of the clinical use of phenothiazines and antipsychotic agents."[57]

The drive to find a chemical that would effectively alter schizophrenic symptoms led to vitamins, introduced by Dr. A. Hoffer of Saskatchewan, Canada, in 1957. This treatment, which maintained schizophrenics on high doses of niacin or nicotinic acid (three grams a day) for a long period, claimed marked improvement in acute cases, with somewhat less spectacular results in chronic schizophrenics.[58] Proceeding along the lines laid down by Linus Pauling, in using *megavitamin* doses for various illnesses, Hoffer, Osmond, and others have asserted that with long-term treatment (two years on daily doses of 3,000 milligrams niacin, B_3, and vitamin C) "long-term prognosis was greatly improved."[59] The ascendance of megavitamin therapy into a field called *orthomolecular psychiatry* captured the imagination of families with schizophrenic patients, leading to the establishment of Schizophrenia Associations promulgating Hoffer's methods. As with all empirical treatment, megavitamin therapy was fitted with a theory, in this case a biochemical one. It is asserted that "kryptopyrrole" (the *mauve* factor) produces a metabolic deficiency in the brain, susceptible to megavitamin dosage. The complex chemistry of brain tissue precludes any one chemical disarrangement to be held responsible for the disease schizophrenia in spite of the current enthusiasm for megavitamins.

However, other psychiatrists have been unable to duplicate Hoffer's results; Wittenborn *et al*, at the New Jersey

State Hospital, Marlboro,[60] were led to conclude that "present findings are discouraging" in the expectation that a two-year treatment with niacin would aid schizophrenics in public hospitals. In Canada, where megavitamin treatment has had extensive trials, Dr. Ban reported after a careful review that "no patient groups (apart from pellagra...) responsive to nicotinic acid treatment has as yet been identified."[61]

That Americans are a drug-using people is by now a banal statement. Whether for insomnia, nervousness (anxiety and tension states), or depression, legal over-the-counter drugs (as apart from prescriptions by physicians, which reached 214 million in 1970) were consumed by thirty-five to forty million persons in the U.S.A. during 1967.[62] When caffeine, nicotine, and alcohol are added, the total picture justifies the accusation that America is virtually a *drug culture.* Self-medication in milder forms as an American trait cannot be discounted as a means of mental healing.

It is a pointed commentary on the democratization of psychologic and medical knowledge that widespread self-treatment among youth, and some adults, followed the success of tranquilizing drugs in mental diseases. Although barbiturates and bromides had been a surreptitious panacea for depression and anxiety for years, solace for the millions could be obtained, since World War II, on a non-prescribed basis through the illicit traffic in drugs. The habit of self-administered medication was given a tremendous stimulus with marijuana and hashish smoking, a practice confined to a few jaded sensualists and bohemians until the 1930s. Its appearance among blacks and Latin Americans in our larger cities, limited at first to musicians and demi-monde habitués,[63] swelled among youths until by 1970, it is estimated, approximately twenty million persons had indulged to a greater or lesser degree.[64] Polls taken during the late 1960s among college students, servicemen in and out of combat (Vietnam), adults in large cities, all attest to the "explosive increase in marijuana smoking" in the period 1969–1971.[65] Coincidentally, LSD (lysergic acid), which has been a vehicle for psychiatric experiments since 1949, gradually gained prominence under the leadership of Dr. Timothy Leary. His "turn on, tune in, drop out" slogan in the 1960s attracted youths with a wish to experience the "higher existential meanings" of life—not as an antidote to ennui and apathy but as an entrance to a richer experience, "the answer to the universal problems facing man."[66]

Although D-lysergic acid was originally a research tool in schizophrenia, its mind-expanding function soon became known to hippiedom. Dr. Abrahamson and his group at South Oaks on Long Island, New York, had successfully combated the emotional blocking of chronic schizophrenics with the drug.[67] Working in the early 1960s, they found that low doses of LSD 25 loosened "infantile bonds" and permitted discussion of emotional problems with the patients. Conversely they found that high doses produced a "cosmic-mystic experience." The attainment of this *psychedelic* state, which drowned out boredom and achieved an existential level described as the "where it's at" attitude, leaked out to youth. As a black market developed in LSD and other drugs, a subterranean cult evolved throughout this country and Western Europe dedicated to psychedelic drugs. Since the federal government withdrew permission for research use of LSD, the black market has taken over, adding mescaline, amphetamine, heroin, and cocaine to its offerings. Self-treatment for depression, for ennui, and as a subtle form of rebellion against the establishment became a nationwide fad. Sedatives ("downers"), benzedrine ("uppers"), glue-sniffing, psychedelics (hashish, peyote, mescaline, psilocybin), opium, heroin, and cocaine became the "open sesame" to an expanded world. Often the reactions reached the level of a "bad trip," a euphemism for toxic reactions reaching the level of brief or extended psychoses...or death.

During the late 1960s drug usage was pandemic.

Youths developed an acquaintance with the effects of drugs by studying publications of pharmaceutical houses, through experimental self-dosage and exchange of information on the street or at centers such as Synanon, Daytop, Aquarian Efforts, and similar lay organizations. Self-medication assumed its place alongside professional prescribing. The significant difference between the self-treatment of youth in the 1960s and 1970s and that of other decades is that esoteric knowledge was no longer confined to researchers and medical specialists.

Self-medication among the young has several roots; an obvious one is the coalesced rebelliousness against prevailing restrictions on pleasure-seeking as a value in life imposed by the mature population. Reaction to what Klerman has called "Pharmacologic Calvinism," i.e., "whatever drug makes you feel good must be bad,"[68] is apparent in sexual freedom and the easy display of aggression, as well as in drug usage. Circumvention of the law, combined with the promise of pleasure, represents an "in-ness," a private universe that unites American youth in all parts of the country like the invisible ether that is said to pervade space. Held together by values that flout society, by a special language, a type of dress and adornment, and a routine of behavior, this unique subculture provides a sense of solidarity to drug users. Here he or she is safe; the commonplace is evaded, boredom suppressed, excitement and exhilaration enjoyed in an atmosphere of togetherness. In this situation, drugs that have the function of preserving accepted norms cannot be called therapeutic.

When, however, anxiety erupts due to body image distortions, frightening hallucinations, changed time relations, depressed or absent sexual impulses, and feelings of unreality, drugs are resorted to as treatment. Marijuana is bypassed, "uppers" replace "downers," and the fear that drugs may lead to harassment by the police or distraught parents becomes a real hazard. At this point stronger drugs like heroin or cocaine may be employed as the reality of being "hooked" looms before the user. This realization may impel the user to seek medical attention or he or she may be forced to this extremity by law enforcement agencies. In hospitals, methadone clinics, communes such as Youth for Christ, or special hospital groupings such as *the Family* (Mendocino State Hospital, Ukiah, California), the addict is treated by detoxification and psychotherapy.

Thus self-medication leads in a circuitous way back to medical attention. The individual who self-prescribes drugs inevitably finds him or herself involved in rehabilitative efforts by the community. The slow process of personality reintegration begins with whatever medical, social work, and psychiatric resources are available. This new problem of community health, an offshoot of the American drug culture, calls for revised or new programs of treatment, a perennial challenge to the psychotherapist.

Notes to Chapter 15

1. Walter Bromberg, *The Nature of Psychotherapy: A critique of the Psychotherapeutic Transaction*, New York, Grune & Stratton, 1962, p. 13.
2. J. H. Kellogg, *Neurasthenia, or, Nervous Exhaustion*, Battle Creek, Michigan, Good Health Pub. Co., 1915, p. 21.
3. Walter Alvarez, *The Neuroses: Diagnosis and Management*, Phila., W. B. Saunders, 1951, Chapter 26.
4. Logan Clendening, *The Human Body*, New York, A. A. Knopf, 1928.
5. J. Wagner-Jauregg, "Treatment of paresis by malaria," *J. Nerv. & Ment. Dis.* 55:369, 1922.
6. G. H. Kirby and H. A. Bunker, "Types of therapeutic response observed in the malaria treatment of general paralysis," *Am. J. Psychiat.* 6:205, 1926.
7. C. A. Neymann, *Artificial Fever*, Baltimore, Thomas, 1938.
8. R. S. Carroll, E. S. Barr, R. G. Barry, and David Matzke, "Aseptic meningitis in the treatment of dementia praecox," *Am. J. Psychiat.* 4:673, 1926.
9. J. Stephen Horsley, *Narco-analysis; A New Technique in Short-Cut Psychotherapy*, London, Oxford, 1943.
10. William Sargent, "Physical treatment of acute war neurosis," *Brit. M. J.* 2:574, 1942.
11. J. Kläsi and W. Oberholzer, quoted in H. D. Palmer, and A. L. Paine, "Prolonged narcosis as therapy in the psychoses," *Am. J. Psychiat.* 12:143, 1932.

12. W. J Bleckwenn, "Production of sleep and rest in psychotic cases," *Arch. Neurol. & Psychiat.* 24:365, 1930.
13. H. D. Palmer and F. J. Braceland, "Six years experience with narcosis therapy in psychiatry," *Am. J. Psychiat.* 94:37, 1937.
14. A. S. Loevenhart, W. F. Lorenz, and R. M. Waters, "Cerebral stimulation," *J.A.M.A.* 92:880, 1929.
15. K. H. Langenstrass, "Treatment of stupor," *Am. J. Psychiat.* 11:447, 1931.
16. F. A. D. Alexander and H. E. Himwich, "Nitrogen inhalation therapy for schizophrenia," *Am. J. Psychiat.* 96:643, 1939.
17. L. J. von Meduna, "Pharmaco-dynamic treatment of psychoneuroses," *Dis. Nerv. System* 8:37, 1947.
18. H. Lehmann and C. Bos, "The advantages of nitrous oxide inhalation in psychiatric treatment," *Am. J. Psychiat.* 104:164, 1947.
19. H. M. Carryer, "The hyperventilation syndrome," *M. Clin. North America* 31:845, 1947.
20. Gabriel Petit, "Curiethérapie des psychoses," *Bull. Acad. de méd.* 109:225, 1933.
21. M. M. Miller, "Cutting down salt in diet relieves sleeplessness," *Science News Letter,* May 27, 1944, p. 343.
22. Erich Lindemann and W. Malamud, "Experimental analysis of the psychopathological effects of intoxicating drugs," *Am. J. Psychiat.* 13:853, 1934.
23. R. G. Hoskins and F. H. Sleeper, "The thyroid factor in dementia praecox," *Am. J. Psychiat.* 10:411, 1930.
24. Karl Bowman and Lauretta Bender, "The treatment of involution melancholia with ovarian hormone," *Am. J. Psychiat.* 11:867, 1932.
25. K. E. Appel, C. B. Farr, and F. J. Braceland, "The Aschner treatment of schizophrenia; a therapeutic note," *Am. J. Psychiat.* 92:201, 1935.
26. E. R. Spaulding, "The importance of endocrine therapy in combination with mental analyses in the treatment of certain cases of personality deviation." *Am. J. Psychiat.* 1:373–384, 1922.
27. Simon Stone, "Evaluation of vitamin E therapy in psychiatric disorders," *Dis. Nerv. System* 11:355, 1950.
28. H. A. Cotton, "The etiology and treatment of the so-called functional psychoses; summary of results based upon the experience of four years," *Amer. J. Psychiat.* 2:157, 1922.
29. N. Kopeloff and C. O. Cheney, "Studies in focal infection; its presence and elimination in the functional psychoses," *Am. J. Psychiat.* 2:139, 1922.
30. L. B. Kalinowsky and P. H. Hoch, *op. cit.,* page 274.
31. Manfred Sakel, "Zur Methodik der Hypoglykämiebehandlung von Psychosen," *Wien. klin. Wchnschr.* 49: 1278, 1936; "A new treatment of schizophrenia," *Amer. J. Psychiat.* 93:829, 1937.
32. Manfred Sakel, "The nature and origin of the hypoglycemic treatment of psychoses," *Amer. J. Psychiat.* (Suppl.) 94:24, 1938 (Proc. 89th Meet. Swiss Psychiatric Association, 1937, translated by S. Katenelbogen).

33. "Insulin for insanity," *Time* 29:28, March 25, 1937.
34. Kalinowsky and Hoch, *op cit.*
35. Ladislaus von Meduna, "General discussion of Cardiazol therapy," *Amer. J. Psychiat. (Suppl.)* 94:40, 1938.
36. Ugo Cerletti, "Old and new information about electro-shock," *Amer. J. Psychiat.* 107:87, 1950.
37. A. E. Bennett and P. H. Cash, "Curarization with quinine methochloride to prevent traumatic complications of Metrazol shock therapy," *Psychiatric Quart.* 15:351, 1941.
38. E. B. Tietz, C. W. Olsen, and W. R. Rosanoff, "The suppression of the motor phenomena of electro-shock and electronarcosis by modification of the current level," *J. Nerv. and Ment. Dis.* 109:405, 1949.
39. Walter Bromberg, Personal observation, 1962.
40. Jonas B. Robitscher, "Psychosurgery and Other Somatic Means of Altering Behavior," *Bull of Amer. Acad. Of Psychiatry and Law*, Vol. II, Mar. 1974, p. 7.
41. Kalinowsky and Hoch, p. 192.
42. John Frosch and David Impastato, "The effects of shock treatment on the ego," *Psychoanalyt. Quart.* 17:226, 1948.
43. Kalinowsky and Hoch, p. 324.
44. Edward Bellamy, *Dr. Heidenhoff's Process*, New York, Appleton, 1880, p. 95.
45. Diogo Furtado, "Notes on Portuguese psychiatry," *J. Clin. and Exper. Psychopath.* 8:1, 1952.
46. Walter Bromberg, Personal observation, Mendocino State Hosp., Ukiah, Cal., 1951.
47. A. Winter, *The Surgical Control of Behavior. A Symposium*, Springfield, Illinois, Chas. C. Thomas, 1971.
48. Quoted in Edward M. Brecher, *Licit and Illicit Drugs*, Mt. Vernon, New York, Consumers Union, 1972, p. 248.
49. Murray E. Jarvik, in Goodman and Gilman, *Pharmacological Basis of Therapeutics*, 4th Ed., New York, Macmillan, 1970, p. 515.
50. Joseph Wortis, "Physiological Treatment (A Review)," *Amer. J. of Psych.* Vol. III, Jan., 1955, p. 515.
51. AMA Drug Evaluations, 2nd Ed., Publ. Sciences Group, Inc. Acton, Mass., 1973, p. 325.
52. *Ibid.*, p. 359.
53. Joseph Wortis, "Physiological Treatment, A Review," *Amer. J. Psychiat.*, Vol. 116, Jan. 1960, p. 595.
54. Rudolf Kaelbing and Donald Larson, "Comparison of Drug Therapy Before and During Psychiatric Hospitalization," *Amer. J. Psychiat.*, Vol. 122, Feb. 1966, p. 900.
55. David B. Feinsilver and John G. Gunderson, "Psychotherapy for Schizophrenics—Is it Indicated?" *Schizophrenia Bulletin*, N.I.M.H., No. 6, Fall, 1972.
56. Harvey C. Stancer, "Position Paper: Psychopharmacology. Yesterday, Today and Tomorrow. A Point of View," *Canadian Psych. Assn. Journal*, Vol. 18, Aug. 1973, p. 371.

57. Ian Stevenson, "The Challenge of Results in Psychotherapy," *Amer. J. Psychiat.*, Aug. 1959, p. 119.

58. A. Hoffer, *et al.*, "Treatment of Schizophrenia with nicotinic acid and nicotinamide," *J. Clin & Exp. Psychopath.* Vol. 18, 1957, p. 131.

59. A. Hoffer, "Megavitamin B, Therapy for Schizophrenia," *Canadian Psych. Assn. Jour.*, Vol. 16, Dec., 1971, p. 499.

60. Richard J. Wittenborn, Emile Weber, and Mary Brown, "Niacin in the Long-Term Treatment of Schizophrenia," *Arch. Gen. Psych.*, Vol. 28, Mar. 1973, p. 308.

61. Thomas A. Ban, "Nicotinic Acid and Psychiatry," *Can. Psych. Assn. Jour.*, Vol. 16, Oct. 1971, p. 413.

62. National Institute of Mental Health Report: Psychotropic Drug Study (Drs. Manheimer, Mellinger, and Balter), 1969, in Brecher, *Licit and Illicit Drugs*, p. 482.

63. Walter Bromberg, "Marihuana Intoxication, A clinical Study of Cannabis Sativa Intoxication," *Amer. J. Psychiat.*, Vol. 91, Sept., 1934, p. 303.

64. Stanley Yolles, Narcotics Legislation. Sub-committee to Investigate Juvenile Delinquency. Government Printing Office, Washington, D. C., 1969, U. S. Senate, Sept. 17, 1969.

65. Brecher, p. 427.

66. John Peterson, "Where's Timothy Leary?" *National Observer*, Mar. 3, 1973.

67. Harold A. Abrahamson, *The Use of LSD in Psychotherapy and Alcoholism*, Intro. by Fremont-Smith, New York, Bobbs-Merrill Co., 1967.

68. Gerald Klerman, in *Communication and Drug Abuse*, ed. J. R. Wittenborn *et al.*, Springfield, Ill., Chas. Thomas, 1970, p. 152.

16

The Psychologic Revolution

As far as mental healing is concerned, the psychologic revolution started innocently enough with Pavlov's experiments in the physiology of the digestive glands, which won him the Nobel Prize in 1904. Before that, physiological psychology, or academic psychology for that matter, had little to do with psychotherapy, with the exception of William James and possibly Stanley Hall. In the eighteenth and nineteenth centuries, philosophers and psychologists struggled to develop clear concepts of the mind as an abstract quality. With the advent of physiological studies of sensation, the mind was brought closer to the body; Professor Boring remarked that the new Germany psychology of the late 1800s was the "offspring of German physiology of sensation and British philosophy of empiricism and associationism."[1]

While the science of psychology was developing on the wings of Pavlov's experiments on dogs and Watson's behaviorism, a new attitude toward the subjective aspect of man's thinking was aborning. Conditioning became the route to changed behavior, not introspection or juggling with emotions and ideas. Time-honored landmarks like *instincts* and *basic emotions* were overturned; behaviorism was the twentieth-century product of a nineteenth-century revolution. Its influence on mental treatment has surfaced in a meaningful way in our mid-century.

Of Pavlov's physiological-psychological investigations, the most significant for the history of mental healing, however, were his experiments on psychic influence on bodily processes, in which he demonstrated that a dog can be made to respond to a neutral stimulus that was associated, after repeated exercises, with a meaningful stimulus such as food. Thus a dog could be "conditioned" to respond to any learning stimulus; by extension via "higher-order conditioning" an animal or human could also be conditioned to complex bits of behavior. When Ivan Petrovich Pavlov graduated in Natural Sciences and Medicine in the late nineteenth century, this type of experiment was far in advance of the physiological psychology of the day.[2] The extremely schematic statement of Pavlov's lifelong work, stated above, represented the foundation for behaviorism, which John B. Watson developed and which became the backbone for today's Behavior Modification Therapy.

Behaviorism actually was the work of several psychologists—Tolman, Hull, and Skinner—but as Herrnstein put it: "John B. Watson defined it, shaped it, promoted it and coined its terminology."[3] Behaviorism aroused tremendous opposition from academic psychologists when first formulated, although its influence was great in education and later in psychotherapy. Watson, the man, was a sport among academicians. Born in rural South Carolina, he lived, worked, won fame, and lost prestige with the same undimmed spirit with which he attacked the prevailing psychology at the turn of the century. The impact of Watson's behaviorism was evidenced in his experiments with children at Johns Hopkins University, where he devised methods for inducing phobias through the conditioning process. In the famous case of Albert, an infant of eleven months who was reported never to have cried except at a loud sound, Watson presented the infant with a white rat with which he played unconcernedly. When the child reached for the animal, the experimenter produced a loud noise by striking a metal bar behind the infant's head. Albert jumped violently, then buried his face in the mattress. After a time, he reached for the rat again—the bar was struck again. Once more the infant jumped violently and began to whimper. In order to condition the child, the white rat was presented at the same time that the frightening stimulus, the noise, was applied. This combination of events was continued for some time. When finally the rat was presented alone, Albert cried and crawled away rapidly.

Other objects—rabbits, pigeons, blocks—were presented to Albert with no unusual reaction; when the rat was presented alone, whimpering followed immediately. Then, to quote Watson,

> A rabbit was suddenly placed in front of Albert. The reaction was pronounced. He leaned as far away from the animal as possible, whimpered, then burst into tears. When the rabbit was placed in contact with him he buried his face in the mattress, then got up on all fours and crawled away, crying as he went. This was a most convincing test.

In short, Watson and his associates proved that a child can build up fears, ordinarily called "instinctive," by a process of conditioning. Enthusiastically Watson outlined a series of experiments to prove that the study of behavior presented a new face to psychology and a new use for the science. If emotional responses, fears, and habits could be "built in," why could not educators and psychologists eliminate the fears that hampered the child's development by reconditioning? The idea was cataclysmic. Fame seemed assured for the young psychologist. Professor Holt said in 1915, "Behaviorism is the one great luminary on the psychologic sky."

Watson's discoveries, announced as the psychology of behaviorism, scattered like shrapnel among introspective psychologists. His rejection of everything they had cherished was more than the academic psychologists could bear. Watson was attacked from many angles with a fury that was not lessened by his own counterblasts. William McDougall, the dean of American psychologists at the time and professor at Harvard, got into violent controversy with Dr. Watson. Their criminations and recriminations were published in scientific journals such as *Mind* and then thrown open to the reading public in the pages of the *New Republic*. Professor McDougall called Watson's theories "lopsided and extreme." School psychologists were also disturbed by his denial of consciousness; still he insisted that animals in experimental tests and children in school learn through the repetition frequency of conditioned reflexes. Learning is not an adaptive conscious process but a series of "right" reflexes.

Watson's behaviorism spread on a wave of revolutionary fervor in education. His theories took the form of a program for social improvement. Educators and publicists rallied to the cause; articles like "Are Parents Necessary?" and "The Heart or the Intellect" appeared in *Harper's Magazine, The New York Times,* and others (1927–1930). Progressive schools embraced behaviorism; the "three R's" were dropped and "emotional training" became a vital part of the new education. Meanwhile, academics continued their attacks on Watson's science. McDougall noted that he could not disregard the experience of a century of introspectionism; for him the pure behaviorism of Watson was "attractive to those born Bolshevists." George Santayana, Harvard philosopher, wrote:

> I foresee a behaviorist millennium; countless millions of walking automatons...all jabbering as they have been trained to jabber, never interfering with one another, always smiling, with their glands all functioning perfectly (which is happiness) and all living to a sunny old age. ...Truly a wonderful exhibition. But alas! I was never brought up to behave.... [4]

Bertrand Russell expressed a contrary view:

> In an American learned periodical I once found the state-
> ment that there is only one behaviorist in the world, name-
> ly, Dr. Watson. I should have said there are as many as there
> are modern-minded men. . . . If you want a child to learn to
> behave in a certain way, you will be wise if you follow Dr.
> Watson's advice rather than, say, Freud's.[5]

Although Watson's individuality puts its stamp on
behaviorism, other experimentalists—Thorndike at Columbia University and Clark Hull at Yale—refined learning
theory and the S-R (stimulus-response bond) theory to
help lay the foundation with today's preoccupation with
Behavior Modification Therapy. Most of the work done by
these savant psychologists remained in the laboratory; as
Hall and Lindzey in reviewing the precursors of behaviorism commented: "It may be an overstatement to say
that the white rat had more to do with shaping the [S-R
bond] theory than have human subjects. . . ."[6] It was B. F.
Skinner, one of the early behaviorists, who brought the
conditioning "science" into relation with man. In his book
Science and Human Behavior[7] he viewed the behavior of individuals and groups as a controllable and predictable enterprise to the degree that behavior could be manipulated. His
thinking led to questioning whether man is indeed "free"
and spontaneous in his actions or conditioned by social
rules more than he would like to admit.

Skinner attacked the assumptions of mental scientists
who try to elucidate the "causes" of behavior; he asked,
"Are nervous anxiety, personality patterns, unconscious
thought observable phenomena or convenient scientific
'fictions'?" His answer was that only the stimuli that bring
about behavior are measurable; some of these stimuli are
embodied in law, religion, and social custom and some in
the early training of the individual. He showed how certain
stimuli are "reinforced" by rewards. Thus if we are conditioned to work diligently, we receive *reinforcement* for that

behavior in the form of money, honor, reputation, etc. On the other hand, we are conditioned to avoid certain stimuli because they are painful, as when we know that stealing will probably be followed by punishment; this he called *aversive* control. Behavioral control operates in society, in the laboratory on animals, and is possible in therapy. Skinner summarized his position succinctly:

> Behavior comes to conform to standards of a given community when certain responses are reinforced and others are allowed to go unreinforced or are punished. [8]

He recognized that a culture in which the individual responds to stimuli beyond his control is "not a very comforting support for... Western democratic thought..." but insisted that a scientific analysis of behavior must take into account these environmental controls.

Some of Skinner's conclusions had political repercussions, but in relation to psychotherapy, the possibility of control through conditioning represented a turning point for psychotherapy wherein the system was rooted in scientific experimental data. The laboratory experimentation by Gantt in Baltimore and Masserman in Chicago solidified the conditioning theory so that Wolpe, Lazarus, and others[9] could apply it to human patients. Thus, Russian psychiatrists following Pavlov, and American therapists following Skinner, adapted learning and conditioning principles to difficult clinical material. The clinicians' interest lay in *changing* behavior, not in searching for causes—in relieving symptoms through reconditioning, not in achieving insight. The new method, which was called Behavior Modification, eschewed depth analysis and psychoanalytic doctrine.

The earliest formulation of a practical clinical method of conditioning was by Joseph Wolpe, a South African, later established in this country. His method of *desensitization* (1958) consisted in carefully analyzing a symptom, e. g., a phobia and regarding the conditions (stimuli) under which it appeared. For example, in a rat phobia, the therapist arranges the stimuli in order of their intensity; did the fear arise on seeing a rat, on seeing a picture of one, on hearing the feared object, on reading of it, on imagining a rat, etc.? This Wolpe called a *hierarchy* of stimuli. Then the patient is relaxed and asked to imagine the weakest anxiety-provoking stimulus. This process is repeated until the patient overcomes his or her fear of rats. In a word, the patient is emotionally desensitized. In the process, if an imagined "scene" proves too disturbing, it is withdrawn. The process is tedious for the therapist but effective for the patient.

The theory on which this practice is based has been briefly stated by Wolpe:

> Reciprocal inhibition principle—if a response inhibitory of anxiety is made to occur in the presence of an anxiety producing stimulus, the bond between the stimuli and anxiety is weakened.[10]

Thus "undesirable behavior is unlearned," for conditioning is merely the learning process in reverse (Wolpe). Contrasting the results of Behavior Modification with those of psychoanalysis, Wolpe claimed his method to have "cured or improved ninety percent" of 210 unselected patients with an average of 30 interviews each.

As noted, treatment by conditioning had been initiated by Russian psychiatrists some years ago in utilizing the lessons Pavlov learned in his laboratory.[11] Since the Russians regarded suggestion itself as a typical conditioned reflex they brought "new, more beneficial cerebral connections" to patients through education, rest, and hypnosis. In a word the Russians translated the notion of an implanted idea, i.e., suggestion, into physiological terms; they spoke of "deliberate excitatory conditioning" that would overcome an earlier inhibition. In this country, Andrew Salter[12] removed symptoms in his patients (earlier inhibitions) by conditioning them to relax at a specified sound. Others employed conditioned reflex in treating alcoholics, the so-called aversion treatment.[13] The alcoholic was offered whiskey or wine at the same time he was given an injection of a drug that caused nausea or vomiting. Thereafter, the smell of liquor would induce a "reflex activity of the centers of nausea and vomiting."

Salter, who spoke of conditioning as a "new and healthy therapy," himself had a predecessor in Edmund Jacobson, a Chicago physician whose "progressive relaxation"[14] was built on a reconditioning of the neuromuscular system of the body. He taught his patients to recognize the residual tension in their muscles, measurable on the kymograph, which accompanied anxiety states. By training them to "relax past the point of apparent relaxation," he virtually conditioned the voluntary and involuntary muscle systems to reduce their subliminal excitation, with the result that the anxiety and nervous tension also disappeared. Jacobson's relaxation methods did not use verbal suggestions or hypnosis; he relied on the effort of the will to achieve relaxation of autonomic (involuntary) muscles in the intestine, stomach, heart, and other internal organs, the site of "anxious" sensations.

In Salter's technique, the breaking of "conditioned inhibitions"—"a seeing what is inhibited and helping it to become motor," i.e., expressed in speech or movement— constituted the essence of his method. He insisted his methods were more economical of time and more certain of recovery than those of depth analysis.[15]

From these beginnings, the popularity of conditioning or Behavior Modification Therapy has grown to the point where it is the treatment of choice in many instances. Phobias, which have been a *bête noir* of psychotherapists, seem to yield to conditioning where analysis, medications, or other methods of treatment have been unavailing. Because Behavior Modification is close to the learning process, even part of the mass of "commonsense" handling of emotional problems in children, its use has spread to such diverse problems as autistic children and airplane phobias.

There are several methods employed in Behavior Modification: two of these are desensitization and operant conditioning, which involves rewards (reinforcement) for "good," that is, desirable behavior and extinction of "bad" habits by repeated deconditioning by denying reinforcements. Obsessions and compulsions have been treated using innovations such as showing attractive female nudes to homosexuals, or the reverse, i.e., attractive men, accompanied by a painful electric shock. Obesity is treated by exposing the patient to delicacies while at the same time delivering an electric shock to his or her acquisitive fingertips; or again, shaming a patient by ridiculing his phobia. In essence, the technique developed by Dr. Wolpe of step-by-step analysis of the stimuli symptom occurring with the system (the hierarchy), relaxation, and gradual desensitization are employed with whatever innovation the therapist finds applicable.

One significant aspect of conditioning is the transfer of methods of training patients to nonprofessionals, for example, parents. In autistic children, where rewards (reinforcements) can vary from cookies to tickling[16] for improvement in destructive behavior, the parent is requested to continue the treatment at home. More and more psychiatric technicians, students, and other laymen are used to condition patients where knowledge of the underlying dynamics is unnecessary. In view of the oncoming national health insurance, wherein third-party insurers will insist on "lower unit-costs" for therapy and patients unable to afford expensive long-term therapy will be encouraged to seek briefer treatments, Dr. Judd Marmor has advised psychoanalysts to "no longer . . . ignore short-cuts to symptom amelioration offered by behavior techniques."[17] That this advice has been heeded is demonstrated by the application of conditioning in many phobia clinics at representative university medical centers. The American Psychiatric Association Task Force, after careful deliberation, gave official sanction to Behavior Modification in these words:

> To summarize the literature as a whole, we conclude that individual subject designs have demonstrated that therapies based on reinforcement principles do produce more improvements than no treatment at all.... Review of the numerous studies of desensitization suggests that this procedure produces measurable benefits to patients across a wide range of problems. [18]

There are other areas of application for operant conditioning that are not specifically psychiatric in type; for example, in the treatment of persistent pain, from chronic neurologic conditions or from a habit-consolidated pain as in persons with chronic arthritis or chronic lumbo-sacral strains. Workers at the University of Washington[19] have developed a program of operant pain conditioning by withdrawing responses to patients exhibiting pain by grimace, moaning, requesting medication, and increasing well-behavior positive reinforcements. The goal is to interrupt the traditional way of managing patients in a hospital where medication is given when pain is complained of (positive reinforcement) by *not* responding in the usual "helpful" way. Thus medication requests are "extinguished" by reducing the frequency of their administration and by placing medicine on a time schedule without relation to the patient's complaints. In other words, pain is not the conditioner of physician-and-nurse attention but well-behavior is. The patient is conditioned towards improvement, or at least, towards a lowered susceptibility to pain. The patients treated in this rehabilitation center have all been certified as having a medically based condition, as back injuries, post-surgical problems, etc.

The widening breach between the medical model of mental treatment and that arising from a scientific psychology is evident in Stuart's claim that Behavior Modification is the remedy for iatrogenic (doctor-caused) illnesses. [20] The extent of the revolution is further seen in Fensterheim's statement that "for two generations [psychiatrists] have been conditioned to think of psychotherapy in terms of deep-seated problems, core conflicts and unconscious impulses," whereas "removal of positive reinforcement is the strongest way of stopping behavior."[21] The fading of psychoanalysis as a treatment of choice and its influence on psychiatric thinking has yielded so swiftly to conditioning that Dr. Alfred Freedman, President of the American Psychiatric Association, could say in 1973: "in the marketplace of modalities [of treatment] psychoanalysis has very little to offer." In spite of this "kiss of death" to depth analysis, attempts are being made to reconcile the "insight-seeking" thrust of psychoanalysis to the "change-producing techniques" of Behavior Modification.[22]

Another offshoot of scientific psychology that influenced psychotherapy to a degree that could be called revolutionary was Gestalt psychology. The movement that eventuated in Gestalt therapy (see chapter 14) started with Max Wertheimer, Professor of Psychology in Berlin and Frankfurt until he was expelled by the Nazi government in the 1930s. Gestalt psychology, usually attributed to Wertheimer, Kohler, and Kofka, German scholars who escaped to the United States during the Nazi reign, was based on experiments in perception. The underlying position stated that "perception of a whole field determined the perception of its parts." An example given is that of a melody that, when altered in key or tempo, can still be recognized; the melody as a whole determines the perception of its parts.[23] This principle is present in mental processes, such as motivation, as it is in visual perception: "what you are doing in toto determines what you do piecemeal." Wertheimer and the Gestaltists rejected behaviorism as a "mechanical coupling of isolated stimuli and responses." Behavior, they assert, results from interaction of a whole organism with a total environment.

These concepts led directly to application in Gestalt psychotherapy as developed by Perls and associates. The "closure" principle, in which the mind has the tendency to complete perceptions, was recognized by Perls as "unfinished business" of the patient. The figure/ground perception, in which the figure in the foreground against an indifferent background is in the focus of interest, was translated as the shifting interest from symptom to environment. The figure/ground concept is particularly important in therapy: for example, the figure in the foreground, say fear, erases body sensation in the background, which slips into unawareness. Gestalt therapists try to bring the background into awareness (body perceptions), thus providing a sense of wholeness to the patient. Perception of the whole organism-in-the-world, a Gestalt concept, when translated into therapy, frees patients to *actualize* themselves, to experience a sense of excitement and enjoyment.[24] (See chapter 14.)

When academic and experimental psychologists turned their attention to psychotherapy, their premises were other than those of clinical psychiatry and medicine. Although they dealt with intelligence tests, personality inventories, learning theory, and projective techniques (Rorschach or Thematic Apperception Tests), their accent chiefly was on understanding the mind, not healing it. With the evolution of a clinical psychology, interest in applying psychological premises to therapeutic problems led to concrete methods. One of the first and most influential of these was Carl Rogers' *client-centered therapy.*[25] By adopting a completely nonthreatening attitude (nonauthoritarian, hence the term "client" rather than patient), the Rogerian therapist permits the client to examine his own life and experiences. The method is called *nondirective* and has been discussed in chapter 13. It is recalled here to emphasize the fact that psychologists working with concepts like the "self" and the experimental field in which it exists have contributed to psychotherapy in a way that may grow rather than diminish. Their work reflects dissatisfaction with the medical model and its substitution by something approaching an untainted relationship between two people. As Rogers put it:

> For the client, this optimal therapy has meant an exploration of increasingly strange and unknown and dangerous feelings in himself... possible only because he is gradually realizing that he is accepted unconditionally.

The net result of three or four decades of the application of clinical psychology to mental problems has been to enlarge the lists of therapists to the end that those trained in psychiatry and those nurtured in psychology use therapeutic methods common to each discipline.

Notes to Chapter 16

1. Edwin G. Boring, *History, Psychology and Science*, ed. R. Watson & D. Campbell, New York, John Wiley & Sons, 1963.
2. Hilarie Cuny, *Ivan Pavlov: The Man and His Theories*, London, Souvenir Press, 1962.
3. R. J. Herrnstein, in John B. Watson, *Behavior, Introduction to Comparative Psychology*, New York, Holt, Rinehart & Winston, 1967.
4. George Santayana, "Living Without Thinking," *Forum and Century*, Sept. 1922, vol 68, p. 731.
5. Bertrand Russell, "Behaviorism," *Century*, Vol. 113, Dec. 1926, p. 148.
6. Calvin S. Hall and Gardner Lindzey, *Theories of Personality*, New York, John Wiley & Sons, 1957.
7. B. F. Skinner, *Science and Human Behavior*, New York, Free Press, 1953.
8. B. F. Skinner, p. 437 *et. seq.*
9. Taskforce Report: Behavior Therapy in Psychiatry, Amer. Psych. Assn., Washington, D. C., July, 1973.
10. Joseph Wolpe, in *The Conditioning Therapies*, New York, Holt, Rinehart & Winston, 1966, p. 12 *et. seq.*
11. K. I. Platonov, *Psychotherapy; Collected papers from the State Neuropsychiatric Institute, Kharkov,* trans. J. Notkin, *Amer. J. Psych.*, Vol. 11, 1932, p. 1206.
12. Andrew Salter, *Condition Reflex Therapy*, New York, Creative Age Press, 1949.
13. F. Lemere and W. L. Voegtlin, "An evaluation of the aversion treatment of alcoholism," *Quart. J. Stud. Alcohol*, Vol. 11, 1950, p. 199.
14. Edmund Jacobson, *Progressive Relaxation*, Chicago, Univ. of Chicago Press, 1929.

15. Andrew Salter, in *The Conditioning Therapies; The Challenge in Psychotherapy*, New York, Holt, Rinehart & Winston, 1966, p. 21 *et. seq.*
16. A Review: Is Conditioning Enough? Evaluating the Effectiveness of Behavior Therapy. *Medical World News*, May 25, 1973, p. 39.
17. Judd Marmor, *Psychiatric News*, publ. by Amer. Psychiatric Assn., Washington, D. C., Mar. 21, 1973.
18. Report: Amer. Psych. Assn. Task Force, July, 1973.
19. John J. Bonica and Wilbert E. Fordyce, "Operant Conditioning for Chronic Pain," National Inst. of General Med. Science, grant GM 15991, 1973. Seattle, Washington.
20. Richard B. Stuart, *Trick or Treatment: How and When Psychotherapy Fails,* Champaign, Ill., Research Press, 1970.
21. Herbert Fensterheim, *Help Without Psychoanalysis,* New York, Stein & Day, 1971, p. 215.
22. Lee Birk and Ann W. Brinkely-Birk, "Psychoanalysis and Behavior Therapy," *Amer. J. Psych.,* Vol. 131, May 1974.
23. Max Wertheimer, "Gestalt Theory," *Social Research,* Vol. 11, 1944, p. 78.
24. Frederick Perls, Ralph Hefferline, and Paul Goodman, *Gestalt Therapy,* New York, Dell Publ. Co., 1951, pp. 56, 118.
25. Carl Rogers, *On Encounter Groups,* New York, Harper & Row, 1970.

17

Therapy for the Soul

RELIGION has always supplied balm for distraught souls; although its aims are not avowedly so, religious contemplation is therapeutic in effect. Immersion in a religious attitude does point the way to a kind of inner harmony and lack of tension. Carl Jung,[1] whose psychoanalysis emphasized the "process of individuation" in treatment, recognized that psychoanalysis and religion held common elements. He called them *self-actualization*, meaning a sense of liberation, the development of one's power over the self, a freedom to live out one's potentialities. As Jung put it:

> Self-actualization means the fullest, most complete differentiation and harmonious blending of all aspects of man's total personality....

This new, yet old, concept of therapy brought in its train an attitude akin to that of religious profession, namely, a turning away from material concerns in favor of intuitive understanding: Rational thought was less important than spiritual feeling.[2]

What this realignment from Western ideals amounted to was a seeking of first principles: hence the infusion of Eastern thinking in therapy as exemplified by Buddhism,

Taoism, and Zen Buddhism. Eastern philosophies recognized that the Western world's stress on rationality has prevented western man from allowing spiritualism, intuition, and emotion to develop within his personality. Rationality has constricted modern man's place in the world, has subdued his fantasy, his "creative mastery of self," and has hence limited his growth or "actualization." For this reason some have turned to Eastern philosophies and religions to gain that serenity that comes of disregarding material things and embracing those of the spirit. This new departure for psychotherapy, never entirely submerged among mental healers of religious persuasion, found its most complete expression in Buddhism, Taoism, and Zen Buddhism.

In contrast to the rational psychotherapy of the Western world, which seeks "causes" and attempts "adjustment" to our social environment, Eastern philosophies are therapeutic in that insight into the essential emptiness of the universe leads to freedom from desire, misery, and anxiety, to a blissful awakening (Mahayana Buddhism). Philosophers and poets have always been inspired by the vastness of Eastern teachings: in the nineteenth century, one Max Mueller translated fifty volumes of Eastern spiritual literature under the title *Sacred Books of the East*; Emerson, Thoreau, and Aldous Huxley have incorporated Eastern philosophy into their world-view. In the latter half of this century, popular interest in Oriental religions has moved like a trade wind over many involved in psychotherapy to the end that the Eastern viewpoint has become incorporated in today's mental healing techniques. Yet Eastern ways of "liberation" cannot be identified as psychotherapy completely. As Alan Watts points out, "the Eastern cultures have not categorized mind and matter, soul and body in the same way as the Western...departmentalization is foreign to them...the separation of the spiritual and material."[3] Eastern religions and philosophies were particularly helpful in the 1960s because of the complaints of "alienation" in which the young especially were enmeshed. The spirit of the times—a shrinking labor market, the pressure of a computerized age, and an interminable Vietnam War with its overreactions in drug usage and ploys at emancipation (Haight-Ashbury, etc.)—made for an acute feeling of not-belonging, an alienation from life. From a dilettante contact with Zen Buddhism or Yoga, those who worked with the young delved into the Eastern philosophies to emerge with a "therapy" that contained ancient wisdom. (See chapter 14.) Primitive Christianity was rediscovered by the Jesus Freaks; Jewish mysticism was rediscovered by the Hasidim. Both groups sought for verities that would stabilize unfulfilled souls. The treasures of the East were racked for answers.

The religions of the East that influenced, or were amalgamated with, modern therapy, were chiefly Brahmanism (India), which teaches of a unity essence underlying the diversity of the world; Mahayana Buddhism (India and China), which stresses that the phenomenal world is illusory; Taoism (China), whose teaching is the unitary principle harmonizing all opposites; and Zen Buddhism (China and Japan), which seeks enlightenment through the stillness of meditation. Zen, particularly, in which meditation led to an insight experience (Satori), won the attention of Jung, Fromm, and Perls because of its nonintellectual grasp of reality and its unlimited awareness. Erich Fromm saw in Zen the "disappearance of the polarity conscious v. unconscious...[the] arriving at the state of immediate grasp of reality...."[4]

Although Eastern practices by gurus are clothed in mysticism, designed to enhance the liberation of normal people, Indian physicians recognize their basic psychologic and physiological truths. Two psychiatrists in Bombay described their work in a psychiatric center utilizing ancient Hindu methods based on Indian philosophies.[5] Treatment starts with relaxation of voluntary muscles to control agitation and restlessness. Gradually the respirations are decreased under the assumption that control of involuntary muscles serving the lungs, heart, and gastrointestinal organs will follow. This procedure is called Pranayama. Breath control is enhanced by posturing the body (Asana) to reduce movement. After several sessions (patients are treated in half-hour sessions, six days a week for six weeks), the patient is led to meditate (Dharana): when effective, it leads to the ultimate state of peace (Samadhi). The practice outlined for psychiatric cases is based on a centuries-old program for mental health. The ancient tradition, reaching back to the Vedic period (1500 to 800 B.C.),[6] was according to an Indian medical historian prescribed by the Sages as a scheme of life to prevent breakdowns. It encompassed four stages: Brahmacharya, training of mind and body; Grahasthya, householder stage, marriage and family; Vanaprasthya, retirement to the forest to cater to the inner needs of man; and Sanyasa, renunciation of life and asceticism. The practices of Yoga and Sufism to reach the desired end state have both a religio-philosophic (purification of the senses and self-renunciation) and a therapeutic aim (a state of inner bliss). The root idea is to bring man back to union with nature, away from his frantic attempts to control nature.

The number of mystical methods for attaining a reunion with the universal spirit are legion. In his *The Book of Highs*, Edward Rosenfeld[7] has gathered 250 ways toward "altered consciousness without drugs." Whereas in previous generations "altered consciousness" was considered a mark of bohemian depravity if sought voluntarily or one of madness if involuntary, nowadays a "high" is the essence of psychologic sophistication. The procedures for attaining greater awareness of the sensory world within, or to put it bluntly a "good feeling," vary tremendously. Whether naive or informed, they range from philosophic reflection to electric stimulation of areas in the brain. Consider Rosenfeld's brief summary of Self-Awareness:

> ... When we continue our usual lifestyles, repeating the same actions over and over, getting tied into habits, not paying attention to either the finer details or the overall

general patterns and trends of existence, we don't notice who is *living* the life.

Consider the Zen Morning Laugh reported by Rosenfeld, a natural activity that may replace the morning meditation of a Zen master:

> The gist of the technique is to arise each morning and assume a standing position. Put your hands on the back part of your hips...Now begin to laugh. Keep laughing. Let your laughter feed off itself and propel itself through your body and out.... [8]

It is likely that many of the procedures collected by Rosenfeld have been used in the past, with or without instruction. However, their multiplicity indicates the vast surge of interest in self-treatment that characterizes the present generation. As has been evident in these pages, mental healing has diffused to the point where it has lost its specificity, its physician-patient (read, donor-recipient) form. The maxim "Know Thyself" has now come to encompass the mind much as nutritional knowledge has come into possession of the populace. This orientation towards the self suggests a turning away from the mechanistic rational view of life to one where nonrational, intuitive forms are basic. Eastern philosophies and the cosmology of the American Indian embody this orientation. Rather than deal with the hundred and one modifications of soul therapy, Transcendental Meditation will serve as a path to the coveted feeling of being "high," a euphemism for a stressless feeling of normality. "Being high," writes Andrew Weil in a foreword to Rosenfeld's book, "might be the most natural condition of all...the euphoria that it is the way things are 'supposed to be.' "[9]

Transcendental Meditation, as taught by Maharishi Mahesh Yogi, founder of Creative Intelligence, aims to achieve a "physical state of deep rest and relaxation while mentally [the devotee] remains inwardly awake and alert."[10] The effect of meditation on bodily functions, metabolism, respiration, biochemical changes, and the like has been studied by medical scientists to the point where physiological changes (for example, reduction of cardiac output) have been certified. University investigators in Europe and this country have proved that T. M. has been responsible for improved auditory ability, increased stability as measured by fewer galvanic skin responses, and improved motor coordination.[11] Moreover, based on the Vedic background, the relaxation achieved exerts a direct effect on the mood, producing a "sense of fulfillment and internal harmony."

The technique, achieved first in groups and then individually, consists in being assigned a *mantra* in secret (a Sanskrit word indicating one's personal guide or talisman), which is repeated during the twenty-minute morning and evening session of meditation. At these times the client assumes a comfortable position, which need not be the cross-legged Yoga stance. He or she then proceeds to permit the mind to shed its stresses, "naturally and innocently," until a feeling of liberation is experienced. The individual repeats his mantra noiselessly to himself while the mind takes its own direction: If a memory or fixed association appears, the client sets it aside consciously. After some practice, the meditator becomes accustomed to this drifting, contentless mental state, achieving a state of "pure consciousness,"[12] interpreted by the Master Maharishi as a "feeling of Oneness"—the ultimate aim of meditation. Meditation is not a form of hypnosis; no trance state is developed, and the meditator reports awareness of his or her surroundings at all times. Increasing numbers of devotees attest to its effect in reducing anxiety and tension, allowing one to meet the stresses of daily life with ease and an "overlying sense of harmony."

The induction of tranquility is aimed at the person who is generally well. In relation to medical conditions, such as high blood pressure, the results are said to be equally good. Reduction of stress-effects is itself therapeutic, in agreement with Doctor Selye's General Adaptation Syndrome, in which stresses produce changes in the ductless glands (adrenals) eventuating in internal diseases. In medical situations, no specific instructions are given beyond those of meditation;[13] its chief value is in the prevention of hypertension, gastric ulcer, and other psychosomatic conditions. From a clinical point of view Transcendental Meditation, practiced as a daily exercise, is nonspecific psychotherapy; from a philosophic viewpoint, it removes the barriers that keep humans from perceiving the "whole reality" about them, i.e., the seen and unseen, rational and supernatural universes.

The utterances and writings of mystics agree that a special state of transcendence permits a view of *nonordinary* reality. To this experience the term supernaturalism has been loosely applied. Carlos Castaneda,[14] an anthropologist working with Don Juan, a Yaqui medicine man in the Mexican border area of the Southwest, delved into the peculiar state induced by drugs (the datura plant or Jimson weed, which contains *stramonium*). Under Juan's guidance he was able to experience the "nonordinary reality" that his medicine man mentor attained: Castaneda was thus led into a realm wherein "the component elements of nonordinary reality had a compelling quality of realness...." The various drugs used—peyote, psilocybin, datura—with their elaborate rituals carried the user over the threshold into the world described as supernatural. The supernatural had its own validity and could bring "knowledge" to the devotee, which united him with all nature.

There are other names for this state of expanded consciousness: It has been called the *oceanic feeling, transcendental realization, cosmic consciousness, peak experience*. Many under the cover of religious exaltation have reached such a state. Doctor Richard Bucke, a British-born psychiatrist practicing in Canada in the 1880s, claims to have been seized with such an experience. One day he was inexplicably and suddenly "wrapped around by a flame-colored cloud,"[15] which he identified as a "light" within his body. Assuming this to be a manifestation of supernaturalism vouchsafed to few men, Doctor Bucke studied the histories of fourteen men covering a span of 3,000 years who had reported similar experiences: Jesus, Gautama Buddha, Walt Whitman, Dante, and Francis Bacon were among this group. He concluded that the "illumination" was in fact a supernatural occurrence, an evidence of *cosmic consciousness*, described in Gautama's words as a "mental state so happy, so glorious that the rest of life is worthless compared with it. . . . " The significant aspect for mental healing of this exalted feeling is its extension beyond ordinary euphoria attending good health and high spirits into a "sense of eternal life . . . a sense of immortality" (Bucke). As has been discussed in chapter 14, many in our day have aspired to this state through the use of mind-expanding drugs without the capacity to attain the divine *afflatus* with which Doctor Bucke's heroes were endowed.

The harnessing of religious ecstasy for treatment purposes has always implied eccentricity or charlatanry for the practicing therapist. Attitudes arising from meditation or flashes of cosmic insight that exclude the material world, except in a sanctioned area such as a monastery, are relegated to an impractical mysticism and are hence outside the reach of rational psychotherapy. An extreme point of view, that of Soviet psychiatrists[16] who follow Pavlovian behaviorism, illustrates the disenchantment with the mystical shared by many Western psychotherapists. Using language couched in Marxist doctrine, one Doctor Pondoev comments that Russian scientific thought is a development

> . . . consciously ridding itself of the taint of Western European influences in the form of mysticism and metaphysics and getting down to the elements of a materialistic doctrine . . . [for] conditioned reflexes . . . shaking to the foundations, metaphysical notions of the soul.

From an opposing viewpoint, Takao Murase, a Japanese

psychotherapist in discussing *Morita*,[17] a type of medita-
tional therapy based on Zen Buddhism, states that "Morita
maintains a very conscious contempt for intellectual,
rationalistic procedures." Obviously the cultural bases
upon which different psychotherapies are erected alter
their reception by patients and hence their effectiveness. As
Murase and Johnson assert: "...failure to take this into
account obfuscates one of the basic explanations for the
efficacy of all psychotherapeutic methods."

Many in today's culture are attracted towards the mystic and cosmic in mental healing. The religions of the East
and of the American Indian (whose ties to nature are a
consequence of their world view) attract some persons who
seek help for feelings of alienation from an on-going society, vague dissatisfactions with their place in the world, and
the anguish of isolation. For these individuals, detachment
from the material world and re-attachment to a universal
spirit answers their needs. For centuries the American Indian medicine man has treated ills of the flesh and spirit
with rituals that partake of a cosmic spirit. The Navajos, for
example, hold a Sing or ceremonial for the patient who is ill
because he is "out of harmony" with nature.[18] Navajo
medicine men may be herbalists, singers, or shamans,
whose rituals are precisely done (a Singer requires 100
hours of ritual chant, which must be letter-perfect).[19] The
basic notion present in all Indian groups throughout the
country is that the mind of the Indian is contiguous to and
identical with the land ("the Earth is our Mother"), animals, and spirit; hence little distinction is made between
"mental" and "physical" illnesses. That the Indian cosmology nurtures ecology makes their view of the natural and
supernatural more appealing: Rhodes, a Pit River Indian,
said "all animals, plants, land and peoples were placed
here by the Great Spirit"—hence manipulation of one in-
jures the others.[20] What is called mysticism is, for the Indian, a true naturalism. Psychology, which is compart-
mentalized (conscious, unconscious, emotion, volition,

cerebration) has no meaning for the American Indian; for him the interrelatedness of thought and emotion is automatic.[21]

It is interesting to speculate whether today's move towards the mystic in mental healing is secondary to intolerable pressures of a technology that threatens to dehumanize our society, or whether it represents a periodic return of the esoteric. Many have noted that the social ambience of a historical period influences the kinds of symptoms presented by patients. Chlorosis (anemia), the Green Sickness of young women during the 1890s, has disappeared; the dramatic hysterias of Freud's time have succumbed to a freer sexual atmosphere; schizophrenics have lost their bizarre utterances and peculiar catatonic postures. Patients seeking help today complain of social symptoms. For such, the detachment from the material world promised by the Eastern religio-therapeutic systems and the "nonordinary" reality of the American Indian religion answer their psychic needs.

Some have suggested that the healer (psychiatrist and other types of "scientific" therapists) may unconsciously alter the clinical picture presented. The modern dynamic psychotherapist who tries to adapt his patient to a nonpalatable world may, in effect, be forcing as a defense the production of new symptoms. Leon Salzman made this point in a recent symposium on *Changing Styles in Psychiatric Syndromes*[22] when he wrote: "... our capacity to heal influences the disorders that require healing."

Therapy for the Soul has justly been described as *antipsychiatric*. Innovators, freed from the constriction of scientific validation, welcomed mind expansion as a legitimate aid in reaching higher, and presumably healthier, levels of conscious awareness of self. More importantly, they have stressed the social nexus in which mental illness arises and have questioned whether the "sane" can rightly lay down rules whereby to judge the "insane." R. D. Laing, a Scotsman practicing in London,[23] opened a new vista in claiming that a psychosis, especially schizophrenia, represents a "strategy for survival" in a disturbed social and family environment. From this position, Laing asserts that schizophrenia "is a set of attributions that some people who are experts in making this set of attributions make about other people." For him, society is mad and the psychiatrist representing society is blinded to the existential world in which the patient lives. To Laing, society's *normality*, for adjustment to which the psychotherapist strives in his disturbed patient, is accomplished by assuming a "false self." He wrote: "... our 'normal,' 'adjusted' state is too often the abdication of ecstasy, the betrayal of our true potentialities...."[24]

What Laing and his associates emphasized was the meaning to the schizophrenic patient of his inner experiences (so-called symptoms). In reality, the patient is retreating from a society which is itself "mad": "psychosis" is a name given, by those in authority, to others who cannot exist in a mad society. The thrust of Laing's treatment for the schizophrenic (with whom he chiefly dealt) is to overturn the usual "adjustment" goal and let the person find his own "authenticity." In the now disbanded Kingsley Hall in London, Laing permitted his patients to sink into a regression (a quest to find his or her true self) and then to rediscover his true self. The therapist's task was only to "guide," never to direct; the process of self-healing constituted a search for the patient's true existential identity.[25] This regression and return to a rebirth has been couched in mystical terms by Laing as a "voyage from outer to inner...a movement from mundane time to eonic time...a return back from immortality back to mortality." In essence Laing is saying that a patient must shed the so-called normal values of society and return to his own base as a person in order to live in our present "mad" world.

Some of the flavor and coloration of the Eastern philosophies enter into Laing's anti-psychiatric treatment methods. Dropping back to eternity to return to our time, the process of rebirth, the "cosmic fetalization to an existential rebirth,"[26] as he put it, partakes of Zen Buddhism. In recent years, Laing has agreed that Transcendental Meditation helped in the psychological rebirth. This fusion of real and non-real, of the rational and supernatural, often observable in the "sick" schizophrenic who has lost his or her ego-boundaries, may be the key to the "alienation" of the human soul.

Existential philosophy, the base from which Doctor Laing developed his view of mental illness and society, insists on the importance of one's individual choice of existence. It is from this framework that patients can nurture themselves back to sanity. Perhaps the best expression of this view of psychotherapy is available in the account of Mary Barnes, one of Laing's patients at Kingsley Hall, who described her return:

> they buried me, entangled in guilt and chocked with anger... schizophrenia, split mind, tormented with distractions; cut off from God; division of self.... From these have I through psychotherapy been released. Different ages, different terms, the world moves, in the eternal breath of God.[27]

Notes to Chapter 17

1. Carl Jung, *Collected Works*, translated by R. F. C. Hull, London, Routledge and Kegan Paul, Vol. 17, 1954.
2. *Tai Wi Chin: The Secret of the Golden Flower*, translated by Richard Wilhelm and Carl Jung, New York, Harcourt, Brace & World, 1931.
3. Alan W. Watts, *Psychotherapy East and West*, New York, Pantheon Books, 1961.
4. Erich Fromm, "Psychoanalysis and Zen Buddhism," in *The World of Zen*, New York, Random House, 1960, p. 198.
5. N. S. Vahia, S. L. Vinekar, and D. R. Doongaj, "Some Ancient Indian Concepts of Treatment of Psychiatric Disorders," *British Journal of Psychiatry*, Vol. 112, 1966, p. 1089.
6. Rao A. Venkoba, "Some Ancient Indian Concepts of Mind, Insanity and Mental Hygiene," *Indian Journal History of Medicine*, Vol. 9, 1964, p. 13.
7. Edward Rosenfeld, *The Book of Highs. 250 Methods for Altering your Consciousness Without Drugs*, New York, Quadrangle/New York Times Book Co., 1973, p. 9.

8. Rosenfeld, p. 73.
9. Rosenfeld, Preface.
10. R. K. Wallace, Maharishi International, University of Los Angeles, California, 1972.
11. Benson and Wilson Wallace, *American Journal of Physiology,* Sept. 1971.
12. Ellen Kaye, "Transcendental Meditation: the High," *Town & Country,* Feb. 1974, p. 102.
13. Harold Bloomfield, M.D., Transcendental Meditation Demonstration, Sacramento, California, 1974.
14. Carlos Castaneda, *The Teachings of Don Juan,* New York, Balantine Books, 1968.
15. Richard Bucke, *Cosmic Consciousness,* New York, E. P. Dutton, 1901, new ed. 1923.
16. G. S. Pondoev, *Notes of a Soviet Doctor,* translated by Basil Haigh. Introduction by I. Galdston. London, Chapman & Hall, 2nd ed., 1959.
17. Takeo Murase and Frank Johnson, "Naikan, Morita and Western Psychotherapy," *Arch. of Gen. Psychiatry,* Vol. 31, July 1974, p. 121.
18. Petersen, "A Conversation with Frank Waters," *Psychology Today,* May, 1973, p. 63.
19. Robert L. Bergman, "A School for Medicine Men," *American Journal of Psychiatry,* Vol. 130, June 1973, p. 663.
20. Walter Bromberg, Personal Observation, Pit River Tribe, Montgomery Creek, California, March 1972.
21. Walter Bromberg, "Self-Image of American Indian: A Preliminary Study," *International Journal of Social Psychiatry,* London, Vol. 20, Summer 1974, p. 39.
22. Leon Salzman, "Changing Styles in Psychiatric Syndromes. A Symposium," *American Journal of Psychiatry,* Vol. 130, Feb. 1973, p. 147.
23. R. D. Laing, in *Going Crazy. The Radical Therapy of R. D. Laing and Others,* ed. Hendrick M. Ruitenbeek, New York, Bantam Books, 1972.
24. R. D. Laing, *The Divided Self. An Existential Study in Sanity and Madness,* Middlesex, England, Penguin Books, Pelican Ed., 1965, p. 12.
25. Morton Schatzman, in *R. D. Laing and Anti-Psychiatry,* ed. Robert Boyers, New York, Harper & Row, 1971, p. 235 *et seq.*
26. R. D. Laing, *Politics of Experience,* London, Oxford Press, 1967.
27. Mary Barnes and Joseph Berke, *Mary Barnes, Two Accounts of a Journey Through Madness,* New York, Ballantine, 1971.

18

The Trail Winds On

ALTHOUGH interminable, the story of mental healing must come to an end with the present. The history of psychotherapy has been tied in the past to priests, monks, kings, philosophers, visionaries; to physicians, mental specialists, and psychologists in the present. It is obvious that this story is not, and never will be, finished. For beyond those whose activities in behalf of nervous sufferers have been traced in this volume, lie other factors involved in the evolution of mental healing. These are social and cultural changes, technological enterprise, even historical epochs; the history of psychotherapy is in fact the history of continuous adaptation to problems of living in all eras.

The insistent cry for help by distraught humans has met with enormously varied responses. Born of conflict and strong emotion, the evolution of mental healing is marked by struggles between "warring sects," by the deification given some, the contumely visited upon others. This aura of emotional agitation has bestowed a vibrant, living quality on psychotherapy, which the author has tried to convey.

In this survey, many twists and turns, many unrecorded failures and successes have been bypassed; of necessity, many lesser figures, on whose shoulders the major protagonists may have climbed, have been omitted. The author has tried to include not only those heroes whose intuition and hard labor fashioned successful techniques but those trends of the times that swayed patients to accept the boons presented. Although influences from far-off places and times have been considered, the main accent was on psychotherapy in the United States. The present scene in this country represents virtually a recapitulation of the entire history of the art and science of mental healing; Americans have always been eager to avail themselves of every type of personal help. This orientation accounts for the probable neglect of much that has transpired in Asiatic or African cultures in mental healing.

With these limitations in mind, the final task could well be to ask *how* mental healing of all stripes functions. To this question there is no agreed-upon answer; each therapist provides explanations based on the particular technique employed. If, however, one looks beyond the technique used, one sees some general human reactions, the extra-technical aspects of psychotherapy,[1] that play an impalpable, but vital, role in successful psychotherapy. The scrutiny of these seldom-considered factors starts with the obvious, i.e., psychotherapy is both an art and a science.

Sometimes the art of therapy outweighs the science, depending on the background, allegiances, and personality of the healer. Modern psychotherapy claims a close relationship to science but it is undeniable that if science depends on qualification and proof, this claim is insecure. Hence the *artful* application of any method rises in importance. The art of any endeavor besides psychotherapy—pedagogy, law, medicine, music, the ministry—relates to the style of application of relevant knowledge. This may relate to the bedside manner, to the approach, the tinge of drama introduced, to personal flourishes and involvements of the practitioner. Before a jury, a class of students, a group of parishioners, a concert audience, or a clinic of patients, the *style*, the *art*, of presentation often spells the difference between success or failure. It seems vital, then, to examine the meaning of artfulness.

Artfulness has two distinct meanings; one indicates a performance utilizing more than ordinary skill or adroitness, the second has the connotation of cunning, even deceit. Reflection will show that mental healing partakes of both meanings, with accent on the former. Examination of the artful application of any technique—and this applies to any one of the myriad methods reviewed in this book—discloses several elements not often discovered. The first of these hidden elements is a deep-seated *service* motive variously called *altruism* or *idealism*. Masserman[2] has alluded to this service motive as one of the "delusions" of mankind, a defense mechanism by which we live. "Man's kindness to man," he states, is "man's Ur-defenses," a primitive postulate of human interaction. Yet, this motive is what keeps humanity from flying apart through the centrifugal force of hostility. It is better stated as an ethical striving attributed to "men of good will."

If the search goes beyond and behind this "ethical striving," the simple wish to help another human being, some interesting unconscious motives are found. These are traces of magical thinking and the operation of omnipotence fantasies, vestiges of our infantile fantasies, common to everyone. The trained therapist is aware of these forces deep within his psyche and tries to control them while intuitive mental healers tend to express these tendencies more openly. Further, a therapist's artfulness depends on his or her inclusion in a craft or guild that confers both a measure of self-esteem and support, and a degree of authority. It is undeniable that these factors aid the narcissistic gratification the healer obtains from success with his clients or patients. Together with magical thinking and omnipotence fantasies, they constitute the baseline on which specific techniques are engrafted, whether depth psychotherapy, hypnosis, behavior modification, or faith healing.

The importance of raising these points, which might be

dismissed as trivial, is that they increase the therapist's sense of *surety* in whatever theory of practice he is using. All therapists like to account for their success on the basis of the correctness of their basic theory, the "science" behind their efforts. They feel less comfortable with the artful components of their work.

How else explain the fact that the *science* of a treatment method becomes scientific mythology a century later? Weir Mitchell's treatment of nervous exhaustion during the 1880s was theoretically sound and practically effective, but was discarded within two decades. Sakel's insulin treatment of schizophrenia during the 1930s rested upon impressive empirical and theoretical grounds, yet it has practically lost its position as a method of choice. There is no need to multiply examples of the fate of once-lauded therapeutic systems. The issue here is that the disparity between the original and later impression of validity of a technique not only depends on lack of scientific verification by others but on the absence of the innovator's artful components. A vital one, already mentioned, is the sense of sureness within the innovator, which aids him in assigning what logicians call *truth-value*[3] to his theories; with truth-value goes a large degree of emotional satisfaction.

If the position of the patient-client is examined with reference to the effect of artfulness in therapy, a complimentary feeling is encountered. Bluntly stated, it is that whatever the therapist does or says is expected to result in the patient-client's improvement from mental troubles. Underlying this attitude, present in all types of mental healing, is the "as if" postulate of Vaihinger.[4] In other words, the patient accepts treatment *as if* what is done will result in benefit. In technical terms, the attitude of the recipient of therapy rests on the presupposition of belief in an "as if" postulate.

This foreshortened analysis of *how* psychotherapy works, which goes beyond the usual explanations of emotional support, insight acquisition, laying bare the unconscious roots of nervous conditions, corrective emotional experience, maturation tendencies, and so forth, admittedly lies upon no measurable data. When one deals with emotions, as all mental healers do, and with the imperishable spirit of mankind, measurable data is difficult to acquire. It is for this reason that scrutiny of the artfulness in therapy promised some partial answers. For it cannot be forgotten that the ever-present element of *hope* in the patient meets the artful elements in the therapist. It is not too much to say that without these two ingredients operating in the background, psychotherapy would be a sterile enterprise.

Karl Menninger, dean of American psychiatrists, has pointed out the significance of hope in the human mind. From a larger frame of reference he places it as "an epiphenomenon of life and the healing arts."[5] As in all things philosophic, the ancient Greeks knew this facet of man. When Zeus, supreme god of the ancient Greeks, placed the secrets of man's soul in a jar to be entrusted to the safekeeping of his devoted subjects, he placed Hope at the bottom, below Evil. Pandora, prurient female, opened the jar, whereupon Evil flowed out with dire results for mankind ever since. However, Hope remained within.

It is this element that Menninger so wisely commented on: "Hope implies process...a going forward, a confident search." As in all of life's activities, so in mental healing, Hope is the final ingredient.

Notes to Chapter 18

1. Walter Bromberg, *The Nature of Psychotherapy; A Critique of the Therapeutic Transaction,* New York, Grune & Stratton, 1962.
2. Jules Masserman, *The Practice of Dynamic Psychiatry,* Phila., W. B. Saunders Co., 1955, p. 481.
3. Susanne K. Langer, *An Introduction to Symbolic Logic,* 2nd Ed. New York, Dover Publ. Inc., 1953.
4. Hans Vaihinger, *The Philosophy of "As If,"* London, Routledge & Kegan Paul, 1952, p. 124.
5. Karl Menninger with Martin Mayman and Paul Pruyser, *The Vital Balance,* New York, Viking Press, 1963.

Index